American Gold Digger

Gender and American Culture

Guided by feminist and antiracist perspectives, this series examines the construction and influence of gender and sexuality within the full range of America's cultures. Investigating in deep context the ways in which gender works with and against such markers as race, class, and region, the series presents outstanding interdisciplinary scholarship, including works in history, literary studies, religion, folklore, and the visual arts. In so doing, Gender and American Culture seeks to reveal how identity and community are shaped by gender and sexuality.

A complete list of books published in Gender and American Culture is available at www.uncpress.org.

American Gold Digger

Marriage, Money, and the Law from the Ziegfeld Follies to Anna Nicole Smith

. . . .

BRIAN DONOVAN

The University of North Carolina Press Chapel Hill

The publication of this book was supported by a grant from the College of Arts and Sciences at the University of Kansas.

The University of North Carolina Press has been a member
of the Green Press Initiative since 2003.

Library of Congress Cataloging-in-Publication Data
Names: Donovan, Brian, 1971- author.
Title: American gold digger : marriage, money, and law from the
    Ziegfeld Follies to Anna Nicole Smith / Brian Donovan.
Other titles: Gender & American culture.
Description: Chapel Hill : The University of North Carolina Press, 2020. |
    Series: Gender and American culture | Includes bibliographical
    references and index.
Identifiers: LCCN 2020013192 | ISBN 9781469660271 (cloth : alk. paper) |
    ISBN 9781469660288 (pbk. : alk. paper) | ISBN 9781469660295 (ebook)
Subjects: LCSH: Fortune hunters—United States—History—20th century. |
    Man-woman relationships—Economic aspects—United States. |
    Marriage law—Economic aspects—United States. | Marriage law—
    Social aspects—United States. | Women—United States—
    Social conditions—20th century. | Culture and law—United States.
Classification: LCC HQ801 .D696 2020 | DDC 306.70973—dc23
    LC record available at https://lccn.loc.gov/2020013192

Cover illustration: *Left to right,* Jane Russell, Charles Coburn, and
Marilyn Monroe in *Gentlemen Prefer Blondes,* directed by Howard Hawks
(20th Century-Fox, 1953). Used by permission of 20th Century-Fox/
Photofest, © 20th Century-Fox.

For Trudy and Randy McAvoy

Contents

Illustrations

Acknowledgments

This book would not be possible without generous emotional support from several cats, notably Possum, Gopher, and Riley. Human beings, too, provided me invaluable help and encouragement along the way. Here, I would like to thank colleagues at the University of Kansas and elsewhere: Tami Albin, Bob Antonio, Beth Bailey, Tori Barnes-Brus, Rebecca Barrett-Fox, Michael Baskett, Katie Batza, Hannah Britton, Marie Grace Brown, Kelly Chong, Lynn Davidman, Dawn Flood, Sarah Gatson, Sara Gregg, Robin Henry, Kathy Hull, Mara Keire, Jon Lamb, Laura Mielke, Joane Nagel, Cathy Preston, Emily Rauscher Katie Rhine, Bill Staples, Nick Syrett, Sherrie Tucker, Akiko Takeyama, and Stacey Vanderhurst. I am grateful for Ann Schofield's support, smart insights, and useful feedback on the introductory chapters. Nikki Perry deserves special thanks for reading every chapter and giving me extremely thorough and shrewd criticism. While all of its weaknesses are my own doing, this book would not have many of its strengths without Nikki's advice.

I am deeply appreciative of Kathy Peiss and Joel Best who have supported my work for many years and were instrumental in helping me move my project from an early stage to its completion.

I delivered papers about gold diggers at different meetings, and I thank these friends and colleagues for their useful comments and questions: Henry Bial, Tom Gerschick, Clarence Lang, Shannon Portillo, and Benita Roth. I am also grateful for research assistants who located material and were willing to have fruitful conversations about what it all meant: Louisa Williams, Samantha Havlin, and Madison Hovis. I want to extend a special thank-you to Elyse Neumann for her help on the final chapters. This book benefited greatly from our many discussions about Anna Nicole Smith.

The Hall Center for the Humanities, the crown jewel of the University of Kansas, was essential for completing my book. Here, I would like to thank Sarah Bishop, Dan Consolver, Richard Godbeer, Andrew Hodgson, Beth McSweeney, Kathy Porsch, Eliott Reeder, and Sally Utech. I benefited from a 2018 Hall Center Humanities Research Fellowship that allowed invaluable time for research and writing.

This book would not be possible without the unselfish labor of several librarians at the University of Kansas. I am indebted to Chris Steadman from Wheat Law Library for helping me locate legal documents and showing me the ins and outs of Westlaw. Sara Morris merits special recognition for routinely going the extra mile to help me find essential material. The book would not be the same without her assistance, and the process of writing it would not have been as pleasant without her friendship.

Jessica Newman was a wonderful editor who believed in this project and always pushed it to be better. It has been a true joy to work with Mark Simpson-Vos on the final stages of this journey. Thank you also to Margaretta Yarborough for careful proofreading and Paula Durbin-Westby for preparing the index.

I am especially grateful to family and friends who have supported me the last several years while I have been working on this book: Aislinn Addington, Lisa Amoroso, Khamisah Barger, Hal Beckerman, Will Berg, Matt Burke, Erica Chriss, Christy Craig, Mary Donovan, Kerry Donovan, Mark Donovan, Mollie Monroe-Gulick, Melinda Hauser, Ann Johnson, Rich Mellinger, Jordan Mills, Jon Russell, Lisa Russell, and (especially) Stephanie Russell. As always, I thank Natalie Donovan for whom words are inadequate to express my appreciation and love. For the last several years, Natalie has been a brilliant sounding board, editor, and gold digger film critic.

This book is dedicated to my in-laws, Randy and Trudy McAvoy, who have given me love and support for over twenty years.

American Gold Digger

Introduction

The American Gold Digger

· ·

Origins of the Gold Digger

Virginia Brooks first heard the phrase "gold digger" amid the cacophony of a raucous Chicago dance hall in the early 1910s. Brooks—political activist, suffragist, and friend of Ida B. Wells—was a Progressive-era reformer who fought coercive sex work, or what was called "white slavery." She received a letter from a concerned mother whose daughter left her rural home in search of employment and excitement in Chicago. The mother worried that her daughter, Mary Holden, had fallen into the hands of "white slavers" and was forced into a life of prostitution. The letter implored Brooks to find her. Brooks formed an alliance with a young woman named Lil who helped her navigate the city's underworld, and Lil accompanied Brooks to a late-night costume ball in search of Holden. In her 1915 book *My Battles with Vice*, Brooks described her alarm at the dancers' seductive moves and the assertive sexual propositions from men. Brooks gained the acquaintance of a young reveler who told her that most men do not care for dancing, but come to "cop off a girl." He said that the men went to the dance to scout for women, and the women looked for money. "Most of 'em are gold diggers," the young man told her. Brooks pointed to a woman sitting in a corner and asked him if she met the definition of a gold digger. The man assured her that the woman, Chrissy Tate, had "been travelin' this route for four years," ensnaring men for their money.[1]

Gold diggers refers to women who are in, or seek, romantic relationships primarily for economic gain.[2] Chrissy Tate, as one of the first gold diggers identified in print, exhibited qualities that would eventually coalesce into the gold digger stereotype of the twentieth century. She was young, appeared sexually charged (wearing a provocative red hat), deceptive ("she's traveled under eight different names"), and manipulative (she could "get money from a 'Gypshun' mummy").[3] The gold diggers recognized by Brooks's companion operated at the edge of prostitution and dating. They were part of urban amusement culture and, freed from the constraints of family, they basked in the thrills of urban life and were exposed to its dangers.

They enjoyed the good times offered by dance halls, amusement parks, and cafes, and their public presence blurred the boundaries between respectable and scandalous behavior. These gold diggers did not necessarily participate in outright sex work, but engaged in "treating" where they exchanged sex or companionship for money and gifts. Vice investigators in New York City, however, distinguished between "charity girls" and gold diggers, regarding the latter as prostitutes. In its earliest formulation, the gold digger stood in a liminal space between sex work and dating, and between vice and respectability.[4]

A casual conversation between a Ziegfeld Follies star and a playwright accelerated the popularity of the term and worked to dislodge it from both its subcultural connotation of prostitution and its literal association with gold mining. Kay Laurell sat with playwright Avery Hopwood in the lobby of the Ritz-Carlton Hotel while they waited for a mutual friend. Laurell spotted another acquaintance enter the hotel and, as the woman walked past, she waved to her and said, "Hello, gold digger."[5] In 1918, when this meeting occurred, Laurell counted among the elite of Ziegfeld Follies performers. For that year's Follies program, Laurell represented the "Spirit of France," standing partially nude atop a gigantic rotating globe in a somber number that referenced the Great War. Her performance as a human statue exploited a loophole in New York obscenity law and garnered her the informal title of "the Girl with the Most Beautiful Figure in the World."[6] Offstage, Laurell socialized with the likes of Helen Hayes, H. L. Mencken, Reginald Vanderbilt, and Clarence Darrow. Hayes remembered Laurell as a poor actor, but "a tigress of a woman" who demanded lavish gifts from her suitors. According to Mencken, Laurell believed that any decent-looking woman could get money from men by sleeping with them, but "she thought it took real skill to get the money and evade the sleeping. This was her invariable custom whenever possible."[7] Laurell's callout to her friend, then, was not an accusation but a self-aware show of camaraderie.

Avery Hopwood had never heard the phrase "gold digger," and he asked Laurell what it meant. "That's what we call ourselves!" she told him. "You men capitalize on your brains, or your business ability, or your legal minds— or whatever other darned thing you happen to have! So why shouldn't we girls capitalize what nature has given us—our good looks and ability to please and entertain men? You men don't give something for nothing—why should we?"[8] Hopwood jotted the phrase "gold digger" on his white shirt cuff and, later, summarized his conversation with Laurell in his personal notebook. A year after his encounter with Laurell, Broadway producer David

FIGURE 1 Kay Laurell (1890–1927), early 1920s, Ziegfeld Follies star. Laurell's casual remark to a friend ("Hey, gold digger") inspired playwright Avery Hopwood to create the 1919 Broadway success "The Gold Diggers." Laurell helped move the phrase "gold digger" from chorus slang to a powerful and popular stereotype. George Grantham Bain Collection, Library of Congress.

Belasco approached Hopwood about writing a play to promote former Ziegfeld Follies performer Ina Claire. Hopwood recalled his encounter with Laurell in the Ritz lobby and produced a script for *The Gold Diggers* in five weeks.[9]

Belasco's assistants urged Hopwood to change the title. The phrase "gold digger" was not in common parlance, and they were afraid that potential audience members would expect a play about prospectors, mining, or the Gold Rush. In its review, *Variety* clarified that "the piece does not concern the mining of precious metal."[10] The 1919 play *The Gold Diggers* follows the travails of three chorus girls struggling to survive in Manhattan. One of the trio summarizes the ethos of the gold digger when she tells her roommates in an early scene, "either you work the men, or the men work you!"[11] *The Gold Diggers* ran for over 280 performances at the Lyceum Theater, grossed nearly $2 million, and earned Hopwood over a quarter of a million dollars in royalties.[12] The play was also a success in London, with Tallulah Bankhead in the starring role. *The Gold Diggers* was remade as a film in 1923 and as a Warner Brothers musical in 1929 (*Gold Diggers of Broadway*). Most of *Gold Diggers of Broadway* is lost, but a surviving clip featured Winnie Lightener portraying a chorus girl named Mabel. In one sequence, Mabel aggressively tries to convince a wealthy lawyer to buy her a car. He insists that he cannot afford to give her a car but, after her hectoring, gives up and declares, "Oh, what's the use." He tries to explain to Mabel that her solicitous behavior imperiled her respectability, especially because they were not engaged. She interprets his clarification as a proposal: "Sweetie proposed! Sweetie proposed!" Viewers witnessed in Mabel the distillation of the gold digger type: frivolous, petulant, childlike, aggressive, manipulative, and unconcerned about her reputation. Despite her obvious lack of sophistication and cultural capital, she was able to exert a strong, almost mysterious, influence over the reasoning ability of the wealthy lawyer.

Hopwood's play was also the basis for Busby Berkeley's *Gold Diggers of 1933*, one of a number of 1930s musicals with the gold digger theme (*Gold Diggers of 1935*, *Gold Diggers of 1937*, and *Gold Diggers of Paris*). Various representations of gold diggers on the stage and screen began to piece together a common cultural understanding of the type of woman who might be called a gold digger. By the 1930s, in contrast to the apprehensions expressed by Belasco's associates, no one at Warner Brothers was worried that the audience of *Gold Diggers of 1933* would misunderstand the phrase "gold digger." Solidified during the course of the twentieth century, the gold digger became a female type, a category of womanhood.[13] Hopwood's original formulation of the gold digger took on a life of its own, tapping into cultural

FIGURE 2 Cover of the satirical magazine *Judge*. By the 1920s, the phrase "gold digger" had shed its connotations with sex work, and its literal association with mining, to become a category of womanhood. *Judge*, July 24, 1920.

fears about social class, gender, and sexuality with a ferocity that he could have scarcely predicted.[14]

This book is about the gold digger stereotype in American law and culture. Throughout the twentieth century, the gold digger was a target, or "folk devil," for white men's anxieties about race, class, and gender relationships within changing socioeconomic contexts. People vilified gold diggers to express concern about shifts in the economy, gender roles, and sexual norms. Tracing the cultural influence of the gold digger stereotype in the United States reveals the porous relationship between law and culture.[15] The proximity of law and culture made the gold digger a social force: popular representations of gold diggers influenced the law and, in turn, the legal tools used by and against gold diggers became an inextricable part of twentieth-century American culture. The gold digger trope created and reflected deep-seated beliefs about dating, marriage, cohabitation, and divorce. Gold diggers generated expectations and worries about the allocation of resources and responsibilities within romantic couples. They became a touchstone through which men and women understood, and misunderstood, economic and social change. Representations of gold diggers—from Anita Loos's *Gentlemen Prefer Blondes* to Anna Nicole Smith's reality TV series—directly connect to the legal realm where individuals and groups engaged in pitched struggles over alimony, inheritance, and the economics of marriage and cohabitation. Over the course of the twentieth century, the gold digger seeped into what Lawrence Friedman calls "popular legal culture."[16] The term gold digger traveled a long way from its humble beginnings as Ziegfeld Follies slang, and it became a misogynistic trope through which everyday people made sense of marriage, money, and law.

The Development of the Gold Digger Stereotype

The gold digger is a stereotype with endurance and inertia. Yet gold diggers are not a freestanding human type; they do not occur in nature as a species. They are visible only insofar as others recognize and label them as gold diggers; gold diggers exist to the extent that people make claims about their existence.[17] Gold diggers are people who have been identified as gold diggers, either through the explicit application of the term or through a set of stock descriptions that invoke the archetypal qualities of the gold digger. Simply put, the constructivist perspective used in this book sees the gold digger as a stereotype leveraged to create social inequality.[18]

The gold digger is a stereotype that labors at the intersections of gender, sexuality, social class, and race.[19] Primarily, however, the gold digger is a gendered stereotype used to make judgments about the behavior and characteristics of specific women. Some men are described as gold diggers, and gold digging is described in same-sex relationships, but the dominant image of the gold digger in the twentieth century is a heterosexual woman who uses her sexuality and charm to seduce a man into a relationship where she can profit.[20] As a social construction, the gold digger stereotype engages in substantial ideological labor to reinforce particular perspectives about women as mercenary and manipulative.

The gold digger stereotype shares a family resemblance with other iconic figures such as the adventuress, the vamp, the Cinderella, and the "dumb blonde." Like the gold digger, the nineteenth-century adventuress used legal tools like breach of promise lawsuits and the implications of common law marriage to extract money from men.[21] Gold diggers supplanted vamps as the premier femme fatale figure in American cinema. Unlike vamps, who destroyed men for unknown motives or merely for the sport of it, gold diggers manipulated men for financial reasons.[22] In some instances, the vamp and the gold digger shared similar modes of self-presentation. The silent screen vamping of Theda Bara in *A Fool There Was* and Louise Brooks in *Pandora's Box* was not too stylistically distant from Barbara Stanwyck's portrayal of gold digger Phyllis Dietrichson in the 1944 film *Double Indemnity*. However, gold diggers sometimes veered away from the intelligence and cunning qualities of the vamp; they appeared on an opposite course, as a naive Cinderella or a dumb blonde. These representations of gold diggers emphasized their childlike immaturity and efforts to cultivate a relationship with men like that of a father and daughter. A self-identified gold digger in Paul Cressey's 1932 study of Chicago nightspots described how "the first impression I have to make is that I'm an innocent little girl in hard circumstances." In her 1929 book *Confessions of a Gold Digger*, Betty Van Deventer described this strategy of self-presentation as "the father appeal," whereby "the man becomes a symbolic father, helping a dependent, lost child." In Loos's *Gentlemen Prefer Blondes*, the protagonist Lorelei Lee said that she refused to think of calling her suitor Mr. Eisman by his first name, and "if I want to call him anything at all, I call him 'Daddy.'"[23] "My Heart Belongs to Daddy," a 1938 song about a gold digger's affection for her wealthy boyfriend, was performed by Marilyn Monroe in 1960 and by Anna Nicole Smith in 1997. Over the course of the twentieth century, gold diggers exhibited a range of emotional affect, from hardboiled aggressor to unsophisticated, childlike naïf.

The gold digger had core characteristics, but she appeared in different guises in distinct social and historical circumstances. As a trickster, the gold digger highlighted contradictions and absurdities within a gender order that denied women social and political opportunities, yet punished them for pursuing relationships that mitigated the problems that they faced as a result of those diminished opportunities. As a folk devil, the gold digger represented a dangerous melding of affective and economic domains. The construction of the gold digger as a folk devil was ultimately more consequential as a mechanism for historical change. Audiences laughed at and identified with gold diggers in movie theaters, but perceived them as a threat in wider society, a threat that shaped legal strategies and outcomes of cases involving sex, marriage, and money.[24] The power of the gold digger stereotype emanated from its dual status as trickster and folk devil, as well as from its simultaneous presence in cultural and legal domains. The circulation of gold diggers within popular legal culture allowed complex arguments and ideas about marriage, gender roles, and the economy to be distilled into an easily identified story or figure. The stylized features of the gold digger function as a shorthand, or "condensing symbol," to account for and to make arguments about complex historical, social, and cultural phenomena.[25]

The gold digger was part of a cluster of women deemed problematic to the public, but the threat she posed varied in degree and intensity across time.[26] The development of the gold digger stereotype in the twentieth century changed with shifting understanding and practices surrounding gender, race, and class. The gold digger did not simply reflect or register those changes. Rather, the gold digger stereotype was part of the cultural language used to promulgate them. The gold digger stereotype had a causal force in shaping the direction of marriage and family law. The desire to thwart or punish gold diggers informed the rationale, rhetoric, and vocabulary of motive for proposed changes—some of them quite sweeping—to alimony, breach of promise laws, laws governing cohabitation, and even probate law and military pension allotments.

The Gold Digger in Twentieth-Century Law and Culture

Folk Devils and Tort Tales

The gold digger stereotype stood as a symbol of general disorder during times of heightened social anxiety about marriage, law, and money. Although the gold digger has a relatively consistent presence through the twentieth century, the stereotype appeared with a white-hot intensity during specific historical moments, especially when older understandings of marriage and courtship were contested, when women asserted new forms of power and access to resources, and when law failed to keep pace with social change. The gold digger was a way to enact, and make sense of, shifting gender roles within marriage and courtship. Cultural representations of the gold digger represented the public face of alimony, breach of promise, palimony, and other legal claims. The gold digger stereotype distorted the conditions of courtship and marriage by pointing to individual behavior, the behavior of alleged gold diggers, as an explanation for structural and economic conditions. The supposedly lavish earnings of gold diggers obscured the mundane reality of divorce and separation in the United States.

In this way, the gold digger acted as a "folk devil" during moral panics about gender, marriage, and money. Stanley Cohen developed the moral panic concept to describe overblown trepidation about distorted or nonexistent enemies, threats, and social problems.[27] Moral panics sometimes arise over imaginary fears like witchcraft or satanic syndicates.[28] Moral panics can also center on real problems, but in a way that exaggerates or distorts their threat or risk.[29] Moral panics prompt citizens to take action against perceived enemies and dangers, and folk devils, individuals or groups designated as the cause of the problem, are the targets of moral panics.[30] As folk devils, gold diggers became the focus of blame for perceived institutional crises around gender norms, the economy, and the family. Gold diggers appeared in roiling moral panics about the state of marriage in the United States. The signature dynamic of moral panic is to misrecognize structural changes and, instead, heap blame on the actions of individuals and historically marginalized groups. People expressed generalized anxiety about changing expectations surrounding marriage, and about transformations in the political economy, through animosity toward alleged gold diggers.

Panics around gold diggers often found expression in the realm of civil law, or torts. Gold diggers were routinely cast in "tort tales," exaggerated stories of lawsuits that worked to epitomize and symbolize dysfunctions in the realm of civil law. Tort tales were circulated through mass media and popular entertainment and thereby became a source of information about the civil justice system. Tort tales sought to tap into a constructed notion of "common sense," and they prompted the stories' consumers to ponder the alleged injustice of frivolous lawsuits, the broken civil justice system, and the stupidity and greed of their fellow citizens. Like moral panics, tort tales deployed narratives that both created outrage and had a tenuous connection to empirical reality. Popular tort tales in the late twentieth century included a man who sued the dairy industry because he had health problems due to an addiction to milk, and a woman who sued McDonald's after spilling a hot cup of coffee in her lap.[31] In these accounts, media reports and tort reform advocates stripped the lawsuits of details that would have given the cases more credibility among the public, and they removed specifics about the case or the outcome that would have made them seem less absurd.[32] Media widely reported these cases as frivolous even though a fuller consideration of them quickly revealed that they had some merit. The bite-sized accounts characteristic of tort tales created an image of out-of-control civil litigation even though the reality did not match the claims.

Many accounts of gold diggers fit the core characteristics of tort tales, especially reports of large, ill-gotten, monetary awards.[33] Stories of gold diggers throughout the twentieth century reported on the extravagant amounts of money gold diggers gained through their strategic relationships. In the 1930s, Rhoda Tanner Doubleday sued her lover for $1.5 million in a breach of promise lawsuit. Although claims for alimony do not fall under the category of torts, the broad characteristics of many gold digger alimony narratives share a strong family resemblance with tort tales. In her contentious divorce in the early 1950s, Eleanor Holm sued her husband Billy Rose for $700 weekly alimony. In the 1970s, Michelle Triola sought $3.8 million in "palimony" from her live-in lover, Lee Marvin. Anna Nicole Smith fought over $474 million from her deceased husband's estate. Commentators deployed the gold digger trope, in varying degrees, to make sense of these legal claims. Also, typical of tort tales, entertainment and mass media entities became prime outlets of gold digger narratives: newspaper reports on sensational trials, movies, and (in some cases) novels. Stories of gold diggers were conveyed through simplistic and media-friendly stories, describing situations where extraordinary events came to represent the status quo.

During the course of the twentieth century, gold digger stories and gold digger tort tales participated in various power relations marked by race and gender.[34] The gold digger, while most obviously a gendered figure, glued together different elements that rationalize discrimination and distract from the origins of social inequality. The gold digger stereotype provoked a misrecognition of structural, demographic, social, political, and legal phenomena and, instead, redirected attention to the character and actions of solitary individuals. Representations of, and narratives about, gold diggers echoed and reproduced the tangled relationships among different dimensions of inequality. In this manner, the history of the gold digger offers significant insights into intersectionality, intersecting forms of race, gender, class, and sexual inequality that shape and direct social life in profound ways.[35]

Gold Diggers and the Roaring Twenties

Moral panic about flapper-era gold diggers reflected and contributed to fears about changing gender roles within, and at the margins of, American marriage. As the average family size declined, and as new employment opportunities for women increased, marriage assumed new meanings and purposes. The rise of the gold digger stereotype in the 1920s coincided with the popularization of romantic love and affection as the central justification for marriage. Early gold diggers also coincided with the move from courtship to dating, a change that started among the working class and trickled up the American class ladder in the early twentieth century. Men and women increasingly rejected Victorianism and made dating and matrimonial decisions based on personal compatibility and common interests. The notion of "companionate marriage" did not suddenly appear in the early twentieth century, but the discussions of companionate marriage expanded and became woven into debates about sex, birth control, and divorce. Companionate marriage was one of several competing definitions and alternative conceptions of marriage in the early twentieth century. For example, Benjamin Lindsey, whose controversial 1927 book *Companionate Marriage* accelerated public discussions of nontraditional marriage arrangements, defended his ideas as a middle ground between older notions of marriage and the more radical concept of "trial marriage." According to both critics and defenders of traditional marriage, gold diggers exploited the internal logic of companionate marriage. The gold digger, through her callous monetary ambitions, called into question the romantic basis of marriage and undermined what sociologist Viviana Zelizer has termed the "hostile worlds perspective," a viewpoint that regards romantic intimacy as a special realm that should be kept separate from the logic and operations of the monetary economy.[36] Gold diggers epitomized the danger of combining romance and economics.

The gold digger emerged as a prominent social figure during the so-called marriage crisis of the 1920s. By the early 1920s, the divorce rate was approximately fifteen times the rate in 1870.[37] As historian William Kuby explains, "concerns over divorce reflected a fear that women were fleeing their traditional roles as mothers and wives, and embracing new legal and social opportunities that had formerly been denied to them."[38] The rise in divorce and the growing acceptance of companionate marriage in the 1920s led to a moral panic specifically about the alimony system. The marriage crisis of the 1920s aligned with and drew strength from the popularity of images and stories about gold diggers. Legal authorities readily drew on the imagery of the gold digger to make claims about the financial and social threats faced by men in the 1920s. For example, a judge from Chicago declared in 1927, "There are too many gold-diggers among divorced women, and half of them aren't deserving of consideration."[39] Cultural production amplified fears about gold-digging alimony seekers. U.S. newspapers ran hundreds of articles about Peggy Hopkins Joyce and her $1 million alimony claim against her former spouse Stanley Joyce. In the 1920s, newspapers reported on greedy chorus girls suing wealthy men for large alimony awards. Alimony, however, was rare and men used a number of contrivances to avoid paying it.

During the 1920s, cultural producers also portrayed gold diggers as a potential threat to the white race. In the early twentieth century, marriage became the central site where discourses of sexuality and race constructed American family norms. The gold digger emerged as a stereotype during an era when the category "white" was in flux and the parameters of racial whiteness were in the process of absorbing ethnicities that were previously considered not quite, or provisionally, white. The creation and popularization of the gold digger stereotype in the early twentieth century coincided with a fundamental change in the way Americans saw race, both in the visual signifiers of race and the way Americans understood racial boundaries and categories.[40] The gold digger reinforced a visual understanding of race through its promulgation of whiteness. Blonde hair was a defining feature of the 1920s gold digger, perhaps exemplified by the protagonist Lorelei Lee in *Gentlemen Prefer Blondes*. Peggy Hopkins Joyce, who was arguably the best-known gold digger of the 1920s, was also known for her whiter-than-white aesthetic sensibility and platinum blonde hair.[41] Discourse about gold diggers in the 1920s, while often not explicitly centered on race, carried racial meaning and was implicated in the creation of racial categories and the lines drawn around them.[42]

Gold Diggers and the Great Depression

In the 1930s, law and culture collided in powerful ways to propel the gold digger into national prominence. By the early 1930s, gold diggers were part of a set of stock characters in Depression-era films. In the context of the Great Depression, gold diggers underscored the connection between sexuality and social class. Newspapers, magazine articles, and movies portrayed gold diggers as interested in using their sexuality for class advancement during a time of widespread downward mobility. Silver screen stars like Jean Harlow and Joan Blondell portrayed gold diggers who manipulated wealthy men in order to avoid the struggles caused by economic scarcity. These depictions were often comedic, and gold diggers sometimes represented quasi-aspirational figures who fought to endure economic hardship and make the best of a dire situation. Their male counterparts were depicted as foolish rich men who got what they deserved and, given the state of the national economy, perhaps did not deserve what they had to begin with. Outside the stage and screen, however, newspapers and litigators portrayed gold diggers less as carefree tricksters and more as a genuine threat to men who were struggling to survive the economic crash.

Stories about gold diggers simplified the complex realities of the Great Depression. The Great Depression stressed American families in unprecedented ways, and both marriage and childbirth rates declined. Gender roles within marriage changed in tandem with men's dwindling ability to act as the sole breadwinner. The economic crisis strained older ideas of masculinity as more women sought employment in the paid labor force, and women faced a backlash from employers and government officials who viewed them as taking jobs that belonged to men. In this context, a set of laws that provided economic protection for women who faced romantic betrayal fell under scrutiny. The best known of these so-called heart balm laws was breach of promise, which created the potential for civil penalties in the event that a man promised to marry a woman but betrayed his marital pledge. During the 1930s, many regarded these laws as, at best, a frivolous excess or, at worst, a malicious tool in the hands of blackmailing gold diggers.

Anxieties about gold diggers led to a nationwide crusade against breach of promise laws. Like the alimony panic of the preceding decade, there was no evidence that breach of promise lawsuits were increasing. In fact, scholars have shown that the total number of breach of promise lawsuits had steadily declined since the nineteenth century. Yet, during the Great Depression, film and newspapers depicted a torrent of breach of promise and other so-called heart balm lawsuits that burdened men who were already financially struggling. The plots of many early 1930s films revolved around gold diggers using breach of promise lawsuits as a weapon to extract large amounts of money from gullible men. In turn, the legal effort to outlaw breach of promise laws, which gained momentum in the 1930s, drew sustenance from exaggerated stories of breach of promise actions in newspapers, magazines, and movies. The gold digger stood at the center of a Depression-era crusade to eliminate an entire category of lawsuit designed to protect women from inequalities built into the patriarchal marriage market. Structural economic changes led to the economic crisis, but the figure of a white woman stealing from men captured the public's attention. Federal monetary policies and the actions of banks were difficult to understand; the plots of gold digger movies were much clearer about where one should assign blame.

Gold Diggers, World War II, and the Postwar Economic Expansion

During the run-up to World War II, marriage rates rebounded from their low during the Great Depression. Men and women were eager to start families to inject stability into lives disrupted by the uncertainty of war. More and more couples married at a young age and the birthrate soared. As young men left their family homes for military training camps and overseas combat, a new moral panic about marriage propelled gold diggers into prominence. Commentators from within and without the military raised the alarm that devious women married numerous servicemen to collect multiple monthly allotment checks from the U.S. Department of Defense. Gold diggers who exploited the U.S. military's system of monetary allotments prompted outcries against so-called Allotment Annies. These women allegedly prowled military posts and encampments, and they preyed on the youth and innocence of American men who were away from their families. The Allotment Annie panic was buoyed by apocryphal newspaper stories and a major Hollywood movie called *Allotment Wives*. Like the distress about alimony and breach of promise in the 1920s and '30s, the widespread distress about Allotment Annies during World War II was overblown and had more to do with anxieties about masculinity than any real threat posed by khaki-crazed young women.

After World War II, the American economy entered into an unprecedented expansion and the family unit took on special symbolic significance as the bulwark against communism and the Soviet Union. Again, the gold digger became a central figure through which men and women negotiated the American economy and its imprint on family life. While Depression-era concerns about alimony and breach of promise lawsuits lingered, the postwar gold digger reflected the preoccupations of marriage and consumerism that engulfed postwar America. Gold digger narratives of the 1950s coincided with opportunities like the G.I. Bill that allowed the white middle class extraordinary economic opportunities and resources. During the 1950s— which served as a kind of bridge between the moral panics of the previous few decades and the upheavals of the 1960s and '70s—the identity of gold diggers expanded to include married women dissatisfied with consumer comforts. Messaging about gold diggers, from newspaper advice columns to popular films, exhorted married women to be happy with what they had.

In the 1950s, gold diggers appeared in popular movies as self-confident, fun-loving, and sympathetic characters. Marilyn Monroe's performance as Lorelei Lee in the 1953 remake of *Gentlemen Prefer Blondes* typified the comedic gold digger of the postwar era. Later that year, Monroe played one of three gold diggers in *How to Marry a Millionaire*, a film that was turned into a successful television show in 1957. Like representations of gold diggers from the 1930s, the gold diggers of the 1950s occupied a double space as figures that represented both comedic tricksters and a threat to the American family. Given the symbolic importance of postwar American marriage as a bulwark against communism, gold diggers represented a potential danger to the domestic sphere. Outside of their portrayals in movies, critics depicted gold diggers as a threat to the fragile ideal of domesticity propagated during the 1950s. The gold digger imperiled a model of family harmony that embodied class and racial elements as well as the more obvious gendered messaging about breadwinners and homemakers. In the early-to-mid-twentieth century, collective panic about masculinity, social class, and racial hegemony coalesced in discourse about white gold diggers as potential race traitors. For example, Charles Wilner's 1952 book *Alimony: The American Tragedy* assailed gold diggers and their damage to "race purity."[43] Gold diggers presented a potential racial danger by undermining the financial security of white men through alimony claims and breach of promise lawsuits.

Late Twentieth-Century Gold Diggers

The images of domestic calm produced by 1950s culture belied a series of contradictions and conflicts that upended the norms of the postwar nuclear family. The growing women's movement overlapped with several legal changes in the 1960s and 1970s that generated trepidation about gold diggers abusing easy divorces and cohabitation laws. The rise of no-fault divorce, where state laws allowed divorces to proceed without one party proving some cause like adultery, generated a new sense of crisis about the state of marriage in the 1960s and '70s. From the 1960s to the 1970s, the U.S. divorce rate doubled.[44] As historian Rebecca Davis explains, critics of no-fault divorce claimed that the new laws promoted "trial marriage," a phrase that harkened back to discussions in the 1920s about the marriage crisis. Many also feared that "palimony," a legal doctrine enshrined by the California Supreme Court in 1976, destroyed the legal obligations of marriage and allowed gold diggers to sue their lovers for alimony-like compensation even if the two were never legally married. Characteristic of moral panics and tort tales in general, the public anxiety about palimony far exceeded the number of successful palimony lawsuits.

The gold diggers of the 1980s and 1990s broadcasted, and helped Americans make sense of, gigantic shifts in the economic and political order commonly characterized as neoliberalism. Stories about Anna Nicole Smith, regarded by many as the quintessence of a gold digger, saturated the media landscape in the late twentieth and early twenty-first centuries. Her marriage to an eighty-nine-year-old billionaire launched a decades-long legal battle over his estate. That Smith was married to someone who made his fortune through a partnership with the Koch brothers makes her part of the history of U.S. neoliberalism. Moreover, her lawsuit, which reached the Supreme Court twice, led to fundamental changes to American bankruptcy law. The trials of Smith, both her legal battles and media brawls, raised questions about deservedness and respectability in the neoliberal age. Late twentieth-century gold diggers were more than women who pursued men for money; they were important emblems and instigators of economic, legal, and cultural change.

Outline of the Book

This book traces a cultural genealogy of the gold digger in the twentieth-century United States and examines key anchor points in the history of the stereotype. The analysis presented in the following chapters uncovers the connections that representations of gold diggers forged among gender, class, and race, and how popular culture and law gave those intersections social force.

Chapter 1 examines concerns about alimony in the late 1920s, a moral panic at which gold diggers took center stage. Historians have described the first two decades of the twentieth century as the "first sexual revolution," a time period which drastically altered attitudes about love, marriage, and divorce.[45] The acceleration of romantic love as the primary justification for marriage coupled with new social and economic roles for women prompted a rise in the divorce rate. As the divorce rate increased, and as the economic basis for family life changed, many Americans expressed widespread concern about men falling victim to alimony-seeking gold diggers. Coinciding with these changes, the parameters of who was considered "white" were in flux, and cultural negotiations of whiteness occurred in gendered and sexualized spaces, like advertising and popular entertainment.[46] Specific white women, like former Ziegfeld star Peggy Hopkins Joyce, came to embody the gold digger and the problem of extravagant alimony awards. Well-publicized stories of greedy gold diggers focused on the high alimony awards sought by Joyce and others but, in reality, alimony payments had not substantially increased. Rather, the social panic about alimony reflected Progressive-era angst about gender, class, and race.

Chapter 2 traces representations of gold diggers during the Great Depression. Distress about alimony persisted, but heart balm lawsuits, particularly actions for breach of promise, garnered massive media coverage. High-profile news accounts featured wealthy men in the entertainment or business worlds who faced lawsuits by women far below their social station. These stories generated a public image of gold diggers engaged in out-of-control litigation. Stories of breach of promise litigation, in both white and African American newspapers, cultivated the notion that heart balm litigation was widespread, grossly unfair, and a public hazard. By the mid-1930s, several states moved to repeal heart balm statutes. During those same years, major film studios produced a bumper crop of movies related to gold diggers and gold digging, often with plots that revolved around women using the law and the threat of lawsuits to extract money from hapless men. Chapter 2 examines how statewide campaigns against heart balm laws drew strength from sensationalized news coverage of breach of promise lawsuits and overlapped with the major themes and plots of early 1930s gold digger films.

The gold digger figure of the 1940s and '50s revolved around a fragile sense of masculinity. Chapter 3 examines the gold digger during World War II and the postwar economic expansion. During World War II, journalists and military officials highlighted the threat from so-called Allotment Annies, women who married multiple servicemen for their military allotment checks. Stories of war brides abusing the allotment system constructed the gold digger as a national security menace. Yet, like the reaction against alimony in the 1920s and heart balm in the 1930s, suspicions about wartime gold diggers far exceeded the actual harm that they caused. In the postwar period, the gold digger revolved around, and attempted to resolve, contradictions about 1950s white domesticity. Gold diggers exploited cracks in the postwar gender order. The sensational divorce trial of Billy Rose and Eleanor Holm revealed the high stakes of marital discord and the limits of postwar domestic compromises. At the same time, Marilyn Monroe emerged as a symbol of whiteness, womanhood, and sexuality, especially for her iconic performance as Lorelei Lee in *Gentlemen Prefer Blondes*. The rise of *Playboy* magazine, which trumpeted the threat posed by gold diggers in its inaugural issue, generated images of gold diggers who threatened hierarchical gender relations. Gold digger imagery during the 1950s depicted deceptive and manipulative women who threatened white masculinity and endangered the assumed quietude of postwar life.

Chapter 4 considers the gold digger in the wake of the sexual revolution. The changes in sexual practices and mores that occurred during the 1960s worked to upend the conservative marital norms of the previous decade. In this context, marriage as an economic institution underwent a renewal not unlike the changes that caused the "first sexual revolution" in the early twentieth century. As more and more couples lived together without the legal bind of marriage, the alimony question assumed new forms. This chapter analyzes the legal battle between actor Lee Marvin and Michelle Triola, a conflict that reached the California Supreme Court and established the concept of "palimony," a form of alimony available to unwed couples. Many commenters, such as writer Nora Ephron, condemned Triola as a gold digger for suing Marvin for financial support. Critics like Ephron regarded Triola's lawsuit as a reproach of the women's movement. Others, like Gloria Steinem and Gloria Allred, championed Triola's cause as highlighting the inequities of modern marriage and divorce. The debate about Triola's status as a gold digger was a referendum on larger questions surrounding women's liberation in the 1970s.

Chapter 5 considers representations of gold diggers in the final decades of the twentieth century. During these years, several changes occurred in American family life, including the erosion of the social safety net, a widening gap between the rich and poor, the widespread adoption of no-fault divorce laws, and the popularization of prenuptial agreements among the middle class. Characterizations of gold diggers during these decades moved away from depictions of plucky women trying to survive economic depression, wartime, or the suffocating doldrums of postwar domestic containment. Representations of gold diggers revealed broad economic and cultural change consistent with the gender, race, and class dynamics of advanced capitalism and neoliberalism. The chapter examines the use of the gold digger stereotype in accounting for Anna Nicole Smith's legal fight over her husband's estate. Model Anna Nicole Smith's protracted legal battle over her deceased husband's wealth speaks to the complex intersection of gender, sexuality, class, and race in the final decade of the twentieth century. Throughout the 1990s, the press and public characterized Smith as both a gold digger and "white trash." As the preeminent gold digger of the late twentieth century, one who consciously modeled her image after Marilyn

Monroe, Anna Nicole Smith was consistently portrayed as a symbol of cupidity and malevolent white womanhood.

The epilogue considers the gold digger as a source of legal culture across the twentieth century. It returns to the constructivist question that animates the core of this book: Why does the gold digger stereotype act as such a powerful cultural force? This chapter also looks at the aftereffects of the gold digger's march through the twentieth century, including the expansion of the gold digger trope in online domains and the amplification of gold digger discourse in African American vernacular and cultural production.

The cultural history of the gold digger shows how the stereotype works to reinforce dominant power relationships and social inequalities by appearing as a threat to marriage, family, and society. The gold digger distilled wider social problems into an easily identifiable caricature. Throughout the twentieth century, individuals deployed the gold digger trope in different ways: to educate, to entertain, and to warn. The gold digger had a dynamic quality and acted as a flexible discursive resource for a range of ideological projects at the intersection of gender, class, and race. From silent movies to digital content, the gold digger has existed for over one hundred years, adapting to new media and forms of entertainment, inserting herself in an ever-shifting set of historical circumstances.

1   The Alimony Panic

The front page of the *Washington Post* for June 4, 1924, cataloged a number of globally important events. A Hungarian anarchist was charged with plotting to kill King George and the President of France. A resurgent Ku Klux Klan posed problems for the upcoming Democratic National Convention. Two wealthy University of Chicago students, Nathan Leopold and Richard Loeb, faced the death penalty for the premeditated killing of a fourteen-year-old boy. And Peggy Hopkins Joyce, former Ziegfeld Follies star, entered her fourth marriage. News about Joyce's latest marriage, which shared prominent space with reports of regicide, child murder, and the Klan, fascinated millions of Americans in the 1920s.[1]

Peggy Hopkins Joyce, also known as Peggy Joyce, was best known as a gold digger, if not *the* gold digger of the early twentieth century. Constance Rosenblum, in her 2000 biography of Joyce, observed, "From the early twenties into the thirties, the name Peggy Hopkins Joyce resonated mightily in the culture."[2] The story of Peggy Hopkins Joyce—her rise in vaudeville, her stardom as a Ziegfeld Follies Girl, and her tempestuous divorce from Stanley Joyce in 1921—found an audience of millions in newspapers, magazines, and tabloids. Peggy Hopkins Joyce's glamorous image, promoted in the press and nurtured by her conscious efforts at celebrity, embodied the gold digger at a moment in American cultural history when that image had wide social salience.[3] Rosenblum contends that "the phrase *gold digger* first attached itself to her" during Joyce's days as a Ziegfeld Follies star.[4] The timing of Joyce's growing notoriety was superb; Americans gained increasing familiarity with the gold digger character type on stage and screen during the years when Joyce's reputation peaked.[5]

Peggy Joyce's public image as a sexually adventurous gold digger eclipsed her acclaim as an actress or stage performer. A feature in *Life* magazine from 1950 listed Peggy Hopkins Joyce, along with Margaret Sanger, Mary Pickford, and several others, as one of the women who influenced the first half of the twentieth century. Despite placing her with esteemed company, the article described Joyce as "an ostentatious Ziegfeld Girl who became famous mainly for marrying millionaires." Marian Spritzer's 1969 Broadway memoir described Peggy as a "pre-Harlow bombshell," but said "she had acquired more public recognition for her skill at collecting millionaire husbands (and for her off-stage exploits) than for any conspicuous acting ability." Kevin Brownlow, in his landmark 1976 study of silent film, simply noted, "Peggy Hopkins Joyce was the subject of numerous scandal stories." Joyce's primary identity as a gold digger has carried over into the twenty-first century. Robert Hudovernik, in his 2006 photographic collection of Ziegfeld Girls, included a photograph of Joyce shot with her back to the camera and her face turned to its profile, looking away from her naked shoulder, draped in pearls. The accompanying caption read: "Ziegfeld girl Peggy Hopkins Joyce, ca. 1924–27, gold digger." Supporting its basic identification of her as a gold digger, the caption described Peggy as "wild and unbridled. Her professional career was men."[6] Depictions of Joyce from the early twentieth century to the early twenty-first century portrayed her deviant reputation as a product of her outrageous conduct; Peggy Hopkins Joyce was a gold digger because she exploited men. Outside of the circular logic of "being famous for being famous," from where did Peggy Hopkins Joyce's celebrity originate? While not discounting Joyce's agency, and Joyce's active role in creating a notorious public persona, she attained iconicity as a gold digger in the context of a widespread panic about men paying unfair alimony to ex-wives. Actions in the legal realm bolstered her notoriety while, at the same time, the scandals surrounding Joyce were used as a justification to reform alimony.

Love, Marriage, and Alimony in the Early Twentieth Century

Alimony is court-mandated financial support paid from one party to another following a couple's divorce. In the early twentieth century, all but four states had procedures by which individuals could seek alimony.[7] In the vast majority of cases, alimony entailed an ex-husband paying toward the maintenance of an ex-wife.[8] Alimony was an important part of family law throughout the twentieth century because it was often the only way to protect women from the economic consequences of divorce. The need for alimony reflected the unequal access men and women had to property and income and, therefore, controversies about alimony encompassed competing perspectives about gender roles and the functions of marriage.

During the nineteenth century, marriage was governed by the legal doctrine of coverture. The husband's authority "covered" a woman's right to own property, earn an income, or use the legal system. Therefore, husband

and wife were a single entity under the law, and the law of coverture created a relationship of dependency of the wife on the husband.[9] In the years before states' Married Women's Property Acts overturned the legal grip of coverture, when married women could not legally own property, alimony settlements were relatively uncontroversial because they kept a divorced woman from becoming a public charge. As women's political and economic opportunities expanded during the first two decades of the twentieth century, critics in various professional domains questioned the fairness of the alimony system. Concerns about alimony in the United States reached a crescendo in the late 1920s in the wake of public scandals surrounding Peggy Hopkins Joyce and other alleged gold diggers. Several states considered alimony reforms to cap the money owed to former wives, limit the length of alimony payments, or make it easier for men to receive alimony. Judges publicly criticized alimony seekers as "parasites," and anti-alimony organizations like the Alimony Payer's Protective Association boasted of thousands of members. Alimony was portrayed in courtrooms, newspapers, and religious sermons as a crisis that threatened to destroy American families and the U.S. social structure. Yet, the public outcry against alimony was, like awards for alimony themselves, anomalous. The rate of alimony payments remained steady throughout the 1920s. In the 2000s, Constance Shehan and her coauthors noted, "In relative terms, alimony awards are currently—and have historically been—rare in the United States." Alimony judgments were not only rare but, when they did occur, were typically granted to women who were unable to work and had children to support.[10] The moral panic about alimony in the 1920s grew from vast changes that were occurring in American families in the early twentieth century.

Beginning in the late nineteenth century, large-scale industrialization and urbanization changed the economic basis of family life.[11] Americans had big families in the nineteenth century as an economic strategy, but the average family size plummeted over the course of the nineteenth century. In 1800, the typical married couple had over seven children per household, which fell to an average of four children per household by the end of the century. Preindustrial labor was divided and managed within families, and the rise of the factory system undermined the place of the family as a singular economic unit. Raising many children no longer held an economic advantage. Breakthroughs in science, medicine, and public health decreased infant mortality and reduced the need for families to have several children in order for a few to survive. By the end of the nineteenth century, these changes altered the economic place of offspring in family life, and a sentimental understanding of children and domesticity accompanied a decline in the size of the average family.[12]

Changes in family structure during the first two decades of the twentieth century accompanied new employment opportunities for young adults. Young unmarried working-class women, including many immigrants or the daughters of immigrant parents, heavily populated the female labor force. The rapid growth of corporations and retail markets created sales and clerical positions for women. Women filled a rising demand for saleswomen, clerks, and stenographers, and many were hired into jobs that had been the exclusive domain of working-class men. In 1890, there were 3.6 million women in the paid labor force, representing about 19 percent of the female population. By 1910, almost a quarter of the U.S. female population worked outside the home. In Manhattan and Brooklyn, for example, the total number of all working women nearly doubled between 1880 and 1900. Income from rising employment opportunities gave working-class women a growing public presence in cities, and the arrival of mobile and uprooted populations of immigrants and wage-earning women generated innovative ideas about companionship, romance, marriage, dating, sex, and childrearing.[13]

Several social factors, including the birth control movement, women's suffrage, a significant rise in women's employment opportunities, and an expanding leisure industry, generated new expectations about the purpose of marriage and family in the early twentieth century. The idea of a personal lifestyle independent from religious, civic, and family obligations competed with the last vestiges of Victorian asceticism, and marriage came to mean something different in this context. Historian Christina Simmons notes, "The older concept of marriage as a sacred and permanent economic and procreative institution, with political, class, and moral functions, that was grounded in larger networks of kin and community, became less salient." Historian William Kuby states how, "Gradually the economic model of mate selection faded from view." Victorianism eroded, and Americans across different classes, and across different ethnic and racial groups, increasingly saw marriage as a place for two people to find personal fulfillment. Experimentation with marriage flourished. New modes of marriage, including the growing prominence of "flapper marriage," African American "partnership marriage," feminist marriage, and trial marriage changed the prevailing understanding of traditional matrimony.[14]

Ideas about marriage that were considered radical in the 1910s were being quickly adopted by men and women from different social strata in the 1920s. Chief among the new frameworks for understanding the functions of matrimony was "companionate marriage." The term companionate marriage was coined by Barnard history professor Melvin M. Knight in 1924 to describe a marriage based around love and intimacy instead of procreation. Colorado judge Benjamin Barr Lindsey's 1927 book *Companionate Marriage* popularized the concept. Companionate marriage emphasized camaraderie, mutual respect, and equality. According to its advocates, companionate marriage entailed having fewer children, adopting a democratic organization for the family, and focusing on the emotional needs of husband and wife. As the companionate marriage ideal grew in the early twentieth century, critics expressed qualms about the use of matrimonial bureaus and matchmaking services. Like concerns about gold diggers, critics of commercialized matchmaking services argued that they corrupted the institution of marriage by encouraging people to leap up the social class ladder by marrying wealthy partners. According to Kuby, marriage services were seen as "a major culprit in the ongoing marriage crisis."[15]

Changing marital norms in the United States caused an increase in the divorce rate and a growing perception that American marriages were in a state of crisis. Historian Elaine Tyler May—who studied case files of Southern California divorces that took place from 1880 to 1930—found many 1880s divorce cases triggered by the husband's or wife's failure to attain the Victorian ideal of femininity or manliness. Many 1880s divorces stemmed from a husband's intemperance or a wife's failure to be "ladylike," but these grounds for divorce were much rarer by 1920. Divorces in the 1920s were often sparked by the inability of the husband or wife to live up to the modern lifestyle expectations of his or her marriage partner. According to May, increasing numbers of Americans sought the glamor displayed in movie houses, but "day-to-day married life did not meet the promises of the Hollywood style." The disjunction between the norms of traditional marriage and the desires created by the burgeoning consumer culture generated domestic dissatisfaction across gender, race, and class lines.[16]

Divorce became a prominent social issue in the 1920s.[17] In 1900, there were over 55,000 divorces in the United States, a rate of four divorces per 1,000 residents. In 1910, the number of divorces increased to over 83,000 but the divorce rate remained relatively stable (4.5 divorces per 1,000 people). The decade between 1910 and 1920, however, witnessed a steep rise in the divorce rate. The number of divorces more than doubled during these years, and the divorce rate increased from 4.5 to 7.7 divorces per 1,000 residents.[18] Changing patterns of family life, women's increased participation in the paid labor force, and new forms of leisure and consumption lowered the social stigma of divorce. A 1920 *Los Angeles Times* editorial ventured, "If one is to judge by the number of sensational divorce suits that are treading on one another's heels and clogging the calendars of the Superior courts, the country has suddenly been inundated by a tidal wave of marital infidelity."[19] Some members of the white middle and upper classes reacted with outsized outrage to shifting marital norms. As the birthrate among so-called native-born whites declined, prominent whites like Theodore Roosevelt trumpeted fears of "race suicide." Historian Kristin Celello observes that "race suicide" rhetoric, "when paired with anxieties about the divorce rate, contributed to a full-fledged sense of crisis in regard to the state of family life in the United States."[20]

The rising number of divorces, coupled with new lifestyle-based justifications for separation, appeared as signs of vast moral decay for many Americans. A 1919 *Los Angeles Times* editorial warned, "Divorce is becoming an increasingly profitable venture for a woman and an increasingly expensive experience for men."[21] An exchange in the editorial pages of the *New York Times* reveals the centrality of alimony in discussions of the marriage crisis and, in turn, its place in women's emancipation. Less than two months after Peggy Hopkins Joyce received voluminous media coverage because of her divorce from a lumber tycoon—and less than three months after the ratification of the Nineteenth Amendment granted national women's suffrage—Samuel Saloman published an editorial in the *New York Times* that criticized women's growing economic and social power. Saloman was a conservative Jewish community leader who publicly excoriated birth control, the teaching of evolution, and communism. He argued in the *Times*, "Under the laws of many of the States the marriage copartnership is a most unequal and inequitable one, with practically all the burdens and obligations on the male and the profits and privileges to the female partner to the arrangement."[22] For Saloman the alimony system was a "howling injustice." He declared, "the divorcée, your true 'parasite woman,' had long tyrannized over the man who conscientiously objected to contribute to her support."[23] Responses to his editorial pointed out that alimony was rare, weakly enforced, and always subject to judicial review.[24] Saloman's editorial nonetheless echoed a common postsuffrage argument about spousal support: If women are now equal to men, why do they need alimony? In what would become a common ideological dynamic in the battle against gold diggers, both proponents and opponents of women's rights viewed the gold digger as a problem for different reasons. For feminists, gold diggers represented a capitulation to the idea that men were economically responsible for women. For antifeminists, gold diggers embodied avariciousness endemic to womanhood.

Simply considering the statistical estimates of divorce, the heightened concern about alimony is unusual. In the early twentieth century, the vast majority of divorces were uncontested.[25] Moreover, alimony was uncommon relative to the number of divorces processed in courts every year. Commenting on post–World War I divorce trends, historian J. Herbie DiFonzo observes, "alimony turns out to have been a surprisingly insignificant factor in the cases."[26] Indeed, the paucity of alimony payments created hardships for divorced women, especially those who were unemployed. Writing about divorce in the late nineteenth and early twentieth centuries, Celello notes, "For wives without independent financial means, the infrequency of alimony allocations meant that divorce could lead to reduced circumstances or even destitution."[27] A government report covering the years 1887 to 1906 showed that only 13 percent of women requested alimony and courts granted it in 9 percent of cases.[28] From 1906 to 1922 the rate of alimony awards rose from 9 percent to nearly 15 percent, but alimony was typically bestowed in instances where the wife was caring for children or unable to work.[29] In the late 1920s, the vitriol that many directed against the alimony system cannot be accounted for by the minor quantitative increase in the alimony rate. The gold digger stereotype performed energetic ideological work to harness misogyny and fears about changing power relationships in marriage, redirecting those feelings toward a singular scapegoat.

Alimony awards were rare, and they were also unevenly enforced and actively resisted.[30] Men avoided paying alimony by taking up residences in neighboring states. Jersey City, Newark, and Hoboken were home to "alimony colonies," allowing men to visit New York on Sundays where "writs in civil processes may not be served on them."[31] A Saturday night railroad run from Philadelphia to New York was referred to as the "alimony train" because it permitted alimony dodgers to arrive in New York in the early morning hours of Sunday and return home before Monday.[32] Men created fake mortgages, transferred holdings to friends, and created dummy corporations to avoid paying alimony. Novelist Faith Baldwin observed in 1928, "An alimony judgment seems to stir up more stubborn resistance and stimulate more resourcefulness than any other kind of conflict that gets people into the courts."[33] Another way men avoided alimony payments was simply to leave the marriage instead of pursuing a legal divorce. Urbanization in the late nineteenth and early twentieth centuries led to a large increase in desertions. Linda Gordon notes how "urban anonymity and geographic mobility meant that men could 'disappear' in a way that was impossible in small-town and agrarian communities."[34] Desertion prevented women from remarrying and, without the support of their husbands, these women faced near-inevitable poverty. Single motherhood compounded the problems of desertion, and child care options like day care were extremely limited. For example, in 1905, there were little more than 200 day nurseries in the entire United States.[35] Moreover, welfare and social support programs were aimed at single mothers and, therefore, single women without children were deemed undeserving of support. Nonpayment of alimony and desertion were, one could reasonably argue, larger social problems than unfair alimony judgments.[36] Despite the dreary reality of postdivorce spousal support in the early twentieth century, major scandals involving alleged gold diggers were the guideposts used by the general public to understand American alimony. The gold digger folk devil shaped the direction of the alimony panic and it provided a raft of arguments used in alimony cases.

The Discovery of Peggy Hopkins Joyce

Marguerite "Peggy" Upton was born in Berkley, Virginia, near Norfolk, probably in 1893, although the exact year is unknown. She lived with her grandmother following her parents' divorce. At the age of sixteen, she dropped out of school and ran away from home with a vaudevillian who performed bicycle stunts. She assisted him on the vaudeville circuit and, in Denver, she met Everett Archibald Jr. Peggy left the bicyclist to marry Archibald, but the union did not last. She spent years in the Northeast reinventing herself as a young woman of refinement, including telling a likely apocryphal story of her enrollment in a finishing school. Her efforts at attaining the requisite cultural capital to break into the upper class paid off, and she met and married Sherburne Hopkins in 1913. Due to their mutual infidelities, she left their plush Dupont Circle home for the excitement of New York City.[37]

Joyce's autobiography, *Men, Marriage, and Me*, depicted her adrift in Manhattan in 1915, penniless and wandering the streets searching for work. Joyce allegedly strolled into Madame Frances's fashionable dress salon, a place Anita Loos described as "a rendezvous for the most expensively kept gold diggers in town."[38] According to Loos, Madame Frances created gold diggers as much as she catered to them: "She would spot some poor, unknown cutie in the backwash of Broadway, send for the girl, and outfit her completely, from garter belts to *robes de style*."[39] Then Frances would

FIGURE 3 Peggy Hopkins Joyce (1893–1957), from her performance in the 1919 play "A Sleepless Night." She met lumber tycoon Stanley Joyce while performing in Chicago. Their divorce battle captured the nation's attention and built Peggy Joyce's reputation as the foremost gold digger of the 1920s. George Grantham Bain Collection, Library of Congress.

introduce the girl to wealthy men at the Stork Club, the Ritz, and other trendy New York nightspots. Frances had the qualities of a matchmaker but, listening to the silences in Loos's description, she also appears to be something of a pimp or trafficker. In Joyce's account, Madame Frances introduced her to Florenz Ziegfeld in 1915, and soon thereafter he made her a star.

Madame Frances possibly introduced Joyce to Ziegfeld, but it is equally likely that Joyce's growing reputation in vaudeville performances caught his attention.[40] From the 1880s to the 1920s, vaudeville was the most popular form of entertainment in the United States. New York's Palace Theater became "the pinnacle of vaudeville" under the ownership of E. F. Albee after it opened in 1913.[41] Joyce worked as a fashion model in the Palace Theatre for the 1915 "Style Show," strolling across the stage in glamorous gowns, surrounded by "the Twenty Most Beautiful Models in the World." She was listed as "Mrs. Sherburne (Peggy) Hopkins," and stories about her second divorce, especially the report that she walked out on her millionaire husband, added to her onstage allure. By April, the show garnered enough success to go on the Keith and Orpheum circuit, the main touring route for vaudeville, guaranteeing her wide exposure. Ziegfeld hired Joyce for the 1917 *Follies* in the New Amsterdam Theatre, and her popularity ensured her participation in his next production, *Miss 1917*.[42]

For many observers, beauty was Peggy Hopkins Joyce's most compelling quality. Peggy Joyce reportedly had little singing or dancing talent, so her vaudeville routines consisted of her wearing extravagant fashions and walking onstage accompanied by an orchestra. Accounts of Peggy Joyce emphasized the extraordinary beauty manifested in her skin, hair, stance, dress, and style. An article about Peggy dining at the Ritz, for instance, described her "generous expanse of throat and gleaming shoulders." A journalist for the *Chicago Daily Tribune* referred to Peggy wearing a black gown: "Against the black depth her white skin, pallidly clear, stood out in refreshing relief." Constance Rosenblum's biography of Peggy Hopkins Joyce presented a typical description of Joyce's gorgeousness: "With her come-hither features and her candy-box coloring, her blonde marcelled bob, her complexion, flawless as alabasters—a cliché that in her case seems to have been true—her creamy shoulders, and the luminous ropes of pearls inevitably twisted provocatively in her fingers, Peggy Hopkins Joyce was a compelling creature, glamorous in a way that no longer exists."[43] Most accounts of Joyce take her beauty as a given quality, seeing her attractiveness as a product of her bone structure, facial symmetry, and slight figure. Taking her beauty for granted in this way potentially elides the racial, class, age, and sexual criteria implicit in the standards of beauty against which the public judged Peggy Hopkins Joyce. Her beauty is an important thing to consider because she not only fit Ziegfeld's image of the "Glorified American Girl," she was involved in its creation. Peggy Hopkins Joyce became part of the language of beauty in the early twentieth century, calling into being a specific understanding of beautiful womanhood. Her physical qualities positioned her in a sexual marketplace, and her image set a kind of market standard for white female sexuality.

Early twentieth-century perceptions Joyce's beauty aligned with dominant notions of racial whiteness. Literary scholar Linda Mizejewski shows that during the first decades of the twentieth century, "the Ziegfeld Girl was one of the many sites where a national white race was being delineated along sexual lines."[44] Mizejewski notes that Florenz Ziegfeld gained a far-reaching reputation "as a prime expert on female beauty" at a time when immigration from southern and eastern Europe to the United States reached a historic peak. From 1900 to 1920, the parameters of whiteness—who was considered part of the "Anglo-Saxon" race—shifted in response to immigration, the migration of African Americans to northern cities, and emergent nativist movements. So-called native-born whites placed immigrants on a racial hierarchy below whites and Anglo-Saxons. The revival of the Ku Klux Klan, the popularity of phrenology and eugenics, and panic over "race suicide" reveal an increased interest in racial purity among self-identified Anglo-Saxons and the "native-born." Ziegfeld's selection of beauty types, Mizejewski argues, paralleled eugenicist efforts to classify racial "types." While eugenics ideology informed understandings of beauty, eugenic thinking also fueled anxiety over immigration, racial and ethnic intermarriage, increasing use of contraceptives, declining white birthrates, and dread about the procreation of the "feebleminded."[45] Peggy Hopkins Joyce as both an emblem of racial whiteness and an archetypal gold digger shows how the gold digger trope tied together and coconstructed a singular, stylized, cultural form that carried significant meanings about social class, gender, sexuality, and race.

Ziegfeld Girls were described as embodying the essential elements of beautiful womanhood: straight noses, small upper lips, blond hair, and creamy white skin. This set of physical criteria excluded many European Jews, and those that might have "passed" were forced to conceal their identities. Pauline Marion Levy, then a Ziegfeld Girl, changed her name to Paulette Goddard to escape her birth name's Jewish connotation. Until her death in 1918, Ziegfeld star Anna Held actively silenced rumors about her Jewish heritage. The acceptance of Fanny Brice into the Ziegfeld organization was predicated on the contrastive role she played next to the Follies Girls. "Fanny Brice's comic genius," writes Mizejewski, "was her embodiment of everything the Ziegfeld Girl was forbidden to be: spontaneous, loud, clumsy, ethnic, Jewish."[46] The Ziegfeld Follies Girl represented a new model of beauty that mirrored and supported a racial hierarchy, and Peggy Hopkins Joyce epitomized the type.

Through her embodiment of normative, beautiful, white womanhood, Peggy Hopkins Joyce also served as a useful point of contrast. Zora Neale Hurston's 1928 essay "How It Feels to Be Colored Me" suggested the extent to which Joyce modeled a potent form of white womanhood as well as how others leveraged that image for uses anticipated by neither Peggy nor her promoters. Hurston wrote that at times, when she felt confident, she strolled Manhattan as if she had "no race." During these times, "Peggy Hopkins Joyce on the Boule Mich with her gorgeous raiment, stately carriage, knees knocking together in a most aristocratic manner, has nothing on me. The cosmic Zora emerges. I belong to no race nor time. I am the eternal feminine with its string of beads."[47] Hurston defined a confident, authentic, black womanhood against Joyce's racial and class privilege.

Vaudeville's esteem faded in the 1910s as people flocked to nickelodeons and moving pictures, and Peggy Hopkins Joyce counted among the vaudevillians who found work in movies.[48] Peggy Joyce's initial screen roles mirrored her flighty and greedy public persona. In an uncredited part, she played a cheating wife in *The Turmoil*.[49] New York illustrator James Flagg cast Peggy Joyce in *Hick Manhattan* and *The Bride*, two of the twenty-plus short films he created from 1917 to 1920. Her portrayal in *The Bride* referenced her supposedly superficial appreciation of marriage in real life. In the film, Joyce's character, a young woman trying to elope against the wishes of her father, refers to marriage as a "charming habit."[50]

Gold digger typecasting followed Peggy in her later roles. Her next film, *The Woman and the Law*, was written and directed by Raoul Walsh. The movie fictionalized the 1917 trial of Blanca de Saulles for murdering her millionaire ex-husband, Jack de Saulles. The story received wide attention in U.S. newspapers, and the murderer looked indistinguishable from Walsh's wife, Miriam Cooper. Winfield Sheehan, an executive at the Fox Film Corporation, urged Walsh to create a film out of the story "while it's hot," and to cast his wife in the leading role.[51] Sheehan hired Peggy Joyce to portray Jack de Saulles's mistress, capitalizing on the actress's notoriety. An intertitle described her character as "that type of woman which infests hotels—her professional smiles drawing men into her web of destruction."[52] Miriam Cooper, Walsh's wife and Joyce's costar, voiced a common characterization of Peggy Joyce: "She wasn't very smart."[53] According to Cooper, Joyce was unaware that she was playing an unsympathetic role during the filming. Cooper recalled in her 1973 autobiography that Joyce flew into a rage a short time into the film's initial screening after discovering her character's true purpose, shouting "where's that son of a bitch? I'll kill him!" Walsh reportedly hid in the ticket booth until Joyce had calmed down.[54] Moviegoers learned about the murder trial from the film, and the trial provided sustenance for the film's narrative. The connection between law and culture cultivated specific understandings about women, marriage, and money.

During the 1918 Broadway season, Peggy Hopkins Joyce appeared in two comedies at the Shubert Theatre (*It Pays to Flirt* and *A Place in the Sun*). On the opening night of *A Place in the Sun*, Joyce missed her cue and delivered her lines a few seconds before the previous scene ended. Her opening night miscue was one of the reasons her costar, Norman Trevor, despised working with her. Joyce recalled, "Of course everyone laughed and I cried and Norman was furious." Her performance received a string of negative reviews but, despite the bad feedback, the Shubert organization arranged another production for Joyce the next year. *A Sleepless Night*, which opened in late 1918, garnered Joyce greater notice in New York newspapers and the celebrity gossip press.[55] Her performance also led to her next, lucrative, marriage.

A Sleepless Night lasted only a few months on Broadway before it traveled to Chicago in 1919. In Chicago, Joyce befriended actress Francine Larrimore while living at the Blackstone Hotel. Larrimore introduced her to Stanley Joyce, a man who had been attending her performances night after night. Peggy Joyce recalled in her memoirs, "He does not laugh very much, only smiles and spends his time constantly looking at me." A reporter described Joyce as a "neat young man, plump faced, pleasant, suave," but Peggy was unimpressed upon first meeting him. She described Stanley as "small and quite uninteresting." "I didn't get a thrill," she told Genevieve Forbes from the *Chicago Daily Tribune*. "My Lord, why should I? I had my career, a good salary, and the promise of a good show for the next year."[56] Stanley Joyce bought Peggy a car to court her and, when she seemed unmoved by the gesture, he gave her a large emerald.[57] Peggy Joyce told a *Chicago Daily Tribune* reporter with her characteristic humor, "I thought the simplest way of getting rid of him was to become his wife."[58]

Peggy Hopkins Joyce ended her relationship with the Shubert organization while *A Sleepless Night* finished its Chicago engagement. Peggy—still married to Sherburne Hopkins—acted to finalize her divorce from Hopkins, and married Stanley Joyce on January 23, 1920. The marriage soured within months and, as the *New York Times* reported, "his violet-eyed bride, Peggy, was not the thoroughly loving wife he believed her to be."[59] Stanley Joyce's chief complaints were Peggy's greed for jewels and furs, her contemptuous treatment of him, and her alleged affairs, particularly during their Paris vacation in the summer of 1920. Peggy claimed in her autobiography that she spent nearly a million dollars in the span of a week, including $200,000 for a diamond necklace and $26,000 for an emerald ring.[60] Although her memoirs exaggerated the pace of her shopping (Stanley claimed that she spent $1.4 million from 1919 to 1921), by all accounts she purchased an impressive collection of jewelry and furs.

Stanley's complaints about Peggy's spending, and Peggy's complaints about Stanley's jealousy and stinginess, signaled relationship trouble, and their problems reached a breaking point during their trip to Paris in May 1920. Peggy allegedly cultivated sexual relationships with a series of men while vacationing in Paris. Ida Smart, a friend from Peggy's Ziegfeld days, acted as her coconspirator, helping to prevent Stanley from detecting his wife's dalliances. Smart cabled Peggy Joyce in code about the travel plans of Peggy's lovers, and Peggy "conjured up make-believe shopping trips and hair dresser appointments to explain her absence to Joyce." Despite Peggy and Ida's efforts, Peggy's affairs with French publisher Henri Letellier and professional tango dancer Maurice Mouvet became well known to her social circle. By August 1920, Peggy Joyce spent an increasing amount of time with Letellier, and their affair was "the talk of Europe's high society." Stanley Joyce left Europe without Peggy, and reports of the couple's marital problems leaked to the press. Months later, the press verified that Stanley sought a divorce and that Peggy wanted one million dollars in settlement. Peggy Joyce secured the services of Weymouth Kirkland, one of the leading trial lawyers in Chicago. A few years before he represented Joyce, Kirkland successfully defended *The Chicago Tribune* against a million-dollar libel suit launched by Henry Ford. Stanley Joyce hired Alfred Austrian, a man with the reputation as "one of the most learned and eloquent lawyers in the city." Armed with Chicago's finest legal representation, Peggy Hopkins Joyce and Stanley Joyce marched toward what the *Los Angeles Times* called "the most sensational divorce case in the courts of the United States in the last quarter century."[61]

Peggy responded to the divorce claim on multiple fronts: she contended that, if she was a gold digger, Stanley made her that way. "He taught me to like expensive things," she told Genevieve Forbes. "It's not my fault, it's his." Joyce claimed, "men were always trying to make me develop a taste for richer, better, more gorgeous things." Peggy Joyce also complained that Stanley robbed her of her independence, telling Forbes, "He wanted to make the world his doll's house, and I was to be that doll." She said, instead of purchasing her expensive fur coats, she "would be much safer and happier in marrying him if I knew he would not drink."[62] Finally, turning the tables on the claim of gold digging, Peggy Joyce argued that Stanley married her for *her* money.[63]

Peggy Joyce also disparaged Stanley's purported adherence to high standards and respectability. In court, Peggy Joyce's attorney alluded to the sexual experience of his client as a way of challenging Stanley's assertions of morality. Her attorney Weymouth Kirkland said, "Did he think at that time he was meeting a social debutante at a pink tea? Did he think she never went out at night without a chaperon? He did not. He knew she was a girl who had to make her own living in the world. He knew she was working as an actress at a theater." Kirkland called Joyce "a stage door Johnny," the slang term describing men who dated chorus girls and waited with gifts for them offstage.[64] The attorney said that Stanley Joyce knew the type of woman with whom he was getting involved. His statement underscored the double bind that women accused of gold digging faced. On the one hand, a woman making "her own living in the world" invited dishonor. On the other, marrying for economic security opened women to accusations of gold digging. The misogynistic logic of the gold digger stereotype gave Stanley Joyce's attorney a powerful cudgel in the courtroom.

Newspaper images bolstered the idea of Peggy Hopkins Joyce as a monstrous gold digger. An illustration in the *Chicago Tribune* depicts Peggy Joyce towering over a small illustration of Stanley Hopkins. Stanley holds up a house as if to offer it to his bride, superimposed over a giant picture of Peggy Joyce.[65]

Another profile of Peggy Joyce's gold digging appeared in the *Washington Post*, titled "Secrets of Vamping." One of the images shows Peggy dangling a tiny man hanging on a piece of string. The wealthy victim—dressed in a tuxedo with tails, a top hat, and a cane—looks up helplessly at a giant Peggy Hopkins Joyce wearing an evening gown with strands of jewels.[66] Peggy peers down at the man with disinterest or, perhaps, disdain. Depictions of Peggy as monstrous, or monstrously seductive, formed a context and explanation for characterizations of her gold digging. With Peggy in charge, there was nothing a normal or reasonable man could do to resist her sexual power. Stanley's wealth could be measured in discrete increments, but Peggy's inimitable and unquantifiable beauty confounded notions of equivalence and commensuration. Fictionalized images of Peggy Hopkins Joyce instantiated more than an opinion about her marriage; they revealed men's anxieties about changing gender and sexual relationships.

Judge Joseph Sabath, a familiar figure in Chicago's divorce court during the 1920s and 1930s, presided over *Joyce v. Joyce* in 1921. Some retrospective evidence indicates that he showed sympathy to neither alleged gold diggers nor their victims. In a 1925 interview he said, "Feminine gold diggers

"Keep them guessing," says Peggy Hopkins Joyce.

FIGURE 4 "Dangle Them." Peggy Hopkins Joyce became a part of the language of beauty and whiteness during the 1920s. At the same time, the national press portrayed Joyce as a folk devil, a threat to rich white men. "Secret of Vamping, Says Peggy Hopkins Joyce, Depends upon Always Keeping the Man Guessing," *Washington Post*, March 18, 1923, magazine section, 3.

usually marry old and wealthy men. In such a case I am in favor of the woman. It is a good lesson for the aged man who thinks he can get a young and lovely wife for nothing." Sabath's observation also demonstrated the place of stereotypes—"feminine gold diggers"—in his legal reasoning. At the hearing, Peggy tried to obtain $10,000 a month temporary alimony and $100,000 for solicitor's fees. Sabath took into account Peggy Joyce's private fortune, estimated at over $100,000, and reached a compromise decision on alimony. He awarded her $1,850 a month pending the final hearing of the suit and $40,000 for her defense.[67]

After her divorce Peggy Hopkins Joyce traveled alone to Paris in the spring of 1922. In Paris, Peggy developed a close relationship with Guillermo "William" "Billy" Errázuriz, a married attaché of the Chilean Legation. Errázuriz shot and killed himself after a long night of drinking with Joyce and Henri Letellier, Joyce's other lover. Newspapers the following morning reported that Errázuriz took his life because of his "unrequited love for Peggy Hopkins Joyce, and for jealousy of Henri Letellier."[68] Errázuriz allegedly loved Peggy Hopkins Joyce since 1916 and, after taking his diplomatic post in Paris in 1921, spent an increasing amount of time with her. She first met Errázuriz during the trial of his sister, Blanca de Saulles, who killed her millionaire husband over a child custody dispute. The murder provided the basis for Raoul Walsh's *The Woman and the Law*, in which Peggy Joyce played the murdered ex-husband's lover. The threads of Joyce's fictional portrayals and her real life tangled again.

On the night of the suicide, Peggy Joyce, Henri Letellier, and Guillermo Errázuriz drank champagne until six in the morning. Peggy danced with both men and, just after leaving the last establishment, she invited Letellier to her suite for a final drink. Errázuriz spoke out before Letellier answered, declaring his love for Peggy. She told him that she loved Letellier, not him, and she bade good night to both men. Guillermo Errázuriz said, "There will be no tomorrow for me," and went next door. Peggy heard a gunshot minutes later. The *New York Times* quoted Peggy Joyce: "Poor Billy was so jealous. I have known him as a friend for six years, but lately he was demanding that I marry him, and when I confessed my love for M. Letellier he seemed to go crazy." In an interview, however, she declared that Errázuriz was "the only man I ever truly loved" and said that she "loved Billy better than any man I ever knew." The Errázuriz suicide garnered extensive attention from the press and the public. The event received its most elegiac description in one of Ernest Hemingway's notebooks. Hemingway wrote six prose poems while living in Paris in 1922 which he later revised for *A Moveable Feast*. "I have seen Peggy Joyce at 2 a.m.," he wrote, "in a *Dancing* in the Rue Caumartin quarrelling with the shellac haired young Chilean (who had manicured fingernails blew a puff of smoke in her face, wrote something in his notebook) and shot himself at 3:30 the same morning."[69] Other representations of the Errázuriz suicide struck a different tone. In the daily papers, the suicide was a source of humor.[70] A two-panel comic featured in the *Chicago Daily Tribune* made light of the Errázuriz suicide by depicting a group of men jumping off an ocean pier after reading the news coverage. "If Peggy keeps on," the captions read, "she's going to drive a lot more people to suicide." The headlines of the newspapers that were held by the men—all about Peggy Hopkins Joyce—poked fun at her overexposure and suggested the inappropriate prominence of the Errázuriz story in the national media.

In the wake of the Errázuriz suicide and new rumors about Peggy Joyce's affair with boxer Jack Dempsey, the Motion Picture Theatre Owners of America adopted a resolution at their 1922 annual meeting barring Peggy Joyce or Jack Dempsey from appearing in motion pictures.[71] The Motion

Pictures Producers and Distributors Association, led by Will Hays, supported the position that no films featuring Peggy Joyce should be screened in the United States.[72] Banned from cinema, Joyce returned to work in vaudeville and was hired by the Earl Carroll Vanities of 1923. Joyce continued to receive news coverage, but media attention to her exploits never burned as brightly as it did in the early 1920s.

Despite her declining popularity, the presence and cultural imprint of Peggy Hopkins Joyce lingered for several years. Peggy Hopkins Joyce made a brief appearance in Anita Loos's 1925 novel *Gentlemen Prefer Blondes*. In the second half of the story, Lorelei meets Henry Spoffard, a moral reformer from New York, who is well known for "always senshuring all the plays that are not good for peoples morals." Lorelei recalls a particular memory of Spoffard spotting Peggy Hopkins Joyce with one of his friends, which prompted him to walk out of a luncheon at the Ritz "because Mr Spoffard is a very very famous Prespyterian and he is really much to Prespyterian to meet Peggy Hopkins Joyce."[73] The Ritz Hotel, where Kay Laurell gave Avery Hopwood the idea for his play *The Gold Diggers*, acted as a site where fictional and real gold diggers collided.

The ban on her movie appearances also softened. In 1926, she starred with Lilyan Tashman and Owen Moore (Mary Pickford's first husband) in *The Skyrocket*, which opened to favorable reviews in February 1926. The *Times* reviewer observed that Joyce "is quite good in her role, but she is not impressive."[74] *The Skyrocket* was Joyce's final appearance in silent film, although her presence lingered still. Two years later, in 1928, Eddie Cantor's popular song "Makin' Whoopee" described the costliness of divorce and referred to Joyce's alleged promiscuity in one of its encore lyrics.[75] Peggy Joyce played herself in *International House*, a 1933 film about investors who descend on fictional "Wu Hu" China in order to witness the advent of the television. In the film, Peggy Joyce notices a group of wealthy men meeting in a train station and tries to join them on their trip to Wu Hu. Joyce discovers that the train tickets to Wu Hu are sold out, so she flirts with a man and eventually convinces him to drive her there. Later, the man's wife is furious to find them together at the hotel. He pleads his innocence, but his wife says in angry incredulity, "Are you having me believe that you were perfectly innocent with Peggy Hopkins Joyce?" The joke, as most moviegoers in the 1930s would have recognized, capitalized on Joyce's reputation for promiscuity. Playing up her stereotype as a gold digger, Joyce reinforced a formulaic understanding of her motives and way of life.

Peaches Browning: The "Acid-Scarred Girl Wife"

In the late 1920s, press reports of Peggy Joyce jockeyed with stories of other supposed gold diggers. The front page of the April 19, 1926, *Chicago Daily Tribune* featured a six-panel comic under the banner "Who Is the Most Interesting Person in the World Today?" The comic featured, along with Mussolini and Henry Ford, Frances "Peaches" Browning and Peggy Hopkins Joyce. The drawing shows a throng packed tightly around a smiling face wearing a hat and furs, noting that "New York City seems convulsed about 'Peaches' Browning, the fifteen year old bride." Peggy Joyce—"who gets married so often the marriage statistics can't keep up with her"—was said to be "a close second" behind Peaches in national notoriety.[76]

The 1926–27 Peaches Browning scandal, where a teenage girl married a fifty-one-year-old Manhattan real estate mogul, amplified the chorus of criticism against perceived alimony abuses. In 1926, Edward Browning married fifteen-year-old Frances Heenan in a secret ceremony designed to derail an investigation by a children's protection society. He called her "Peaches" and she referred to him as "Daddy." The couple became national celebrities from 1926 to 1927, with tabloids playfully documenting Peaches's garish shopping trips and "Daddy" Browning's many eccentricities. In later decades, one can easily imagine sympathy expressed toward Peaches as a victim of pedophilia, rape, and exploitation. Just as easily, one can picture the actions of Edward Browning triggering a torrent of condemnation and a likely prison sentence. Instead, in 1926 and 1927, the national media portrayed Peaches as a conniving gold digger and Edward "Daddy" Browning as a browbeaten victim. The counterintuitive treatment of Peaches and Edward reflected historically distinct attitudes about age, sexual agency, and early twentieth-century understandings of "child brides."[77] To be sure, none of the parties in the Peaches Browning scandal escaped criticism from the American public. The New York City tabloid press made alarming insinuations that Edward Browning molested his ten-year-old adopted daughter as well as ordered Peaches to strip naked and showed her nude pictures of occult figure Alma Hirsig.[78] The dominant characterization of Peaches as a gold digger, however, undercut a now-familiar narrative of victimization, and Peaches's supposed sexual agency neatly aligned with a discourse about gold digging and alimony abuse in the late 1920s. The Peaches Browning scandal shows how the gold digger stereotype redirected potential suspicions about child exploitation by creating (and drawing from) widespread cultural anxieties about marriage and alimony.

When Peaches Browning married Edward Browning in April 1926, Browning was one of the wealthiest men in America. At the time of his death in 1948, he owned hundreds of Manhattan buildings and a fortune of $20 million. Browning was divorced and living with his nine-year-old adopted daughter when he met Frances Heenan at the Phi Lambda Tau sorority high school dance in March 1926. Browning founded Phi Lambda Tau (known as the "Pretty Little Things"). He funded their events and attended nearly every one of their social dances. Browning was immediately attracted to Heenan, and he dubbed her "Peaches" because she appeared to him like "peaches and cream." She, like the other members of the sorority, called him "Daddy." Over the next several weeks, Browning spent a great deal of time with Peaches and her mother Carolyn. Her story, already bizarre, took a tragic turn when, following a telephone call with Edward, Peaches went to sleep and was allegedly awakened by someone throwing a vial of acid in her face. The acid burned her chin and neck, causing severe scars. She underwent multiple surgeries to treat her damaged skin.[79] The account of the acid burn became important in her and Browning's separation trial months later.

Frances and Edward's courtship, with all of its strange and lurid subplots, drew interest from Vincent Pisarra, superintendent of the New York Society for the Prevention of Cruelty to Children. Pisarra filed a suit in New York Children's Court to have Frances's mother declared a neglectful and improper guardian. But Peaches had permission from her parents and, being over the age of twelve, she was legally able to wed.[80] Browning married Heenan in a secret ceremony a little more than a month after they first met, partly in an effort to stymie Pisarra's plan for prosecuting Browning. As the words "peach" and "peachy" became popular slang terms, the news-reading public followed stories about Peaches's extravagant shopping trips and her attendance at professional tennis tournaments, fashion shows, and beauty pageants.[81]

On October 2, 1926, Frances Heenan instructed the doormen and bell-boys at the Browning estate to pack her jewels and clothing (worth approximately $30,000) in a car, and then she drove away with her mother.[82] Peaches made a public statement that she was leaving Edward Browning, and the two parties fought each other through the New York City tabloids. Edward Browning accused Heenan of failing to provide him a child of his own and Heenan accused Browning of destroying her mental health through his various eccentricities and demands. She also introduced the charge that Edward Browning molested his adopted daughter. The allegation carried more weight because of Browning's past. Browning placed an ad in New York newspapers in 1925 to find and adopt a "pretty refined girl, about 14 years old" as a playmate for his daughter Dorothy Sunshine. Browning became enamored with one of the ad's respondents, Mary Louise Spas. He paid her parents and commenced adoption proceedings. New York authorities investigated Browning (because it was illegal to pay for a child), and New York tabloids discovered that Spas was not sixteen as her parents claimed but, rather, twenty-one. Browning had the adoption annulled, but his reputation as a potential pedophile grew.[83]

In New York, the only legal ground for divorce was adultery, and there was no evidence that either Frances Heenan or Edward Browning were sexually unfaithful. Unable to divorce, Heenan sought the closest thing, legal separation. Browning countersued for abandonment. The legal separation trial determined the basis of their separation and the financial obligations of the parties—who was at fault and what, if anything, Browning had to pay Heenan. In November 1926, Heenan's lawyer Henry Epstein filed a motion requesting Browning pay Peaches temporary alimony of $4,000 a month in addition to $40,000 in legal fees. Two weeks after Epstein filed the motion, the judge heard arguments from the parties in front of a crowded courthouse. The judge eventually ruled that Peaches should receive $1,200 a month in temporary alimony and $8,500 in fees. The formal separation trial, where a judge made a final determination in Edward's alimony, began on January 24, 1927.

Like Stanley Joyce's divorce trial, the Daddy-Peaches separation trial gained national press coverage. The trial lasted five days, producing a flood of racy media coverage that vacillated between portrayals of Peaches as an exploited child and depictions of her as a gold digger who took advantage of Browning. The *New York Times* reported, "She looked very much like an overgrown girl who had been hurt and was trying not to cry." A *Chicago Daily Tribune* reporter painted a different picture, incorrectly gave her age as seventeen, and said, "she showed a bit of ironic humor, strangely out of place in one so young—she is only 17 years old [*sic*] now—and a poise that would have done credit to a woman of mature years"; and, "Her mature appearance and her cool eye gave the lie to the baby blonde curls wandering out from under her blue hat." Multiple newspapers discussed her mature, yet affected, speaking style, describing how she preferred a soft *a* sound when pronouncing "dance," and that "pos-i-tive-ly" was her favorite affirmative response. All agreed that the topics discussed in court provoked a mature performance from Peaches. The *Washington Post* reported, "For four hours the acid-scarred girl wife, sometimes in tears, related a tale of marital abnormalities that forced the justice sitting in judgment on her cause to veil his eyes. It covered a wide range. Much of it was unprintable."[84]

Peaches's four-hour testimony levied a list of charges against her husband ranging from the trivial to the horrendous. Of the less serious claims, Peaches Browning testified that Edward engaged in a series of strange behavior that made it impossible for her to live at the estate. Browning, she alleged, treated her like an infant, bringing home a pink frilled teddy bear for her as a gift. When she asked for an automobile, he brought her a toy car. Peaches expressed that she wanted a child of her own and so Edward Browning offered to adopt a "Japanese princess" which "he told her didn't cost much and she could take it walking with her in native dress and get more publicity." Peaches also testified that Browning's sexual aggression constituted a form of insufferable cruelty. On their wedding night, Browning wanted Peaches to walk in front of him naked and he supposedly showed her nude pictures of Alma Hirsig. Peaches's pretrial statements to the press that Hirsig led a "love cult" prompted Hirsig to bring a $150,000 slander suit against Peaches. The suit was eventually dismissed.[85]

Other testimony from Peaches suggested graver themes, including the intimation that Edward hired someone to throw acid on her face.[86] The most serious allegations centered on Edward's relationship with his adopted daughter, Dorothy Sunshine. Carolyn Heenan, Peaches's mother, laid the groundwork for this claim in her pretrial affidavit, which noted that Browning's adopted daughter was "fast approaching full physical development," and stated that "my daughter's husband is sexually abnormal and that a careful analysis of his attentions to Dorothy Sunshine would reveal this." Harry Epstein, at the end of his direct examination of Peaches, bolstered the insinuation that Edward had sexually molested Dorothy Sunshine. Peaches told the court that Edward entered Dorothy's room at two or three in the morning several nights a week, testimony which "caused a dead silence in the courtroom."[87]

Although Peaches gave potentially damaging testimony against Browning, the press and the courtroom crowd held her up for harsh criticism. Peaches and her attorney sought to show that Edward's many eccentric behaviors wrecked her nerves, but Browning's attorney John Mack easily defused Peaches's stories by noting their triviality. For instance, Peaches testified that when she asked Edward Browning for a dog, he brought her a watch with three tiny clay puppy charms. During his cross-examination of Peaches, Mack asked, "The pups, now, did they cause you any mental

FIGURE 5 Peaches Browning (1910–1956), January 1927. In later decades, sixteen-year-old Frances "Peaches" Heenan would likely be considered a victim of sexual exploitation for her marriage to a fifty-one-year-old real estate mogul. In the late 1920s, cultural critics and the press portrayed Peaches as a ruthless gold digger. George Grantham Bain Collection, Library of Congress.

anguish?" "No, not the pups particularly, but it got worse," she said. "The pups got worse?" the attorney quipped, to the delight of many in the courtroom. The *Los Angeles Times* reported, "When the courtroom broke out in laughter, the young woman, who had consistently held to a dignified attitude, retorted 'This is no joking matter to me.'"[88] Judge Albert Seeger held a thin grip on the proceedings, and the crowd was prone to excited outbursts. Edward Browning's attorney capitalized on the lax atmosphere.

Edward Browning's defense strategy aimed to obliterate Peaches's claims to respectability by detailing her prior sexual experiences. With a strategy akin to rape and seduction defenses, Browning delved into her romantic past in order to sully her reputation and, ultimately, establish her culpability for the separation. Peaches's diary formed the primary source for this line of attack. The *Chicago Daily Tribune* reported at the time, "They will resort to the tactic of calling as many of these boys mentioned in the diary as they can reach." Edward Browning's attorney told the judge, "I will show that this woman has a past. We propose to show that this young woman was accustomed to being unclad and had been intimate with young men before her marriage."[89] Tales of heavy drinking, casual sex, nude parties, and general debauchery created a portrait of Peaches Browning as a sexual agent—a "woman" with a sexual past—not a teenager.

The efforts to portray Peaches as sexually immoral likely influenced the judge's decision-making. Judge Seeger ruled in favor of Edward Browning, maintaining that Peaches unjustifiably abandoned him, and he denied that Edward owed Peaches any alimony. Like the press reports of the trial, Judge Seeger juxtaposed statements about Peaches's young age with insinuations about her consensual sexual experience. Seeger described Peaches as an "infant of the age of sixteen years," but said, "The defendant had been in the habit for about a year of attending dances, theatres, motion pictures and restaurants with young men and without a chaperon." The judge's decision also raised doubts about the acid burn incident, hinting that Peaches may have burned herself to garner sympathy from Edward. He noted that Browning "paid large sums of money for medical treatment to numerous physicians both before and after the marriage." Seeger also rejected as "groundless and particularly vicious" the theory that Edward Browning molested his adopted daughter. As for the claim of intolerable cruelty arising from Browning's many eccentricities, Seeger wrote, "Many of the charges of alleged cruelty are too trivial to warrant the belief that if true they could in any way have affected the defendant's health or peace of mind." The judge's decision portrayed Edward Browning as the exploited party, not the teenage girl. His legal reasoning exposed several things: prevailing anti-alimony attitudes, the trivialization of childhood sexual abuse, a legal system that protected men at the expense of women, and a gender ideology that scorned signs of women's sexual agency.[90]

The judge's rationale, at least in part, rested on the logic of capital exchange. According to his line of reasoning, Peaches was unjustified in leaving Edward because he showered her with economic, cultural, and social capital. By "introducing her into good society, allowing her to play golf and tennis and furnishing her with the implements with which to play," Edward provided Peaches with all of the social advantages that the wealthy and well-connected enjoy. The legal ruling portrayed Edward as Henry Higgins in *Pygmalion* or Daddy Warbucks in the then-popular *Little Orphan Annie* serial comic strip: he sought to transform a dewy-eyed working-class girl into a cultured woman of high society. Seeger explained, "She enjoyed a life of ease and pleasure during her life with plaintiff, taking her breakfast in bed and enjoying all the pleasures that money could buy and that the plaintiff could lavish upon her. She gained twenty pounds in weight." The comment about her weight dovetailed with news reports noting Peaches's plump face and "barrel-shaped" legs. During a time when dominant notions of femininity entailed thinness and athleticism—exemplified in Gabrielle Chanel's modern swimwear styles—observations about Peaches's weight gain highlighted a social exchange gone awry. Edward granted her a new standard of living, and gave her opportunities to golf and play tennis, but she misapplied these resources and became slothful. In this calculation, Browning's wealth and generosity secured a modicum of honorability, despite his strange habits and craving for public attention. Judge Seeger said that Edward Browning "may be a man of peculiar character, tastes and ideas," but it was a fair and equitable relationship. The judge noted that "he endowed her with his property, lifted her out of poverty and gave her every attention up to the very day of her leaving him." The judge also blamed Peaches's mother for the failed relationship. He said that Edward's "treatment of the defendant and her mother was uniformly kind and considerate, but there was no limit to their demands," and that the mother and daughter "falsified, exaggerated and magnified to such an extent as to render their testimony entirely unbelievable."[91]

Peaches received harsh condemnation outside the courtroom as well. She moved to leverage her newfound notoriety by becoming a vaudeville performer but, with her damaged reputation, her plan received public scorn. In a "person on the street" feature in the *Chicago Daily Tribune* a reporter asked if the Chicago City Council should "bar 'Peaches' Browning from appearing as a performer in a dance café?" One man said that she already has had too much publicity. A woman commented, "Chicago does not need 'Peaches.'" A nightclub in Pittsburgh bowed to pressure from civic and religious organizations to cancel one of her scheduled appearances. The Motion Picture Theatre Owners Association of Western Pennsylvania and West Virginia barred her performing in any of the 400 theaters they oversaw.[92]

The public reaction to the judge's ruling was consistently in favor of Edward Browning's legal victory, and many observers used the ruling as an opportunity to criticize gold diggers. Prominent newspapers heaped scorn on the child bride. Harry Carr, a writer for the *Los Angeles Times*, declared, "Peaches Browning deserves even less than she got." He referenced Pisarra's investigation in another column: "The various humane societies had best start on an entirely new tack in this 'Peaches' Browning case. Instead of protecting the kindergarten classes from the middle-aged realty dealer, it is he who needs protection." In his 1927 survey of American law, William Armstrong Fairburn referred to the Browning case as the "most sensational and most disgusting divorce," and declared, "This is certainly the 'Gold-Digger' era." In an unsubtle reference to Peaches's mother, he blamed "mother-in-law gold diggers, using girls of fifteen or sixteen as 'bait.'" R. F. Wingard, in his letter to the *Chicago Daily Tribune*, showered praise on Seeger's ruling. He said, "If Chicago judges followed his decision we wouldn't have as many women gold diggers looking for divorces and large alimony." Others insisted that the ruling did not go far enough to relieve Edward Browning of financial obligation. Richard Harding Armstrong, writing for the *Virginia Law Register*, referred to Browning's preliminary alimony award as inspiration for other gold diggers: "'Peaches' Browning solemnly left the court-room a poor little unhappy, disillusioned woman. Yes, it seems sad indeed that one so young should come to such an end. She is suing her aged husband and all she has now in the world is an income of three hundred dollars a week, which was awarded to her as alimony. Now, if we are desirous of cutting down the divorce rate, how in the world do we expect to do it by offering such enormous prizes to the successful party?" For Armstrong, "The Browning case is just an ordinary case with extraordinary characters. Others, daily meet the same fate." Armstrong advocated a national divorce law that would abrogate an ex-husband's alimony obligation if the ex-wife was childless and able to work.[93]

The comments from Richard Armstrong illustrate how images of gold diggers and gold digging—propelled by stories about Peggy Hopkins Joyce and Peaches Browning—thoroughly entered the discursive repertoire of judges and lawyers during the late 1920s. A judge from the District of Columbia observed in 1927, "It seems to me that this business of divorce is to a large degree the business of gold-diggers." He said, "As far as I have it in my power, I am going to discourage the gold-diggers and I intend to remove temptation from the paths of those who are doing the digging." Chicago judge Chief Justice Harry A. Lewis set a "far-reaching precedent" in 1925 by denying alimony in cases where the women are childless and healthy. He said, "This gold-digging trade in blasted marital alliances by women, who have failed as much as their former mates in making the dead union a success, must stop." New York Supreme Court Justice Selah B. Strong declared in 1926, "alimony evil turns wives into parasites, liars, cheats, money grabbers, and contributors to immorality on a wholesale scale," and he urged the public to "get actively behind a movement for adequate revision of the statutes relating to marriage and divorce." Driven by the Peaches Browning and Peggy Hopkins Joyce scandals, a movement was underway by the late 1920s to reform the alimony system.[94]

The 1927 Alimony Panic

Many Americans perceived a vast alimony crisis despite the relative scarcity of alimony claims, the barriers to receiving alimony, and the social and economic conditions that disadvantaged single women compared to single men. In this way, the anxiety about alimony has characteristics of a moral panic. Prominent comments from novelists, jurists, professors, and journalists described alimony as one of the greatest problems facing the United States. An article in the *Washington Post* in May 1927 observed, "Popular disgust with the alimony provisions of the divorce laws has been growing rapidly in the last few months," and that "the alimony question is one of the most serious problems of our time." A 1927 *Wall Street Journal* editorial captured the anti-alimony mood among American men: "These days a man about to marry must figure whether he can afford not only matrimony but alimony." In advance of a 1927 Pennsylvania town hall meeting sponsored by the Alimony Payers' Protective Association, John Gasteiger described alimony as "the plague of the country." That same year, a New York architect maintained, "the alimony question is one of the most serious problems of our time."[95]

Critics framed the alimony problem as a consequence of gold diggers. Enemies of alimony accused conniving women of using divorce settlements for their own personal gain. In contrast to the statistics on marriage and postdivorce legal settlements during this time period, alimony critics claimed that the majority of women receiving court-mandated spousal support were conniving gold diggers. Reverend John H. Williams told the *Los Angeles Times* in September 1927, "Gold digging is growing more insidious every day and deserves our immediate attention." An Ohio newspaper in 1928 reported "that the familiar 'gold-diggers' far outnumber all other alimony receivers." In a 1927 article in *Harper's*, Dorothy Dunbar Bromley argued that "gold diggers" were "by far the most numerous" of all the women seeking alimony. She noted, "Their number is increasing so rapidly—at least here in the East—as to be a disgrace to the courts that are supposed to mete out justice." Bromley, a feminist and birth control advocate, viewed alimony as out of step with women's independence. Similarly, in 1927, novelist Fanny Hurst described alimony-seeking women as "parasites" and argued, "The vast army of women seeking divorces are mainly after easy alimony from men they have ceased to love—surely one of the most despicable forms of barter that can exchange human hands."[96] Hurst's critique of alimony stemmed from her advocacy of marriage decoupled from economic and child-bearing motives. When her 1915 "trial marriage" to Jacques Danielson was revealed in 1920, the press criticized the couple's unconventional arrangement for providing a bad role model to younger men and women.[97] Hurst's and Bromley's comments on alimony show that the alimony system came under fire from both traditional moralists and from those who advocated models of marriage liberated from calculating economic exchanges between husbands and wives. For traditionalists, alimony reduced marriage to a crass economic connection unmoored from its spiritual and procreative roots. For feminists like Hurst and Bromley, alimony represented an outdated system of marriage where men exchanged money for women's reproductive and domestic labor.

Critics assailed the alimony system for several social problems facing the United States in the 1920s. Most notably, many observers blamed the rising divorce rate on the alimony system. According to this argument, alimony enticed women to remarry multiple times in order to collect payments from two or three ex-husbands. A law clerk from Ohio claimed, "divorcees have developed a highly skillful technique of marrying, divorcing and suing for alimony, then remarry some wealthier man, divorcing and suing again for alimony." A pastor from Indiana singled out Peggy Hopkins Joyce in an antidivorce sermon he delivered to the First Presbyterian Church of Michigan City. He said, "These Peggys of our time are doing more than all of our egotistical newly rich and the plutocrats who cut wages and waste profits, to prevent a return to any kind of normalcy. More than anything else, they are the reason why six hundred wedding rings were smashed in one court in Chicago last year." He also compared Joyce to prostitutes in Chicago's red-light district. Others argued that the alimony created disincentives to remarry. A Chicago judge declared that women stayed single and lived "riotously and often immorally," with "the ex-husband paying for the liquor, the gigolos, and the love nest." The requirement for alimony payments, critics charged, ruined men's businesses and financial security, and it turned alimony into a tool of "polite blackmail."[98]

Alimony critics feared—in addition to financial and material problems generated by profligate postdivorce spousal support—gender disequilibrium created by the alimony system. Robert Ecob, New York architect and founder of the Alimony Payers' Protective Association, declared that alimony gave

American women "political rights far, far ahead of any a man has." A representative from the National Sociological League, an "organization to fight injustice in the present alimony laws," stated, "The modern, much publicized 'equality of the sexes' is an empty phrase" because "a gold-digging, vindictive, heartless wife has everything in her favor when the case goes to court." A 1927 article about the Chicago Anti-Alimony League noted that "many Chicago judges" viewed the alimony system as out-of-date as "a horse and buggy." New York Supreme Court Justice Selah B. Strong argued in 1926 that alimony was appropriate in the age when "the business woman hadn't been invented or discovered," but women's suffrage and new economic opportunities for women obviated the need for postdivorce spousal support. Critics portrayed alimony variously as an invitation to divorce, a cruelty inflicted on men, and an antiquated practice out of sync with new understandings of marriage.[99]

According to some, like novelist Faith Baldwin, the alimony system also posed a threat to the white race. Baldwin called the alimony system "the ultimate refinement of gold digging" and claimed, "There is no doubt that this business of alimony is getting to be a serious menace."[100] Faith Baldwin's 1928 novel *Alimony* narrates the problem of gold diggers and the U.S. alimony system through the toils and interconnected lives of several New Yorkers. *Alimony* describes the demise of a five-year marriage between Stephen and Charlotte Dane, and Charlotte's quest to live off of Stephen's alimony. Charlotte carries the physical hallmarks of a gold digger. Baldwin describes how she possesses "the blond childlike quality of prettiness," and how she could enchant a man with "her soft white throat which her dark dinner dress left uncovered." When she confronts Stephen about obtaining a divorce, she "looked like a tired child, her blond hair crushed against her cheeks." Stephen refuses to grant her a divorce, even though he regards his young wife as "a parasite" who is "ruining him with her extravagance, her demands, her hysteria."[101]

Charlotte's friend Helene refers Charlotte to Max Wertheim, a "well-groomed little Jew" who is "God's gift to alimony-hunters." Baldwin describes Wertheim as a "sleek, dark gentleman" who was "just about as clever as they come." Wertheim hires a detective to document phony evidence of Stephen's affair with his secretary, Eve Harkness. Stephen and Eve have a friendship that deepens as the novel progresses, but Stephen remains faithful to Charlotte despite "her ceaseless, restless extravagance" and "the continuous leakage of his hard-won resources." Charlotte threatens to name Eve as a "corespondent" in the divorce unless Stephen agrees to admit to adultery (the only legal grounds for divorce in New York). He submits to the "entirely vulgar manufacturing of the evidence" by sitting half-dressed on a hotel bed with a woman hired for the purpose of creating grounds for the divorce. A man enters the room to take a photograph of the "couple." Stephen knows he "had perjured himself" but did so "in order that Eve might keep her honest eyes fixed upon the face of the world." Due to the "indefatigable Max," a judge rules that over half of Stephen's income must be paid to Charlotte as alimony.[102]

Stephen falls in love and marries Eve, but they realize that they cannot afford to raise a child, and Stephen's attempt to earn a promotion fails when his employer learns that he is divorced "on statutory grounds." Eve's millionaire stepfather, Thorpe Bedford, accuses Charlotte of "legal gold digging," and works to attain for Stephen a new, higher-paying job. Charlotte finds out through a mutual friend about Stephen's enhanced salary and, again, secures the services of Max Wertheim to gain more alimony. At court, Charlotte "looked very blond and very childlike and most appealing. And the Judge was susceptible to childlike and appealing blonds." Not surprisingly, the judge decrees that Stephen needs to pay Charlotte more monthly alimony. Time passes and Stephen and Eve struggle to raise a family while Charlotte pursues a fulfilling singing career. Bedford intervenes again, engineering a set of circumstances to allow Charlotte to marry her wealthy boyfriend, thereby relieving Stephen from having to pay her alimony.[103]

The novel uses the gold digger trope as a contrastive device to highlight the abuses of the alimony system. Charlotte admits, "I'm a vain woman. I'm selfish, I love comfort and luxury—all the things money can buy." She stands in contrast to Eve, the apotheosis of true womanhood: "a girl who never shirked responsibility, who'd keep her vows just as she'd keep her house— dusted, immaculate, protected." Eve and Charlotte represent opposing models of 1920s womanhood. Charlotte longs for a mink coat, an ermine wrap, and a diamond bracelet. Eve sacrifices her pride and seeks help from her stepfather so that she can be a full-time mother. While Charlotte pursues excitement and material comforts, Eve's willingness to protect her child "makes for the continuation and the good of the race." In the novel, the gold digger anchors intersecting social locations based on race, gender, and social class. As exemplars of the white, middle-class, nuclear family, Stephen and Eve are rescued by appealing to the better nature of Thorpe Bedford, a man who became rich due to the expanding economy of the 1920s. Max Wertheim, meanwhile, exerts "his racial pride in possession of a rare and costly object," Helene's hand in marriage.[104] Baldwin portrays gendered deviance in terms of race. In contrast to Eve's propagation of the white race through the birth of her child (Junior), the gold digger and her accomplices either resist racial reproduction or engage in racial contamination. During their five-year marriage, Charlotte refuses Stephen's intimacies and abdicates her motherly gender role. Helene's engagement to Max occurs during a time when Jews clung to "probationary whiteness" and were regarded as inferior to "native born" whites.[105] *Alimony* draws together the racial threat underlying the gold digger's repudiation of femininity. Baldwin's novel, written during the height of the U.S. alimony panic, sketches a cast of characters who stand in for, and help explain, the wide-ranging economic, social, and legal changes facing American families in the late 1920s.

Other prominent figures in the 1920s used racialized language to criticize the alimony system. The president of Illinois's anti-alimony society referred to the alimony system as "legalized white slavery." White slavery, or forced prostitution, was a heated public issue during the Progressive era. The reference to white slavery is notable because reformers portrayed the victims of white slavery as naive white women from the countryside who, seeking employment and opportunities in the city, were trapped by villainous immigrants. The white slavery panic reflected anxieties about new gender norms and changing racial and ethnic relations. The idea of alimony as "white slavery" inverted the stock anti-prostitution narrative to cast white women as a severe menace. In this way, critics drew a connection between alimony and one of the biggest concerns of the early twentieth century.[106]

For William Armstrong Fairburn, the racial threat of gold diggers stemmed from deep dysfunctions in gender relations. Fairburn was a British-born polymath who attained wealth and recognition in the early twentieth century for inventing a safe and profitable way to manufacture matches. In his treatise on American law, Fairburn struck out against both "campus sheiks and bathing beauties" as embodiments of moral decline among American youth.[107] He also railed against couples who refuse to have children for promoting "race suicide." "The operations of the female gold-digger," he lamented, "now dominate courtship." The age of the dowry, he explained, has been replaced by the age of alimony and, instead of a dowry, women come to a marriage with nothing but a "pick and shovel."[108] The invocation of race suicide fears demonstrates how the gold digger stereotype engaged in racial meaning-making during the 1920s. Through their purported abuse of the alimony system, gold diggers posed a threat to white men and, ultimately, the perpetuation of the white race.

Alimony Martyrs and Anti-Alimony Activism

Some women, like Peggy Hopkins Joyce and Peaches Browning, were the public face of gold diggers and thereby represented alimony abuses in a general sense. Likewise, specific men came to represent the archetypical gold digger victims. Sam Reid, or "Alimony Sam," was perhaps the most well-known victim of gold digging during the 1927 alimony panic. In 1925, Phoebe Brownell married Sam Reid, and the couple had a child named Zada May. Reid's wife sued for divorce in July 1925 after being married less than a year. Phoebe Brownell was granted custody of their child and the judge demanded that Sam Reid pay $40 a month for support ($20 in child support and $20 for alimony). Reid refused to pay, was held in contempt of court, and sentenced to an indeterminate jail term. Reid was troubled by the amount the judge required him to pay, but he was also outraged by the fact that his child was living with its maternal grandmother, not his ex-wife. According to Reid, he was willing to pay four times the amount required by the court, but only if Zada was placed in a "good Christian home." Reid stayed in jail for six months before his case became a lightning rod for anti-alimony sentiment. By December 1927, Reid was receiving hundreds of letters of support from other men.[109]

Reid's ex-wife remarried, which renewed his resolve to stay in jail. He petitioned the California governor, C. C. Young, for a pardon, but was refused. Ultimately, Sam Reid stayed in the Glenn County Jail for over three years. The *Hamilton Evening Journal* referred to Reid as California's "most famous case" of alimony injustice. The *Oakland Tribune* called him a "folk hero."[110] A grocery store called The Twentieth Century Market ran an "Alimony Sam Says" feature in their advertisements, showcasing witty quotations allegedly from Sam Reid.[111] The *San Antonio Light* reported that admirers sent Reid "a flood of encouraging letters from all over the nation—and many of them from women—bidding him keep up courage and continue his one-man filibuster on behalf of altering the prevailing alimony system."[112]

A World War I veteran and formerly clean-cut infantryman, Sam Reid grew out his beard as a form of protest. He explicitly portrayed himself as a martyr, declaring, "I shall never pay. It's not the money; it's the principle. What if I am here for life? I'm the first martyr to a great cause." He also had support from at least some of the men trusted to keep him in jail. Sheriff Roy Heard became friends with Reid during Reid's imprisonment. When

Reid's army friends were having a reunion in San Francisco, Heard escorted Reid from jail so he could attend the event. The Glenn County Bar association charged Heard with contempt of court and fined him $250. On October 28, 1928, Reid's friends from his infantry unit paid the back alimony Reid owed, which allowed him to finally leave the jail. Once free, Reid gained employment as a surveyor for the State Highway Commission at San Luis Obispo. In 1931, Reid found himself again facing legal action from his ex-wife. Sam and Phoebe's young daughter, Zada May, died, and Phoebe sued Sam for approximately $780 for medical and burial expenses. He refused to pay.[113]

Jailed men on the opposite coast staged a similar protest. Three men imprisoned in Brooklyn's King's County Civil Jail formed the Alimony Payers' Protective Association in January 1927. John G. Gasteiger, Frank F. Fiorini, and Hyman A. Proe—all incarcerated for failing to pay their ex-wives alimony—applied to the Secretary of State for a charter. They declared that the organization would protect men against the estimated "100,000 vindictive wives" living in New York. The *Washington Post* doubted the effectiveness of the New York organization, commenting, "It is not likely that the bomb hurled by the Alimony Payers' Protective Association into the ranks of the gold diggers' union will create anything like havoc among the members of that blithe and winsome band who, observing that gentlemen prefer blondes, have boosted the peroxide industry to the peak of production." The reference to Loos's novel demonstrates fluidity between legal and cultural fields, and the levity of *Gentlemen Prefer Blondes* allowed the writer to cast the serious question of postdivorce support in comedic terms.[114]

In Chicago, the fight for alimony reform was led by Dr. Vernon P. Cooley, a forty-seven-year-old dental surgeon. He created the Alimony Club in July 1927 and led their first meeting in August. Approximately sixty people attended the meeting, pledging their support for the club's "war on gold diggers." Cooley's crusade grew out of his experience with Chicago's divorce court following the demise of his first marriage to Margaret Melter. Cooley graduated from the University of Illinois College of Dentistry in 1904 and established a successful practice, earning a yearly income of approximately $12,000. By 1920, he had been married to Margaret Melter for over ten years, but trouble in their relationship reached a breaking point in September 1922 when Melter filed for divorce, alleging that Dr. Cooley "began a course of cruel and inhuman conduct toward her." In his counterclaim, Cooley argued that his wife was a habitual drunk. Melter hired a detective agency to watch her husband, and she accompanied the detectives when they raided the apartment of Cooley's alleged lover, Anna Klein. Melter and the detectives discovered Klein, in silken underwear, in the bedroom with Cooley. The judge found Cooley's explanation unpersuasive and allegedly murmured that his conduct was "disgusting." Judge Hurley awarded Margaret Melter a divorce and decreed that Vernon Cooley pay her permanent alimony of $100 each month. A year later, Cooley successfully petitioned to have his alimony payment reduced by half.[115]

In 1926, Vernon Cooley asked the Superior Court of Cook County to have his alimony requirement completely vacated, premised on the theory that Margaret Cooley's immoral behavior following the divorce should effectively nullify her right to permanent support. Cooley cited three events that supposedly proved Margaret's unwomanly conduct. In the first incident, in October 1924, police stopped Margaret and a man named William Fisher for drunk driving. An officer testified "that her talk was incoherent, and that she smelt of liquor; that her clothes were in a disorderly condition; that she used profane language, and called him a vile name." Over a year later, the same officer stopped Fisher for drunk driving and found Margaret Melter and another woman in the backseat. According to the officer, "it looked like a booze party." Next, in April 1925, a federal agent accompanied three police officers on a raid of Margaret Melter's apartment. They found Fisher and Melter sharing a bed and, upon further searching, discovered two quarts of whiskey and three pints of moonshine. The testifying officer depicted Melter as highly intoxicated: "She would try to get hold of them, and would dance and curse them, and would break into a laugh." The officers arrested her for fornication, but a jury found her not guilty.[116]

Margaret Melter denied these events occurred and maintained that, even if she was guilty of moral misconduct, her right to alimony should remain intact. The Illinois Supreme Court eventually ruled that there was "a preponderance of evidence" that Margaret Melter was guilty of drunkenness and illicit relations with William Fisher, but that the payment of alimony was "merely a pecuniary matter, is not in any way affected by what may be called, the moral quality of her post-divorce conduct." The court reasoned that the economic relation of dependence and support existed as a separate entity apart from the laws governing moral conduct.[117]

Press reports suggested that the Cooley decision, by ruling that a woman's legally established immorality does not jeopardize her right to alimony, was a massive victory for Illinois gold diggers. Cooley told the *Chicago Daily Tribune* that he knew of many men "whose former wives are living riotously on the alimony which this infamous decision imposes on them forever." In

Chicago, he maintained, unjust alimony payments extracted more than $3 million a year from ex-husbands.[118] Vernon Cooley decided to create an alimony club of angry ex-husbands to fight for changes in Illinois alimony laws. Over fifty people showed up to the first meeting and the rally gained national press coverage.[119]

Bessie Cooley, Vernon's second wife, played a particularly active role in the Alimony Club of Illinois. "A modern Joan of Arc has risen in the person of Mrs. Bessie Cooley," a reporter for the *Ogden Standard-Examiner* wrote: "Her cry is: 'Down with alimony gold digging.'"[120] A sense of injustice or self-interest may have motivated men's participation in Cooley's organization, but the participation of women in the anti-alimony group is less straightforward. Why would women join an organization that sought to weaken or eliminate their rights to continued economic support? Beyond pecuniary motivations, it is easy to envision Bessie defining herself against the drunk and disorderly Margaret Melter. In the politics of respectability that surrounded the alimony debate, Bessie Cooley's advocacy of alimony reform worked to prove that she was not a gold digger.

Other women from Chicago made performances of respectability by taking public stands against gold digging. For example, the *Chicago Daily Tribune* published a picture of Martha Fjellander, a sixteen-year-old girl whose parents moved from Sweden to the United States in 1904.[121] The image shows Fjellander smiling and pointing to the door sign for the Alimony Club of Illinois. Just as Bessie Cooley embraced the anti-alimony cause to define herself against the adulterous gold diggers like Margaret Melter, one can easily imagine Martha Fjellander positioning herself against Peaches Browning. The picture of Fjellander appeared just a few months after newspapers reported that Browning was arrested for disorderly conduct for cursing at a police officer who stopped her for speeding.

In New York, some men pushed for a change in the state alimony law because, as one explained, "In these days it is getting so that many women marry men only because of their cash alimony value." Justice James F. Smith of the District of Columbia Supreme Court said, "If a woman is not able to support herself, she can have enough alimony for that purpose, but for no other purpose. As far as I have it in my power, I am going to discourage the 'gold digging,' and I intend to remove temptation from the paths of those who are doing the 'digging.'" Assemblyman Hackenberg of New York City introduced a bill to limit the payment of alimony to "one year for a woman under the age of fifty, unless she's been married longer than ten years or had children under the age of eighteen." Hackenberg said that the alimony "privilege" was becoming "a menace to public morals" because, "The idea of the marriage institution is that man and wife shall live together and propagate the race." Assemblyman John P. Nugent, Democrat of New York, presented two bills before the Assembly Codes Committees "designed to provide relief for alimony payers." Nugent claimed that the present alimony law was "dynamite in the hands of gold-digging women."[122]

· · · · · ·

Discussions of Peggy Joyce and Peaches Browning fit with, and contributed to, a series of changes in alimony, divorce, and American marriage. The marriage scandals of Joyce and Browning, as well as explicitly fictional portrayals of gold digging found in novels like *Alimony* and *Gentlemen Prefer Blondes*, represented important cultural spaces wherein to make claims about social class, race, gender, and sexual respectability. Images of gold diggers and alimony martyrs cultivated new interpretations of marriage law in the early twentieth century. Representations of gold diggers and gold digging in the 1920s inspired anti-alimony activism and created a socio-legal context amenable to alimony reform. Alimony came to be seen as a national problem, and it became an issue upon which to delineate masculine and feminine respectability.

The alimony panic did not result from an increase in expensive, court-ordered alimony awards; the alimony panic was caused by the fear and vilification of gold diggers. Journalistic and popular discussions of gold diggers during the 1920s shaped the language and frames of reference for judges, juries, and legal authorities in their approach to the alimony question. The gold digger—as a lens to think through changes in power relations, and as a bridge between culture and law—prompted alimony critics to oversimplify the causes of structural change, to distract from the root causes of deep problems, and to attribute economic and legal transformations to the individual temperaments and personalities of alimony seekers.

A few days before the stock market crash of 1929, a Columbia University psychology professor observed, "No subject perhaps is of more vivid, vital interest to men and women today than alimony." By 1929, California, Oregon, Iowa, Ohio, and Washington passed laws "against wives who seek divorces for the sake of alimony." A writer for the *Los Angeles Times* declared, "The days of the gold digger are numbered."[123] The campaign against alimony, however, did not abolish gold digging or perceptions of gold digging, and the gold digger stereotype certainly did not disappear during the Great Depression. On the contrary, the 1930s witnessed a proliferation of gold diggers in print, in court, and in an increasingly popular form of entertainment: the movies. The gold digger reappeared in a new cultural context shaped by extreme resource scarcity, and she had a direct influence on the abolition of seduction, breach of promise, and other heart balm laws in the early 1930s.

2 The Crusade against Heart Balm

In September 1934, a typist named Frances Singer sued acclaimed crooner Rudy Vallee for $250,000. Her lawsuit accused Vallee of "breach of promise," alleging that Vallee agreed to marry her but later broke his pledge. Singer claimed that, through his songs, Vallee used a "musical code system assuring her of his undying love and matrimonial intentions." Vallee told reporters that he had never met Singer and called the suit "crank" litigation. He said that Singer "alleged the obviously absurd charge that I made love to her over the radio."[1] The suit, which was ultimately unsuccessful, garnered national press coverage.[2] Although the details of the case were unusual, litigation for "heart balm" (breach of promise, seduction, alienation of affection, and criminal conversation) received vigorous media coverage in the Depression-era United States.

Reports about the lawsuit against Vallee coincided with a movement in various states to eradicate heart balm lawsuits. By the mid-1930s, several states rushed to eliminate them, citing their abuse in the hands of gold diggers. Heart balm laws were state statutes that allowed for lawsuits to be launched against individuals who disrupted or betrayed a romantic relationship. Following the lead of Indiana and New York, several states outlawed legal action for heart balm. There is no evidence, however, that heart balm lawsuits were either abused or increasing in frequency.[3] In fact, historians have shown that heart balm suits declined substantially from the end of the nineteenth century.[4] Moreover, threats women faced in public life, like sexual violence, exploitation, and workplace discrimination and harassment, received far less public attention compared to consternation about gold diggers abusing heart balm lawsuits.[5] The gold digger stereotype played an important role in generating disproportionate concern about heart balm laws during the 1930s. In particular, the gold digger stood as a lightning rod for colossal cultural and structural changes during the Great Depression. Gold diggers and gold digging comprised a discourse used to communicate and understand the impact of the Great Depression on marriages and families, and the gold digger appeared as a central trope in wildly popular Depression-era movies.

Heart balm refers to four categories of law: criminal conversation, alienation of affection, seduction, and breach of promise. With slight differences among them, they are lawsuits based on the betrayal of, or interference with, an intimate or romantic relationship. Both criminal conversation and alienation of affection were lawsuits levied against outsiders who allegedly ruined the plaintiff's intimate relationship. Criminal conversation suits were usually initiated by a husband against his wife's lover, and they were uncommon. According to one commentator in 1935, criminal conversation cases "rarely reach the courts." Like criminal conversation, action for alienation of affection was often, but not necessarily, triggered by adultery. Plaintiffs pursued alienation of affection suits against individuals who disrupted a valued personal relationship. Sometimes a meddlesome in-law launched these suits, but more often than not they were used against romantic rivals. According to Depression-era journalist Mary Winn, alienation of affection suits were a "weapon generally employed by one woman against another."[6] "Seduction" described a situation where a man promises to marry a woman, she has sex with him based on that promise, and then he refuses to marry her. Seduction was one of the most popular forms of civil litigation in the nineteenth century.[7] Seduction laws were also included in the criminal statutes of several states, and they were used to prosecute instances of sexual violence that fell short of the strict requirements of first-degree rape.[8] Men accused of seduction could be sued by their alleged victim and, depending upon state law, they could be arrested and tried for criminal seduction. Seduction was similar to breach of contract because both hinged on the denial of the man to make good on a proposed marriage. Unlike breach of promise, however, seduction required a sexual connection between the plaintiff and defendant, and it was contingent on the woman's prior virginity. Seduction laws illustrated that, although heart balm statutes aimed to help women, they embodied sexist assumptions about gender roles, romance, and marriage.

None of the four forms of heart balm received as much attention and consternation as the breach of promise lawsuit. Breach of promise actions, where a woman sues a man for backing out on a promise to marry her, were a product of English common law and a staple of nineteenth-century civil litigation in the United States. Breach of promise law was an amalgamation of contract law and torts; breach of promise refers to both a broken contract and damages experienced by the plaintiff. The damages in the nineteenth century revolved around marriageability and the realistic prospect that the woman would be unable to find a new suitor if she was rebuffed by an older one. Opportunity cost was a central harm of nineteenth-century breach of promise suits; a woman was unable to search for a proper suitor if she was waiting for the fulfillment of another's promise to marry.[9] This conception of the damage wrought by a man's breach of promise changed over time as women acquired greater political, economic, and social rights. In the twentieth century, the injuries caused by a man's broken marriage promise revolved around emotional harm, hurt pride, and mortification, and less around the question of the woman's marriageability.

The gender and class dynamics of breach of promise actions made plaintiffs vulnerable to attacks on their character and respectability. Similar to stock defenses against rape and seduction, defendants in breach of promise cases sometimes assailed plaintiffs' morality and chastity. For example, actor Bettie Butler launched a $125,000 breach of promise suit against director Al Rogell after Rogell married Irma Warner, the former wife of Warner Brothers producer Jack Warner. Butler's attorney argued that she remained unmarried for two years waiting for Rogell to marry her and, when she learned of his new marriage to Irma Warner, she became "shocked and made seriously ill." According to her attorney, news of the marriage caused Butler "humiliation and disgrace which she will suffer the remainder of her life." To counter the lawsuit, Rogell's attorney sought to obtain testimony in a deposition that Butler "associated with other men and was a night club habitué." The attorney also claimed, "she had staged the 'dance of the seven veils' before men in her apartment," a charge she denied. Butler eventually dropped the charges and the parties settled the case out of court.[10] As this case shows, breach of promise lawsuits often acted as referendums on the social and sexual respectability of plaintiffs and defendants. Journalistic storytelling about heart balm actions, like the case against Al Rogell, forms an important context for the timing and fervor of the campaigns against heart balm laws in the 1930s.

The inclusion of breach of promise under contract law, and the principle that contracts must be blind, meant that these lawsuits were, in theory, gender neutral. In practice, breach of promise suits were almost exclusively initiated by women. As a gendered form of litigation, breach of promise laws represented and created assumptions about men, women, and marriage.[11] The breach of promise lawsuit underscored women's economic dependence on men and the role of marriage in securing and maintaining a favorable class position. According to Lawrence Friedman, "It was a remedy for respectable, mostly middle-class women who had been seduced and abandoned."[12] The use of breach of promise lawsuits, especially in an era marked by enthusiasm for companionate marriage (which supposedly un-moored matrimonial considerations from economic ones), reflected the po-litical and economic constraints women continued to face in the early twentieth century.[13] Marriage was a path to avoid poverty, and—especially during the Great Depression—promises of marriage contained economic as well as romantic implications. In this way, breach of promise suits struc-tured, and were structured by, the intersection of gender and class. A unique combination of economic and cultural factors, in which gold diggers were deeply entangled, buoyed alarm about heart balm lawsuits and led to the crusade to abolish the statutory basis of heart balm laws. The connec-tion between law and culture gave the gold digger a fundamental role in channeling misogyny and economic anxiety toward the abolition of laws designed to protect women from financial hardship.

Marriage and the Great Depression

The Great Depression, and its particular effects on American family life, roared in the background of heart balm panic. On October 29, 1929, a day eventually dubbed Black Tuesday, panicked brokers traded over sixteen mil-lion shares of stock and the Dow lost $14 billion of value. The Great De-pression was the gravest financial crisis of the twentieth century and its damage reverberated worldwide. Unemployment, homelessness, and hun-ger became major social problems. Bank failures caused nine million fami-lies to lose their savings. By the winter of 1932, approximately thirteen million people, nearly a quarter of the workforce, were unemployed. There was no end in sight. The election of Franklin D. Roosevelt in 1933 fostered some optimism, but the implementation of the New Deal and the pace of recovery lagged behind the hopes and needs of most Americans.[14]

The Great Depression affected all Americans, but its impact was felt un-equally among people in different categories marked by class, race, ethnic-ity, gender, and rurality. The Great Depression had a wide influence on gender relations, and men and women had distinct experiences coping with the economic calamity. Marriage and divorce rates decelerated and, in an era before the widespread availability and legality of birth control, sex among married couples declined.[15] Historian Rebecca Davis observes that, during the Great Depression, "The American family seemed to be crumbling under the weight of financial and psychological strain." According to his-torian Susan Ware, as the Depression stressed the institution of marriage, "women's roles at the center of the family took on even greater significance."

The loss of status men experienced as out-of-work breadwinners created unprecedented threats to their sense of masculinity. Accordingly, women outnumbered men in asking the government for financial and material assistance. Historian Robert McElvaine notes, "Men might be as pleased as women to receive help, but their expected sex role made it more difficult for them to ask." One of the many social side effects of the Great Depression was the perceived crisis of masculinity engendered by the collapse of economic security. Men continued to retain unmatched economic, political, and social power, but they believed their manhood was under assault, and this perception prompted strategies to strengthen their status in relation to women. The vilification of gold diggers and the attempt to abolish the legal tools of gold digging were important elements in this effort.[16]

Morris Dickstein, in his acclaimed 2009 history of the Great Depression, argued, "Most observers agree that women fared better than men during the Depression."[17] Dickstein's comment, however, is a misleading characterization of the reality American women faced in the 1930s. Women often fared better in the paid labor force—they increased their presence in the work force by over 4 percent from 1930 to 1940—but it is improper to conclude from employment figures that women had an easier time during the Great Depression. Compared to men, women worked longer hours for less pay. They faced intense public antagonism for occupying positions in the working world that would otherwise have gone to men, even though they were primarily employed in fields that were the exclusive domain of women, like nursing and teaching.[18] Over 75 percent of school districts in the United States refused to hire married women, and over half of school districts had a policy of firing single women once they became married.[19] Women's work was more contingent than men's work. As historian Elaine Abelson explains, "They lost jobs at a higher rate than did men in the early years of the collapse, were often unable to find other sources of income, and were routinely discriminated against in public employment."[20] State and federal lawmakers who moved to limit married women's opportunities in government worsened the plight of women during the Great Depression. Moreover, banking, insurance, and other white-collar industries practiced severe discrimination against married women and restricted the number of women they hired.

Historian Linda Gordon contends that the focus on statistics and unemployment figures obscures the unique struggles faced by women during the Great Depression, especially those who were single mothers. Although almost all states had mothers' aid programs, most local areas had no programs at all, and only seventeen states received state funding. Existing programs were strained or exhausted by the early 1930s. Single women without children were also vulnerable because organizations and programs offering a social safety net, like the Children's Bureau, were created for women with children. The threat of having to engage in sex work to survive loomed over impoverished single women during the Great Depression. As an African American commentator told Studs Terkel, sex work and pimping "were a necessity. Survival. Women had to sell their bodies for twenty-five cents, fifteen cents." Women, compared to men, faced unique forms of gender-based violence and degradation during the Great Depression.[21]

The Great Depression upended taken-for-granted heterosexual relationships between men and women.[22] It undermined the financial security that marriage traditionally offered women, and it called attention to the economic basis of the institution of marriage in stark new ways. At home, women were in charge of managing increasingly delicate household budgets, as well as being saddled with housework and child care. Despite the introduction of home electricity and labor-saving devices during the 1930s, women spent an enormous amount of time each week on housework.[23] Given this precarious situation, marriage represented a tentative bulwark against economic privation. What some perceived as gold digging, others saw as a survival strategy. The ire against heart balm lawsuits, particularly breach of promise cases, cannot be understood outside the financial crisis that plunged the United States into a decade-long economic depression. Observers used the gold digger trope to make sense of economic changes that threatened the role and ideology of male breadwinning. Newspaper stories, like the reportage on Rudy Vallee, were a part of this but, as the financial crisis worsened, Americans learned about lucrative breach of promise lawsuits from a novel source: the movies.

Heart Balm, Gold Diggers, and Pre-Code Cinema

A fundamental transformation occurred in American entertainment during the march toward economic disaster in the final years of the 1920s. The 1927 release of Al Jolson's *The Jazz Singer*, the first movie with spoken dialogue and synchronized sound, marked a cultural sea change.[24] The growth of motion pictures with sound moved haltingly and awkwardly from the introduction of the first "talkies," but movies soon became America's preeminent form of entertainment, and over 90 million Americans went to the movies every week during the final years of the 1920s.[25] The dominance of film in

1930s American culture was not a foregone conclusion because the Great Depression severely limited Americans' discretionary spending. In fact, movie attendance dropped as the Depression deepened. By 1933, only 50 million Americans went to the movies per week. Thousands of movie houses closed their doors and banks took over previously independent production companies.

Despite dwindling audiences, the opening years of the Great Depression were an incredibly important time for the advancement of movies as an artistic form, a vehicle for social commentary, and a mode of mass entertainment. American movies, especially those released during the first half of the decade, made bold statements about women's roles, poverty, crime, and other social issues. During the so-called pre-Code era, from 1929 to the full imposition of the Motion Picture Production Code in June 1934, American filmmakers deployed themes and characters that celebrated social deviance and sexual openness. Gangsters were glorified, villains sometimes escaped punishment at the end of the film, and sexual promiscuity did not invariably lead to bad consequences. During those four short years from the end of 1929 to the first half of 1934, the boundaries of what was acceptable to show onscreen was wider than it would be until the 1970s.[26]

The 1932 film *Red-Headed Woman* starring Jean Harlow vividly illustrates how pre-Code films pushed the boundaries of sexual explicitness and depicted sin without consequences. Harlow portrays a conniving gold digger who uses sexual entrapment to move up the class pecking order. Written by Anita Loos, the film follows Lillian Andrews, or "Lil," as she breaks up a marriage, carries on affairs, and threatens to blackmail men in order to improve her social standing. Lil sets her initial sights on her boss, Bill Legendre. She steals Legendre's work mail from his secretary's desk and, knowing that his wife is out of town, goes to his house. She sidles up beside him on a large couch. He begins to dictate a letter about a coal shipment, but she distracts him with her exposed legs. The scene fades and cuts to a close-up of Lil crying, presumably because they just had sex. She says, "Can't a girl cry a little bit when she's happy?" Bill's wife Irene learns of Bill's dalliances with Lil and they eventually divorce. Bill and Lil marry, but Lil seeks to move higher in the class hierarchy and sets her sights on a coal baron named Charles Gaerste. She sleeps with Gaerste and blackmails him. *Red-Headed Woman* ends with Lil in Paris, speaking French, living the high life, and entering into the back of a limousine with an older man. The film conveys the message that she has not suffered any repercussions for her actions and is continuing her gold-digging ways unscathed.

Gold diggers like Lil reigned supreme in pre-Code cinema. By the 1930s, Hollywood produced a flood of movies about young women increasing their class status through strategic relationships.[27] Sociologist Stephen Sharot notes, "Most of the heroines in the cross-class romance films are virtuous, but the sexually empowered woman who manipulates men, who came to be known from about 1915 as a 'gold digger,' appears frequently in the films of the early 1930s." According to Roger Dooley, the gold digger is one of the most prevalent of the "stock company of stereotypes that continually recurred in 1930s films." For contemporary film and literary scholars, the gold digger trope in pre-Code films often worked as a subversive cultural force.[28]

Contemporary reappraisals of 1930s gold digger films underline the agency, moxie, and protofeminist impulses of gold-digging protagonists.[29] Film and literary scholars have highlighted the subversive potential of the gold digger stereotype in pre-Code cinema. For example, Lea Jacobs contends that gold digger films from the early 1930s "helped to construct the immoral, cynical, and sexually aggressive gold digger as a heroic figure." Pamela Robertson describes the gold digger performances of Mae West as a kind of "feminist camp." Jessica Hope Jordan recognizes in Jean Harlow's gold digger films a "proto-feminist agency." In her analysis of Harlow's portrayal of gold digger Kitty Packard in George Cukor's *Dinner at Eight*, Jordan argues that Kitty symbolizes the hope of economic rebound and an end to the Great Depression.[30] Through her hypersexual whims and unabashed consumerism, Kitty Packard and other gold diggers lampoon both patriarchal gender ideals and excesses of consumer capitalism. Jordan's interpretation contrasts sharply with the way that some feminist film scholars in the past have characterized Harlow's performances as antifeminist.[31] For Jordan, the gold digger acts as an ironic counterforce to society's hypocrisies.

Pre-Code gold diggers also trumpeted a new threat in Depression-era America. Armed with a savvy appreciation of the combined power of sex appeal and civil law, the gold diggers of pre-Code cinema wield heart balm lawsuits against naive and unsuspecting mates. In the 1932 film *Lawyer Man*, a talented and corrupt attorney uses his skills to launch expensive breach of promise suits against wealthy men.[32] Also released in 1932, the film *Breach of Promise* centers on a young woman named Hattie who baselessly sues a wealthy politician for breach of promise and ruins his life. Unlike many pre-Code gold digger narratives where the gold digger escapes punishment, Hattie confesses to perjury and is sent to prison. *Havana Widows*, released in 1933, features two out-of-work chorus dancers who travel to Cuba after a friend tells them that the "place is positively reeking" of millionaires. She

FIGURE 6 Ginger Rogers, publicity still for *Gold Diggers of 1933*. The musical comedy *Gold Diggers of 1933* counted among the many Depression-era films about gold diggers. Different plot points in *Gold Diggers of 1933* reflected fears about gold diggers abusing the legal system. Courtesy of PhotoFest.

tells her friends to find a lawyer named Duffy who specializes in breach of promise suits. Mae West portrays a circus performer named Tira in *I'm No Angel*. Tira sues her former lover for breach of promise after a misunderstanding led to their break up. Her attorney assures her that the case will be a "cinch" because of all the evidence she has collected that prove their love affair. *Gold Diggers of 1935* was released after the imposition of the production code but features a breach of promise plot where, echoing the details of Singer's lawsuit against Rudy Vallee, a secretary requests that her wealthy boss autograph song lyrics he has written. She intends to use those lyrics as a makeshift love letter in court. These films show the legal themes and issues that swirled around the gold digger figure during the Great Depression. They also suggest how pre-Code films helped construct the gold digger as both a folk devil and trickster during the early 1930s, the same years when heart balm lawsuits came under fire from lawmakers.

The popularity of the Warner Brothers film *Gold Diggers of 1933*, and the importance of this film in constructing the gold digger type, merits special consideration. *Gold Diggers of 1933* was one of several Busby Berkeley musical comedies that focused on the tribulations of the Great Depression.[33] It was shot in forty-five days and became the second most lucrative film for Warner Brothers in 1933.[34] Based on the Avery Hopwood play *The Gold Diggers*, the backstage musical focuses on three out-of-work chorus girls, Carol, Polly, and Trixie. Barney Hopkins (played by Ned Sparks) raises everyone's hopes by announcing the creation of a new show, but he lacks the money to fund it. Polly's boyfriend (and songwriter), Brad, gives Hopkins $15,000 for the show, but only if he casts Polly in a leading role in the show and, most mysteriously, if Brad can pay in cash. The chorines wonder what Brad is hiding from his past, how he has the money, and whether or not he is really an out-of-work songwriter as he says. Trixie, showing Polly a recent newspaper clipping, suggests that Brad might really be a bank robber.

Their suspicions rise on opening night when Brad refuses to step in at the last minute to play a key role after one of the actors is unable to perform. Trixie implores Brad to take the stage. "Listen, I don't care even if you have to go to jail after this performance," she says.[35] Trixie strongly implies that he cannot let the chorus girls down because, if he does, they will have to resort to sex work to survive. "God knows what will happen to those kids. They'll have to do things I wouldn't want on *my* conscience. And it will be on *yours*."[36] Trixie's entreaties prevail, Brad steps in to perform in the musical number "Pettin' in the Park," and Barney's musical is a smash hit. The revelation at the end of the show—that "Brad Roberts" is really Robert Treat Bradford, a "Boston Blue Blood"—propels the drama in the second half of the film. Brad was hiding his identity, not because he was a criminal, but because he wanted to strike out on his own to pursue his true passion, songwriting, independent of his family's influence. Brad's wealthy brother (J. Lawrence Bradford) and Faneuil Peabody (the family lawyer) descend on Manhattan in order to dissuade him from show business. They threaten to cut him out of the family estate if he continues his relationship with

Polly, a "cheap little show girl." Brad, giving voice to the dominance of companionate marriage and modern notions of romantic love, tells his brother, "Listen, that's pretty much of an old-fashioned idea. Families don't interfere with love affairs nowadays."[37] Meanwhile, Polly's friends Carol and Trixie set their gold-digging sights on J. Lawrence and Faneuil in an effort to prevent the men from interfering in Brad and Polly's relationship. Their gold digging, the film emphasizes, aims to benefit Brad, Polly, and the multitude of men and women involved with the musical production; they are not doing it for purely self-centered ends. J. Lawrence mistakes Carol for Polly and, trying to end "Polly's" relationship with Brad, he tries to woo her with his wealth in order to prove to Brad that Polly is a shameless gold digger. J. Lawrence and Carol then fall in love. Trixie and Faneuil pair together. With Brad's relationship to Polly no longer threatened, all three women find love, romance, and success.

Film scholars have generated different opinions about the political and ideological implications of *Gold Diggers of 1933*. Arthur Hove argues that, at its core, "the film is little more than a commonplace variation on the boy-meets-girl theme that has been with us since the romances of the Middle Ages." For Hove, the exuberant song and dance numbers that punctuate the plot points of *Gold Diggers of 1933* are a mere "visual tutti-frutti" with no discernible political valence. Andrew Bergman contends that *Gold Diggers of 1933* was escapist fare that tried to reaffirm the American Dream and give hope to movie audiences during the Great Depression. The film allowed its audience to "drown its sorrows in legs and glitter, and plumes and teeth and sweet harmonizing." Others discern a more ominous quality to the film. In a 1982 essay, Paula Rabinowitz uses Marx's concept of commodity fetishism to locate the film in "the complex of advanced capitalist-patriarchy." Rather than being a carefree musical, the film "can be seen as a sinister vehicle for the perpetuation of both women's and working class passivity." Rabinowitz argues that the song and dance routines are misogynistic because they turn chorus girls into objects ogled by men. The film's escapist and fantastical features praised by Bergman and Hove are precisely what Rabinowitz finds ideologically insidious.[38]

The most useful analyses of the film highlight the nascent feminist aspects of its themes and characters. Patricia Mellencamp uses the theories of Sigmund Freud, Michel Foucault, and Laura Mulvey to excavate the meaning and significance of the film. Ultimately, for Mellencamp, the film celebrates women's agency. She notes, "the women move the narrative forward, finding a backer for Barney's show and husbands for themselves, albeit through manipulation, trickery, deceit, and seduction." Likewise, film scholar Pamela Robertson regards the movie as a form of feminist camp. Robertson argues that Trixie and Carol make justifiable use of their sexuality to control men: "In pretending to be gold diggers, the women play up on the trope by suggesting that it is only an act."[39] True to the gold-digger-as-trickster construction, the women of *Gold Diggers of 1933* leverage what they have to make the best of a bad situation.

A less appreciated characteristic of the film is its legal and economic themes. The force of law, both criminal and civil, structures the characters' motivations and drives key plot points. The film features the persistent presence of police. Indeed, the film opens with police interrupting Fay's musical number "We're in the Money" and seizing the props and scenery of Barney Hopkins's production. Hopkins demands the police stop, but one of them responds, "Tough luck, brother. I'm from the sheriff's office. Legal attachment to collect for creditors. *Corpus delicti*—or seize the body!"[40] In a play on the literal and legal meaning of corpus delicti, another man grabs Carol's arm. Carol protests but the man takes the chair from under her and comments that it will look good in the sheriff's office. Police reappear in various scenes throughout the film, such as the roller-skating chorus in "Pettin' in the Park" and the "Remember My Forgotten Man" finale. Also, in one of the final scenes of the film, J. Lawrence brings a detective to arrest his brother for an illegitimate marriage to Polly, a threat he calls off after Carol appeals to his better nature.[41]

Gold Diggers of 1933 fuses the construction of the gold digger with her ability to launch and thwart lawsuits. Within the domain of civil law, the socio-legal constraints and opportunities of marriage run throughout the film. In the original shooting script, Trixie comments on the effect of the Great Depression on her alimony payments. She states, "Even love is not what it used to be. When show business was slow, I used to live on my alimony. Now I can't collect a cent of it. Married three of them against a rainy day. Now it's pouring and they haven't an umbrella between them!" Poverty obliterates the legal mechanism by which Trixie receives support. Trixie depended on alimony to survive when her work was sluggish, not to live lavishly as suggested by the late 1920s alimony panic. Similarly, Barney Hopkins receives help for his show when an associate of his obtains a divorce; the impending divorce freed the man to support Hopkins's play as an investor. However, Hopkins laments, the investor and his wife "had become reconciled—and she don't want him fooling around in the show business. And there I am, holding the bag."[42] The Great Depression overturned the financial security normally promised by both marriage and the alimony system. Although Barney and Trixie are comedic characters, their laments allude to the serious way in which the Great Depression upended individuals' survival strategies.

Another scene, one that appears in the shooting script but not the final version of the film, suggests the economic consequences of marriage and the financial constraints that structure matrimonial decisions. The script calls for a montage of women receiving the news that Barney Hopkins needs chorus girls for his upcoming production. A nurse leaves a patient in the middle of taking his temperature, a nude model abruptly walks out of a drawing session at an art school, and a shop girl abandons her demonstration of "unbreakable" glassware by smashing it on the ground. In the fourth and final scene of the montage, a woman tightly embraces a man who says, passionately, "I'll gladly marry you—Tuesday." The script calls for the woman to pull back briefly. The women "then sighs and gives in" to his caresses. Just then, the phone rings with news of Hopkins's production and "her face lights up." She hangs up the phone, breaks free from the man's embrace, and then "slaps his face hard" before walking out of the room.[43] The woman initially gave in to the man's promise to marry and the presumed security that it would offer her, but after learning that she could become one of Barney Hopkins's chorus girls, she rejected him as repulsive. Economic anxiety was the key thing keeping her in the relationship and generating her performance of affection and sensuality.

The threat of a breach of promise suit motors the dramatic action in the second half of the film. Faneuil Peabody, the Bradford family lawyer, warns J. Lawrence about the true character of the chorines. Mirroring the language of the late 1920s alimony panic, Peabody declares to J. Lawrence, "I know these show girls. They're just little parasites, little gold diggers."[44] When Peabody confronts Carol (whom he mistakenly thinks is Polly, Brad's girlfriend), he asks, "How much do you want to release his brother [Brad] from his promise to marry you?" The precise wording of the question—"to release his brother from his promise to marry you"—mirrors broader societal apprehensions about alleged gold diggers using breach of promise suits to extort money from wealthy men.[45] The breach of promise suit is a comic device within the plot structure of the film, but it is a type of lawsuit that many regarded as a genuine menace.

A final scene pivots on the threat of a seduction lawsuit. Carol encourages J. Lawrence to get drunk and, after he passes out, she and Trixie drag him to Carol's bed. He wakes up the next morning convinced that he had sex with Carol. Trixie accuses him of trying to "ruin a young girl's future" and demands that he write a check for $10,000, a payment Carol later rejects because she has fallen in love with him. The phrase "ruin a young girl's future" draws on the language of seduction and ruination, and carries the idea that premarital sex destroyed a woman's respectability and her future prospects on the marriage market. In a similar scene in the original script, but not in the final film, Trixie hires a man named Gigolo Eddie to barge in on her and Peabody and pretend to be Trixie's husband. "If I was you," Gigolo Eddie tells Peabody, "I'd take out my checkbook." The payment would be, presumably, to forestall a lawsuit for "criminal conversation," which is a form of litigation that allows a husband to sue his wife's paramour. Trixie, however, demands that Gigolo Eddie leave and declares her love for Peabody. Fay approaches the three of them to participate in the ruse, but Gigolo Eddie waves her away. "The deal's off," he says. "They're going to get hitched." From beginning to end, the interplay among love, law, and money provides the film with its core subject matter and sources of humor. Literary and film critics have, understandably, concentrated on the film's protofeminist themes. A focus on the film's legal and economic leitmotifs suggests the film's place in reflecting and contributing to mounting alarm about heart balm laws.[46]

Breach of Promise Tort Tales

As films with gold digger themes showed in movie theaters across the country, and as the despair of the Great Depression deepened, both the white and African American press popularized breach of promise stories. Typical of tort tales in general, stories about heart balm suits emphasized their frequency and expense. Theodore Apstein, secretary of the National Divorce Reform League, described an explosion of these lawsuits: "There was a rising market in wounded affections, and thousands of love-letters were taken from safe boxes. A new profession was created, and men started to pay large sums to keep their clandestine dalliances from the courts." He declared, "One began to read almost daily of a new breach of promise suit."[47] Headlines broadcast the high stakes of broken hearts: "Cleveland Dancer Wins $10,000 Heart Balm"; "Seeks $75,000 Heart Balm"; "Woman Tells of Marriage Promise in Suit for $50,000"; "Tells of Love and Liquor in $100,000 Suit"; "Heart Balm Award Huge."[48] These stories coincided with growing outrage against heart balm lawsuits and an organized effort to outlaw them. In the early 1930s, the press and public increasingly portrayed heart balm suits as a "racket" or form of blackmail.

Similar to accounts of alimony abuses during the late 1920s, stories of heart balm suits often raised the specter of Ziegfeld Follies performers bilking respectable men out of their hard-earned money. One story recalled Evan-Burrows Fontaine, former Follies dancer, unsuccessfully suing Cornelius Vanderbilt Whitney for one million dollars in a breach of promise action. Another Follies dancer, Betty Kaege, sued actor Alan Dinehart for $250,000 after he married another woman, but the suit was settled out of court. Journalist Mary Day Winn held out Follies performers for particular contempt: "Bachelors had best be on their guard when they feel the urge to send effusive epistles to secretaries, clerks, cloak models, widows or most dangerous of all, fair alumnae of the Follies Chorus." Apstein baselessly speculated that "girls of the theatre" initiated 80 percent of the breach of promise suits in the United States. He described the efforts of Follies performer Judy O'Day, a woman who sued a man for breach of promise because he went against the suggestion of an astrology report that predicted their compatibility: "To the astonished court she brought data on Pisces and Virgo as well as other constellations to substantiate her claim of breach of promise." Like the suit against Rudy Vallee, this story of outrageous litigation, this tort tale, highlighted the absurdity of the lawsuit and suggested that men were vulnerable to conniving women.[49]

Newspapers regaled readers with stories of high-profile heart balm defendants. For example, a woman named Lilian Mendal sued Frederic Gimbel, co-owner of Gimbels department store, for breach of promise for two million dollars, which resulted in a $250,000 verdict. Rhoda Tanner Doubleday, divorced wife of publishing giant Felix Doubleday, brought a $1.5-million breach of promise suit against Chicago multimillionaire Harry F. McCormick in 1935. Her suit settled out of court for $65,000, although early press reports erroneously stated that the amount was close to $100,000. Colette Francois, who sued movie mogul Arthur Loew for $100,000, was less effective. A jury of twelve men decided the case in Loew's favor. Film producer Harry Joe Brown, who was best known for producing Errol Flynn's first film, married actor Sally Eilers in the early 1930s. He wrote love letters to another woman, Marjorie Gay, who later levied a $100,000 breach of promise action against him. The jury, after seven hours of deliberation, awarded Gay $5,000.[50]

The breach of promise lawsuit against violinist David Rubinoff drew wide press coverage, including an article in *Life* magazine. Rubinoff made his radio debut in 1931 (with Rudy Vallee as his introducer), became a popular radio performer, and headlined a free concert in Chicago's Grant Park for an audience of tens of thousands. A woman named Peggy Garcia sued him for $100,000 because he purportedly broke a marriage promise. Garcia, one journalist commented, "served in the ranks of the large army of New York's amusement blondes" by working as a hatcheck girl at the Cotton Club and taxi dancer at the Blue Bird Hall. Rubinoff's attorney successfully fought the lawsuit by investigating Garcia's past and proving that she was married to a tombstone salesperson from Astoria named Michael La Rocca. La Rocca's wife testified in New York City's Court of General Sessions, and Peggy Garcia was charged with bigamy.[51]

The African American press also published accounts of costly breach of promise lawsuits. As in the white mainstream press, these narratives invoked themes of class mobility and respectability. A 1930 case in Newark, New Jersey, alleged that William Henry Washington, a "wealthy and prominent" physician, promised to wed twenty-three-year-old Ethel Cannon. He told Cannon that he would marry her after his wife died but, instead, he married a white woman. Harkening back to the 1926 Peaches Browning scandal, the trial uncovered letters where Washington referred to Cannon as "Peaches" and she referred to him as "Daddy."[52] The court awarded her $20,000 of the $75,000 she originally sought. In another case, Alice Piper, a twenty-two-year-old white nurse from Iowa, sued Alvin Jefferson, a sixty-year-old African American doctor, for $10,000 in a breach of promise suit. A writer for the *Chicago Defender* hailed Jefferson's character by describing him as "mild mannered" and "showing every evidence of culture and refinement." Piper's respectability, however, was jeopardized by her lawsuit. Her former employer described her as "extremely refined," noting that she "read only the best books and was never out once after 9:30 at night"; yet Jefferson's defense attorney called her "unsophisticated" and stated "Alice Piper's motive was to get more money." Jefferson called her "eccentric and queer," and said, "I doubt if she will ever be able to find work again in Des Moines or the state of Iowa." The jury deliberated for eight hours before deciding to award Alice Piper only one dollar in damages. Piper's attorney, an African American man, decried the decision. He said that she would have received from $500 to $5,000 if Jefferson was a white man.[53] Social class and gender constituted the dominant themes of heart balm torts, but the actions against William Henry Washington and Alvin Jefferson demonstrated that race sometimes played a direct role in heart balm narratives. The gold digger acted as an intersectional node, tying together claims about social class, race, and respectability into a single cultural form.

'Heartbreaker'

ASKS $10,000 FOR BROKEN HEART

FIGURE 7 Heart balm litigants, Alvin Jefferson and Alice Piper. A 1936 breach of promise suit brought by a white nurse, Alice Piper, against Alvin Jefferson, an African American doctor, underscored the issues of class, race, gender, and respectability at the core of the 1930s "heart balm" debate. *Chicago Defender*, February 29, 1936, 4.

The proliferation of news reports about heart balm lawsuits during the 1930s led to specific criticisms of the practice. Many described heart balm lawsuits as a tool of blackmail and noted that the threat of having love letters read aloud in open court created an incentive for men to pay outrageous quantities of money. Some speculated that 90 percent of heart balm cases were settled before trial for this reason.[54] A writer for the *American Weekly* argued that men will pay high sums in order to "buy back mortifying love-letters or pictures which they know will be exhibited in court and shame them regardless of whether the jury awards any damages or not." A writer for the *Charleston Daily Mail* noted that letters that might say something negative about a man's family or employer "can make the scion of an old and respected family of wealth shell out a neat bag of hush money." A journalist in Madison, Wisconsin, satirized the efforts of women to earn heart balm by touting a fictitious "Institute of Applied Heartbalmry," a school that promised to teach women "how to appear intelligent. How to make an octogenarian propose. How to make men write passionate love letters. How to preserve them for use at the trial." Mary Day Winn, a writer for the *Billings Gazette*, cautioned that men were vulnerable at every stage of love and romance. A woman can sue a man for breach of promise if he changes his mind about marriage during the engagement phase. If he obtains a divorce, he faces "alimony or a debtor's jail." Finally, if the man seeks to remarry, his first wife can sue his second wife for alienation of affection.[55]

Another critique of heart balm statutes highlighted their capricious nature. The damage awards, these critics maintained, varied based on the beauty of the plaintiff. Good-looking plaintiffs had a higher rate of success and garnered larger jury awards. These decisions were irrational, critics reasoned, because the largest awards went to the women who were best able to find another suitor. Winn stated, "it is a well-recognized fact in legal circles that the prettier the plaintiff, the larger the award she will get from a masculine jury—a highly uneconomic basis of decision." Critics alleged that male jurors were particularly vulnerable to heart balm plaintiffs' manipulations. Alma Whitaker wryly observed, "United States male juries can be sumptuously sympathetic and gallant about feminine tears and other fellows' money."[56]

Critics used the language of gold digging and gold diggers to portray breach of promise suits as a national menace. In 1930, Mary Day Winn warned against the "large army of American gold diggers" using breach of promise suits. In 1935, Frank A. Garbutt, a wealthy Los Angeles industrialist, advocated "adequate protection for poor weak susceptible men from the wiles of designing alimony and heart-balm gold diggers." Writing about the move to "outlaw gold digger suits for heart balm" in Illinois, the editorial page of the *Chicago Tribune* stated, "Suits for alienation of affection and breach of promise of marriage have become a stench in the nostrils of everyone except gold diggers and unscrupulous lawyers who supported themselves on this kind of practice." Some of the rhetoric about gold digging heart balm hunters was rooted in straightforward misogyny. Roi Ottley, one of the most well-known African American writers and journalists of the first half of the twentieth century, stated in a 1934 article about heart balm, "Women, in the main, are parasites." He said, "I am not the man to say that all women should go back to the home, but do say the majority are fitted for no better."[57] Some, like Ottley, used criticism of heart balm suits as a vehicle to pursue an antifeminist agenda of limiting women's political and social power.[58]

Other heart balm critics attacked the laws as failing to keep pace with women's emancipation. The problem was not, as Roi Ottley contended, that women were leaving the domestic sphere to enter male-dominated social, political, and economic spaces. Rather, women's well-deserved social progress made heart balm laws antiquated and symbolic of a time when women were little more than chattel. A 1935 editorial in the *Christian Science Monitor* observed, "Women now have the legal right to collect their own wages, enter into business contracts, own property in their own name and in general to provide for themselves independently of men. One way they can prove their equality is by not asking for the kind of protection breach of promise laws are meant to give." Theodore Apstein noted the common law roots of heart balm, and that heart balm laws were designed to prevent women from becoming public charges once their marriageability was destroyed by seduction or a broken matrimonial promise. Heart balm actions rested on the premise that women were defenseless and that their station in life depended on the good graces of their male suitors. "Now," Apstein writes, "the times have changed, thus making the old reasoning inapplicable. The adoption of universal suffrage; the entrance of women in important places in the professions, in business, in industry, and, more lately, into high public offices, has altered their status from that of the weak dependent into the independent and self-sufficient equal of man." *Chicago Daily Tribune* columnist Antoinette Donnelly stated that breach of promise suits always had a "most distasteful tang." "It simply does not belong in an era in which women work alongside men as competitors," she concluded. Like alimony reform in the late 1920s, heart balm came under attack from misogynist critics who thought women had too much freedom (like Ottley) as well as those who championed women's rights and regarded heart balm as an undignified throwback to a repressive era (like Apstein and Donnelly).[59]

The changing status of heart balm lawsuits replicated the gendered politics of respectability.[60] The decision to engage the civil justice system when a romantic bond was damaged or betrayed gave (primarily) white middle- and upper-class women a mechanism to restore their status. In the context of the Great Depression, however, the idea that working-class women could use heart balm lawsuits as a survival strategy, as a "racket," alarmed reformers. Although it was once a tool to preserve middle- and upper-class respectability, critics reframed heart balm as an instrument of blackmail and malevolence in the hands of the lower classes. Heart balm opponent Theodore Apstein contended, "Sensitive and refined women hesitate to sue for breach of promise because the defense is permitted to attack their characters and often their motives. Designing and vicious parties seldom have such qualms." Nathan Feinsinger, a law professor at the University of Wisconsin, observed that heart balm laws provoked disapproval because the presumption that the plaintiff was always "a person of refined sensibilities and irreproachable character" was increasingly untenable. The apparent class-based diversity of heart balm plaintiffs, and the perception of gold diggers abusing the court system, stoked critics' complains.[61]

The Repeal of Heart Balm

Fueled by anger from multiple directions, public sentiment turned sharply against heart balm laws in the 1930s. In 1935, the year when Congress created the National Labor Board through the passage of the Wagner Act, feminists and clubwomen urged heart balm reforms as part of a progressive social policy to draw the country out of the Great Depression. The National Women's Party (NWP) counted among the most vocal advocates for heart balm reform. The NWP was formed in 1916 and, after the passage of women's suffrage, turned their efforts to other aspects of women's equality. In 1935, leaders in the NWP stated that heart balm suits "should be laughed out of court." They grouped heart balm reform with the need for equal pay for equal work and fair opportunities for women's employment and property. Grace Hudson, president of the Los Angeles District of the California Federation of Women's Clubs, speculated that the majority of women in the General Federation of Women's Clubs supported heart balm reform. She said in 1935, "it is high time that the American woman, who is steadily winning the equality she deserves, stopped racketeering." John Coontz, a journalist for the *Charleston Daily Mail*, observed in 1935, "Headed by women's clubs and female legislators throughout the United States, the war against the unscrupulous members of the fairer sex is coming out into the open and woe is the breach of promise suit." He conjectured, "So widespread is the feminine assault that prediction is made breach of promise suits will, before long, be as extinct as the dodo." While he was wrong about the ultimate fate of breach of promise laws on a national level, he correctly assessed the role of female politicians in several statewide efforts to repeal heart balm laws.[62]

The sole congresswoman from Indiana, Roberta West Nicholson, introduced the first anti–heart balm bill in the country. The governor signed it

FIGURE 8 Critics of "heart balm" lawsuits claimed that gold diggers saved their suitors' love letters and used the threat of a breach of promise lawsuit as blackmail. An editorial cartoon in *The Lincoln Star* shows the animosity toward gold diggers common during the 1930s. *The Lincoln Star*, April 7, 1935, 35.

into law in March 1935. The legislation outlawed breach of promise, seduction, alienation of affection, and criminal conversation lawsuits. The law also prohibited litigants from naming any corespondents—third parties implicated in adultery or seduction—except from a direct order of the court. Nicholson gave an impassioned speech for her new law and, roused by the novelty of a woman speaking before the Indiana legislature, a roar came from packed galleries, prompting the Speaker of the House to pound his gavel and declare, "I want absolute quite in this chamber. The author of this bill is a lady and she can't talk very loud." Newspaper accounts commented on her modest dress, and how she began to deliver her remarks softly and slowly but assumed "more confidence as she continued to talk."[63]

Nicholson's remarks before the Indiana legislature echoed both the popular and feminist critiques of heart balm lawsuits. She stated that half of heart balm suits never reached the courts. As such, these suits functioned as tools of blackmail, allowing women to compel men to pay large sums of money lest embarrassing love letters be read aloud in open court.[64] She said, "I am convinced most actions for breach of promise and seduction have extortion as their chief motive. This I seek to prevent through adoption of this bill." Nicholson also assailed heart balm suits for their deleterious effect on public morals. She said that she wanted young people to understand that "marriage is a divine sacrament, not a commercial agreement." "Love and respect and affections," she continued, "are not transferable, negotiable commodities." Nicholson maintained that the understanding of romance in crass economic terms, an understanding induced by heart balm laws, summoned "a sordid and vulgar conception of marital affairs in the minds of the immature." "I am not a professional moralist," she said, "but I have attempted to set up a deterrent to irregular relationships by removing the prospect of pecuniary profit from them."[65]

Nicholson's remarks before the Indiana legislature also played on the respectability politics rumbling beneath anti–heart balm agitation. She described her bill as "progressive legislation, in keeping with the times." "As I see my bill," she said, "it is symbolic of a change in attitude toward women. We don't want to see inferior women pull down our sex." Feminist supporters of heart balm reform drew a firm boundary against allegedly disrespectable women—like Peggy Garcia and other "amusement blondes"—who engaged in litigation against their lovers and suitors. For example, Kathleen Norris gave enthusiastic support for Nicholson's bill. Norris was the author of ninety-three novels and one of the most prolific journalists of the first half of the twentieth century. Although Norris's gender politics were complicated (she opposed birth control but supported women's suffrage), she regarded female heart balm plaintiffs with unequivocal contempt. In 1935, she wrote, "When we pick up our morning newspapers and see the injured woman, when we study her vapid face and her permanent wave, we know perfectly well that not a natural tear has ever fallen from those bright calculating eyes, that the thick lacquer of that soft, characterless mouth has never been jeopardized by a tremble." Norris focused on the hair and makeup of the allegedly typical heart balm plaintiff as markers of frivolity and dishonesty. She also invoked the notorious personalities of Peggy Hopkins Joyce, Peaches Browning, and Rhoda Tanner Doubleday to suggest that heart balm suits demeaned all women. She lamented, "It is humiliating to balanced women to read, day after day, of the Peaches and Rhodas and Peggys whose fantastic affairs of the heart are spread so lavishly over the front pages of the morning paper." She observed, "Not the most desperate poverty would force a woman of any fineness to such a step." Norris aligned herself with opponents of heart balm as a way to distinguish herself and her achievements from gold diggers. Speculation about the sway of "the most desperate poverty," a condition from which Norris was removed her entire life, underscored the social class dynamics central to the gender politics of heart balm reform. For heart balm critics, what was once a relatively acceptable method of maintaining class and gender respectability became a tool of debasement and blackmail among working-class women, chorus girls, and others who were trying to marry above their social position.[66]

The success of her bill brought Nicholson a small amount of fame. She gave a talk to an organization of professional women in Chicago a few weeks after the passage of her bill titled "Aching Hearts of Itching Palms." She exclaimed in her speech, "It seems to me that we should say to these gold diggers and shyster lawyers, as did the Queen in 'Alice in Wonderland,' 'Off with their heads!'" Nicholson regarded the anti–heart balm campaign as the biggest thrill of her political career, and news reports indicated that she planned "to extend her crusade against 'gold diggers' to the remainder of the nation." Indeed, *American Weekly* referred to Nicholson's bill as the "mother of all others," noting that multiple states had considered heart balm reform following Indiana's lead.[67]

Nicholson's bill received support from newspaper editorialists and politicians across the country, but the new law came under fire from other quarters. Some believed an unfounded rumor that Nicholson initiated her bill because her father-in-law, a well-known Indiana novelist, was involved in a heart balm suit.[68] Others attacked the law on legal grounds. Bernard Sandier acted as legal counsel for Colette Francois, a twenty-two-year-old woman who sued movie mogul Arthur Loew. Sandier described heart balm actions as a "fundamental right" and ventured that, without access to the courts, aggrieved parties would use the "unwritten law" to resolve their conflicts. The "unwritten law" was a legal norm that excused men and women from attacking or killing adulterers who interfered in their marriages.[69] Likewise, a legal scholar writing in the *Illinois Law Review* argued that, without recourse to heart balm actions, "victims or their male relatives may resort to self-help." The dean of Barnard College mused that a better solution to the problem of heart balm might be, not legislative reform, but to have all-women juries for heart balm trials: "It would be difficult for a hard-boiled adventuress to convince a jury of her own sex that she was just an innocent, trusting slip of a girl who did not understand what it was all about."[70]

In spite of its critics, Nicholson's bill served as a model for other states. In New York, John McNaboe designed a bill based on Nicholson's legislation

THE OLD DIGGINGS AIN'T WHAT THEY USED TO BE.

FIGURE 9 By 1940, ten states across the country had passed laws prohibiting breach of promise and other "heart balm" lawsuits. Many viewed a ban on heart balm as a victory against gold diggers. *St. Louis Post-Dispatch*, March 22, 1935, 2E.

in Indiana. McNaboe was a forty-two-year-old attorney who was elected to the New York State Senate after serving as an assistant district attorney for three years. Soon after his arrival onto the State Senate, McNaboe served as a member of the Hofstadter Committee, which examined corruption in the police and courts of New York City. He framed the heart balm bill as a method to sweep away connubial corruption. McNaboe claimed that the legislation "marks a new era in social justice." McNaboe stated that his law took aim at "a tribute of $10,000,000 paid annually by New York men to gold-diggers and blackmailers."[71] McNaboe's heart balm bill attracted many supporters (including Eleanor Roosevelt) but it also faced stout opposition in New York.

In contrast to the ready acceptance of Indiana's heart balm reform legislation, New York's legislature engaged in a fierce debate that lasted over an hour. Rhoda Fox Graves, the only woman member of the State Senate, voted against the bill, but did not give a reason for her vote. Elmer Quinn, a representative of the Lower East Side and best known for cosponsoring groundbreaking antidiscrimination legislation in the 1940s, opposed the bill. He said that the new law would unfairly protect the "coal-oil Johnnies, the rich philanderers, the stuffed shirts," and that heart balm torts allowed wronged women to hit a man "where it hurts most, in the pocketbook." New York lawyer Bernard Sandler argued that outlawing heart balm would contribute to male sexual predation. He warned that women who favored the law "will realize before long they are cheating themselves of the rights and remedies they have had for 300 years. They will regret it, especially when they see all the old satyrs stalking their daughters. The satyrs will have an open field." The bill eventually passed on a 36-to-9 vote that crossed party lines. Governor Lehman signed bill on March 29, 1935, promising to end "a fruitful source of coercion, extortion, and blackmail."[72]

New York's 1935 heart balm law faced two major court challenges to its constitutionality. In the first case, a nurse named Catherine Fearon levied a $25,000 suit against Charles Treanor, a retired insurance broker, for breach of promise and seduction. Fearon's lawyer argued that New York's heart balm law was unconstitutional because it interfered with a protected right to make contracts. In 1936, the New York State Appellate Court upheld the law banning heart balm in *Fearon v. Treanor*. The court noted the state's interest in regulating marriage: "From time immemorial the State has exercised fullest control over the marriage relation, justly believing that happy, successful marriages constitute the fundamental basis of the general welfare of the people." They cited, "Thoughtful people who have given attention to the matter have long realized that the scandals growing out of the actions to recover damages for breach of promise to marry constitutes a reflection upon the courts and a menace to the marriage institution, and thereby a danger to the state." The reference to "the scandals" demonstrates the Court's consideration of the public image of heart balm laws, not simply their analysis of doctrinal issues related to contracts and legal obligations. Scandal refers to a public perception, not just a collection of wrongdoing. The heart balm scandal was created through journalistic tort tales, gold digger movies, and feminist and antifeminist activism and, therefore, the appellate court's decision underscored the proximity of law and popular culture in legal decision-making. The State Supreme Court affirmed the ruling and, on appeal, the U.S. Supreme Court refused to consider the case because it did not involve a substantial question of federal interest.[73]

A second case in 1937 specifically took aim at the ban on alienation of affection suits. Lawrence Hanfgarn sued George Mark for $30,000 for alienating his wife's affection. Hanfgarn claimed that his wife sought a divorce after she had carried on an affair with Mark. Hanfgarn's attorney argued that New York's ban on heart balm lawsuits was unconstitutional because it violated common law rights. Echoing Senator Quinn's testimony against the law two years earlier, he dismissed the heart balm ban as a way "to protect a few rich defendants from newspaper publicity." The trial court denied the motion to dismiss the husband's alienation of affection action. The state court upheld Hanfgarn's right to sue and struck down the constitutionality of New York's anti–heart balm law. The dissenting opinion argued that heart balm actions "are in the main founded on fraud," that "general knowledge and public opinion support this view," and, therefore, the New York Legislature has a reasonable basis for barring such lawsuits.[74] On appeal, the decision was reversed. Irving Hubbs, writing for the unanimous opinion of the Court of Appeals, reaffirmed the state's power to regulate and control marriage. Hubbs deployed the feminist critique of heart balm used by Kathleen Norris, Roberta West Nicholson, and the National Women's Party. He stated that the laws were out of step with the "almost unlimited extension of the rights of married women brought about by statutory enactments and social advancement."[75] The court concluded that heart balm laws, rooted in men's property rights over their wives, were inconsistent with the new reality of marriage relations. In this manner, the court's analysis paralleled public discussions about the abuses of heart balm and the changing roles of women. Like *Fearon v. Treanor*, the court's language and reasoning mirrored the outside influences that constructed the heart balm controversy. The establishment of heart balm reform was propelled by a larger conversation about women's roles in marriage, the labor market, and American culture.

Other states, following the lead of Indiana and New York, introduced legislation to reform or eliminate heart balm. Maryland's only female senator, Mary Risteau, introduced a heart balm bill in March 1935. Lawmakers in Iowa also pursued anti–heart balm legislation. Iowa's anti–heart balm bill included a provision that imposed a fine from $100 to $1,000 for merely threatening to sue. Alma Smith and Blanch Hower from Ohio introduced a bill modeled after Nicholson's legislation. Hower related a story to the *Mansfield News Journal* about "a refined young woman, a graduate of Wellesley, who had a cocktail party." At the party, a male guest allegedly hugged her and gave her a "light little kiss," which prompted her husband to sue the man in a $20,000 alienation of affection suit. In April 1937, Eudochia Bell Smith from Denver sponsored a heart balm bill in the Colorado legislature. When it passed, she said, "That's the end of the gold digger in Colorado courts." The following month, less than two weeks before the nation reeled from the sudden and premature death of actor Jean Harlow, star of popular gold digger films, Democratic Congresswoman Katherine Foley from Lawrence, Massachusetts, introduced an anti–heart balm bill in her state, declaring that such lawsuits were nothing but a "gold digging racket."[76]

. . . . . .

By 1940, ten states across the country had passed legislation to eliminate or restrict heart balm lawsuits.[77] The rush to outlaw heart balm laws was not a consequence of a sudden increase in such suits or a rash of impoverishment caused by breach of promise actions. Like the alimony panic of the late 1920s, the fear of gold digging exceeded the reality of it. Some scholars have attributed the anti–heart balm movement to shifting notions of gender, sexuality, and the family.[78] The decline of the Victorian feminine ideal and the rise of new modes and intensities of sexual expression in the 1920s and 1930s strained the legitimacy of breach of promise actions.[79] In this understanding, the anti–heart balm movement was rooted in the modernization of gender and sexuality.

Yet explaining the agitation against heart balm by pointing to changing gender and sexual norms only provides part of the picture. The broad shift in sexual mores was well under way by the 1920s, and the rejection of sexual Victorianism began to occur—at least in major U.S. cities—by the 1910s. The linkage between gender ideology and legal change is important and essential, but insufficient to explain the timing of the heart balm backlash in the 1930s. The public's momentum against heart balm, which reached a crescendo in the middle and late 1930s, was driven by a confluence of structural and cultural dynamics. The Great Depression heightened the precarious position of women's paid labor, contributed to a crisis in masculine identity, and strained the politics of respectability that surrounded marriage as a path to avoid poverty. As historian Larissa Werhnyak's meticulous research has shown, the female politicians who opposed heart balm primarily came from upper-class backgrounds.[80] The heart balm issue allowed these women to establish their privilege by positioning themselves against gold diggers who sought meritless class advancement. At the same time, the panic over heart balm developed from a series of tort tales, well-publicized (yet atypical) stories in local and national newspapers about high-stakes breach of promise lawsuits. The gold digger trope—amplified by a bumper crop of pre-Code films featuring breach of promise lawsuits—provided a vocabulary of motive for the alleged problem of women abusing the court system for economic security. The anti–heart balm campaign took direction from popular representations of gold diggers, and gold digger narratives created a ready-made scapegoat through which the public could understand the heart balm debate.

3 Gold Diggers and Midcentury Domesticity

· ² ·

The trouble began in 1940 when Archie and Rose Crist, along with their two children, moved into a house across the street from Walter and Clara Swick. A friendship developed between the Crists' nineteen-year-old son Herbert and the Swick's adopted daughter Marjorie. Before long, Marjorie and Herbert fell in love. The sixteen-year-old Marjorie tried to impress Herbert with her maturity, told him that she was scheduled to audition for the Metropolitan Opera Company, and described herself as "the Judy Garland of Columbus." Herbert exhausted his savings to buy Marjorie a $140 ring. The two of them traveled to Kentucky to marry and they moved in with the Swicks upon their return. The Crists never approved of their son's marriage and allegedly pressured him to obtain a divorce. Archie Crist refused to speak to his new daughter-in-law. Rose Crist called Marjorie "adopted trash" and "nothing but a damn little gold digger." Perhaps from the influence of his parents, Herbert asked for Marjorie to return the ring he purchased for her and then he left town. Herbert's father filed for divorce on his son's behalf.[1]

The Swicks filed an alienation of affection suit against the Crists alleging that they conspired to destroy Marjorie and Herbert's marriage. A jury was persuaded by the claims that Archie and Rose Clara treated their daughter-in-law cruelly and poisoned their son against her. They awarded the Swicks $1,250. The Ohio Court of Appeals reversed the decision. The court ruled that, although the in-laws treated their daughter-in-law terribly, the venom they hurled at Marjorie occurred after Herbert had left town. The court affirmed that the acts and statements of Archie and Rose Crist "were obnoxious in the extreme," but Herbert's parents were not legally responsible for harming the marriage. From the court's perspective, Marjorie Crist was not a gold digger, but neither was she entitled to compensation for her in-laws' matrimonial meddling.[2]

Crist v. Crist was a minor affair that barely made a dent in Ohio case law. The saga of Marjorie Crist, however, reveals a few things about the gold digger stereotype as it moved into the 1940s and '50s. The gold digger no longer called to mind a restricted class of villains and victims, of Ziegfeld Follies stars and lumber tycoons. The gold digger could be a sixteen-year-old girl seeking a $140 ring.[3] The gold digger was now a creature of the middle class. The case also shows that, despite the robust campaign against heart balm laws in the 1930s, heart balm lawsuits still made it to trial and found jurors sympathetic to heart balm plaintiffs.

Concerns about alimony and heart balm lingered into the 1940s and 1950s, but they did not attract the organized attention of activists like they did during the 1920s and 1930s. In some ways, the 1940s and '50s acted as a bridge between the early twentieth-century moral panics about American marriage and the turmoil sparked during the "long 1960s"—a period of rapid social change starting in the late 1950s and extending into the 1970s. Nevertheless, the gold digger persevered during the middle of the twentieth century, performing the alchemic social role of providing a simple, individualistic explanation for large economic and social changes. Gold diggers in the 1940s and '50s reflected and supported fears about the effect of world war on the American family, fears about women and heterosexual desire undermining the war effort, and postwar anxiety about masculinity, family, dating, and changing women's roles. This chapter traces the life of the gold digger stereotype during the 1940s and 1950s. It connects mid-century social changes—World War II, the G.I. Bill, the Cold War, and the postwar economic expansion—to the new frontiers of the gold digger stereotype and the proliferation of gold digger narratives found in movies, television, magazines, and newspaper advice columns.

World War II and Allotment Annies

During World War II, gold diggers allegedly undermined the war effort by fleecing military men. The United States lurched into World War II after Japanese forces attacked Pearl Harbor on December 7, 1941. World War II engaged the full attention of the civilian population, and the war effort involved not only the mobilization of troops and munitions but the reimaging of family and marriage. Material production shifted to bolster military armaments, and ideological production moved to boost the morale of Americans at home and abroad. Inevitably, men and women recrafted marriage and romance under the cloud of war. Young couples, faced with the prospect of an uncertain future, raced to the altar. In 1942, the percentage of Americans getting married peaked, prompting concern about the growing number of young married couples. University of Chicago sociologist Ernest Burgess warned of "considerable risk in wartime romance" and cautioned,

"Romantic patriotism won't help in the long run."[4] Despite warnings from elders, wartime marriages and childbirth soared. Men found love abroad, too, and the phrase "war bride" increasingly referred to interethnic couples often united across enemy lines.

Public opinion about war brides shifted over the decades. According to historian Susan Zeiger, "War brides in the 1920s were stigmatized as prostitutes or 'gold diggers,' women who had taken advantage of innocent American 'boys.'"[5] The public's attitude toward war brides softened following World War II. The War Brides Act of 1945 allowed Asian war brides to immigrate to the United States regardless of immigration quotas.[6] War brides from other nations were viewed as cultural authorities who could help ease international tensions. After the war, many American men regarded war brides as model wives because, unlike American women, they did not take jobs that were seen as belonging to men. Public policy and public opinion, however, favored certain war brides over others. Several state antimiscegenation laws prevented marriages between whites and African Americans, Native Americans, and those of Latinx descent.[7]

The conflict abroad opened new employment opportunities for women, but this created a dilemma for the domestic war effort. The United States needed women to fulfill responsibilities typically bestowed to men, yet the completion of those roles strained deeply entrenched gender norms. As historian Maureen Honey has noted, wartime propaganda walked a difficult path because military efforts to increase domestic support for the war potentially clashed with prewar cultural narratives about class and gender. War propagandists negotiated the desire to keep women ensconced in the domestic sphere while simultaneously motivating them to work in the service of American military victory. Honey explains that the dominant image of the gold digger, popularized through 1930s films, was particularly ill suited for the new task: "the gold digger with her materialistic focus was a counterproductive character at a time when the government wanted to inspire energetic industriousness in the civilian population, particularly among young working-class women." The gold digger stereotype backfired because it generated public distrust about the very class of women most likely to take war jobs. She explains, "Therefore, one of the first things writers faced was transforming the gold digger into a model of patriotic devotion without sacrificing her dramatic usefulness." In this context, the image of Rosie the Riveter emerged as an iconic representation of women's participation in the war and their entrance into heavy industry. Although most women in the wartime workforce attained clerical and service jobs, the rugged look of Rosie the Riveter served as a rallying point and allowed women to envision themselves in heretofore forbidden domains. One of the most recognizable pieces of World War II iconography developed out of a contrast with the 1930s gold digger.[8]

But the gold digger did not go away during World War II. In the 1940s, the gold digger appeared in the form of the "Allotment Annie," a woman who married multiple servicemen and enriched herself from their military allotment payments. Congress changed the allotment system in 1942 in order to provide financial support for the wives and children of men fighting in World War II.[9] A wife could receive $50 a month, with $22 coming from the serviceman's pay and the remainder coming from the government. The gigantic scope of the allotment system managed by the War Department Office of Dependency Benefits opened itself up for abuse.[10] In their 1945 book *Wartime Racketeers*, Harry Lever and Joseph Young observed, "any 'Allotment Annie' willing to hustle a little and take unto herself a mere half-dozen husbands—all foreordained to absenteeism—may bask in an income of several hundred dollars a month without greater effort than occasionally opening the mailbox." A writer for the *St. Louis Post Dispatch* warned, "This war has produced a considerable quota of women who make a career of this crime." Another commentator lamented the "hundreds of Allotment Annies" who abused the military compensation system during World War II. Columnist Clifton Williams from Norfolk, Virginia, argued that servicemen were facing high rates of divorce upon their return from fighting overseas because "all too many girls did not marry because of reasons of love." The women, he explained, "were thinking along the mercenary lines of service allotments, casualty insurance, etc. Disappointed now that their husbands didn't get killed in the service, and facing the prospects of having to live with them, the girls would rather be free than to bother." Critics portrayed the Allotment Annie as a threat not only to the deceived men but to the national fabric.[11]

News reports about Grace Reinert were typical of the outrage expressed over Allotment Annies. Twenty-year-old Reinert lived in Washington, D.C., and worked at a filling station. She married a Kansas City police officer when she was fourteen, but the union ended in divorce. When she was eighteen, she married a sailor who was later killed in Pearl Harbor. Her third and fourth marriages to two sailors, one in D.C. and one in Norfolk, Virginia, allowed her to double her collection of allotment payments. Her connivance ended when a government inventory of allotment records uncovered her two marriages. Police arrested her for bigamy.[12] News reports portrayed her as a relentless flirt who maliciously seduced naive soldiers. According to one source, "For several days Grace was the sensation of the District of Columbia jail as she languidly paraded her charms, becomingly attired in a sweater, riding breeches, and boots." She complained of illness and officials sent her to the Gallinger Municipal Hospital Psychopathic Ward in Washington, D.C., where she escaped within an hour.[13] Days later, San Diego police discovered her working as a waitress. Upon her arrest in San Diego, she unsuccessfully appealed to the police to wait to book her because she was "supposed to go on a hike with the cutest little sailor boy" later in the day. One source described how, when U.S. marshals accompanied her on the train ride from California to D.C., she left her chaperones to flirt with soldiers and sailors ("anyone garbed in khaki or blue").[14] Federal officials returned her to Washington, D.C., and she was found guilty of bigamy and sentenced to prison.

The Allotment Annies' danger stemmed from both the aggressiveness of young women and the naïveté of young men. These stories portrayed men as gullible and effortlessly swayed by attractive young women. One article described the men as "blithely ignorant" of allotment wives. Another source claimed, "A soldier or sailor about to ship out is an easy target for their wiles." Grace Reinert allegedly told reporter Ruth Reynolds that willful young women purposely attained jobs near big naval bases like San Diego or Norfolk and "that way she meets a lot of sailors, and those young kids off the farms for the first time are easy pickings." For example, Elvira Tayloe, a seventeen-year-old "blonde temptress," worked "as a dime-a-dance girl at one of Norfolk's hot spots." Tayloe supposedly seduced and wed six sailors, collecting $300 a month in allotment money. While accounts of Allotment Annies characterized the women as seductresses, they portrayed the military men as foolish and lacking sexual agency. Allotment Annies hurt national security by preying on men's natural, yet ungovernable, sexual desires. In this way, putatively normal heterosexual impulses, combined with wartime gold digging, allegedly posed a danger to military readiness.[15]

Historian Ann Pfau notes that gold-digging bigamists were "rare in real life" but "received a great deal of press attention."[16] Consistent with other moral panics that accompanied the gold digger in earlier decades, Allotment Annies represented more of an ideological projection about womanhood and gender than a response to a real social problem. Nonetheless, some military and political leaders regarded Allotment Annies as a grave concern. In June 1943, Edwin C. Johnson, a Democratic senator from Colorado, voiced trepidations about immoral women marrying servicemen at a

Senate committee hearing on military affairs. John Sparkman, a representative from Alabama, urged the military to make it easier for servicemen to terminate allotment payments to dependents. Military leaders pushed back against these senatorial interventions because they worried it would overextend their responsibilities, forcing them to perform the functions of a domestic relations court.[17]

The problem of Allotment Annies received Hollywood treatment when Kay Francis starred in the 1945 film *Allotment Wives*. Reviews and marketing for the film emphasized its realism. One ad called it, "A blast at the most nefarious racket ever conceived by woman," and promised the film would show "the whole vicious story of the thousands of service men who were betrayed by them." A review in a Texas newspaper called it "an exploitation picture exposing a current and flourishing racket."[18] Using the imagery of gold mining, the film opens with a description of the workings of the Newark, New Jersey, Office of Dependency Benefits (ODB) and the potential for abuse: "Never in history was there such a gigantic stream of gold accessible to avaricious and criminal elements. It looked easy, and the scramble to get greedy fingers into the stream was on."[19] Rather than an isolated problem of some women marrying men for their allotments and family allowances, the film depicts a mob-affiliated syndicate where scores of "unscrupulous women" seduced, married, and fleeced unsuspecting servicemen.

An early scene in *Allotment Wives* shows General H. N. Gilbert and Colonel Peter Martin discussing the problem of allotment abuses. Gilbert tells Martin about the suicide of a mutual acquaintance who returned home from the war only to discover that his fiancée had married three other servicemen. Martin, who has experience as an investigative reporter, agrees to travel to the Pacific Coast to break up the allotment conspiracy. He meets Sheila Seymour (played by Kay Francis), a savvy businesswoman who runs a beauty salon, manages a military canteen, and is well connected to high society. Unbeknownst to him, Sheila also leads an allotment wives syndicate through her canteen. She discovers that he works for the ODB posing as a journalist, and reasons that she can protect herself and her organization if she keeps him close and cultivates his friendship. When he confides to her that he is an undercover investigator trying to break up the allotment racket, she pledges her help and assures him, "I may turn out to be your ace in the hole."

Allotment Wives portrays Sheila Seymour as a hardboiled businessperson who is competent, but ruthless. In the first half of the film she is shown at a luncheon, charming wealthy donors at her canteen. Going over details about her beauty salon with her assistant, she makes a series of high-powered decisions, including the move to sue one of her competitors. In the next scene, she opens a door to a secret room to meet her comrades in the syndicate. She demands reports from five men in suits seated around a large desk. She learns that her syndicate has earned $37,000 from operations in the Northwest Territories. When she asks about Texas, her associate tells her, "We're tilling a rich vineyard down there. Thirty-three sweet maidens so far, operating around the various camps, all acquiring sheaves of husbands." Seymour runs her operation with merciless aggression. She orders the assassination of a former associate to prevent him from speaking to the police, she shoots and kills a rival, and, in one of the final scenes, she raises her gun to fire at Peter Martin, the undercover investigator, but is shot and killed by police. Sheila Seymour embodies many of the general characteristics of a femme fatale from a film noir, but the wartime context heightens her malevolence. For example, Seymour appears onscreen for the first time in the film wearing a black dress decorated with prints of lady's slipper orchids. The flowers, emblems of both East Asia and femininity, mark her as exotic and foreign. As one of Martin's coinvestigators tells him, the Allotment Annies are "like Japs and Germans, rotten to the core and incurable." Sheila Seymour's oversight of the allotment wives racket reveals her to be not just an isolated gold digger but a national threat on par with foreign military adversaries.

By contrast, Sheila's relationship with her teenage daughter Connie highlights her nurturing side, and underlines the dominant ideological messages about work and womanhood prevalent at the middle of the century. Sheila's extensive financial commitments—her legal ownership of the beauty salon, the management of the canteen, and role as "the big cheese of Allotment Wives Incorporated"—keeps her estranged from Connie. In an early scene, Sheila spots Connie, drunk, walking into a bar with a soldier and tells her associate, Whitey Colton, that it is "so hard to look at myself twenty years ago. Just the way I started." They take Connie home and, worried that her daughter will follow her into a life of crime, Sheila beseeches her to stay in school and promises her that they will soon go on a vacation to get away from it all. But Connie quickly falls under the influence of Sheila's rival, Gladys Smith, over a series of hard-partying weeks. Connie becomes an Allotment Annie, and is targeted in Martin's efforts to shut down the syndicate. Sheila and Connie share a tender moment in the hours before Martin and the police finally put a stop to the allotment racket. In a scene more reminiscent of a mother-daughter melodrama like *Stella Dallas* or *Mildred*

Pierce than film noir, Connie and Sheila embrace and Sheila tearfully tells her to "just remember I've always loved you. I've always loved you from the bottom of my heart." The film's conflicting portrayals of Sheila Seymour as a ruthless criminal and an affectionate mother epitomized the complicated and inconsistent messages women received during wartime about their duty to home, country, and the war effort. These messages implored women to be motherly and domestic, but to work for the national good. They told women to be sexy and available, but not to seduce men. Sheila Seymour, as the matron of a squad of Allotment Annies, represented a wartime-specific form of gold digging, one that engaged in ideological work around the edges of gender, social class, and race and ethnicity.

Gold Diggers in the Postwar Transition

The gold digger stereotype operated in a changed domestic landscape following the war. In August 1945, just a few months before the release of *Allotment Wives*, the bombing of Hiroshima and Nagasaki hastened the end of World War II. The divorce rate accelerated during and after World War II, reaching a peak of nearly eighteen divorces per 1,000 marriages in 1946.[20] At the same time, both married and unmarried women sustained the wartime economic expansion by entering the workforce. Much of the American public perceived these trends as threatening a traditional way of life. As Jessica Weiss explains, "Despite this steady growth in married women's employment since 1945, Americans persist in viewing changes in women's work and family patterns as new."[21] By the end of the 1940s, the gold digger was used to critique both the growth of women's paid employment and the shaky foundations of the American family. *Good Jobs for Good Girls*, a 1949 book described by the *Los Angeles Times* as "a facetious etiquette manual for gold diggers," instructed women on how to manipulate men into providing them with care and luxury. *Good Jobs for Good Girls* used the gold digger trope to mock the growing numbers of women who sought employment in the postwar era. Arguing that, "Work is bad for woman's figure, posture, and digestion. It is ruinous, in the long run, to her personality," the book proposed "a higher career": marriage. The book cautioned, "But it must be a marriage to a man who enjoys gratifying your every whim, and who always has the funds necessary for this good purpose." *Good Jobs for Good Girls*, dotted with illustrations and short rhymes, included cheery advice for women to ensnare a husband in different occupational domains. For example, reminiscent of the strategies used by breach of promise liti-

FIGURE 10 From Harford Powel's *Good Jobs for Good Girls*, a satirical guide to gold diggers in 1949 that urged women to "marry for property!" Discourse about gold diggers during the postwar period revealed fears about both the imposition and destabilization of heterosexual domesticity. Harford Powel, *Good Jobs for Good Girls*, Vanguard Press, 1949, 100.

gants in the 1930s, the book advised women to hold onto incriminating love letters: "never tear up his letters; are his letters full of pash? guard them in a secret cache." The illustrations in *Good Jobs for Good Girls* showed various scenes of female dominance: a woman dragging a man to the altar, a woman riding a man as if he were a horse, and a woman clutching a man's money as his spirit rises to heaven. These images strove for humor but they also unwittingly uncovered anxieties about masculinity that plagued white middle- and upper-class men in the middle of the twentieth century.[22]

The gold digger also lurked in the dating market. A lighthearted piece in a 1949 issue of *Ladies' Home Journal* observed that teenaged gold diggers might suggest taking a cab "when a boy's budget barely allows busfare," expect lavish dining options, and demand "orchids or nothing." The gold digger trope was used to make sense of, and push back against, the increasing importance of money in dating. Historian Beth Bailey has explained how dating in the United States became defined by the willingness of both young men and women to spend money and participate in consumer culture. The distinction between an orchid or carnation corsage was vital because it worked to establish a girl's value in an increasingly consequential and complex dating system.[23]

Just as *Good Jobs for Good Girls* and *Ladies' Home Journal* deployed the image of gold diggers to discuss the place of women in the postwar American economy, attorneys, litigants, and judges used the gold digger trope to make sense of the role of women in the home. A 1949 case in Missouri illuminates the incompatible messages women received in the postwar period and the countervailing constructions of masculinity invoked by the gold digger stereotype. In 1949, the Springfield Court of Appeals in Missouri took up the question as to whether Gwendolyn Stokes received adequate alimony from her divorce. In *Stokes v. Stokes*, a two-to-one decision affirmed the lower court's ruling for Gwendolyn to collect $3,250 instead of the $7,500 she sought. The Appellate Court's majority opinion granted broad discretion to the lower court to interpret Stokes's deservedness, and it argued that her poor behavior could act as a limiting factor in the alimony decision. In dissent, Justice James C. McDowell concurred that Gwendolyn Stokes's behavior should influence the amount of alimony she was awarded, but he had a completely different understanding of her role in the divorce and the unhappy marriage. The divergent perspectives articulated in the appellate decision revealed conflicts over gender roles within marriage, the dynamics of femininity and masculinity at the middle of the century, and the place of the gold digger stereotype in making sense of it all.

Gwendolyn Zimmerman was a thirty-two-year-old medical technician when she married her childhood friend Rayburn Stokes. Although Rayburn did not earn a salary, he owned a farm and houses worth a considerable amount of money. Rayburn also drank heavily and, a year into their marriage, Gwendolyn persuaded him to take the "Keely Cure," a then-popular approach to alcoholism that involved a daily regimen of injections with a gold and chlorine compound. Ray quit drinking but became hostile, emotionally distant, and sometimes violent. They divorced and a trial court granted her alimony. After consulting with a new attorney, Gwendolyn made a motion to set aside the divorce in order to obtain a new trial and a higher alimony award. At the request for the new trial, her attorney testified about her "desire to make Rayburn pay and pay and pay." In refusing to set the original decree aside, the court said, "I think she wanted a lot more money than she got from the [original] Court."[24]

In the appellate ruling sustaining the original alimony award, the Court observed, "she was not entirely blameless in their marriage difficulties." She drank with Rayburn in the first year of their marriage and a hysterectomy caused her to be irritable and moody. She loved Rayburn's sons from his prior marriage, but had different views of child-rearing, and she resented the meddlesome involvement of Rayburn's sister in their household affairs. The Court concluded that Gwendolyn "was continually nagging her husband about the children's conduct and about the visits of his relatives." Moreover, she brought nothing financially to the union except her monthly salary of $275 and yet spent lavishly on furniture and clothing. "The inference that she was extravagant," the Court said, "is inescapable." The Court cited the argument in *Knebel v. Knebel* that "under modern economic and social conditions, practically every avenue is open to the wife that is open to the husband." Mirroring anti-alimony arguments from prior decades, the Court's opinion stated that the economic and social gains made by women relative to men decreased the need for postdivorce spousal support. Gwendolyn could work, was earning a healthy wage doing so, and did not need more alimony.[25]

In his dissenting opinion, James McDowell presented an entirely different picture of the marriage and Gwendolyn's proper role in it. He underlined her authority as a mother to Rayburn's children, her mental and physical fragility, and Rayburn's cruelty as factors that the Appellate Court should consider. While the plaintiff argued that Gwendolyn was overly strict with his two young boys, Justice McDowell characterized these instances as moments where Rayburn blocked Gwendolyn from administering proper discipline. McDowell noted that Gwendolyn required hormone shots to recover from her hysterectomy, had a nervous breakdown, and attempted suicide. He also recalled testimony from the first trial that Rayburn "threatened to whip her, did strike her and that he threatened to kill her on different occasions." According to McDowell, Raymond's abuse, coupled with her nervous condition and lack of resources, should have persuaded the court to grant Gwendolyn a hefty alimony award. He said that Rayburn "tries to leave the impression that plaintiff is a gold digger," but "there is no foundation for this contention."[26]

The conflicting perspectives on the status of Gwendolyn Stokes as a gold digger reflect the double binds women faced at the middle of the twentieth century. Women, especially white women, enjoyed modern economic and social conditions characteristic of the expanding postwar economy, but dominant gender norms implored them to be content in their roles as homemakers. Gwendolyn Stokes was placed in a no-win situation. The appellate court deemed Gwendolyn unworthy of a large alimony award because she could earn her own wage, but she was also expected to take care of the home and child care. She was compelled to raise Rayburn's two boys, but she was criticized if she exerted her authority. The majority court referred to Gwendolyn's mental and physical impairments as a reason to limit alimony because they contributed to her marital problems, while the dissent referred to her condition as evidence of the husband's abuse. Numerous causes of her "nervous condition" are noted in the appellate record—the surgery, hormone shots, suicidal tendencies, and her husband's misconduct—but, taken together, her maladies resembled the "problem that has no name" that Betty Friedan identified a decade later in *The Feminine Mystique*. The legal question about whether Stokes was deserving of a higher alimony award or whether she was a gold digger speaks to the unresolvable demands of postwar femininity. The case, which took place on the cusp of a new decade, presaged the cultural construction of the gold digger during the middle of the twentieth century. Stokes was caught between the cultural demands of domesticity and new pathways of agency and independence. She enjoyed material comforts derived from an economy supercharged by the G.I. Bill, but in a context where a woman's place in the workforce, marriage, and wider society was profoundly unresolved.

Gender, Marriage, and the Postwar Economic Expansion

Following the war, marriage and childbirth increased and the United States entered a period of domestic retrenchment. The gold digger trope embodied conflicting notions of masculinity and femininity during the 1950s, and concerns about gold diggers reflected fears about both the imposition and destabilization of heterosexual domesticity. During the postwar period, the gold digger threatened to undermine domestic tranquility by demanding the comforts of 1950s economic expansion without the perceived sacrifices those comforts required. The image of the gold digger during the 1950s became embedded in the construction of the postwar family. The gold digger, as so many dumb blondes who appeared in television, movies, and magazines, made white womanhood appear undeserving of postwar, middle-class comforts, and she comprised part of a cultural apparatus that seemed to threaten white masculinity. As men's magazines, popular movies, and other cultural products warned, gold diggers were no longer found primarily among the ranks of chorus girls. The gold digger moved into the middle-class family matrix. She was a girlfriend who demanded orchid corsages and steak dinners. She was a housewife who no longer conformed to the mold of domestic calm crafted during the 1940s and '50s.

The conclusion of the war marked the beginning of breakneck economic growth and a profound alteration of American families. The total value of goods and services produced in the United States rapidly expanded along with per capita income and wages.[27] Increasing numbers of families attained middle-class status. Single-family homeownership grew at an extraordinary rate. The growth in first-time home ownership for families surpassed the increase for the previous 150 years. By 1960, well over half of American families owned homes and over half of the population earned a middle-class income. More women, including married women, entered the paid labor force. In fact, despite the push for men to reclaim the jobs they had given up during the war, by the early 1950s there were approximately two million more married women in the labor force than at the height of wartime.[28] The postwar period also witnessed a reversal of Depression-era demographic trends. Approximately 50 million babies were born in the fifteen years after 1946, ushering in the postwar baby boom.[29] The marriage rate increased nearly 50 percent in 1946.

New legislation was directly responsible for many of the economic and demographic changes during the 1950s. In particular, the Servicemen's Readjustment Act of 1944, or the G.I. Bill, provided a bounty of benefits for World War II veterans, including low-cost mortgages, tuition assistance, low-interest loans, and generous unemployment compensation. Benefits from the G.I. Bill were available to 40 percent of the male population between the ages of twenty and twenty-four. By 1956, nearly 8 million veterans had used the G.I. Bill education benefits, igniting tremendous growth in university enrollments. These gains came at the expense of women: publicly funded day care centers were closed, qualified female college applicants were rejected to make room for the influx of male applicants, and significant numbers of employed women were fired.[30] The racial impact of the bill was also uneven, and scholars continue to debate the role of the G.I. Bill in relieving or exacerbating economic and social inequalities between African Americans and whites.[31] That one of the authors of the bill, John Rankin, was an outspoken racist limited the full potential of the legislation in improving the life chances of the million or so African Americans who served in World War II. The benefits of the G.I. Bill, while neutral in theory, were primarily used by white men. Therefore, descriptions of the 1950s as a time of unparalleled economic advancement need to be considered in the context of ongoing racism and discrimination, as well as the valorization of heterosexuality.[32] The legislation that underwrote the legal construction of the gold digger during the 1950s—the law that generated the scene of apparent domestic calm that the gold digger threatened to disrupt—was tangled in a complex set of policies and ideologies inflected by race, gender, and class inequality.

Economic prosperity, propelled in part by the G.I. Bill, led to a boom in consumer spending and a symbolic intensification of the nuclear family as the primary fount of meaning and joy. In her landmark study *Homeward Bound*, Elaine Tyler May persuasively draws a connection between the Cold War push to contain the Soviet threat and domestic containment.[33] The elation that marked the end of World War II coincided with new global and domestic anxieties. The use of nuclear weapons to force Japan to surrender, coupled with the decaying wartime alliance between the United States and the Soviet Union, gave way to distress about an atomic future.

The dominant picture of 1950s American domesticity existed in an uneasy relationship with the reality of men's and women's lives. Women's magazines and cultural commentators encouraged women to embrace their role as happy housewives, yet mass media images of joyous homemakers and upright breadwinners were more of an ideological projection of the way some people wanted life to be rather than a reflection of the way Americans were living. Popular culture during the time (and decades later) enshrined the 1950s family as the epitome of the "traditional family." Historian Jessica Weiss shows that families in the 1950s had a dynamic quality that is obscured by cultural representations of the era as a time of mass conformity. As Stephanie Coontz explains, the 1950s family was "a historical fluke, based on a unique and temporary conjuncture of economic, social, and political factors."[34] Moreover, the apparent stability of the 1950s nuclear family came at significant costs to women. Married women were expected to abandon their ambitions in service of their husbands and children. The prevalence of shared breadwinning meant that many women—women who worked in order to support their husband's education or to keep up with the increasing consumer demands of middle-class American culture—were caught between cultural ideals and economic necessity.[35] Meanwhile, unmarried women were expected to marry young and fulfill the cultural expectations of the newly "traditional" family unit.[36]

The War of the Roses

Divorce cases vividly displayed the gender conflict that beset families in the 1950s. While cases like *Stokes v. Stokes* escaped public notice, others received sustained interest from U.S. newspapers. No divorce in the early 1950s garnered more attention than Eleanor Holm's divorce from Broadway producer and multimillionaire Billy Rose. Decades later, movie critic Rex Reed referred to Holm as "the swimming gold digger," but during the divorce trial, the status of Holm as a gold digger was an open question, not a foregone conclusion.[37] The battle over Holm's public image sheds considerable light on the contradictory messaging about femininity and marriage in postwar America. The case shows the circumstances in which the gold digger stereotype worked and, importantly, did not work as a controlling image of white heterosexual womanhood.

Eleanor Holm first gained notoriety in 1928 as a fourteen-year-old Olympic swimmer with a formidable backstroke. She earned a gold medal for the U.S. team in 1932. A year later, Eleanor Holm married Arthur Jarrett, orchestra leader at the Cocoanut Grove nightclub. Holm catapulted to national attention at the 1936 Olympics, but not for her talent in the pool. On the ship bound for Berlin, Holm caused a scandal by drinking and socializing with reporters on the upper deck. U.S. Olympic team leader Avery Brundage claimed that Holm was horribly drunk and he dismissed Holm from the team for violating a rule against drinking. Holm recalled, years later, that her expulsion from the team was in retaliation for turning down a pass he made at her. His abuse of power and his denial of her chance at Olympic glory caused her to have ill will toward Brundage for the rest of her life, but Holm leveraged the media attention she received into full-blown celebrity status.[38] She portrayed herself as a young woman who loved a fun time and a cold drink. She teased reporters, telling them, "I train on champagne and cigarettes," and "I've always swum better on a little liquor." The scandal gave her notoriety and a degree of fame that allowed her to dip her toes into the world of movies and entertainment. Holm took screen tests at various Hollywood studios and briefly performed in the Ziegfeld Follies.[39]

The publicity over the drinking scandal strained her marriage and Arthur Jarrett divorced her in 1937. In his divorce complaint, Jarrett stated that Eleanor's dismissal from the Olympic team caused him enormous embarrassment and prevented him from obtaining work in radio and theater. He also cited an incident in Long Island when she stayed out all night drinking and lost a fur coat worth $1,800. He could not collect insurance on the coat, he purported, because to do so would provoke humiliating publicity. He also claimed that she took all of the money they received from joint theatrical appearances "without giving him spending money." Her dishonor at the Olympics might have strained the marriage, but her status as a bread-winner, her infidelity, and her nascent gold digger tendencies all contrib-uted to the relationship's decline.[40]

At the time of their divorce, Holm was carrying on an affair with the-ater director and impresario Billy Rose. Rose, capitalizing on the growing popularity of women's synchronized swimming, invested in producing the-atrical water shows. Eleanor Holm starred in Rose's 1937 Great Lakes Expo-sition Aquacade, and they fell in love. The affair between Rose and Holm became fodder for Broadway gossip especially when, as several newspapers insinuated, Holm accompanied Rose to Canada for a business trip and the couple checked into a hotel under misleading names. In 1938, Rose divorced Fanny Brice, the legendary Ziegfeld performer and comedian. Their nine-year marriage was largely peaceable, but passionless. Rose bristled at her greater notoriety and loathed his identity as "Mr. Brice." For her part, Brice was incensed by Rose's affair with Holm. That year, as Rose's marriage with Fanny Brice dissolved, Eleanor Holm briefly flirted with an acting career, starring in *Tarzan's Revenge*, a 1938 release by the Twentieth Century Fox Film Corporation. She allegedly left the filming before its scheduled end because a stunt involving a live alligator made her nervous.[41]

Billy Rose married Eleanor Holm on November 14, 1939, in a ceremony witnessed by forty reporters and photographers. After a four-month hon-eymoon in Miami Beach, they established two estates. The couple owned a costly house on Beekman Place in New York City and a mansion on Mount Kisco in Westchester County, New York. Like Mary Pickford and Douglas Fairbank's "Pickfair" in Beverley Hills, Holm dubbed the Mount Kisco es-tate "Roseholm," and it became "one of the showcases of New York."[42] Billy had a solidly domestic vision for Eleanor's future, and he had Holm sign a marital agreement that promised she would not work again.[43] According to Rose, "Eleanor's future will be devoted exclusively to being Mrs. Rose and making good coffee."[44] Nonetheless, Holm and Rose created an exception to their marriage contract and Holm made dozens of appearances at the 1939 New York World's Fair in Billy Rose's Aquacade show. A 1940 feature in *Life* magazine featured Holm smiling broadly on a bed in their fourteen-room house in New York City. The article detailed the luxurious interiors of their Beekman Place estate, noting the $2,000 Sheraton sofa, the Modi-gliani that hung over the bedroom mantel, and Eleanor's collection of over 300 bathing suits. The union of Rose and Holm continued in harmonious splendor, with the couple referred to as "one of the happiest in show busi-

FIGURE 11 Eleanor Holm, 1938, publicity photo for *Tarzan's Revenge*. Actor and Olympian Eleanor Holm was remembered by movie critic Rex Reed as "the swimming gold digger" for her alimony suit against Billy Rose during the 1950s. Yet, at the time, the status of Holm as a gold digger was much contested. Courtesy of PhotoFest.

ness." Pampered and housebound, Eleanor Holm lived a version of the midcentury ideal for white American women.[45]

Billy Rose made a tremendous amount of income when the musical *Gentlemen Prefer Blondes* opened at his Ziegfeld Theatre on December 8, 1949. *Life* magazine called the show, "Broadway's first musical-comedy smash hit of the season." The musical grossed nearly $50,000 a week and ran for 740 performances over twenty-two months. For a New Year's Eve celebration, Rose turned the Ziegfeld Theatre into a nightclub and invited a list of stars, including Carol Channing, who played Lorelei Lee in the lead role.[46] For the night, he christened the club "Chez Eleanor." Behind the happy façade, however, the marriage of Holm and Rose deteriorated because of his cavorting with actresses and showgirls. According to his sister, sleeping with single women was "his favorite indoor sport" for most of his career.[47] Their relationship was also imperiled by Eleanor Holm's reputed anti-Semitism, which expressed itself with particular ugliness when she was drunk.[48] Rose's

Jewish identity became more intense and self-conscious after the world learned about the horrors of the Holocaust. Yet, Holm tried to prevent Rose's involvement in Israel, including thwarting Rose's fundraising for a $250,000 publicity campaign for the newly formed nation.[49]

Their marriage reached a breaking point when Rose initiated a very public affair with actor Joyce Matthews, the former wife of comedian Milton Berle. On a July evening in 1951, in an event the press referred to as the "Joyce Matthews incident," Matthews locked herself in the bathroom of Rose's penthouse apartment above the Ziegfeld Theatre and slashed her wrists. Police arrived to find her face down and unconscious and, after applying tourniquets to her arms, called for an ambulance. At this moment, Billy Rose said, "Now is the time to have a wife. I'm going to call Eleanor now." She allegedly made the suicide attempt because Rose refused to divorce Eleanor and marry her. She also feared that Broadway gossip about her affair with Rose would cause her to lose custody of her six-year-old daughter. But, when journalists asked why she attempted suicide, Matthews quipped, "I just love razor blades." According to the *Los Angeles Times*, the suicide attempt and the public disclosure of the affair "projected Rose into a drama rivaling many of those he produced on stage." Billy and Eleanor's thirteen-year marriage headed towards divorce court. Their split was hostile. National newspapers referred to the aggressive pretrial maneuvers of both parties as "The War of the Roses."[50]

In court and in the press, Billy Rose portrayed Eleanor Holm as a thieving gold digger. She locked him out of their Beekman Place mansion and, according to Rose, absconded with art and antiques worth hundreds of thousands of dollars. He accused Holm of manipulating the press and feeding reporters stories "as a prelude for huge monetary demands." Rose, ignoring the advice of his attorney, attacked Holm on several fronts. According to Rose's sister, "Billy's blows were low and dirty." Among the attacks was an affidavit that "purported to show that she joined in sex parties, sometimes with other women." Rose also filed a motion in California court to verify that Holm's first marriage to Jarrett was invalid because the bandleader did not meet California's residency requirement for marriage. If Holm's marriage to Jarrett was illegitimate, Rose's attorney reasoned, then she could not possibly be legally married to Rose. Holm's attorney Louis Nizer hit back with a fiery press statement. His remarks summarized the confusing legal web Rose had spun: "So, Mr. Rose, at the same time pretended to be married to Joyce Matthews who was not his wife, argued that he was not married to Eleanor Holm Rose who is his wife, and finally claims that not being married to her, he nevertheless wants a divorce from her." Nizer's statement and Rose's impetuousness tilted public opinion in Holm's favor.[51]

Holm told the press that she was willing to work out a divorce settlement, but Rose refused to negotiate because he held a "clenched fist on the dollar." Rose continued to ignore advice from his attorney to be quiet and issued a statement to the press to counter his avaricious image. Marbled with sarcasm, the statement enumerated the treasures and indulgences Rose afforded Holm. He started, "Eleanor is absolutely right. Compared to me, Scrooge is a philanthropist." Rose elaborated, "The pictures on the wall were horrors—the works of hacks like Rembrandt, Hals, Velasquez, and Renoir." He mentioned that he gave Holm $17,000 for "pocket money" and an $80,000 sable coat. In the battle over publicity, the statement may have served its purpose in underlining Eleanor Holm's greed but, as a legal artifact, the press release utterly backfired. Nizer replied, "Mrs. Rose is indebted to Mr. Rose for having provided the evidence of their high standard of living, upon which permanent alimony will be awarded at the trial." The details of their riches proved the opulent lifestyle to which Eleanor was accustomed, and it made it increasingly difficult for Billy to avoid paying a weighty sum in alimony. Years later, Nizer remarked, "The incident was a good illustration of the errors a client can make when he masterminds his own contest."[52]

An atmosphere of intense excitement enveloped the courthouse on the day of the trial, and journalists jockeyed to access the extra telephone wires that were newly installed in the building for the occasion. Hundreds of spectators, reporters, and photographers gathered in the front of the court building, but the assembled throng was quickly disappointed. Rose's counsel asked for a conference with the judge in an attempt to settle. The public nature of the divorce gave Eleanor and her lawyer an advantage, and Rose worried that his affair with Joyce Matthews would be aired in open court, further damaging his already shaken reputation. The attorneys worked out a settlement agreement whereby Holm limited her divorce claim to exclude mentioning Joyce Matthews. Rose, in turn, agreed to make a public apology in open court. The financial arrangement required Rose to pay $600 a week and $200,000 over a ten-year period. Decades later, Holm downplayed the enormity of the alimony settlement, observing that she received the alimony payments during a time when Rose held over $15 million in assets. His biographer observed that the settlement "barely tapped his fortune." Nonetheless, newspapers the following day featured a photo of Holm leaving the court building with a beaming smile.[53]

According to her attorney, Holm "received an ovation from a huge crowd that filled the corridors." Joyous public attention followed Holm and her lawyer as they made their way to the Algonquin Round Table for celebratory cocktails. "Feelings were so intense," Nizer alleged, "that many women sobbed." Public opinion favored Holm, her attorney mused, because of "the ingrained American tradition of fair play."[54] Billy behaved unchivalrously and was excoriated in the public eye. But Eleanor Holm's upright reputation during the War of the Roses speaks to the relational and contrastive qualities of the gold digger trope. Eleanor's restrained comportment, encouraged by her attorney, stood in stark relief to Billy Rose's braggadocio and his relentless assaults on her character. She fulfilled postwar expectations of feminine domesticity by giving up work and devoting herself to home, but he rewarded her devoutness with infidelity and smears to her public name. Eleanor's victory elicited strong emotions not because most women could identify with her wealth or fame but because she occupied a sympathetic position in the ideological and material lattice of postwar America. Although far more famous, Holm was similar to Gwendolyn Stokes, insofar as both women made a series of compromises in order to embody a midcentury feminine ideal but were punished for their desires.

Eleanor Holm's whiteness and Billy Rose's Jewishness constituted another important contrast that can help explain why Rose was publicly criticized and why Holm largely escaped the label of gold digger. Awareness of the Holocaust caused a decline in anti-Semitism in the United States during the postwar period. Some historians point to the 1950s as the moment in American history when American Jews shed their racial otherness and were accepted as "white." Considerable anti-Semitism nonetheless lingered and, when Billy Rose married Eleanor Holm, the Jewish intermarriage rate (the percentage of American Jews marrying someone of a different faith) hovered around one to two percent. Holm was fourteen years younger, and several inches taller, than Billy Rose. According to historian Mark Cohen, her "sleek sexual allure" set her apart from her husband, and their physical differences accentuated the perceived social differences in their religion and ethnicity.[55]

Eleanor's esteem in the public eye, and her evasion of being branded as a gold digger despite the enormous alimony award she received, also stemmed from yet another contrast. Joyce Matthews stood as the "other woman" in the Rose-Holm divorce proceedings and this inescapably made Eleanor Holm the aggrieved party. Joyce Matthews, whom the public held as less talented than Holm and therefore less deserving of Rose's wealth, was arguably the real gold digger in the whole affair. Holm's attorney seemed to imply as such when he said, "A man who is caught with the proverbial blonde is hardly in a position to take the offensive against his wife."[56] The phrase "proverbial blonde" harkens back to the gold diggers of the 1920s and '30s: the "amusement blondes" referred to in the heart balm debates and the protagonist of *Gentlemen Prefer Blondes*. At the time of Holm's divorce settlement, January 1954, the reference to blondes had strong resonance in the wider culture. By the conclusion of Eleanor Holm's divorce battle, the fame of Marilyn Monroe reached epic proportions in part due to her stardom in *Gentlemen Prefer Blondes*. Labeling Joyce Matthews as the "proverbial blonde" implied that she, not Eleanor Holm, was the real gold digger.

Gold Diggers and the Postwar Masculinity Crisis

White men in the postwar period, while maintaining unrivaled political, social, and economic power, perceived various threats to their authority. The history of American masculinity has produced different perspectives on the causes and consequences of the postwar "crisis of masculinity," and some have criticized the language of crisis altogether.[57] Nonetheless, many men regarded a burgeoning feminist movement, mass consumer culture, and a white-collar corporate working world as a threat to their sense of individualism, manliness, and way of life. Women's increasing presence in the paid labor force during the 1950s generated anxiety among heterosexual men as they attempted to reconcile cultural messaging about male breadwinning with the realities of both shared breadwinning and the pressures to purchase a middle-class lifestyle. In her landmark study of American marriage and marriage counseling in the twentieth century, historian Rebecca Davis observes, "Men's positions in these postwar households were fraught with ambiguity: marriage counselors' advice evinced little confidence that a husband's masculinity could survive his wife's paid employment or shared household leadership."[58] Characteristic of hegemonic masculinity in general, midcentury masculinity was defined in opposition to traits and cultural forms perceived as feminine. Public intellectuals and commentators portrayed the stereotypical conformity of the 1950s as feminizing, and so there were efforts to revive older models of masculinity that were popular toward the end of the nineteenth century, models of masculinity that were created in response to an earlier "crisis" of masculinity during the 1890s. The gold digger trope became a useful image through which to define American manhood in the 1950s.

In 1952, as newspapers gave thorough coverage of Eleanor Holm's divorce battle with Billy Rose, Dr. Charles Wilner published a screed called *Alimony: The American Tragedy*.[59] The book, which was mentioned in the *New York Times* and favorably reviewed in *The International Journal of Sexology*, aimed for a historical and sociological meditation on the alimony question.[60] Laced with unvarnished misogyny and references to white racial purity, Wilner argued that alimony undercut men's natural authority in the public and private spheres. The alimony system posed a grave danger, not only for the men who had to pay it but for American society and white civilization. He argued, "militant feminism and its alimony laws contribute strongly to the bastardization of racial castes and cultures." White men, Wilner reasoned, will marry outside their race because they suspect that white women, emboldened by feminism, will marry them for money, seek a divorce, and pursue alimony. He wrote, "Even a brief investigation of interracial marriages will show that the main source of the evil can be ascribed to unbridled feminism and its alimony laws." Citing racists and eugenicists like Robert Shufeldt, Madison Grant, and Arthur de Gobineau, Wilner argued that feminism and alimony laws led to poisonous racial integration and societal decline.[61]

Wilner based his arguments about alimony and marriage on the premise that women are inferior to men. He wrote, "researchers agree that emotional balance in woman is unstable," and that women's "brains are in their wombs." Because of feminism, "too many women are becoming bold and breastless Amazons, impossible for men to live with." In this context, alimony laws became tools for fraud and sin, "tending to make a mockery of marriage and hasten the disintegration of the family." Wilner drew a comparison between modern marriage and prostitution. He argued that alimony may have been justified in the past when women's economic and business opportunities were limited, but now, "almost every field of endeavor is open to them. And they control over seventy per cent of the national wealth." In a "strange bedfellows" moment, he cited Fanny Hurst, a writer who made a similar argument about alimony during the 1920s, but from a position of celebrating feminism rather than lamenting it. The alimony system, he contended, needed serious reform. He wrote: "Such laws may have meaning when children are born of a union and the wife is rearing citizens for the State. But they lack logic when they favor the young, childless, self-supporting gold-digger, or the woman who, sometimes, because of previous promiscuity, is unable to bear children." Wilner's expressions of racism and sexism were entirely unremarkable for 1952, but his use of the gold digger trope shows its protean quality in tying together various anxieties. The gold digger, in Wilner's analysis, serves as a docking port for the racial, gender, and sexual fears that existed at the middle of the twentieth century. His book also exposed the perceived crisis of masculinity that occurred during the postwar period, a set of deeply felt apprehensions that motivated the readers of Wilner's rants. Wilner's criticism of gold diggers, and the professed threats to masculinity that they augured, was echoed in popular magazines of the 1950s, including *Playboy*.[62]

Hugh Hefner published the first issue of *Playboy* toward the end of 1953, and the first featured article was about the dangers of gold diggers. "Miss Gold Digger" was a broadside attack on gold diggers and the state of alimony awards in the early 1950s. The article was authored by Burt Zollo writing under the pseudonym Bob Norman. Zollo was instrumental in helping launch and raise money for *Playboy*. Before working with Hefner, Zollo was a writer and publicist at *Cornet* and *Esquire*, the latter of which served as a template for the new magazine. Zollo, far from being a victim of gold digging, was happily married at the time he penned his article. Years later, his son stated that Zollo "personally didn't endorse the values exposed in the article" but knew what Hefner wanted and had a perceptive sense of the historical moment in which he was writing.[63]

Reminiscent of anti-alimony sentiment during the 1920s, "Miss Gold Digger" groused about women who married men solely to accrue huge alimony awards after a divorce. But, the article maintained, the threat of alimony had changed. Unlike the "frivolous flapper days" when alimony was "reserved for little floozies who periodically married and divorced millionaire playboys," gold diggers were targeting men of ordinary means. *Playboy* cautioned that "alimony has gone democratic" and "the modern gold digger comes in a variety of shapes and sizes." The magazine that celebrated the sexuality of the "girl-next-door" warned in its first issue that the girl-next-door might be after its readers' alimony: "The 1953 variety gold-digger may be a chorus cutie or she may be Miss Plain Jane from across the street. All American womanhood has descended on alimony as a natural heritage." *Playboy* described alimony-seeking gold diggers as a danger to men from all social classes and backgrounds.[64]

The magazine reiterated the critiques against alimony and heart balm from decades earlier by emphasizing the economic and social gains made by women. The article stated: "The whole concept of alimony is a throwback to the days when grandma was a girl. A couple of generations ago, this was a man's world, and a nice young woman without a husband had a difficult time making her own way. Nothing could be further from the truth in 1953. Even the simplest wench can make a handsome living today." Alimony, the author claimed, discouraged women from seeking work after their marriage, and the system penalized working women because it limited their alimony in comparison to their freeloading sisters.[65]

The article deployed different stories of alimony abuses to underscore the dangers of the gold digger. It told of a television director who "was overpowered by a 37" 25" 37" brunette" and, five years later, found himself sued by "his 37" 30" 37" wife." The implication of giving the woman's measurements, which became *Playboy*'s standard way of referring to women, was that while the man's wealth increased, his wife lost her attractiveness and gained weight. The presumed transaction between the man's wealth and the woman's attractiveness went astray. Characteristic of the gold digger problem in general, the exchange of beauty for wealth tilted in favor of women. Men in fast-paced careers were not the only ones at risk. The article described a truck driver who faced a six-month jail sentence for falling behind in his spousal support payments. Indeed, the article warned, "the less a man makes, the deadlier alimony becomes."[66]

Consistent with critiques of alimony from earlier decades, "Miss Gold Digger" held up judges for special scorn. The article relayed the story of a wealthy man in the furniture business who had a three-month marriage to his attractive secretary. The ex-wife demanded alimony in accordance with the comforts to which she was accustomed, but the ex-husband protested due to the short length of the marriage. The man lost his plea to limit alimony because, as the article explained, logic fails "when the lady is a full-busted blonde in a low cut dress and the judge is on a very high bench looking down." The Marilyn Monroe look, blonde hair and large breasts, unnaturally influenced judges as much as it influenced the men who marry gold diggers. In fact, "after reviewing a number of the court decisions, one wonders whether some of the ex-wives didn't show up for the proceedings wearing bathing suits." "Miss Gold Digger" concluded with a number of steps that aimed to eradicate alimony abuses and protect men from greedy women. Noting the wide variations in state alimony rules, the article advocated a total overhaul of alimony laws at the national level. The author also offered men advice on how to avoid being hit with unfair alimony judgments, including leaving town, offering the ex-wife a financial incentive to remarry, and threatening to destroy her reputation in open court. In the article, the gold digger stereotype expressed men's sexualized fears about women's power, and it was used to justify hostile actions against women who sought postdivorce financial support.[67]

In the 1950s, the threat of the gold digger appeared not just in men's magazines but also in outlets aimed at a wider audience. In a 1955 letter to columnist Molly Mayfield, a man who signed off with "Sort of Old-Fashioned" complained about college-educated women. He explained, "College girls are frustrated, fanatical, and neurotic—not to mention gold-diggers, lousy cooks, poor housekeepers, and generally unfit to assume the duties of wife." In summarizing contemporary women, he said, "her only thoughts are of a career, glamour, world travel, and finding a rich 'sucker' to foot the bill for a life of luxury." The columnist invited women to respond and published three letters that she described as "fairly typical." One woman wrote, "So I'm a gold-digger. That's why I worked for three years after we were married, and happily put my entire salary into the family stock to help us get on our feet financially." Another explained that she paid for the marriage license, the priest, and the organist for their wedding, and, "Once we did go boating, and he bought me a cup of coffee twice. So, I'm a gold digger?" They coupled their objections to being accused of gold digging with assertions that they upheld the household. In this way, the responses to "Sort of Old-Fashioned" did not constitute a wholesale rejection of traditional 1950s domestic ideologies. Rather, the women objected to being labeled as gold diggers simply because they wanted to enjoy the fruits of their education and the postwar economic boom. The warnings about gold digger wives that appeared in popular periodicals represented a subtle refashioning of the gold digger image. Instead of young women who married for money, or divorced for alimony, gold diggers could be married women who demanded too much from their husbands.[68]

The reimagining of the gold digger as a dissatisfied housewife was exemplified in *Who's Right?*, an educational short film released in 1954. *Who's Right?* focused on the basis of marital harmony and the expectations men and women have of one another that generate resentment in a marriage. The film, produced by McGraw-Hill as a supplement to their textbook *Marriage for Moderns*, focuses on a fictional couple married for eleven months. It opens with a narrator describing a man's view of his wife. Honey Carson is "spoiled, selfish, self-centered." He describes her as having "uncontrollable temper flare ups at the slightest imagined provocation. Heartless, scheming, always ready to attack the unsuspecting male." According to

Frank Carson, his wife is "a megalomaniac. She's a gold digger." In the next scene, Honey appears in her bedroom and looks around. "Gold digger?" she thinks. "All I'm trying to do is make the house livable. Make myself look human. Make the meals edible with what little money we have." Looking at her closet, she says that she purchased most of her dresses before she ever married Frank. She laments her poor shoe collection, and notes that one pair was resoled twice. Making a reference to Monroe's signature song in *Gentlemen Prefer Blondes,* she muses, "If diamonds are a girl's best friend, I'm sure alone in this world."[69]

The scene then shifts to Frank in the living room. He thinks aloud, "I'm just a slave around here. I work all day earning the money to keep things going. I bring it back so she can spend it." He complains that she picked out all of the furniture, but there is not a decent chair for him to sit in. According to Frank, Honey "runs around all day with her friends buying things." Meanwhile, he is tasked with helping around the house: "I've practically gotten two full-time jobs." Presented as a discussion starter, the film ends without resolving the conflict between the husband and wife. The short film, released during a brief, nationwide downturn in 1954, reflects the burden of prevailing gender roles in the 1950s and the rising expectations about social class and consumerism during the postwar economic expansion. The film uses the phrase "gold digger" as a critique of consumer desires within marriage, where both parties presumably come from a similar class background. It does not refer to a mismatched or unbalanced relationship between, say, a chorus girl and an oil tycoon. In *Who's Right?* the phrase "gold digger" performs different categorical labor than it did in the 1920s and 1930s.

The film's reference to "Diamonds Are a Girl's Best Friend" from *Gentlemen Prefer Blondes* reveals the centrality of Marilyn Monroe in the cultural imagination of the early 1950s and the essential position she held in the cultural genealogy of the gold digger. *Who's Right?* was part of a constellation of elements that revolved around Marilyn Monroe, cultural forms that invoked Monroe without necessarily mentioning her. The phrase "diamonds are a girl's best friend" was used in advertisements from dress shoes to pianos.[70] According to one of many of her biographers, in the mid-1950s, "Pictures, interviews and news of Marilyn Monroe flowed in an uninterrupted cascade."[71] The stardom of Monroe, the archetypal "proverbial blonde" of the mid-1950s, was an unparalleled cultural touchstone that was intimately bound up with the image of the gold digger.

Marilyn Monroe and the Postwar Masculinity Crisis

Marilyn Monroe played a unique role in the cultural history of the gold digger. Inspired by Jean Harlow, she inherited and amplified "blonde bombshell" iconography from decades earlier. Monroe epitomized the "dumb blonde" stereotype and served as a template for others to model their persona and aesthetic. Monroe also starred in *Gentlemen Prefer Blondes*, arguably the most significant gold digger movie of the twentieth century. Monroe's performance reflected a particular postwar gold digger, one engaged in material consumption made possible by the 1950s economic expansion and guided by the contradictions of 1950s femininity. Marilyn Monroe's life and work are inexorably enmeshed with the cultural history of the gold digger.

Marilyn Monroe also functioned as an emblem of racial whiteness. On an aesthetic level, Monroe's platinum blonde hair, white clothing, and radiant teeth created an exaggerated image of white womanhood. As Richard Dyer explains, Monroe was "the most unambiguously white you can get."[72] On a social and psychological level, Monroe represented both the fears and desires of white heterosexual men. They feared that the combination of her seductive power and purported lack of intelligence would corrupt the rightful place of white men at the top of the social hierarchy. Monroe's film roles, especially later in her career, portrayed her as a threat to men. In her depiction of a psychopath in *Niagara*, as well as her comedic performance as a nameless woman leading astray a married man in *The Seven Year Itch*, Monroe's characters undermined the power and authority of the white men who came within her dangerous orbit.

Marilyn Monroe's performances as a gold digger in *Gentlemen Prefer Blondes* and *How to Marry a Millionaire* during the mid-1950s established her as the foremost sex symbol in America.[73] In Elaine Tyler May's study of postwar American culture, she writes, "Perhaps the most telling saga of the transformation of female sexuality in the popular culture is the career of Marilyn Monroe." Overlapping ambiguities and contradictions created the ideological and cultural force of Marilyn Monroe's persona. One set of contradictions involved her projection of innocence and experience. Monroe was at once a childlike naïf and sexual siren. Early in her film career, Groucho Marx referred to her as "Mae West, Theda Bara, and Bo Peep all rolled into one!" A related set of paradoxes revolved around her status as an agent and object. Monroe and her on-screen roles simultaneously represented a target

FIGURE 12 Jane Russell, Charles Coburn, and Marilyn Monroe in a publicity still for the 1953 film *Gentlemen Prefer Blondes*, one of the most important gold digger films of the twentieth century. Monroe's iconic performance as Lorelei Lee solidified her star status as well as her typecasting as a gold digger and dumb blonde. Courtesy of PhotoFest.

of sexual desire and a trickster. Monroe was both a sex symbol to be consumed by male lust and a subversive gold digger who gets one over on the men who ogle her. American film scholar Will Scheibel points to the existence of "self-awareness, irony and contradiction" in her personal and cinematic performances during the early and middle 1950s when her sex symbol image was at its peak. For Lisa Cohen, "Marilyn Monroe's star persona partakes of these tensions between sexual display, on the one hand,

and domestic containment on the other." Laura Mulvey describes Monroe as "emblematic of contemporary American society's obsessions and repressions." As the gold digger extraordinaire, Monroe was in a unique position to stand in for and participate in the double-edged quality of 1950s gender ideology. Marilyn Monroe generated and worked to resolve incongruous messages about domesticity, sexuality, and consumption engulfing the white middle class in postwar America.[74]

Marilyn Monroe, born Norma Jeane Mortenson in 1926, had a highly unstable family life and cycled through multiple foster homes. A family friend named Grace McKee assumed custody of Norma Jeane after Norma Jeane's mother was committed to a psychiatric hospital. Grace McKee had a tremendous influence on the child and, from a very early age, cultivated Norma Jeane as a future movie star. McKee put Jean Harlow, the gold digger in *Red-Headed Woman* and *Dinner at Eight*, before Norma Jeane as an idol for her to emulate. Grace told her, "One day, you'll be perfect—like Jean Harlow." In the mid-1930s, after seeing Harlow in *China Seas* and *Libeled Lady*, Grace copied Harlow's distinct white color scheme, bought only white clothes for herself and Norma Jeane, and briefly toyed with the idea of dying ten-year-old Norma Jeane's hair platinum. "Grace was captivated by Jean Harlow," Monroe said, "and so Jean Harlow was my idol." According to one of her biographers, Grace was fixated with "the transformation of Norma Jeane into Jean Harlow."[75] The role model stuck, and Monroe aped Harlow well past her childhood. She sought out the hairdresser who dyed Harlow's hair and, like Harlow, she stopped wearing underwear. Talent scouts, executives at Fox, and others in the entertainment business also regarded Monroe as an incarnation of Jean Harlow. Hollywood reporter Sidney Skolsky, for example, tried to convince Monroe to star in a biopic about Harlow, but the project never materialized.[76]

At a New Year's Eve party celebrating the start of 1949, twenty-two-year-old Marilyn Monroe met Johnny Hyde, the executive vice president of the William Morris Agency. Hyde, fifty-three years old and afflicted with a serious heart condition, was obsessed with Monroe and was determined to marry her. Monroe carried on a sexual relationship with Hyde, but felt no great affection for him as a lover. Monroe regarded Hyde as a kind of father figure who could help her navigate the difficult path to Hollywood stardom. Monroe biographer Donald Spoto observed that Monroe made a strategic decision to refuse Hyde's marriage offer because "she would be called a gold digger, not only romancing for her career but even marrying a man known to be gravely ill." Hyde acted as a mentor for Monroe and helped secure roles for her in two major films: *Asphalt Jungle* and *All About Eve*. The publicity she garnered through these performances helped Hyde negotiate on her behalf with Twentieth Century Fox, but he died at the age of fifty-five not long after finalizing the details of her film contract.[77]

Monroe's film roles, combined with a scandal about posing nude, propelled her stardom. In the early months of 1949, Monroe finished her fourth movie, *Love Happy*, and was looking for a way to meet her car payments and other expenses. She called photographer Tom Kelley and scheduled a photo shoot for a Pabst beer poster. Months later, Kelley contact Monroe to see if she would pose for artistic nudes. She agreed and earned fifty dollars for her efforts. The photos from that session spread across the world and became some of the best-known nudes in the history of photography. Images from the shoot were reproduced in various formats, such as playing cards and keychains, and the most popular photo from the shoot, *Golden Dreams*, was the centerpiece of a calendar that circulated nationwide.[78]

The nude photos presented a potential problem for Marilyn Monroe three years later. In 1952, news leaked that Marilyn Monroe, then a rising star, was the model in the 1949 Kelley photo shoot. In early March 1952, Fox executives heard rumors that the nude woman on the cover of the John Baumgarth Company calendar was none other than Marilyn Monroe, and she was called into the front office of Fox. Monroe admitted she was the cover model of the calendar and immediately launched a stealth campaign to contain the potential crisis. She arranged a meeting with a journalist from the *Los Angeles Herald Examiner* and, allowing her own account to lead the way and shape the narrative, admitted that she posed nude for an "art calendar."[79]

Monroe adroitly handled the potentially damaging media attention and managed to turn the negative publicity into a positive affirmation of her as a striving and starving artist. She gained publicity of which her publicist could only dream.[80] Monroe claimed that she was hungry, in between movie roles, and feared her car would be repossessed. Besides, she reasoned, Kelley's wife was in the room when the photos were taken, and despite the exposure of her breasts, the images were tasteful and classically composed. The *Golden Dreams* incident speaks to Monroe's savvy, intelligence, and understanding of the finicky aspects of Hollywood stardom. Those weeks in 1952 also exposed contradictions about postwar gender and sexuality that Monroe reflected and helped create. That the *Golden Dreams* image failed to generate a poisonous uproar during the hegemony of the Motion Picture Production Code, the Legion of Decency, and McCarthyism, echoes conflicted ideas about sexuality that circulated in the 1950s. On the one hand, the image conveyed sexual availability: *Golden Dreams* showed Monroe draped over dark red cloth, fully nude, with her left breast directly facing the camera. She had an arched back, closed eyes, half-opened mouth, and arm extended over and behind her head. The image was explicit. On the other hand, the image was no more salacious than the *Esquire* pinups that entertained servicemen during World War II. She was like a wholesome postwar "sweater girl" without the sweater. Americans could express shock about Monroe's nude modeling while simultaneously embracing it. This contradictory quality of Monroe's early celebrity carried over into her on-screen roles with tremendous force.

Having turned a potential career calamity into radiant publicity, Monroe's stardom continued to shine bright into 1953. *Gentlemen Prefer Blondes* was the twelfth film of her career. According to one of her biographers, the performance as Lorelei Lee "forever enshrined her in memory as the luscious, nubile gold digger, apparently witless but in fact savvy about the ways of men, misers and millionaires."[81] Her incarnation of Lorelei Lee helped to typecast Monroe as the true inheritor of Jean Harlow, a dumb, but seductive, blonde bombshell. According to film theorist Laura Mulvey, "*Gentlemen Prefer Blondes* launched Marilyn Monroe as the sex symbol of the epoch."[82] The movie popularized the gold digger stereotype, reviving the blonde gold digger image that had remained somewhat dormant after the national crusade against heart balm laws in the late 1930s.

The movie *Gentlemen Prefer Blondes* was based on the 1925 novel by the same name. A brief consideration of the novel—for both a fuller appreciation of the film and the cultural genealogy of the gold digger stereotype—is warranted. *Gentlemen Prefer Blondes* is a sprawling travelogue told in the form of Lorelei Lee's diary. The novel describes Lorelei's relationships with men and her friendship with Dorothy, the straight-talking foil to Lorelei and the conscience and voice of the novel's author, Anita Loos. Many believed that Anita Loos modeled Lorelei after 1920s gold digger Peggy Hopkins Joyce, but the real-life inspiration of Lorelei Lee is exceedingly murky.[83] Regardless, the novel was a success, and *Blondes* garnered enthusiastic praise from esteemed literary figures such as James Joyce, Aldous Huxley, Edith Wharton, and William Faulkner.[84] Contemporary scholars have also extolled Loos's representation of Lorelei Lee's agency and power.[85] A less-appreciated aspect of the novel centers on Lorelei Lee's manipulation of the law, particularly her threat to launch a breach of promise lawsuit against her lover Henry Spoffard.[86] Legal scholar Mary Coombs observes that, for many people in the 1920s, Lorelei was not a heroic protofeminist with agency and power but "was considered representative of real plaintiffs by various critics."[87] Like other gold diggers of the twentieth century, Lorelei Lee's status as either a trickster or folk devil wavered based on the reader's relationship to marriage, money, and law.

The film *Gentlemen Prefer Blondes* follows the broad outline of the novel, and it features two American showgirls, Lorelei Lee (played by Marilyn Monroe) and Dorothy (played by Jane Russell), traveling to France on a cruise ship. Lorelei Lee intends to wed the wealthy Gus Esmond, but his father, fearing his son's fiancée is a gold digger, hires a private detective to follow her aboard the ship. The detective, Ernie Malone, falls in love with Dorothy and, although Dorothy is attracted to the detective, she notes his interest in Lorelei and suspects he is up to no good. As in the novel, the tension between the two friends revolves around Lorelei's insistence on marrying for money and Dorothy's insistence on marrying for love. Lorelei lays bare her materialism in her performance of "Diamonds Are a Girl's Best Friend" after the ship arrives in France. The iconic musical number shows Lorelei Lee wearing a satin pink dress surrounded by men in tuxedoes. Perhaps hinting at the future legal trouble ahead for her in the film's plot, Lorelei sings, "There may come a time when a lass needs a lawyer, but diamonds are a girl's best friend."[88]

The structure of the film mirrors the meandering quality of the novel, with song and dance numbers punctuating different, disconnected, storylines. One plot revolves around Sir Francis Beekman, and Lorelei's schemes to get his wife's diamond tiara. Lady Beekman notices that the tiara is missing and accuses Lorelei of stealing it, so Dorothy impersonates Lorelei to protect her friend. In the courtroom scene later in the film, the judge informs "Lorelei" that she is being charged with grand larceny. She responds, "You're so much more intelligent than poor little me." When the judge demands she answer the charges, she says, "It was just all a terrible misunderstanding. You see, judge, sometimes life is very hard for a girl like I, especially if she happens to be pretty like I and have blonde hair." In this scene, Dorothy pulls the expectations one has of the dumb blonde into a plea for her (Lorelei's) innocence. She uses her beauty to influence the legal system, and she allows the audience, who knows she's really a brunette wearing a blonde wig, in on the joke. Her action represents an essential feature of Lorelei and the gold digger trope she embodies: the manipulation of the legal system to extract money from men and the manipulation of men to garner favor from the legal system. As it turns out, Beekman has had the tiara all along. The film ends with a double wedding, with Lorelei marrying Gus and Dorothy marrying the detective Ernie.[89]

As Susan Hegeman notes, the film *Gentlemen Prefer Blondes* "has been an important site for feminist scholarship."[90] A central issue in these discussions is the film's reproduction or repudiation of the "male gaze." Laura Mulvey established the concept of the male gaze in her highly influential 1973 essay, "Visual Pleasure and Narrative Cinema."[91] Mulvey uses psychoanalytic theory to show how Hollywood films position women to be sexual objects looked at by male (heterosexual) viewers. This "to-be-looked-at-ness" is a major characteristic of cinematic storytelling in the studio era. In the decades following the publication of her essay, the theory of the male gaze spread to other domains of cultural and scholarly inquiry while, at the same time, the male gaze concept faced scrutiny and revision by film scholars, including by Mulvey herself. The question of the male gaze in *Gentlemen* parallels and mirrors the dual qualities of the gold digger as a folk devil and as a trickster. Marilyn Monroe represents both a threatening force poised to destroy men as well as a playful and harmless figure participating in consumerist pleasures. The gold digger as a malleable construct was one that Marilyn Monroe utilized particularly well.

Mulvey created the male gaze as a theoretical construct in the 1970s, but reviewers and the public certainly recognized Marilyn Monroe's role as a sex object in *Gentlemen Prefer Blondes* at the time of its release. A writer for *Saturday Review* described a sneak preview of the film at New York's Roxy Theatre: "It was difficult not to notice that every time Miss Monroe, in full calendar colors, wiggled, crooked a finger, or so much as batted an eyelash . . . a loud series of moans, groans, and sighs rose from every part of the theatre." *Catholic World* described the film as "a frank, often bawdy, musical comedy which capitalizes heavily on the physical endowments of its two stars. The kids should be sent to the nearest Western." One of Monroe's dresses in *Gentlemen Prefer Blondes* drew scrutiny from Joseph Breen, head of the Motion Picture Production Code. In a memo to Fox, he complained that the outfit did not adequately cover Monroe's breasts. Censors, critics, and the ticket-buying public regarded the bodily spectacle of Jane Russell and Marilyn Monroe as a defining feature of the film.[92]

Feminist film criticism of *Gentlemen Prefer Blondes* echoed familiar arguments about gold diggers as, on one hand, a problematic folk devil and, on the other hand, a trickster who uses her agency to undermine societal constrictions. For some feminist film scholars, Monroe's performance inevitably activated the degrading male gaze. Molly Haskell acknowledged the satiric aspects of Monroe's performance, but characterized Lorelei Lee as a "tootsie" and a "masturbatory fantasy." Lorelei was, according to one of her biographers, "all body; no thought; little feeling; all whispery, high voice and no sensibility."[93] Yet many scholars who commented on the movie's appeal to stereotypical male fantasy recognized the unevenness of the film's apparent sexism.[94]

Film scholars Lucie Arbuthnot and Gail Seneca observe that Monroe and Russell were frequently costumed in high-necked sweaters and shot in medium close-ups that focused on their shoulders and face. The move by Howard Hawks to deemphasize their bodies to the extent that he does is notable given the "mammary madness" of the 1950s.[95] For Arbuthnot and Seneca, these cinematic moves make the friendship between the two leads the main text of the film. Cultural studies scholar Lois Banner also maintains that the central lesson of *Gentlemen Prefer Blondes* is the value of friendship. Humanities scholar Lisa Cohen takes the argument a step further to read *Gentlemen Prefer Blondes* as a film with strong queer themes, citing the courtroom scene where Dorothy impersonates Lorelei and the double wedding finale where the framing of the shot makes it seem as if Lorelei is marrying Dorothy instead of Gus.[96]

The crosscurrents created by the film, the way that it simultaneously invites the male gaze and destabilizes it, is characteristic of the gold digger's complex qualities. Monroe's Lorelei used her sexual agency to buck the chauvinistic impulses of postwar America, but she also reproduced, or at least participated in, the sexism inherent in 1950s American consumer culture. In this way, Monroe's portrayal of Lorelei, characteristic of the gold digger's historical and liminal role, mediated the tensions in 1950s postwar America. She pursued both material abundance and traditional heterosexual marriage. She sought after men, but mocked them in the process. She upheld the norms of 1950s domestic ideology while radically subverting them.

Independent of any film scholarship, *Gentlemen Prefer Blondes* solidified Marilyn Monroe's star status. According to Douglas Spoto, "never before, in the history of the world, had someone other than a great ruler or head of state received such celebration."[97] Quick to capitalize on her popularity and keeping with the Monroe-as-gold-digger formula, Twentieth Century Fox cast Monroe in *How to Marry a Millionaire*, produced in 1953. *How to Marry a Millionaire* was one of the first films released in CinemaScope, representing a new production process and aspect ratio that offered a more immersive viewing experience by generating a greater than usual visual depth and a sense that the screen arched around the viewer's visual field. Other major film studios adopted CinemaScope's wide-screen perspective in an effort to compete with the rising popularity of television. *Millionaire* was a major success and Fox's second-largest box office earner.[98]

Based on the Pre-Code gold digger film *The Greeks Had a Word for It, How to Marry a Millionaire* follows the adventures of three women in pursuit of wealthy suitors. Schatze, Loco, and Pola rent a New York City penthouse in order to attract rich men, but have difficulty reaching their goal. Loco brings home a gas station attendant who helped carry her groceries, but Schatze sets her straight: "I don't want to be snobbish, but if we begin with characters like that we might just as well throw in the towel right now." She tells her companions, "a gentleman you meet among the cold cuts is simply not as attractive as one that you meet, say, in the mink department at Bergdorf's." By dispensing advice, Schatze assumes a leadership role among the trio, and the other women listen to her because of her experience with marriage and divorce. In an early scene, Loco learns that Schatze recently returned from Reno:

> *Loco*: Oh, then you must be loaded.
> *Schatze*: No. Mine was one of those divorces you *don't* read about. The wife finished second.
> *Loco*: But that's against the law isn't it?

The notion that Schatze did not receive a hefty alimony award, and Loco's amazement at the current state of marriage law, speaks to the ongoing debate about the fairness of postdivorce spousal support. The humor in the exchange comes from Loco's astonishment that Schatze is not "loaded" due to a large spousal support award. The reference to "those divorces you don't read about" also recognizes that seemingly unfair alimony awards to women received the most publicity and became, like the cautionary tales in *Playboy*'s "Miss Gold Digger" article, reference points for the public's understanding about alimony in general. The film's primary theme, however, centers on the expectations of marriage and the relative roles of love and money in structuring romance.

The women pledge that they are not going to be foolish like Schatze and marry for love, yet they find it hard to meet eligible rich men. Schatze wonders what they are doing wrong, but Pola surmises that New York men are to blame. "I don't think it's us," she tells her friend, "I think it's the men these days. They're getting more and more nervous, especially the loaded ones." Pola's comment identifies anxieties at the intersection of masculinity and social class. The heightened nervousness of the "loaded ones," the men who should be freest from economic concern, reflected the increasing pressures brought by the conformity demanded of corporate life.[99] Men's nervousness also stemmed from the backlash against the perceived gains made by women during World War II. The gold digger tied together the worry about economics and eros that confronted white middle- and upper-class men in the 1950s.[100]

During the course of the film, the women pair off with different suitors and, in each case, they toggle between their attraction to a rich man and their truer love for another man of more modest means. Loco is entangled with a fraudulent oil tycoon with a shady secret, but falls for a man she met on a flight to Kansas City. In another plotline, Pola accepts an invitation to a winter lodge with a married man but, once there, she falls in love with a park ranger. She mistakes the park ranger for a rich landowner after he shows her a picturesque view of the tree line, but he confesses that he does not "even own a bush." Schatze has her eyes set on an old and wealthy man, J. D. Hanley, but is beset by advances from Tom Brookman, the "gas pump jockey" who helped Loco with her groceries. Brookman is, unbeknownst to the women, a multimillionaire. Schatze goes on several dates with Brookman and, although she finds him attractive, she thinks that their relationship is doomed. After their date at a diner, she tells him, "It's no use Tommy boy. Just as soon as I finish this horse burger, I never want to see you again." She proceeds with the marriage to Hanley but, upon learning that her two friends married for love, has second thoughts and calls off the wedding.

The film ends with the marriage of the women and, in one of the final scenes, the three couples enjoy dinner at a cheap diner. Brookman pays the tab with a $1,000 bill and reveals his true class status to his new wife. In *How to Marry a Millionaire*, the women seek rich men, but learn to be content with the middle class. They begin as gold diggers but wind up as love-dazed housewives. Schatze, who married whom she thought was a gas station attendant, is rewarded for favoring romance over riches. Pola wanted the rich man, but found love and comfortable serenity with the modest park ranger. In this way, the film encouraged its viewers to celebrate the booming 1950s economy, but to be content with what they have.

Marilyn Monroe scholar Amanda Konkle locates the film within the contradictory messages about domesticity during the postwar period. The film mirrors 1950s prescriptive literature where "women were encouraged to become housewives, but they were also encouraged to be sexual creatures." Indeed, the title of the film plays on the proliferation of "how to" marriage manuals published in the postwar period. Konkle notes that the film engages in an "interrogation of the boundary between the Cinderella stories and the gold-digging narrative."[101] In contrast to gold digger stories from the 1930s, the women seek millionaire husbands, not to pull themselves out of Depression-era economic despair, and not to return to work as chorus girls, but to participate fully in the go-go consumer culture of the 1950s.[102] They use the same methods as 1930s gold diggers, but have consumerist, instead of survivalist, motives.

The success of the film *How to Marry a Millionaire* inspired the creation of a television series by the same title. The series ran for two seasons from 1957 to 1959. *How to Marry a Millionaire* followed the formula of a situation comedy wherein each episode offered up the premise of one of the women marrying a wealthy man but, after a series of misunderstandings or odd situations, the marriage prospect sours. The episodes open with a voice-over describing a source of riches or something associated with the upper class, like yachting, an oil field, or gambling at Monte Carlo. The voice-over describes the hard work required to participate in the signifier of wealth, but a woman's voice interrupts the man and suggests "another way" to acquire the wealth—marrying it. Each episode, following the introductory credits, begins with an establishing shot of the penthouse apartment where the women struggle to pay rent and scheme over marriage and class mobility. All three women are gainfully employed. Greta is a production assistant for a television game show, Mike is a secretary for a Wall Street concern, and Loco is a model who works for various advertising campaigns. Their careers, however, are only a temporizing move until they secure rich husbands. This state of mind is exposed in an early episode in season one ("Loco the Heiress") where Loco is mistakenly informed that she is set to receive a large inheritance from a deceased relative.[103] All the women plan to call their employers and quit their jobs but, ultimately, the bad news is revealed. That the three women plan to profit from one of their moments of good fortune is characteristic of the show's emphasis on female friendship. They view the snagging of a rich husband as a collective endeavor and, if one of them succeeds, the others are expected to benefit from it. The women share an oath: "On my honor, I promise to do my best to help one of us marry a millionaire. All for one and one for all so help us Fort Knox."[104] The television show inherits and extends the theme of the power of women's friendship from *Gentlemen Prefer Blondes* and the film *How to Marry a Millionaire*.

The show also illustrates the cultural role of the gold digger figure at the zenith of 1950s gender norms. Specifically, it speaks to the crisis of white

FIGURE 13 Publicity photo from the television series *How to Marry a Millionaire* (1957–1959). Loco Jones (Barbara Eden), Greta Hansen (Lori Nelson), and Michelle "Mike" McCall (Mary Anders) scour the Dun and Bradstreet reference book to search for prey. Representations of gold diggers in the 1950s reflected anxiety about white masculinity during the postwar economic expansion. Courtesy of PhotoFest.

masculinity in the postwar period and the tension between marrying for love and marrying for security. In "Alias the Secretary," Loco, Mike, and Greta struggle to pay for groceries.[105] Greta suggests that they move into a cheaper apartment, but Mike reminds them of the grand plan: "The more expensive the mousetrap the richer the mouse." The women notice men moving into an empty adjacent penthouse. "Maybe it's a rich mouse," Loco optimistically observes. They learn that the new tenant is Abner Doncourt, a millionaire from Idaho who made his fortune in lumber. He and his secretary Steve Chandler are in town for a short time to finalize a corporate merger. The reaction to their new neighbors verifies the money-oriented bent of the trio. Mike muses, "Imagine, a millionaire next door. How convenient." "Yes," Greta says, "we could always run over for a cup of money." The women agree to invite the men over for cocktails but, upon receiving the invitation, Doncourt becomes nervous. He wants to swap identities with

Steve because, he says, "For once I want to find someone who likes me just for myself." The men arrive at the penthouse for drinks and hors d'oeuvres with the women and, keeping with the plan, Steve introduces himself as Abner and Abner introduces himself as Steve. When the women gaze upon the man whom they think is Abner, they superimpose a bag of money onto his image (a running gag on the show). When they look at the real Abner, who they mistake as the secretary, the bag of money reads "No Sale." The women fawn over Steve because of his presumed wealth, thus affirming Abner's predictions about the superficiality of the women he commonly encounters. Loco, however, finds herself drawn to the real Abner despite his alleged lowly status as a secretary. When she makes a date with him for the following day, her roommates protest and pressure her to cancel. Mike and Loco discuss the matter:

> *Mike*: Abner J. Doncourt is our target. You forget about that secretary.
> *Loco*: But he's so nice!
> *Mike*: Nicer than a million bucks?

Mike tells her, "We're not paying all this rent to meet underprivileged secretaries." Greta agrees: "It's as simple as this honey: why settle for chow mein when you can get caviar?" Their plan predictably backfires, the business deal collapses, and the men leave town.

Unlike earlier representations of gold diggers in films like *Red-Headed Woman* or *Gold Diggers of 1933*, the women of *How to Marry a Millionaire* get neither love nor money from their gold digging. They are punished for their gold-digging intentions in episode after episode, but their failure sustains their consciences and allows them to continue their schemes. Loco, who is the trio's token dumb blonde, wants to marry for love and affection, but is talked out of it by her friends. The foundering of their plan, and the hint of Loco's good intentions, secures the virtue of the lead characters. Their status as *failed* gold diggers absolves them of the opprobrium one might hold for someone like Peggy Hopkins Joyce or Lorelei Lee. They also refuse to use the tools of typical gold diggers, like breach of promise lawsuits. In the episode "Day in Court," Steve speaks on behalf of her two friends and tells an ambulance-chaser lawyer, "we don't sue."

"Alias the Secretary" also stands as a commentary on 1950s masculinity and its pressures for corporate conformity. When Loco meets Abner (who she confuses for Steve), she asks him, "I've never talked to a man secretary before. What's it like?" Abner, posing as Steve, responds that a "man secretary does the same things any other secretary would do." Loco muses, "Well, isn't that confusing? Who sits on whose lap?" The punchline played on gendered assumptions about employment and the audience's presumed familiarity with office romance and the sexualized status of women secretaries, especially before second-wave feminism. While Steve Chandler is employed in an occupational role that diminishes his masculinity, Abner Doncourt occupies a position where the three women quite literally cannot see him without visualizing his wealth. "It isn't easy being a millionaire," he explains. "You never know how people feel about you." Abner and Steve represent a dialectic of postwar masculinity where wealth eroded one's individuality, but lack of wealth was feminizing. Both men have considerable social and economic power when compared to women in the 1950s, but the men experience the tension between wealth and individuality as a crisis of masculinity. In the 1950s, the gold digger trope—in magazines, film, and television—was used to explain and negotiate that perceived crisis.

· · · · · ·

On August 19, 1956, Catherine Heenan found her daughter Peaches Browning lifeless on the bathroom floor of their shared apartment in midtown Manhattan. Peaches, who remarried and went by the name Frances Willson, never regained consciousness. She died after four days in the hospital, at the age of forty-six. She faded from public view after her brief time in the spotlight during the Roaring Twenties, married and divorced three times, and struggled with alcoholism. No one knows the circumstances that led to her death, but it is likely she slipped, fell, and (because eight hours had passed before her mother took her to the hospital) suffered from irreparable trauma. The autopsy reveal a brain hemorrhage, cerebral compression, and liver damage.[106] Peaches Browning, as one of her obituaries noted, was in "one of the most publicized marriages of the mid-Twenties," and "the litigation that followed symbolized an era."[107] Less than a year later, Peggy Hopkins Joyce succumbed to throat cancer at the age of sixty-four. As the gold digger icons from the early twentieth century faded from public view, novel ones took their place.

The gold digger construct assumed new forms as the United States recovered from the Great Depression and entered World War II. Marriage and childbirth increased following the war, and the United States entered a period of domestic retrenchment. The gold diggers of the mid-twentieth century exposed ideological tensions and contradictions created in the crisis of World War II and its aftermath. A kiln of Cold War gender anxiety forged new representations of gold diggers. Prescriptive literature and popular culture exhorted women and men with a series of incompatible messages. Women were urged to prioritize the needs of their husbands and seek sexual fulfillment, but embrace motherhood as the highest goal. They were told to consume and partake in the riches of postwar abundance, but be grateful for what they had. Men, for their part, received conflicting messages about the pleasures of bachelorhood and the desirability of marriage. Men were torn between, on the one hand, a celebration of individuality and, on the other, pressure to join corporate work culture. Popular cultural depictions of the 1950s, captured in family situation comedies like *Father Knows Best* and *Leave It to Beaver*, portray it as a time of conservatism, conformity, and stability. While these representations contained a grain of truth about the forces of domestic containment, it was also a time of roiling conflict and tension, and the gold digger trope was used to address questions about to whom postwar wealth should flow and how proper men and women should act in the Cold War era.

Women whose status as potential gold diggers was called into question, like Gwendolyn Stokes and Eleanor Holm, showed the relational quality of the gold digger trope. Although these two women were from vastly different class backgrounds, they shared a common womanhood through their whiteness and the behavior of their husbands. Although they might be gold diggers, their susceptibility to the gold digger label was undercut by the failures of their husbands to uphold midcentury norms of masculinity. Their alimony battles show that constructions of the gold digger depended upon understandings of men and masculinity as well as notions of women and femininity.

Midcentury gold diggers sowed the seeds of a shift in hegemonic gender ideology. The precise vessels of the alleged gold digger threat during the 1950s, Marilyn Monroe and *Playboy*, generated the conditions for a broad set of social changes that engulfed the United States in the subsequent decade. According to historian Carrie Pitzulo, *Playboy* "acted as a bridge between the traditionalism of the previous era and the modern celebration of personal freedom and fulfillment." Lois Banner described Marilyn Monroe as "a rebel pointing to the radicalism and sexual rebellion of the 1960s." According to Banner, the public regard of blondes in the late 1950s—brought on by the popularity of hair dyes and "Marilyn clones" like Jayne Mansfield and Mamie Van Doren—were "bellwethers of the era's sexual revolution."[108] The next chapter will address the place of the gold digger amid the sexual revolution of the 1960s and 1970s.

4 Gold Diggers of the Sexual Revolution

Concern about gold diggers routinely appeared in newspapers and advice columns during the 1960s. Newspaper columnists in the early 1960s warned about gold diggers corrupting the dating pool. A columnist in 1960 cautioned that women in the dating market needed to lower their expectations and not to be a financial burden on men. A "pretty would-be popular girl" who cannot find a steady boyfriend should examine her behavior to see if her dinner dates are too expensive because "nobody loves a gold-digger." Pulitzer Prize–winning columnist Hal Boyle griped that gold diggers have sullied Valentine's Day. The day "is acquiring a vinegar flavor, replete with a dash of hemlock and arsenic" because of "the gold-diggers who make a racket out of Valentine." Many young women, Boyle claimed, sent out cards to numerous men and "in return they expect to get back gifts ranging from a $15 compact to a $50 bottle of perfume—or even a mink wrap, if they're traveling in the big leagues." In a 1963 "Dear Abby" column, the mother of a twenty-year-old man complained about the expensive gifts her son gave to his fourteen-year-old girlfriend: "I told our son tonight that if this little gold-digger has to have a $40 present he can quit school and go to work." She wondered why the girl's mother did not "keep her in where she belongs?" The columnist did not comment on the age difference between the twenty-year-old man and the fourteen-year-old girl, but told the letter writer that she should not blame the girl's mother for her son's frivolous spending.[1]

During the early 1960s, advice columns also warned older adults about the risks of encountering gold diggers in the dating world. In a 1962 Dear Abby column titled "Never Trust a Gold-Digger," Abigail Van Buren counseled a fifty-five-year-old man in a relationship with a forty-seven-year-old woman. The woman married an elderly rich man in Miami "for his money," but promised to marry the letter writer after the man died. Van Buren told the man to "head for the hills" because the woman is a "gold digger." In a 1963 column, Van Buren cautioned a sixty-seven-year-old widower to downplay his wealth when seeking a mate. The man worried about becoming "a Sugar Daddy to a gold-digger," and Van Buren told him, "He who advertises sugar attracts flies." In a letter to columnist Sally Shaw, adult children expressed worry about their widowed father dating a "notorious gold-digger" thirty years his junior. "She drives around town in Dad's new convertible" and he buys her expensive jewelry.[2]

The threat posed by foreign gold diggers also appeared in early 1960s advice columns. A concerned mother wrote to Dorothy Dix with fears about her son's infatuation with a young woman from Germany. The girl made empty promises to travel to the United States to wed the young man, but requested money every time she wrote to him. Dix stated, "the facts indicate that your son has been taken over by a gold-digger." Like rhetoric about meretricious war brides, anxieties expressed about foreign gold diggers featured them as jeopardizing the hard-earned money of American men. In an inversion of the fear of foreign gold diggers, counsel about gold diggers sometimes referred to women from other countries to stress the greed and unreasonable expectations of American women. A man wrote to Dear Abby in 1961 to express that he "longs for the paradise of the Orient because all American women are all gold-diggers." For some, all women, foreign and domestic, potentially posed a threat as gold diggers. In a 1961 Dear Abby column, a man shared a cautionary tale about his brother who married a Korean woman while stationed in Korea during the war. After they returned to the United States, she spent all of his money and "was running him like all the American women run their husbands." In a 1963 column, Ann Landers offered advice to a young boy from Europe who invited a girl to the prom. The prom date asked that he pay for her dress, corsage, and "other expenses." Landers told him that it was not customary for the boy to pay for everything. "In America, girls do not ask such favors," she explained, "unless they are cheap little gold-diggers." Gold diggers in advice columns of the early 1960s reflected postwar apprehensions about both the oversized expectations in modern marriage and the increasing monetization of dating. As the 1960s progressed, discourse about gold diggers constituted a way to talk about larger social forces undermining postwar notions of marriage, family, and gender roles.[3]

In the second half of the 1960s, a series of events shattered the illusion of postwar calm, and it set into motion a new era. Several events and developments worked to expand rights and access to justice for women and historically subjugated groups: the founding of the National Organization for Women in 1966, the adoption of raising consciousness as a key feminist practice, the creation of the National Abortion Rights Action League in 1968, the election of Shirley Chisholm as the first African American woman to serve in Congress, and the proliferation of feminist activist organizations such as the Chicago Women's Liberation Group, the New York Radical Women, the Women's Equity Action League, and the Redstockings.[4] The political movements of the late 1960s worked on a broad range of topics and, in so doing, cast a spotlight on problems inherent in the institution of marriage. Some feminist activists took an aggressive stance against marriage. Women's liberation organizations disrupted bridal fairs in San Francisco, one group in New York City affixed "Fuck Marriage, Not Men" stickers in subways, and some women, like Ti-Grace Atkinson, advocated the abolition of marriage and compared it to slavery.[5] Discontent extended well beyond activist circles. Rebecca Davis observes, "The economic model of marital happiness, already fraying at the edges in the 1950s, began to unravel completely as women voiced their displeasure with the sexual division of labor."[6] Notions of "traditional marriage" were under attack in the 1960s, and many welcomed the institution's demise.

The sexual revolution and social justice movements of the 1960s affected American marriages in a number of ways. The loosening of sexual mores brought about a new image of the typical American family. Some young people in the United States chose to live communally, shrugging off the nuclear family unit that was so essential to the code of postwar family order. The availability of birth control decreased the risks of nonmarital sexual experiences. The 1965 *Griswold v. Connecticut* Supreme Court decision legalized birth control for married couples and fortified a right to personal privacy. Seven years later, the Supreme Court affirmed the legality of accessing birth control for all citizens regardless of marital status. Gays and lesbians, buoyed by waves of collective action and resistance against state oppression, including the New Year's Ball raid in San Francisco in 1965, the Black Cat raid in Los Angeles in 1967 and, most famously, the Stonewall riots of 1969, demanded recognition, social acceptance, the decriminalization of same-sex sexual activities, and an end to discrimination in housing and employment. Individuals with alternative sexual and gender identities created their own forms of family and made important steps toward the legal recognition of their relationships.[7]

Collectively, the impulses of the sexual revolution and social justice movements of the 1960s expanded the definition of the traditional family. Love and companionship existed and flourished outside the parameters set by the breadwinner and homemaker. The sexual revolution was most visible in major U.S. cities, but the sexual revolution reached across the United States and into small towns and rural environs.[8] The upheavals of the 1960s contributed to and coincided with large-scale trends in marriage, work, and family formation. By the 1970s, there were new expectations about marriage, sex, and courtship, and many—like those in the 1920s—shared a common fear that the institution of marriage was in a state of crisis.

Marriage and Divorce Revolutions

A widespread perception that the institution of marriage was under attack gripped Americans in the 1970s. By the 1960s, postwar demographic trends made a series of dramatic reversals. Between 1960 and 1980 the rate of marriage declined by 25 percent and the number of divorced men and women increased by 200 percent. Fewer people sought marriage, and those who did marry did so at an older age.[9] Compared to the 1950s and early 1960s, more wives worked outside the home and more homes were led by single parents. The divorce rate also increased. Nearly half of all marriages in the 1970s failed and, in 1975 alone, there were over one million divorces.[10] By the 1970s, and accelerating in the 1980s, the public, legal, and political nature of marriage underwent a transformation. During the 1970s, the revolutionary changes in marriage and divorce in the United States were buttressed by three trends that had important implications for the image of the gold digger: no-fault divorce, cohabitation, and prenuptial agreements.

The most important development in family law during the 1970s was the rise of no-fault divorce. Under the traditional fault system of divorce, one party had to show a cause for the collapse of the marriage by proving that the other party made some kind of egregious mistake in the relationship. For example, before 1969, California recognized seven grounds for divorce: adultery, extreme cruelty, willful desertion, willful neglect, habitual intemperance, incurable insanity, and the conviction of a felony. The fault system was dysfunctional for several reasons. As a basis for alimony, the division of property, and child custody, the fault system interjected an accusatorial process into a situation that did not always require the assignation of blame. The necessity to prove that one member of the marriage was at fault required dubious methods to gather lurid evidence. Couples who amicably sought to terminate their marriage had to create some kind of legal grounds to end the union, even if it meant lying. Couples contrived scenarios to "prove" adultery or mental cruelty. For example, like the plot point in Faith Baldwin's 1928 novel *Alimony*, couples seeking a divorce on friendly terms might hire a photographer to take a photo of the husband sitting on a bed with another woman to prove "infidelity." Beyond the reputational consequences of these arrangements, the husband and wife also risked criminal penalties for engaging in "collusion."[11] The chronic dishonesty impelled by the traditional fault system of divorce, as well as the growing legal recognition of marriage as a contract instead of a sacred bond, contributed to a nationwide push to change divorce law.

California led the way in transforming national divorce laws from a fault basis to a no-fault system. In 1969, California became the first state to institute no-fault divorce. The California Family Law Act of 1969 recognized "irreconcilable differences" as a legal justification for divorce, acknowledging that both parties could be jointly responsible for the breakdown of a marriage. California's law became a nationwide model. By 1973, eight states adopted a pure form of no-fault and seven states listed "incompatibility" as legal grounds for divorce.[12] Divorce moved away from considerations of interpersonal grievances and drifted toward economic calculations. Divorce, as described by the *Los Angeles Times* in 1977, is "a business for appraisers, tax men, experts in corporate liquidation, and business lawyers."[13] By 1985, all states and territories in the United States had adopted some form of no-fault divorce.

Changes in family law had mixed results for married women seeking divorce in the 1970s. Although divorce became easier, and the law granted women a presumed measure of equality, the short-term outcome for divorced women undermined their financial security. Despite its recognition of formal equality between men and women, the no-fault system favored men in various ways. No-fault divorce made it easier for men to exit a marriage and it sparked a growth in do-it-yourself divorces. A company called Divorce Yourself distributed low-cost divorce kits, a trend *New York* magazine said in 1976 was "starting to sweep the country."[14] Once divorced, women tended to find that their standard of living plummeted while men's standard of living actually improved.[15] The adoption of no-fault divorce laws in the 1970s also weakened the system of alimony. The no-fault ethic quashed older rationales for alimony, and fresh legal burdens were heaped on divorced women. One of the traditional justifications for alimony was a reward for virtuous behavior. In theory, this cut both ways, imposing moral demands on both men and women. For example, states usually prevented women from receiving alimony if they were found guilty of adultery. In practice, however, the putative formal equality instantiated by no-fault divorce solidified preexisting gender inequality.[16] According to Lenore Weitzman, the implications of no-fault divorce "had a radical effect" on the amount of alimony women received and on attitudes toward alimony in general.[17] Women seeking alimony now had to show, not just that they were wronged by their partner, but that they could not find a job. Under this new conception of divorce, courts based alimony on the wife's future employment prospects instead of her past living arrangement. Courts also became more reluctant to award long-term alimony to divorced women.[18] Moreover, those women who did, in fact, earn alimony were worse off than their husbands; one study in 1975 showed that twice as many upper-class men, compared to similarly situated women, were able to maintain their economic position following a divorce.[19] A 1974 study of alimony collection in Connecticut indicated that it took upwards of a year for a woman to receive payment if her husband lived in the same state and much longer if he was out of state. Many women failed to collect any money at all regardless of a court's decree.[20]

No-fault divorce coincided with a shift in public opinion away from traditional understandings of alimony. Survey data from the late 1970s show scant support for the notion that a woman deserved alimony for her years of work as a homemaker, her lost opportunities, or because her husband promised her support.[21] Attorneys in the no-fault era increasingly counseled their female clients to give up on their quest for alimony and to "get on with building their new lives."[22] No-fault divorce laws changed alimony in a number of other ways, including the language used to describe the awards. Now, more frequently called "spousal support," alimony awards were granted for shorter periods, and permanent alimony was exceedingly rare by the 1980s. Also, the overall frequency of alimony awards and the amount of monetary payment significantly declined after the adoption of no-fault divorce. Weitzman's data show that judges more often awarded alimony to housewives (compared to women in the paid labor force), but only if the woman had been married for ten or more years.[23]

Historical and social scientific studies in the 1980s and 1990s demonstrated the problems of no-fault divorce, but observers at the time also noticed its unfair outcomes wrapped in a language of gender equity. One attorney noted in 1973, "The irony is that in terms of women's lib, equality costs women money: the wife is not being treated more equally, and she often gets a lot less than she did before."[24] Feminists argued that no-fault divorce wiped away men's financial duties while doing nothing to change a woman's homemaker obligations.[25] The stigma of divorce undermined women's financial security in a number of ways. Despite the reputed embrace of egalitarian gender ideologies during the 1970s, divorced women faced considerable stigma when seeking loans and credit. One journalist in

1974 commented, "A divorced woman trying to buy a house probably will have to have a credit record of surpassing purity."[26] In short, assurances of legal equality did not keep pace with the lived reality of women's lives. Lingering norms and assumptions about women's roles as wives and mothers were used to limit their options and imperil their economic security despite legal guarantees otherwise. This is a consequence of what historian Alison Lefkovitz terms "expansionist" notions of equality. The expansionist approach, advocated by liberal feminism, and adopted with vigor at the federal level during the 1970s, sought formal, legal equality between men and women without the necessary changes to create substantive equality. For example, the Supreme Court's 1979 ruling in *Orr v. Orr* made it unconstitutional for states to have an alimony system that denied men benefits.[27] The ruling expanded formal gender equality between men and women, but granted men potential financial assistance at a time when spousal support for women nose-dived.

A second trend affecting marriages and families in the 1970s was the rise of unmarried cohabitation. According to some studies, the number of Americans living together as unmarried twosomes increased more than eightfold from 1960 to the mid-1970s.[28] By 1978, more than a million people lived together as unmarried couples.[29] Experts considered the possible causes of the spike in cohabitation: uncertainty created by the Vietnam War and the draft, fear of commitment among the young, rejection of parents' lifestyles, and individuals mounting an intentional challenge to postwar gender roles. Many cohabitators viewed marriage as a failed institution and regarded marriage as corroding true love. Regardless of the cause, the stigma surrounding cohabitation had faded considerably by 1979. According to journalist Dorothy Storck, average Americans, not just "actors, artists, or revolutionaries," regarded living together as an acceptable alternative to marriage or, at the very least, a crucial stage before marriage.[30] As historian Elizabeth Pleck explains, by the end of the 1970s, cohabitation was decriminalized in most states and the practice was portrayed in an uncritical fashion in movies and other forms of popular culture.[31] Moreover, cohabitation was no longer seen exclusively in terms of a training ground for marriage; it was regarded by many as a legitimate lifestyle choice.

Finally, increasing divorce rates and the rise of no-fault divorce meant that prenuptial agreements, which gained in popularity beginning in the 1970s, acquired heightened significance. The growth of prenuptial agreements, or "prenups," was a trend consistent with an emerging understanding of marriage as a contractual agreement instead of an institution primarily legitimated by government or religious entities. Moreover, courts gave increasing solidity to premarital agreements through the affirmation of "binding prenups," prenups that are not subject to state or judicial alteration unless they are procedurally flawed.

Like no-fault divorce, the enforcement of binding prenups treated marriage as a contract immune to state intervention, thereby exacerbating preexisting inequalities between parties who are presumed to be autonomous and equal. The presumption of legal neutrality reinforced social inequality because the partner with the most money, which in the 1970s was almost always the man, could write the terms of the prenup in his favor. The gold digger stereotype loomed over the creation and enforcement of prenups, undermining the potential of prenuptial agreements to further equality between husbands and wives in the event of a divorce.[32] The stereotype also stigmatized women who gained spousal support after a divorce. Feminist legal scholar Sharon Thompson writes, "The stereotype operates by labelling women with no mercenary intent as gold diggers simply because they have received a share of marital assets that they did not directly earn."[33] In this way judgments about prenuptial agreements, as well as the initial creation of prenups, tilted in favor of the moneyed spouse.[34]

Many attorneys noted the growing popularity of prenuptial agreements in the late 1970s and early 1980s. In 1977, a practitioner of family law in New York City estimated that requests for prenuptial agreements had grown three to five times since the start of the 1970s.[35] Ever more lawyers specializing in matrimonial work advocated that all couples seeking marriage should execute a prenuptial or antenuptial agreement.[36] Downplaying or ignoring the inequalities prenups could create, commenters tried to fit the growth of prenuptial agreements into the guiding ideals of the 1970s, such as personal fulfillment and feminism. One attorney, writing in 1976, argued that prenuptial agreements allowed couples to structure their marriage "in a manner more suited to their needs and values." In 1977, another attorney claimed that prenuptial agreements "reflect a growing consciousness of parity in marriage." A self-identified feminist stated that she liked the idea of prenuptial agreements because they allow her to define her marriage in way that "was not oppressive." In response to those hesitant to use a prenuptial agreement because of its "coldly legal approach," a writer for the *Los Angeles Times* said that one "need only remember the case of actor Lee Marvin."[37]

Lee Marvin, Michelle Triola, and Palimony

In an audacious move, Michelle Triola sued her ex-boyfriend, Lee Marvin, for monetary support, even though the couple had never been married.[38] On a fishing expedition to San Blas, Mexico, in 1964, Marvin supposedly promised his girlfriend that he would share his life with her. Years later, Michelle Triola described the agreement in court: "what I have is yours, and what you have is mine."[39] The legality of that pledge, the extent to which Marvin owed his live-in girlfriend any money, and whether or not Michelle Triola was a gold digger, were part of a churning conversation about the effect of the sexual revolution on American marriage. Numerous Americans perceived the Marvin case as having cataclysmic effects and, for many, the case was an emblem of both sexual and legal liberalism. This understanding of the case, what Pleck calls "the myth of Marvin," overestimates and misstates the impact of its legal outcomes.[40] While the case centered on an implied marriage contract, the Marvin controversy shared some of the qualities of a tort tale, a misleading story about a lawsuit that lays bare a society supposedly in turmoil. The timing of the case also coincided with a growing perception in American society of a "litigation crisis," the idea that Americans were assailing one another with frivolous lawsuits.[41] Perceptions of the Marvin case, however distorted they may have been, are important for understanding the linkages among money, law, and marriage after the turbulent 1960s. Opinions about the lawsuit constituted a referendum on gold digging and cohabitation in the wake of the sexual revolution.

Michelle Triola had lifelong aspirations of entering show business, and she embarked on a professional performing career shortly after graduating from high school. When she was eighteen, she tried to make her mark as a dancer in Las Vegas and Reno, and eventually toured with the Barry Ashton Dancers. She started her professional singing career in 1957 by performing at a supper club in Beverly Hills and (allegedly) Playboy Clubs in Chicago, Tucson, Phoenix, and Miami.[42] Triola also claimed that she performed in European nightclubs, including a four-month stint at the Kit Kat Klub in Rome, earning approximately $300 to $1,000 a week, although the details of her engagement could not be verified.[43] In 1964, she worked on the film *Synanon* as a background performer and stand-in.[44] Her career was unremarkable by Hollywood standards, but it put her in contact with many entertainment luminaries.

On the advice of her parents, she married actor Skip Ward when she was twenty-seven years old, but the union lasted less than a year. Her marriage was brief, but it introduced Triola to a social circle populated with celebrities like Burt Reynolds and Nancy Sinatra. After her divorce, Triola took small roles in order to maintain her connection to Hollywood and the entertainment field. In 1964, Triola worked as a stand-in and extra on the set of *Ship of Fools* where she met Lee Marvin. Despite being married, Lee began a relationship with Michelle. Marvin's bond with Triola evolved as quickly as his acting career, and he moved into a Malibu beach house with Triola in 1965. Some critics dubbed 1965 as "The Year of Lee Marvin" because of his ascendancy as a leading man.[45]

In 1966, Marvin embarked on a seven-month appointment in London to film *The Dirty Dozen*. Marvin did not want Triola on the film set because he feared that she did not comprehend the job, its long hours and lack of privacy. He worried she would not adapt to the "camaraderie, or the family, locked-in style we live."[46] Instead, Marvin encouraged her to work on her singing while he stayed in London. She followed his advice and took a ten-week contract to perform in Hawaii. She later described the separation as "sheer torture" and commented on the costly telephone bills they amassed.[47] While Marvin claimed he supported her singing career, she recalled that he demanded that she join him in London. She said that Marvin gave her an ultimatum: travel to London or forget the relationship.[48] Triola left Hawaii to visit Marvin on the film set, but it only increased the stress in an already tense relationship. Their conflicting memories of the separation became a key part of their separation trial years later.

Marvin found Triola "fun to be with," but observed that the relationship became more difficult after they returned to Malibu. In 1967, Marvin divorced his wife Betty, started "hanging around with a freaky crowd," and became extremely depressed.[49] Part of his depression stemmed from strain in his family life. Marvin's children disapproved of the divorce and his relationship with Triola. Although newly single, Marvin was in no rush to marry his girlfriend. Triola, however, initially wanted a legal marriage because unmarried cohabitation went against her Catholic upbringing. He convinced her that the marriage certificate was a needless formality. As she told *Ladies Home Journal*, "how could a piece of paper make us any happier than we were?"[50]

The relationship began to buckle by the end of the 1960s. Triola complained about Marvin's drinking and he was distressed by her controlling behavior. On film sets, Triola ingratiated herself with different members of the cast and crew, and then deliberately caused conflict. When he confronted Triola about her behavior, she threatened to kill herself or blackmail

FIGURE 14 Michelle Triola and Lee Marvin, 1960s. After they broke up, Michelle Triola sued her partner Lee Marvin for $1.8 million for "palimony." Gloria Steinem and Gloria Allred hailed Triola as a feminist fighter. Others, like Nora Ephron, castigated her as an uncouth gold digger. Courtesy of PhotoFest.

him.[51] Marvin said that the relationship had been terrible in its final few years, but he felt trapped in it.[52] He finally broke up with her in 1970, and the turmoil from the breakup extended for several weeks. In one incident, San Diego police arrested Triola for disturbing the peace after she pursued him in her car.[53] Marvin claimed that Triola was emotionally abusive. He said that she threatened to "kill herself, wreck my career, make statements to the press, things of that nature. She would cause deep embarrassment to me and my children."[54] Marvin said that she demanded $50,000 and then, later, $100,000 to leave him alone.[55]

Marvin reasoned that offering her money was the best way to sever the relationship. Working through his attorney, Marvin agreed to pay Triola $800 a month with the stipulation that she not speak to the press about their relationship. As Triola described it, she received the money "on the condition that I be a good little girl and not bug Lee."[56] She complained that her monthly payment failed to sustain the lifestyle to which she had become acquainted. Nonetheless, she accepted the payments, and Triola and Marvin assumed a level of normalcy for over a year. During this time, Marvin resumed a relationship with his first wife, Pamela.

Marvin terminated payments to Triola after he suspected that she was a source for unfavorable stories about him in Hollywood gossip columns. Marvin's business manager contacted Triola and informed her that the monthly payments were ending. Triola was stunned. She said years later, "It was impossible for me to face the fact that everything Lee had promised me during our relationship was untrue." She called Marvin who, at the time, was living with Pamela. According to Triola, Pamela took the phone and went on a tirade. She told Triola that the payments were ridiculous, she was entitled to nothing, and should find herself another boyfriend. For Triola, this insufferable indignity sparked her into action. She contacted celebrity lawyer Marvin M. Mitchelson. He helped Triola handle a personal injury case a few years before her breakup with Marvin, and rumors circulated that, earlier in their acquaintanceship, Mitchelson and Triola staged accidents to generate profitable lawsuits.[57]

Marvin Mitchelson played an outsized role in the legal action against Lee Marvin, and the case boosted his already considerable notoriety garnered from representing Hollywood celebrities. As a young adult, Marvin Mitchelson wanted to become a renowned actor, but instead pursued fame through a career in law. After graduating from the University of California at Los Angeles in 1953, he became exposed to both the worlds of law and Hollywood by working as a process server in Los Angeles. He served papers to famous Hollywood figures such as Joan Collins, Sophia Loren, and Louis B. Mayer. It was difficult to gain access to those defendants, so Mitchelson donned costumes and crafted ingenious schemes to serve them with papers. Casting aside his Hollywood dreams, he graduated from law school and quickly made a name for himself with a case about indigent legal representation, a case that reached the Supreme Court in the early 1960s.[58] Finding that "divorce proceedings are often as emotion-charged as murder trials," Mitchelson began to practice family law.[59] In one of his biggest cases, Mitchelson served as cocounsel with Roy Cohn to represent the wife of American lyricist Alan Jay Lerner in a divorce and custody battle. In that case, Cohn and Mitchelson squared off against Louis Nizer, the attorney who represented Eleanor Holm in her divorce battle with Billy Rose. Mitchelson was an accomplished and well-known celebrity divorce lawyer by the time Michelle Triola met him in 1959.[60]

Marvin Mitchelson saw the monetary and fame-enhancing potential of the case and agreed to represent Michelle Triola. He claimed that Lee Marvin owed Triola financial support because the two lived together in a state akin to marriage. California was one of many states that had abolished common-law marriage. Therefore, Mitchelson and Triola's claim was not based on established case law. Rather, Mitchelson argued for an innovative category in family law that the press later named "palimony." As a combination of "pal" and "alimony," palimony referred to a form of alimony available to unmarried couples. Palimony recognized a communal and romantic relationship between two cohabitating adults, but it constituted a trading of resources beyond a sexual connection. Before the 1970s, courts routinely interpreted monetary exchange within nonmarital forms of companionship as "meretricious" and similar to prostitution. Palimony, Mitchelson argued, was a form of compensation capable of rectifying the historic power imbalance between men and women. With cohabitation on the rise, women of the 1970s were saddled with the demands of living together without the legal protection afforded by marriage and the possibility of alimony. For Mitchelson, palimony created a way to balance the scales of power and usher in the unfinished promises of the women's movement and sexual revolution. And the case had the potential to make him very rich.

Marvin and Triola fought in court for most of the 1970s. The conflict between Lee Marvin and Michelle Triola resulted in two separate, but connected, legal battles. The first battle centered on the mere ability of Triola to bring a lawsuit against Marvin. Since California did not recognize common-law marriage, it was unclear whether Triola had legal standing to initiate a suit against Marvin. The court confronted a seemingly simple question: Did she have the legal ground to take him to trial? On this front, the case reached the California Supreme Court and affirmed Triola's legitimate right to sue. The California Supreme Court, however, only confirmed that Triola had the lawful ability to sue, but the question of what Marvin was obligated to pay her, if anything, was left to a trial judge. The second legal fight was the civil trial. At the conclusion of the lengthy trial, Marvin was ordered to pay Triola $104,000, a significant sum, yet far less than what she sought. Both declared victory, but Lee Marvin emerged as the ultimate winner after he won his appeal.

The years-long legal struggle between Marvin and Triola received colossal media coverage. Although Martin was arguably victorious, the outcome in the court of public opinion was mixed. The question of whether or not Michelle Triola deserved any of Lee Marvin's wealth, and the question of whether or not Michelle Triola was a gold digger for seeking it, reflected gains made by feminists after the sexual revolution regarding the value of women's paid and unpaid work, as well as the lingering influence of conservative ideologies of respectability and domesticity. The status of Michelle Triola as a gold digger for desiring financial support from Marvin without the legal formality of marriage depended on a kaleidoscope of elements revealed in the two legal contests.

The California Supreme Court and Nonmarital Support

Michelle Triola's lawsuit against Lee Marvin appeared to die before it ever had a chance to be heard by a judge or jury. On December 4, 1973, Superior Court Judge William Munnell granted a motion by Lee Marvin's attorney to dismiss the suit without full consideration. The judge reasoned that Marvin's prior marriage made Triola's lawsuit "contrary to public policy" because it deprived "the legal wife of her community property." While the judge recognized the growing acceptance of premarital and nonmarital cohabitation, the era within which Triola and Marvin began their relationship was different. The judge said, "Even if our society has changed so that a relationship such as this might be sanctioned today, in 1964 it certainly was not the law." Triola and Mitchelson immediately filed an appeal. In July 1975, the Second District Court of Appeals upheld the lower court's dismissal of the suit. Marvin Mitchelson spun the decision in the best possible light. He said, "I actually never have been so happy about a ruling because this means the Supreme Court will have to take it." In December 1976, the California Supreme Court overturned the ruling of the lower court in a landmark decision that gave legal weight to Mitchelson's palimony theory.[61]

Associate Justice Matthew Tobriner, a liberal jurist who favored gay rights and affirmative action, wrote the Marvin decision. Friend-of-the-court briefs by feminist law professors and attorneys likely influenced his ruling.[62] The opening sentence of the majority opinion in Marvin v. Marvin acknowledged the momentous increase in couples living together without marriage. The decision noted that the Courts of Appeal have been torn between two perspectives articulated in California family law, one that abided by community property standards for unmarried couples and one that rejected that standard. While courts in the Marvin case had refused to apply California's Family Law Act to adjudicate the controversy, another case developed alongside it with different results. The First District Court of Appeals decided a case in 1973 that ruled that Paul Cary and Janet Forbes needed to divide their property equally. The Cary-Forbes case involved a couple who lived together for more than eight years, had four children, but were not legally married. When they separated, a trial court determined that their property should be equally divided, as decreed by the 1969 Family Law Act, regardless of who was at fault in upending the relationship. Paul Forbes appealed the decision, arguing for a "pre-1970 notion that the law must leave the parties where it finds them."[63] In a 1973 decision, the Appellate Court upheld the lower court's ruling and demanded that the couple divide their property equally. Two years later, a California appellate court came to the opposite conclusion in a different case, Estate of Atherley.[64]

The Marvin case allowed the California Supreme Court to put forward a definitive ruling about the division of property among unmarried couples and, therefore, resolve a legal ambiguity about the laws governing marriage and cohabitation. The court ruled that California's 1969 Family Law Act (which instituted no-fault divorce) only covered marital relationships and, therefore, a judicial process should guide the distribution of property of an unmarried couple. The California Supreme Court reasoned that courts can enforce written or verbal contracts unless they are based explicitly on an exchange for sexual services. Moreover, in the absence of a written or verbal contract, courts can examine the conduct of the parties to discern whether or not there was an implied contract. The Marvin ruling stated, "The fact that a man and woman live together without marriage, and engage in a sexual relationship, does not in itself invalidate agreements between them relating to their earnings, property, or expenses."[65] The ruling walked through and refuted arguments made by Lee Marvin's attorneys, including the claim that Triola's lawsuit violated the community property rights of Betty Marvin, Lee Marvin's then-wife. The court observed that Betty could have asserted her community property rights by divorcing Lee. The court also rejected the argument that the union of Triola and Marvin was meretricious and based on a trade of sexual services for money. The court noted that it was commonplace for unmarried couples to have sex, and that they could have valid agreements about property as long as they did not orient them on an explicit sex-for-property agreement.

Observers across the country perceived the California Supreme Court's 1976 ruling to be monumentally important. Some legal experts and members of the media described the decision as undoing the traditional basis for marriage. A judge from New York compared the impact of the *Marvin* decision to the Supreme Court's decisions in Miranda v. Arizona and Brown v. Board of Education. In *Cosmopolitan*, Marcia Seligson declared that Marvin Mitchelson was "largely responsible for significantly altering the state of American marriage and male/female relationships forever." A writer for the *Chicago Tribune* predicted that the California Supreme Court's judgment would give rise to the family law equivalent of ambulance chasers because the ruling encouraged lawyers to seek "women jilted by well-heeled lovers" in pursuit of large settlements and contingency fees. The exact implications of the ruling for cohabiting couples, however, remained shrouded in ambiguity.[66]

Experts on law and relationships capitalized on the confusion created by the California Supreme Court's decision. Professionals in Los Angeles organized a workshop entitled "Living Together (in California)" that was attended by over one hundred people. The event, led by Marvin Mitchelson, centered on "the psychological, social and legal aspects of the changing man-woman relationships as exemplified by the Lee Marvin case." Similarly, the University of California at Los Angeles offered an extension course called "Marriage Without License." Wealthy celebrities took especial note of the ruling. Mitchelson described a "panic" among actors and musicians that the lawsuits could become "a well-publicized fad."[67] Marvin Mitchelson reported "overwhelming concern among the rock people" about potential lawsuits, especially after Rod Stewart and Alice Cooper were sued by their former lovers.[68] Other entertainers, like Flip Wilson and Nick Nolte, also faced Marvin-style lawsuits.

Lawyers braced themselves for the new climate created by the 1976 Marvin ruling. The ruling, according to one New York attorney, "arrested the legal community's attention." Another attorney reported receiving dozens of calls from unmarried men and women inquiring about their legal obligations in the wake of the court's judgment. A writer for the *New York Times* speculated that hundreds of "disgruntled live-in spouses throughout the country" were emboldened by the court's ruling and busy filing lawsuits against their former live-in partners.[69] *People* magazine described a "legal stationery store" that had a "Cohabitation Contracts in Stock" sign in their storefront window. The magazine baselessly claimed "a thousand plus cohabitation suits have been filed in California alone."[70] Some predicted a surge of similar cases across the country.[71] Similarly, one lawyer compared the "Marvin Doctrine" to a "large stone thrown into a quiet pond." "As the ripples widen," he said, "all sorts of relationships will be affected. No couple, married or unmarried, will remain untouched by the judge's pen."[72] Alfred

Song, a distinguished member of the California Legislature, declared that the Marvin decision "radically alters the basis of all unmarried relationships within the state." He said, "I doubt any of us can imagine the consequences of the court's action."[73] For many, the California Supreme Court's ruling was a bomb whose anticipated explosion was damaging, widely felt, yet scarcely understood.

The California Supreme Court's Marvin decision left a much smaller imprint on law and American society than commentators in the late 1970s predicted. According to Elizabeth Pleck, "Marvin did not open the floodgates of litigation, and its impact was relatively short-lived."[74] Post-Marvin, relatively few couples created written agreements about how to divide property and resources in the event of a breakup, and implied or verbal agreements still faced difficulty in court despite their legal validity.[75] The Marvin ruling may have helped decrease the cultural stigma associated with romantic cohabitation, but it did not lead to the rash of lawsuits many observers feared. If anything, it prompted some state legislators to make preemptive moves to limit the precedent-setting force of the California ruling. The Marvin decision garnered a hostile response from lawmakers, especially in the South and Midwest.[76] In Illinois, the decision in Hewitt v. Hewitt rejected the Marvin doctrine altogether and affirmed that post-breakup financial support was only available if the couple were previously married. In the Hewitt case, a woman named Vicky Hewitt, who had lived with Bob Hewitt for sixteen years but never became legally married, demanded an equal share of their property when the relationship failed. The Appellate Court, quoting heavily from the California Supreme Court's Marvin ruling, sided with Vicky. The Illinois Supreme Court, however, ultimately ruled in favor of Bob Hewitt, arguing that the relationship was "meretricious" and that Vicky was entitled to neither half of their property or spousal support. Bob Hewitt's attorney observed, "It's the pendulum starting to swing back the other way."[77]

The Los Angeles Trial of Lee Marvin

The California Supreme Court's ruling did not make any judgment as to whether Lee Marvin owed Michelle Triola any compensation; it only allowed for Triola's lawsuit to advance. Her suit against Lee Marvin took another three years to reach its conclusion. With the approval to move forward from the California Supreme Court, Marvin Mitchelson filed a lawsuit on behalf of Michelle Triola. Claudia Luther, a journalist who provided full coverage of the trial for the *Los Angeles Times*, accurately anticipated that the "trial will quickly deteriorate to the level of a sensational and nasty domestic argument played out in public."[78] Over sixty witnesses testified during the eleven-week trial, generating over 8,000 pages of testimony and costing taxpayers an estimated $30,000.[79] The legal proceedings also imposed a physical toll on its participants. Lois Goldman, Lee Marvin's attorney, developed diabetes during the ordeal, Lee Marvin battled with recurring colds and flu symptoms, and Mitchelson at one point collapsed and had to be carried out of the courthouse in a stretcher after an overpowering coughing fit. On at least two occasions, Michelle Triola began sobbing and had to leave the courtroom.[80]

Michelle Triola's initial suit asked for over $3 million, but Mitchelson ultimately arrived at a figure of $1.8 million, half of the $3.6 million Lee Marvin had earned while Michelle and Lee lived together.[81] During the trial, Mitchelson tried to add a count of fraud to the initial claim, asking for $1 million in punitive damages because Marvin attempted to deceive Triola by telling her that he loved her when he did not mean it. The judge denied the request.[82] Mitchelson made big demands, but he portrayed the litigation as about something more than money. The trial, he declared, would affirm the social acceptability of living together without marriage.[83] Mitchelson was correct that the trial involved more than money, but the cultural imprint of the court's action extended well beyond the legitimacy of cohabitation. The three-month trial served as a symbol of the sexual revolution and a statement about women's property rights in an era of no-fault divorce and widening employment opportunities for women. A careful analysis of the claims made in the Marvin case, even the seemingly trivial ones about Triola's cooking and Marvin's drinking, captures broad understandings of marriage, law, and money in the 1970s. Testimony about Michelle Triola's avarice, her domestic career sacrifices, and her demands for money from Marvin show how gender stereotypes, including conceptions of gold digging, shaped the trial and its outcome.

The central claim of Triola's case was that she had an implicit agreement with Lee Marvin that he would take care of her the rest of her life regardless of whether or not they stayed together as a romantic couple. She tried to prove that what she had with Marvin was similar to a legal marriage and, therefore, she deserved all of the benefits that marriage entailed. The case involved the weighing and evaluation of the couples' domestic and monetary responsibilities, their treatment of one another, and the meaning of love. Consequently, the trial revolved around several core components, including

Triola's legal name change to "Marvin," Marvin's love and alleged promises to support her, her housewifely care for Marvin, Triola's mental anguish, and her career sacrifices.

A key element in Michelle Triola's case was her name change to "Michelle Marvin" two weeks before the relationship ended and Lee kicked her out of the beach house. To underscore the significance of the new name, and to emphasize that both Lee and Michelle regarded their union as one of marriage for all intents and purposes, Mitchelson entered into evidence a series of bills and checks in the name of "Michelle Marvin" and "Mrs. Lee Marvin."[84] On the witness stand, Triola gave conflicting reasons for the name change. She claimed that she changed her name at Lee's suggestion in order to make it easier for them to travel abroad. In her original petition to the court, she stated that she adopted the new name because she was an entertainer known professionally as "Michelle Marvin." During the trial, however, she said that she was always known professionally as "Michelle Triola." Lee Marvin's defense team tried to weaken the claim that her name change represented a solidification of the relationship. In fact, Lee Marvin testified that he encouraged Michelle to keep her original name because adopting his last name would be embarrassing for himself and his family.[85] Lee Marvin's publicist, perhaps influenced by discussions about the widely publicized murder-suicide that occurred in the Jonestown cult just three months prior, testified that Michelle had "probably brainwashed" him into calling her "Michelle Marvin."[86]

Triola's case also centered on Lee Marvin's promise to love and care for her. Marvin sent Triola eight love letters during the time he filmed *The Dirty Dozen* in England. The letters, Mitchelson contended, showed that Marvin and Triola had an implied contract based on mutual love. In one letter from 1966, Marvin sketched a scene where he was "the first man in history" found guilty of "robbing a 33-year-old cradle." A judge, he speculated, would sentence him to live with Triola forever, a fate that he would happily accept. He wrote, "Well, guess we will have to spend the rest of our lives hiding in bed. Hmmm." Mitchelson argued that Lee Marvin's promises to love Triola proved the substance of their bond and constituted an implied contract; the letter was proof of Marvin and Triola's agreement. On the stand, Lee Marvin said that he made "an idle male promise" and that the letter was primarily about sex.[87] Marvin said that he may have declared his love to Triola, but it was not significant. He said, "I may have said it on a number of occasions. I might have meant it on some."[88] When Mitchelson questioned Lee Marvin about the meaning of love Marvin responded with an analogy of a fuel gauge. Young and frivolous love was at the "empty" end of the spectrum and true love was at the "full" end. When asked about his love for Triola, he characterized it as a "one-quarter full—boyfriend-girlfriend feeling."[89] While these letters showed that Marvin had feelings for Triola, they failed to prove that the couple had a give-and-take relationship characteristic of marriage, and a letter where Lee purportedly asked Michelle to give up her singing career never materialized.[90] Testimony about love created a colorful moment in the trial, but it failed to offer decisive evidence of Marvin's degree of commitment one way or another.

On another front, Mitchelson portrayed Triola as a devoted housewife. He claimed that she provided her partner with care much like a traditional wife would support a husband and, therefore, was entitled to support just as a wife would be entitled to alimony. This testimony brought into focus a range of her domestic practices, including cooking, cleaning, and caring for Lee. On the witness stand, Triola expressed raw sensitivity about her reputation as a competent cook. She said that she prepared elaborate meals for Marvin and his friends, including trays of food for the cast and crew of one of Marvin's films. Marvin countered, "I never remember her carving a roast."[91] She later told the press that, of the many things raised during the trial, Marvin's criticism of her cooking was especially perturbing. Recalling the comment about the roast, she said, "I'll never forgive him for that."[92] Testimony about her cooking, while seemingly inconsequential, was directly relevant to the legal questions raised by the plaintiff and was important for the emotional tone of the trial. Talk of cooking worked to establish Michelle Triola's housewifely role.

Similarly, Lee Marvin's drinking was another area where Mitchelson sought to establish Triola's authenticity as a housewife. According to Mitchelson, Lee was too drunk to perform his job without Michelle's help and, in turn, Michelle's career was held back by Lee's drunkenness.[93] Mitchelson called witnesses to attest to Marvin's excessive drinking. Edna McHugh, a friend of the couple (and Eddie Cantor's daughter), stated on the witness stand that Marvin was often drunk when the three of them had dinner together. She described an occasion when Marvin was so intoxicated that he fell over, hit his head, and had to be treated at a hospital. Triola claimed that Marvin's excessive drinking prompted her to attend Al-Anon meetings, boil the alcohol out of his liquor, and patch up personal and professional conflicts created by his alcoholism. His drinking was an integral part of the reciprocal relationship the couple shared, and her protection of Marvin when he drank was part of the agreement the two had about their domestic arrangement.[94] Triola claimed that she cared for Marvin when he was drunk in the same way a wife would look after a drunk husband.[95]

Marvin's attorneys addressed accusations about his drinking in a few ways. Marvin's professional agent stated on the witness stand that Triola drove Marvin to drink through her "badgering." One of Marvin's attorneys also noted that, contrary to the claim that "he was virtually awash with alcohol," the defendant starred in several major films that all required physical vigor and mental concentration. Marvin's legal team also contended that Triola was the one with the substance abuse problem. Marvin testified that she overdosed on pills and threatened to commit suicide. On the witness stand, Marvin called Triola "a doper" and attested that she used marijuana and Percodan.[96]

Another area of conflict concerned Triola's career sacrifices. Michelle Triola was a true wife, Mitchelson contended, because she gave up her career aspirations for Marvin. Marvin's attorneys solicited testimony to counter the image of Triola's burgeoning career thrown sideways by Marvin's demands. The defense called singer Trini Lopez as a witness. He testified that Michelle Triola had a poor voice and that he was only being polite when, years earlier, he praised it. Lee Marvin's attorneys also solicited testimony from Sam Distefano, the musical director for the Playboy Clubs for most of the 1960s. Distefano said that Triola performed for only one two-week engagement at the Playboy Club in Phoenix, and her performance rating was so low they refused to hire her again. In contrast to the image of lost career opportunities, Lee Marvin spoke of the sacrifices he made for her career, including setting up a record company for her and introducing her to people in the entertainment business.[97]

Finally, the defendant and plaintiff traded claims of mistreatment. The competing testimony resembled the standards of fault in traditional adversarial divorce cases: infidelity and mental cruelty.[98] From the plaintiff's side, Triola testified that she became pregnant three times while living with Marvin and that he compelled her to have abortions which caused her to be sterile. Marvin allegedly pressured her to have an abortion during the first two pregnancies, and the third pregnancy ended in a miscarriage.[99] During one of their fights toward the end of their relationship, Triola screamed at Marvin that he had "killed her babies."[100] The plaintiff called her gynecologist as a witness, and he testified that she was sterile because of an abortion she had in 1967. Marvin said that he never asked her to abort the pregnancy.[101]

From the defense's side, Lee Marvin alleged that Michelle Triola was serially unfaithful to him with a young man named Richard Doughty. As a

Peace Corps volunteer, Doughty worked with the fisheries on the island of Palau while Marvin was filming *Hell in the Pacific*. Marvin befriended him and obtained a job for him on the film crew, which thrilled Doughty because he had aspirations of becoming an actor. At the trial, Doughty claimed that he had sex with Michelle Triola over two dozen times. Under direct examination, Doughty said that he felt guilty about it, but Triola threated to have him fired from the film if he did not continue with the affair. Their relationship persisted when he returned to the United States and, in fact, he lived with Marvin and Triola for a brief period. Marvin and his attorneys used Doughty's testimony to suggest that Marvin's union with Triola was not a robust, loving relationship approximating marriage.[102]

Lee Marvin's second wife Pamela claimed that the testimony of Doughty, and the plaintiff's effort to undermine it, was "the most traumatic part of the trial."[103] Marvin Mitchelson attacked Doughty's testimony in several ways. He suggested that Doughty gave false testimony as a favor to Marvin.[104] Mitchelson and Triola also argued that the affair never occurred because Doughty was gay. Mitchelson called a witness who testified that she saw Doughty at a gay bar and that he was "often seen in the company of other homosexuals."[105] Triola told reporters outside the courthouse that she "never saw him make a pass at any girl, to tell you the truth."[106] The trial judge openly questioned the weight placed on testimony about Doughty's sexuality and mused that Doughty could be bisexual.[107] The testimony about Doughty fit the broader pattern of the conflicting trial strategies. Triola and Marvin Mitchelson resurrected an appearance of domesticity befitting earlier decades of American history. Triola painted herself as a housewife—Mrs. Marvin in law and form—putting her talent and future on hold, cooking, caring for Lee, and patching up for him after he drank. For this, she claimed that she was left emotionally abused and sterile. According to Lee Marvin, Triola was manipulative, unfaithful, and unable to cook a simple roast.

During the first week of April 1979, lawyers for both parties submitted more than ninety pages of briefs to Los Angeles Superior Court Judge Arthur K. Marshall.[108] The attorneys made closing arguments the following week. In a ruling that allowed both sides to claim victory, the judge declared that Marvin owed Triola $104,000 for "rehabilitative" purposes so that she could learn new skills and gain meaningful employment. He arrived at the sum by considering the highest weekly salary she ever earned ($1,000) and computed it for a two-year period.[109] This was far less than the $1.8 million she originally sought, but Triola and Mitchelson beamed smiles as they held up a copy of the *Los Angeles Times* with the headline, "$104,000 for Michelle." Lee Marvin successfully appealed the ruling and Michelle Triola earned nothing from her legal efforts. The case was an unqualified victory for Marvin, and public opinion seemed to be on his side.[110] Although the trial finished in late April of 1979, the conversation sparked by the trial extended well beyond the judge's decision.

Constructing Gender and Social Class in *Marvin v. Marvin*

The Marvin case attracted a mountain of media attention. Although the legal import of the case was less than anticipated, wide swaths of the public perceived that the trial had broad social stakes. A consideration of the cultural response to the conflict demonstrates the extent to which the gold digger trope, and the gendered and sexualized fears that it embodied, directed the course of and reaction to the trial, its context, and its participants. The response to the trial suggests how the women's movement and sexual revolution changed the perception of romantic and monetary exchange, but also how those changes were continually challenged and contested. Michelle Triola, depending upon one's view of her legal case, was a champion of women's rights or a gold digger who set back the advancement of women.

Many observers in the 1970s regarded Michelle Triola as a gold digger. According to attorney Joel Sonelick, the American public viewed Triola's lawsuit as a "boon to female gold diggers and an affront to the institution of marriage." Writer Nora Ephron tagged Triola as a gold digger in the *Washington Post*. In her 1979 article "The Gold Digger Standard," Ephron called the trial "the living definition of tackiness." She compared Triola unfavorably to the gold diggers of the 1920s and '30s. Triola was a gold digger, Ephron concluded, but one who fell short of the implicit code of conduct that governed classy, cocktail-sipping gold diggers from earlier decades. She said she would "like to think that gold diggers have standards, and that no decent gold digger ever expected that her big bald tycoon would go on providing her with goodies after the relationship was over." Referencing Triola's award, Ephron stated that she respected traditional gold diggers much more than Triola because they refused the role of victim. Ephron wrote, "She [Triola] got $104,000 for it, but as old-fashioned notions go, I prefer mine. I'll take a gold digger with a swizzle stick over a victim with a lawsuit any time."[111]

Nora Ephron's argument placed Triola in a rhetorical bind. Ephron contended that Triola degraded herself by presenting herself as a victim and by involving the law in a relationship problem that the couple should have resolved informally. Yet, if she had not pursued a legal remedy to her situation, she would have been left with no opportunity whatsoever to shoulder the substantive economic inequality created by formal legal equality. Nora Ephron, a Wellesley graduate who was, at the time, married to famous Watergate journalist Carl Bernstein, judged Michelle Triola's sexual respectability through a lens of class-based propriety. Ephron had firsthand experience with sexism, most notably when editors at *Newsweek* refused to give her a writing job because the magazine had a stated practice of not hiring women. She also used legal mechanisms to seek recompense, joining in on a class action lawsuit against the magazine. She judged Triola by a different standard. Her class privilege caused her to view Triola's lack of cultural capital as a failing of her gender.

Other cultural commentators sharply criticized Michelle Triola and her cause. Art Hoppe's *San Francisco Chronicle* column implied that Triola was a gold digger, if not a prostitute. Popular entertainment also lampooned Triola. On *The Carol Burnett Show*, Burnett performed a biting parody of Triola and her allegedly poor singing skills. Johnny Carson, an ardent supporter of Lee Marvin, regularly skewered Michelle Triola on his nightly comedy show.[112] The portrayal of Triola as a gold digger and prostitute peaked with a *Saturday Night Live* satirical news segment featuring Jane Curtin and Dan Aykroyd. Curtin defended Triola: "times change and so does the nature of relationships." The intended comedy and the biggest laughs from the studio audience, however, came from Aykroyd's evisceration of her as a promiscuous gold digger—a "swamp sow"—one who was after Lee Marvin's "last three million dollars." "I guess what you and Michelle are saying," Aykroyd claimed, "is that when you're on your backs the meter is running." The enthusiastic response to Aykroyd's joke echoed and contributed to sexist fears about the status of women after the sexual revolution.[113]

Public criticism of Michelle Triola represented the intersectional world of the gold digger trope and its judgments about gender, sexuality, race, and social class. Characteristic of discourse about gold diggers in general, the relationship between Marvin and Triola was portrayed as a lopsided deal. Triola did not have the requisite female beauty needed to match and form an equitable union with Lee Marvin's star stature. Accordingly, many observers claimed that Triola lacked the intelligence, culture, and classiness needed to make the relationship a fair one. Journalists and newspaper columnists from across the country upbraided Triola for her unintelligence and trashy demeanor. Reporter Claudia Luther observed that Triola "looks more like a well-to-do matron than the wife of a movie star." Nora Ephron mocked "short, pudgy Michelle." Columnist Bill Raspberry said, "Her behavior was as dumb as his was contemptible." Novelist and then-newspaper columnist Ann Rinaldi declared, "She was a stupid woman from the word go." With characteristic condescension, George Will surmised that Triola "disregarded society's settled judgment, codified in law, about behavior that is socially important and morally sound."[114] A set of *Los Angeles Times* person-on-the-street interviews echoed the notion that Triola was an undeserving gold digger. The opinion that she deserved no compensation "was a far from uncommon response." For example, a twenty-eight-year-old woman from El Sereno said, "If he was an ordinary guy and not some movie star, she would never have even tried. She just wanted the publicity."[115]

In addition to her personal failings, many commenters portrayed her legal action as trashy and uncouth. An editorial in the *Los Angeles Times* compared the trial to a soap opera and said that both parties should be embarrassed. An editorial in the *Iola Register* titled "Sorry Spectacle" called the case "tawdry" and hoped for "a quieter way to set a price on failed love." George Will ridiculed Marvin's love letters that attorneys read aloud in court and declared that the Marvin case "is the sort of litigation society does not need." California politicians speculated about the case and its deleterious effect on public morals. State Assemblyman Walter Ingalls from Riverside (who was arrested years later after soliciting sex from a plainclothes police officer in a park bathroom) compared unmarried women living with their lovers to sex workers. The plaintiff and the defendant, by laying their private life out to public examination, were deemed tacky and trashy.[116]

Several cultural critics detailed another problem with the case beyond the personal failings of its participants. Newspaper columnists and other cultural authorities argued that the very nature of the trial corrupted true love. In a column that invoked Shakespeare, Art Buchwald said that, "since the Lee Marvin decision Juliet wants something in writing." In the wake of the Marvin ruling, Sue Mittenthal imagined "the unmarriage ceremony" where participants would be flanked by lawyers, and the ceremony "is sealed not with a kiss but with the stamp of a notary public, and the unwed partners live contractually ever after." Writing at a time when prenups were increasingly popular, Jacque Jones, a writer for the *Los Angeles Times*, lamented, "Even less affluent live-in couples are being advised to sign contracts and agreements about breaking up before they even begin. Whatever happened to romance, not to mention trust?" Terry Clifford from the *Chicago Tribune* said that the Marvin decision "unleashed a new form of social disease," because "couples don't court anymore; they go to court." Steve Brill from *Esquire* stated that the Marvin case "injects lawyers and courts into yet another area of life where we may be better off without them." Humorist Joan Beck mused, "Couples who now think they have fallen in love are urged not so much to wait for the preacher as to wait for the lawyer." Articulating what Viviana Zelizer has termed "the hostile worlds" perspective, these observers argued that a bright line should separate the legal realm from the domain of love and romance. In these analyses, law, lawsuits, and lawyers corrupt true love and have a poisonous effect on romantic companionship. Public figures used the Marvin case to criticize the creep of legalism into romance, but they often had difficulty separating the flamboyant personalities of the litigants from profound changes to divorce and community property law that had taken place in the prior decade. They focused on personal behavior, and the need to use legal mechanisms to prevent gold digging, instead of the broad economic, demographic, and legal transformations that undergird the changes in law. In this way, the gold digger image helped play its usual cultural work of distraction by drawing attention to individual conduct instead of structural processes.[117]

Several commenters viewed the case as symbolic of women's place in society. For many, the case was a setback for hard-fought gains made by women during the sexual revolution and the women's movement of the late 1960s and early 1970s. Though hardly an unbiased observer, Pamela Marvin contended that Triola was "about as far as you can get from the ideals of women's liberation." In a person-on-the-street interview for the *Los Angeles Times*, Rhonda Gale-Wilzig, a twenty-six-year-old worker for the California Assembly Speaker's office, said that the case was "a step back for the women's movement." She noted the symbolic importance and precedent-setting quality of the case: "It's a shame that Michelle was the test case. She wasn't a very viable symbol." Jacque feared that the standard set by the case "could set women's integrity and gains as individuals back twenty years." She reasoned that the lawsuit seemed like a sham in an era where "healthy and capable women are learning that they can have both career and marriage." Similarly, Ann Rinaldi in the *Indianapolis Star* opined, "One can't help thinking that instead of making one giant step for womankind, as Michelle set out to do, she has done just the opposite. She has set the '70s woman, with her free lifestyle, back a long way." In these comments, the understanding of Triola's action as a mercenary strategy for advancing her class position fortified the gendered meaning of the trial. In other words, her lawsuit ostensibly set back women's rights because it was a trashy ploy to rise in class. These critiques echo concerns expressed by female heart balm critics during the 1930s. Both sets of writers misidentify their class privilege as a form of gender respectability, propelling them to criticize women who fell short of class-based standards of propriety.[118]

Others regarded Triola as a positive symbol of the women's rights movement. The case was resolved during the final days when state legislatures were considering the Equal Rights Amendment, and so the Marvin trial represented a lens to project different perspectives on the subject of women's rights. While some feminists like Nora Ephron described Triola as a disgrace to womanhood, others latched onto her as an emblem of women's continuing struggles in the 1970s. Gloria Allred, who on one occasion walked arm in arm with Triola into the courthouse, used the case to criticize sexist media representations of women. She said, "His career is praised. Hers is laughed at," adding, "It seems that men who engage in a career are respected while women who work become the subject of bad jokes." A twenty-three-year-old Los Angeles City Hall worker called the press coverage "abusive" and compared the trial to a rape case where the full burden of proof fell on the victimized woman. Gloria Steinem claimed the ruling would help women. She said, "I think women will now be far more likely to insist on a financial agreement in writing before they give up their careers or wash even one dish—and that's probably healthy."[119] She also lashed out at the defendant and said, "Lee Marvin seems to be the one who needs rehabilitating—in the form of a short course in truth-telling."[120] Jane Dunbar, chair of the Los Angeles County Commission on the Status of Women, said that the case had a positive impact by encouraging women to become independent from men.[121] Shelly Mandell, president of the Los Angeles chapter of the National Organization of Women, praised the decision for its recognition of women's unpaid household labor, noting that the amount of the ruling approximated $17,000 a year for the duration of Marvin's relationship, which "a lot of studies have shown that that's roughly what housewives are worth." Mandell's analysis of the case echoed a larger public conversation about women in the labor force who did the majority of household work and child care when they returned home from their paid jobs. This discussion accelerated with the women's movement in the 1970s and was later named the "second shift" in sociologist Arlie Hochschild's book by the same title.[122]

Regardless of the cross-cutting political interpretations of the Marvin case, the plaintiff and her attorney certainly framed their legal effort as a feminist cause. Michelle Triola portrayed herself as a champion of women's liberation, in part to buck the image that she was "an old-fashioned gold digger."[123] Triola said, "I am proud to have paved the way for other unmarried women."[124] She told talk show host Tom Snyder, "If you had relationships that took a man away from the job market for seven years there'd be a *law*."[125] Marvin Mitchelson depicted the case as a tool for gender equality. Homemakers, he argued, would be recognized as equal contributors in their relationships and would henceforth be entitled to a fair division of the couple's property. In a column he wrote for the *Chicago Tribune* in 1981, Mitchelson explained that "true independence" for women can only be attained through economic parity secured through legal agreements.[126]

Popular culture used the Marvin case as a reference point into the 1980s. For example, palimony formed the basis of an episode of the highly successful television comedy *The Love Boat*. Creators of *The Love Boat* structured every episode around multiple storylines, each with their own title and team of writers. In an episode that aired on April 5, 1980, the story "The High Cost of Loving" was based on the Lee Marvin scandal. The episode opens with a man identified as Mr. Massey (played by Steve Kanaly) talking with his attorney before boarding the ship for a weeklong cruise. The attorney warns him not to take the trip. "That Lee Marvin decision?" he intones. "Murder for wealthy guys like you." The attorney admonishes him, "After all, the court made you pay off your last live-in girlfriend almost half a million bucks!" Massey assures his lawyer that it will not happen again, but the lawyer hands him a file and says "just in case." He warns him, "before you even shake hands with a girl be sure she signs one of these releases freeing you of any legal obligations." The reference to "that Lee Marvin" decision nearly a year after the initial ruling of $104,000 makes plain the cultural power of the case.

The episode places Massey in a series of situations that test his pledge to his attorney. In each, the fear of palimony either subverts Massey's sexual desires or drives women away from him. In one scene, he stares at six women doing a calisthenic routine led by the ship's cruise director, Julie. The camera shots alternate back and forth between, on the one hand, Massey staring at the women and, on the other, women bending over to do a toe-touching exercise. The camera zooms in a little bit with each alternation to suggest his intensifying lust of the bikini-clad women. He gives a look of frustration, pointedly turns his head away from the women, and pulls out a $460,000 receipt from his last palimony case to remind him of the financial perils of romance and to quell his sexual desire. In another scene, Angela, a blonde white woman in a blue bikini, emerges from a Jacuzzi. She introduces herself to Massey and asks him to dry her back. Angela tells

Massey that she teaches at a boys' school and has been in quarantine for six weeks because of a measles outbreak. She says, "I really like men. I've been locked up a long time, so I came aboard to catch up on some serious socializing." At the juice bar, Angela propositions Massey: "Let's play. Your court or mine?" Massey asks her, "Would you mind signing a form? Just a little piece of paper. It's not for me. It's for my lawyer." She tells him to hurry. Massey walks to his cabin to retrieve the form but, when he returns, he finds Angela embracing and kissing another man in the Jacuzzi. The next set piece of the story unfurls a similar scenario. In a booth at the ship's restaurant, Massey embraces a woman and asks her to his cabin. "One little thing," he says. "I have something I'd like you to sign first." She looks incredulous: "You want me to sign something?" "It's nothing," he reassures her, but when he turns to grab a pen from his coat, she slinks away. The story depends on, not only the audience's awareness of palimony and the Marvin case, but their amused pity for the man's struggles to find sexual companionship on litigious turf.

Another scene underscores the societal implications of palimony and the Marvin ruling, and the alleged threat gold diggers pose to men and norms of masculinity. Massey congregates at one of the ship's poolside bars with Isaac (the bartender) and Adam (the ship's doctor). Isaac comments on the number of "good looking ladies" on the ship and tells Massey that he ought to "be out there socializing." He responds, "The only friendships I can be interested in are with men." Isaac and the ship's doctor look to him with shock from the suspicion that he is revealing himself to be gay. "Oh?" they inquire, followed by laugh track. "No, you don't understand," he says. "You see, men are decent. What you see is what you get. But them." He points to the women lounging by the pool. "Look closely. Each one of them has this invisible wire pulling you right into the courtroom. They should be forced to wear price tags just like everything else you have to pay for." The doctor offers a comforting cliché that "the best things in life are free." "Free?" Massey asks, and then shows the two men a cancelled check for $460,000: "This is what I had to pay my last girlfriend." He tells the men that he keeps the check near him to remind him that there are "other things in life besides girls." Isaac observes, "If guys start giving up girls, we're going to be out of business." At the personal level, the threat of palimony strains Massey's heterosexuality. His legal need for homosocial companionship in order to avoid litigious women throws his sexuality, however briefly, into questionable terrain. At the societal level, Isaac's observation about the potential chilling effect of palimony underscores a panic about the destabilizing effect of law, specifically women using the law in courtship, in the romantic economy. The episode shows how, continuing into the 1980s, representations of palimony in popular culture constructed the gold digger as a personal and social menace.

During the 1980s, both Michelle Triola and Marvin Mitchelson tried to move on with their lives after the Superior Court's decision. Mitchelson unsuccessfully sought to recoup his financial losses by suing Lee Marvin for $500,000 for court costs on the premise that the case was in the public interest. Triola appeared on a few television game shows and began work on a memoir.[127] In 1980, Triola told the *Los Angeles Times* that "she has found a new life as an author, lecturer on women's rights and—most importantly—as a 'survivor.'" Beverly Hills police arrested her later that year for shoplifting from a department store. She was fined and placed on probation.[128] Following Lee Marvin's successful appeal of the $104,000 ruling against him, the plaintiff attempted to take her cause to the California Supreme Court, but the court refused to consider the case.[129] In October 1981, after nearly a decade of court action, the case finally reached its conclusion. Although Mitchelson never won a single palimony suit, he used the publicity surrounding the Marvin trial to obtain new clients. By the late 1980s, Mitchelson was, according to the *New York Times*, "arguably the most famous lawyer in the world."[130] Marvin Mitchelson was not shy about showing off his wealth, as exposed in his expensive suits, fleet of luxury automobiles, $5 million mansion, and in-office Jacuzzi. But trouble followed his success. Years of cocaine abuse and professional negligence led to multiple tax liens and investigations by the IRS and the State Bar of California. In 1979, *Cosmopolitan* described Mitchelson as "something of a knight-errant for women," and noted he "really does view himself as a feminist."[131] Yet, by the early 1990s, no fewer than eight women accused Mitchelson of rape, including former palimony clients. His embrace of the women's rights movement was a predatory ploy to hide his greed and misogyny. He was never tried for sexual assault but, in 1993, authorities convicted Mitchelson on charges of felony tax fraud for failing to report over $2 million in income. He spent thirty months in prison in Lompoc, California.[132]

· · · · · ·

At least twenty Marvin-style lawsuits had been adjudicated by 1978, with some states aligning their rulings with the California Supreme Court and others affirming traditional property laws. Meanwhile, different state legislatures made efforts to prevent their state judicial systems from adopting the palimony standard. Representatives in Illinois, for example, introduced a bill that would have required couples who lived together to have a written contract in order to receive post-separation support; implied contracts, as supported in the *Marvin* ruling, would be legally unenforceable. In California, Alfred Song unsuccessfully introduced a bill intended to create a legislative end run around the Marvin decision. Song's bill would have prohibited a court from considering whether an unmarried couple was cohabitating. It would have enforced a presumption that unmarried couples intended to keep their property separate. During a hearing for the bill, Marvin Mitchelson countered that Song's legislation was an "unrealistic giant step back toward the Dark Ages."[133]

As Elizabeth Pleck, Lawrence Friedman, and others have shown, the legal and substantive impact of Lee Marvin's legal ordeal was relatively modest. The ruling did not remake divorce law in the way that critics feared. It did not lead to a flood of litigation among dissatisfied unmarried couples, nor did it bolster women's rights. The distance between the impact of the case and its colorful, anxiety-provoking publicity meant that the trial of Lee Marvin was more important as a story about gold diggers and litigation. The Marvin trial mirrored a growing concern with frivolous lawsuits and a perceived expansion of the law into domains where it did not belong. Observers projected their complaints and fears about the legal system onto the case, all the while unwittingly exaggerating the impact of the litigation on their own lives. The trial was legally inconsequential, but its cultural importance left a powerful imprint. The conflict between Triola and Marvin allowed for a distillation and projection about demographic changes that shook up American marriages. Public discourse about the trial, and the rhetoric about gender and social class that constructed Michelle Triola as a gold digger, was a cultural way to come to terms with structural change in the 1970s. The expansionist perspective of gender equality cultivated a legal approach that viewed couples as business partners, not as individuals held together by religious, familial, or state-sanctioned bonds. The heart of the *Marvin* case, the claims about an implied promise, was about a breach of contract as much as it was about something resembling marriage. The ordeal of Lee Marvin and Michelle Triola foreshadowed the legal and political dimensions of marriage in the 1980s. As Alison Lefkovitz explains, "By the mid-1980s, state legislators were taking an individualist, even neoliberal, approach to family obligations."[134] The next chapter explores the connection between neoliberalism and the gold digger construct in the late twentieth century.

5 Material Girls

Marilyn Monroe's gold digger archetype moved into the 1980s and '90s with boundless vitality. Madonna, Anna Nicole Smith, and others took up the mantle of Marilyn Monroe and gave the gold digger renewed energy appropriate for the late twentieth century. Madonna's song "Material Girl" attained massive worldwide success after appearing on her 1984 album *Like a Virgin,* and it reached number two on the Billboard Hot 100 in the United States. The music video mimicked Marilyn Monroe's 1953 performance of "Diamonds Are a Girl's Best Friend" in *Gentlemen Prefer Blondes.* In the video, Madonna, like Monroe, wears a pink strapless dress with matching pink arm-length gloves and sings about her love of wealth. The video's set mirrors Monroe's, replete with dancing men in tuxedoes flanking her performance. The lyrics of "Material Girl," what Prieto-Arranz calls "a hymn to materialism," reflect the self-conscious greed of the 1980s and the raw pursuit of luxury.[1] She croons about her rejection of the boys who make a pass at her, saving her attention only for the "boys who save their pennies."[2] Yet, the "Material Girl" music video tells a story that contradicts the message of the lyrics. In the video, she rejects the gifts the men offer her and, in the end, she falls in love with a rich man who appears to be poor. In an unconscious nod to *How to Marry a Millionaire,* Madonna is rewarded for her embrace of true love over material wealth.

"Material Girl" was emblematic of the cultural and economic climate of the 1980s, and scholars have vigorously debated its meaning and importance. Some have used the video to draw a contrast between Monroe and Madonna, noting Monroe's victimization and Madonna's power and agency. Nonetheless, the broad lines of the academic discussion of "Material Girl" replicated the debate about *Gentlemen Prefer Blondes* and the male gaze. Wakako Masuda argues that Madonna's video reverses patriarchal gender roles because the protagonist functions as the wealth object that men pursue instead of the other way around. Before becoming a fierce critic of Madonna, Camille Paglia contended that Madonna was a true feminist for using her sexuality to retain control over her life. For Georges-Claude Guilbert, Madonna is a quintessential postmodern figure. The "Material Girl" video satirizes and plays with sexuality, engages in postmodern strategies like pastiche, and routinely undercuts the reality of its purported message. Like other representations of gold diggers, Madonna's "Material Girl" was a flexible text onto which its viewers, academic and otherwise, could project varied arguments, ideologies, and pleasures.[3]

Madonna released the "Material Girl" video during the height of the so-called Greed Decade, a decade marked by corporate malfeasance, deep welfare cuts, and an expanding gap between the rich and poor. Accounts of the era tend to focus on the agency and notorious personalities of white-collar criminals like Ivan Boesky and Michael Milken. Yet, the shift in wealth was widespread and beyond the control and strategies of junk bond profiteers and corporate raiders. During the 1980s, the richest fifth of the population increased their collective wealth by $25 billion while the bottom fifth lost about $6 billion.[4] Structural economic transformations coincided with, and drew strength from, an ethos that put the acquisition of wealth above all else. Economic changes in the 1980s—the continuation of a large-scale shift from manufacturing to an economy based on services, the liquidity of capital, and the expansion of communication technology—created qualitatively new instruments for economic growth and exploitation. At the same time, conspicuous consumption embodied in the "yuppie" social type eroded the communitarian and antimaterialist impulses of the 1960s and '70s.

The declining power of organized labor, the deregulation of industry, and the dismantling of state welfare policies—changes captured in the concept "neoliberalism"—remade the United States. Neoliberalism is an expansive concept but, at its core, it describes the simultaneous retreat of state regulation and the expanding power of economic markets to shape public and private life. Despite the fact that many of these changes were scarcely felt by Americans in the early 1980s, all sectors of society experienced the effects of neoliberalism even if the individuals involved lacked the sociological vocabulary to account for it. David Harvey isolates the years 1979 and 1980 as a possible "revolutionary turning-point in the world's social and economic history."[5] The changes Paul Volcker made to the U.S. Federal Reserve in 1979, and the election of Ronald Reagan in 1980, set in motion cataclysmic shifts to the world economy and its institutions. These transformations were not just hardwired into political economic structures, and they were not simply the result of historical inertia; they were created and accelerated by culture, propaganda, and other elements in the realm of ideology. Changes occurring in the political economy were propelled by complicated ideological work that pitted a quasi-religious faith in the free market against folk devils and stereotypes like the "Welfare Queen" and "white trash." The cultural work of the gold digger image, and the trajectory of women labeled as gold diggers during the 1980s and '90s, needs to be seen in this context.

Critiques of greed and materialism, and accounts of wrongdoing and corruption stemming from economic and political elites abusing their power, appeared in several media outlets during the 1980s.[6] Nonetheless, ideological production in the United States tended to displace anxiety about economic excess onto members of the lower class and African Americans. The promulgators of white-collar deviance faced their share of scorn, but some of the anger about economic inequality and the state of the country were directed at twin cultural constructs that reflected the racial, class, and gender anxiety of the age: the Welfare Queen and white trash. Stories about Welfare Queens and white trash caused a public misrecognition of economic circumstances and worked to justify moves to restrict public assistance. As Harvey explains, under neoliberalism, the successes and failures of individuals are increasingly interpreted "in terms of entrepreneurial virtues or personal failings" instead of being a result of structural or systemic conditions. Accordingly, in mass media and political culture, blame for the perceived problems of greed were moved onto those who lacked political and economic power.[7]

The Welfare Queen of the 1980s has its origins in Ronald Reagan's presidential campaign in the late 1970s. Like the concerns about Allotment Annies during World War II, Americans accused Welfare Queens of using fraud to get money they did not earn. On campaign stops, Reagan worked the Welfare Queen into his speeches, playing on gender and racial prejudices to characterize the public benefits system as enriching the undeserving. In a stop in New Hampshire in 1976, he referred to "a woman in Chicago" collecting welfare (and Medicaid and food stamps) under eighty assumed names. Reagan stated that she gained tax-free income in excess of $150,000 a year. Reagan used reporting from the *Chicago Tribune* about Linda Taylor, a woman charged with defrauding Illinois welfare programs, to construct the Welfare Queen stereotype. Reagan considerably distorted the details of her case in order to make a sustained attack on welfare policy and to gin up resentment against the poor. According to historian Julilly Kohler-Hausmann, "Ronald Reagan seized on the caricature, stripped it of its context and peculiarity, and gave it national visibility." The Welfare Queen was a late twentieth-century folk devil full of gender, race, and class meaning.[8]

The Welfare Queen, like the gold digger, acted as a shorthand for flaws in law and public policy. Although the actual race of Linda Taylor was ambiguous, the way in which Reagan talked about her contained unmistakable racial signifiers. The debate about welfare in the 1980s revolved around racial stereotypes and images of African American family dysfunction, even though data show that African Americans were in the minority of welfare recipients. Ange-Marie Hancock argues that the Welfare Queen was more than a simple stereotype. Rather, it was a "public identity" used for the advancement of apparently neutral public policy goals. Concretizing the Welfare Queen image during his presidency, Reagan gave a name to "long-standing beliefs regarding single, poor African American mothers."[9]

Like the Welfare Queen, the social category "white trash" did significant ideological work during the 1980s and '90s. It crafted the boundaries of social respectability, marked the deserving from the undeserving, and performed a cultural sleight of hand that highlighted personal failing to obscure structural antecedents. The category "white trash" has a long history that stretches back to the 1850s. The category of white trash demarcated rigid class lines and designated those who fell into the group as dangerous, contagious, and licentious. White trash denoted class instability and racial polarization; white trash were downtrodden, but they defined themselves against both African Americans and white elites. The category refers to a racial and class location, but it also captures a constellation of cultural practices. After World War II, the stereotype took its modern shape, with characteristics that included living in a trailer, eating fatty foods, and sexual promiscuity. During the development of Johnson's Great Society programs, the cultural construct of "white trash" delineated the deserving from the undeserving poor.[10]

The gold digger in the 1980s and '90s needs to be understood alongside the Welfare Queen and white trash stereotypes. Both the Welfare Queen and gold digger are gendered stereotypes that perform ideological work in the advanced capitalist era. Like the Welfare Queen, the gold digger abuses an unequal exchange relationship where she gains money that she does not deserve. Whereas the gold digger exploits a single man or set of men, the Welfare Queen takes advantage of the state and abuses a slew of taxpayers. The gold digger is also similar to white trash because both lack the cultural capital required for respectability, and sometimes the stereotypes explicitly overlap.[11] The mixture of white trash and gold digger creates a potent cultural construct that fuses racial and social class into something more than the sum of its basic parts. The concept of white trash, whose existence solidifies and justifies class distinctions based on illusions of deservedness, reinforces the core elements of the gold digger, a woman whose sexuality makes a constant—but failing—purchase on class-based respectability. Working together, the two stereotypes create a figure of tremendous inter-sectional weight and complexity. In this context, it is not surprising that Anna Nicole Smith, regarded by many as the epitome of a white trash gold digger, dominated the media landscape in the late twentieth and early twenty-first centuries.

The Koch Brothers and the Rise of Anna Nicole Smith

Think tanks and other instruments and institutions of ideological produc-tion during the 1980s and 1990s greased the move toward radical free mar-ket dominance. Yet, the ground-level push for a blend of conservative and libertarian policies occurred decades before the full realization of neolib-eralism. Organizations like the John Birch Society, created in 1958, protested a communist danger discerned in every corner of American political and social life. Men of extreme wealth, including the candy manufacturer Rob-ert Welch and the oil and cattle tycoon Fred Koch, heavily funded the John Birch Society during the late 1950s and 1960s. Koch played a crucial role in promoting conservative free market ideals, using his wealth to finance his political goals. Fred's company, Koch Industries, grew from innovative oil extraction and refinery techniques. Ironically, the company made enormous profits early in its history by collaborating with Stalin and the Soviet Union. Yet, Fred Koch's experiences in the Soviet Union made him a lifelong anti-communist agitator, and he learned to distrust most forms of government, especially state intervention into private economic activity. In 1960, Koch used his fortune to print over two million copies of his self-published book, *A Business Man Looks at Communism*, which claimed that communists had infiltrated public education, labor unions, modern art, and both the Demo-cratic and Republican parties.[12]

Two of Koch's four sons, Charles and David, carried on the legacy of their father's political and corporate vision, building Koch Industries into the sec-ond largest private company in America. The Koch brothers (as they were often called) were educated in a radical version of neoliberal, free market, and libertarian ideals. Charles Koch was particularly well versed in laissez-faire political and economic theory. He resigned from the John Birch Soci-ety in 1968 and found a renewed purpose in the Freedom School, a fringe group with Bircher leanings, but one with a more radical perspective on

American history, economics, and human nature.[13] At the Freedom School, Charles Koch immersed himself in the philosophies of Austrian laissez-faire economists Ludwig von Mises and Friedrich Hayek. The Koch brothers sought to put their libertarian ideals into action, funding think tanks and organizations like the Cato Institute, the Center for Libertarian Studies, and the Institute for Humane Studies. Jane Mayer explains, "As their fortunes grew, Charles and David Koch became the primary underwriters of hard-line libertarian politics in America."[14] They played a vital role in the Tea Party movement in the 2010s and emerged as a formidable force shaping twenty-first-century U.S. elections.

By 2009, Charles and David Koch were each worth an estimated $14 billion.[15] Much of the Koch Industries fortune grew from a strategic partnership they formed with Texas oil mogul J. Howard Marshall II. In 1959, as Fred Koch was writing his book about the dangers of communism, he purchased a 35 percent interest in the Great Northern Oil Company. Located in Rosemount, Minnesota, the refinery processed about 40,000 barrels a day of Canadian crude oil. Investment in Great Northern propelled the Koch family fortune. The purchase also solidified a business relationship between the Koch family and J. Howard Marshall II, an accomplished oil tycoon who cofounded the refinery in 1954. After his father's death in 1967, Charles approached Marshall with a plan to exchange Koch Industries stock for the majority share in Great Northern (renamed the Pine Bend Refinery). Charles said, "I generally do not like partners, but Howard Marshall is an exception." Marshall returned the praise, recalling, "Charles had all of his father's ability plus some."[16] Marshall was one of a select few who sat on the board of trustees for Koch Industries.

In 1980, J. Howard Marshall helped Charles thwart a corporate coup by Frederick and Bill Koch. The incident is important because it hardened the competing alliances between members of the Koch and Marshall families. Bill Koch wanted the company to have greater liquidity, and the Koch Industry practice of investing profits immediately back into the company did not leave him the money to which he felt entitled. Also, Bill expressed concerns that Charles was leading the company in troublesome directions. Toward the end of the 1970s, the company faced investigations by the Department of Energy and the Internal Revenue Service (IRS), creating the potential for looming civil penalties, and the possibility of criminal prosecutions, on the horizon. If Bill and Frederick could rally enough stakeholders in the company, they could wrest control from Charles and David and correct the wayward path of Koch Industries. J. Howard Marshall's son,

Pierce Marshall, sided with David and Charles, so Frederick and Bill tried to enlist the help of J. Howard Marshall's other son, J. Howard Marshall III, to try to dissolve the board of directors and take the company public. Pierce and J. Howard Marshall III each owned 4.1 percent of Koch Industries, a gift of stock that the elder Marshall gave them on the occasion of their respective marriages. J. Howard Marshall learned about the attempted takeover. With less than a week before the scheduled shareholders meeting where Bill and Frederick intended to complete their plan, J. Howard Marshall flew to Los Angeles to confront his son. He bought his son's shares of Koch Industries at an inflated rate, and tipped the balance of power back to Charles and David Koch. When he returned to Houston, J. Howard Marshall cut his namesake out of his will, a decision that, years later, drove J. Howard Marshall III into an alliance with Anna Nicole Smith against his brother Pierce Marshall.[17]

The aftermath of the attempted corporate coup strengthened Pierce Marshall's association with the Koch brothers. By the late 1990s, however, their business relationship strained under the weight of complex litigation. Former fashion model Anna Nicole Smith, who was married to J. Howard Marshall for fourteen months before his death, sat within striking distance of the Koch Industries wealth. According to a writer for the London *Independent*, "The corporate house that Marshall built, Koch Industries, is little short of panicked at the idea that a provincial nobody, with little to recommend her apart from her studied physical resemblance to Jayne Mansfield and her silicone-enhanced breasts, might soon hold a significant interest in its stock and, conceivably, be clamoring for a seat on its board."[18] The preeminent gold digger of the late twentieth century, Anna Nicole Smith, faced off against the promulgators and primary beneficiaries of neoliberalism in the United States. Understanding Anna Nicole's story can tell us about the cultural life of neoliberalism. Her rise and fall illustrate how the gold digger stereotype connects to the political, economic, and legal conditions of the late twentieth and early twenty-first centuries.

Typical accounts of Anna Nicole Smith's stardom begin with her squalid childhood and poor Southern roots. Details of her struggles serve as an ineffaceable part of her persona, and they accentuate her later celebrity and serve to rationalize her downfall. Vickie Lynn Hogan, who later changed her name to Anna Nicole Smith, was born in 1967.[19] She lived in Mexia, Texas, with her aunt. A 1993 article in *People* described how Smith's aunt gave her five dollars in food stamps to buy candy in exchange for helping clean her house.[20] Smith reportedly stole toilet paper from a local restaurant because her aunt could not afford to buy any.[21] Later in her life, Smith said that she "didn't have a childhood" and, like her idol Marilyn Monroe, she had a troubled relationship with her mother.[22] She also had a tough time finding friends and feeling comfortable in school. Anna Nicole Smith dropped out of high school and became a server at a fried chicken restaurant. She met her first husband, Billy Wayne Smith, working at Jim's Krispy Fried Chicken, and Smith married him in 1985 at the age of seventeen. A year later, she gave birth to her son Daniel and divorced Billy Wayne. Billy Wayne claimed that two core elements of her public image flowered in her late teens: her gold digging and promiscuity. He said, "Anna liked to spend a lot of money. She would go out and buy fancy clothes and make-up a lot, probably a bit too often because she would ask me for my money when hers was spent." Billy Wayne claimed, "She's a gold digger and everyone in this town knows it." Wayne alleged that Smith cheated on him with other men just weeks after they were married: "She was seeing guys every time she had the chance."[23] According to Smith, Wayne was abusive, a charge he only halfheartedly denied.[24]

Following her divorce, Smith moved to Houston to be near her family. She failed to find steady work, so she applied for a job as a nude dancer at a men's club called Rick's Plaza. According to her half sister Donna Hogan, Smith acquired the job with aspirations of furthering her gold digging. She said, "Anna began to boast to friends that she would soon land a wealthy man."[25] She worked at Rick's off and on for three years, but the owner refused to give her work during the more lucrative evening shift. His hesitance was allegedly because of Smith's relatively flat chest and her tendency to drink on the job.[26] In 1991, Smith used the money she had saved to purchase breast implants and found work at another strip club called Gigi's Cabaret. Again, the manager relegated her to the day shift. The daytime work schedule, however, turned into the opportunity of a lifetime.

Anna Nicole Smith's second husband, J. Howard Marshall, was an accomplished legal scholar and sharklike investor. He graduated magna cum laude from Yale Law School in 1931. With a brilliant grasp of law and finance, he served as the assistant dean of the Yale Law School from 1931 to 1933. During that time, he produced scholarship in an emerging field known as legal realism. Legal realism, which developed in the 1920s, dialogued with social scientific methods and theories to consider the influence of law on society and culture. It challenged formalistic approaches to law in favor of utilitarian methods of legal reasoning. At Yale, Marshall learned about a 1931 case, Champlin Reining Company v. Oklahoma Corporation Commission, which concerned the federal regulation of state oil production.[27] This case sparked a lifelong interest in the economic and legal aspects of the oil industry, and prompted him to leave the academic world for government and private positions in the oil business. From 1933 until the early 1950s, Marshall worked as the legal counsel to the president of Standard Oil, helped develop U.S. energy policy during World War II as head attorney for the Petroleum Administration for War, and assumed leadership positions at major oil companies, including Ashland Oil and Refining Company (now Ashland Inc.) and Allied Signal (now Honeywell). Marshall's life took a new turn in 1961. He moved to Houston, divorced his wife Eleanor Pierce, and married Bettye Bohannon.[28] In Houston, Marshall also connected with his old friend Fred Koch, whom he knew from his time in Washington, D.C. Marshall learned that Koch had made a fortune through the invention of a new gasoline refining process and Marshall wanted to strike a deal with him. Marshall made a stock trade with Koch—"the best deal I ever made," according to Marshall—giving him a 16 percent stake in Koch Industries.[29] According to some estimates, J. Howard Marshall held over a billion dollars in assets by the early 1990s.[30]

Before Anna Nicole Smith came into his life, J. Howard Marshall met with his mistress, Jewell DiAnne "Lady" Walker, at least three days a week. Marshall's relationship with "Lady Walker" (as she was known in the Houston society press) is significant because it foreshadowed the legal problems he encountered with Smith and typified his financially indulgent habits on women with whom he was infatuated. Toward the end of 1982, as Jerry Reed's song about an unfair alimony award, "She Got the Goldmine (I Got the Shaft)," topped the country music charts, Marshall met and fell in love with Lady Walker.[31] Prior to their relationship, Walker's fourth husband moved out of state and left her with three children to raise and scant financial support. At the age of forty-two, Lady Walker took a job as a topless dancer at the Chic Lounge strip club in Houston. Marshall met Walker at the club and she gave him a private dance. In his own words, Marshall "was blinded by love" and, within weeks, he purchased her a Cadillac El Dorado, a new house, and a diamond ring.[32] J. Howard Marshall spent approximately $2 million a year on Lady Walker, and she eventually owned an impressive jewelry collection and three Rolls-Royce automobiles.[33] According to a writer for *Texas Monthly*, "that she soaked him financially, with an enthusiasm and artistry bordering on brilliance, is indisputable."[34] Lady Walker became ensconced in the Houston social scene and she gained a reputation as a sophisticated socialite.[35] Marshall's many love notes to Walker gushed with adoration and passion. He said that he wanted to marry her, but feared that divorcing his wife, who suffered from Alzheimer's disease, would kill her. Marshall, indeed, never had the opportunity to marry Lady Walker. She died in July 1991 at the age of fifty-one due to complications from cosmetic facial surgery, and Marshall's wife Bettye died two months later.[36]

The deaths of his mistress Lady Walker and his wife Bettye rushed Marshall headlong into depression. Making matters worse, Marshall discovered that Lady Walker had cheated on him during their entire ten-year relationship. She left most of her $5.8 million estate to her children Cerece and Starr, but she also left a truck, $30,000, and a diamond bracelet to her lover, Dale Clem. News of Lady Walker's infidelity spurred J. Howard Marshall into action. He teamed up with his son Pierce to sue Lady Walker's heirs (and some of her friends) in an effort to recover the riches he had bestowed upon her during the previous decade. Journalist Mimi Swartz convincingly speculates that Marshall was aware of Walker's affairs, but was attempting to recover money in an effort to address looming IRS problems resulting from unreported gifts.[37] Marshall also sued her private jeweler for usury, a suit that dragged on long after J. Howard Marshall's death.[38] Marshall's legal action against Lady Walker's heirs froze their assets, and they were unable to pay taxes on the properties Marshall had given her. From this advantageous position, Marshall pressured Lady Walker's children to settle the case in 1993. They kept two houses and her jewelry, but Marshall recovered most of the money and Lady Walker's fleet of luxury automobiles.[39] By the time the legal conflict with Lady Walker's heirs had resolved, Marshall was dating, and spending enormous sums of money on, another young woman.

When J. Howard Marshall met Anna Nicole at Gigi's Cabaret in October 1991, he was eighty-six years old and she was twenty-four. Smith developed a relationship with Marshall initially through her topless dancing and personalized attention. Emotionally vulnerable, he bonded with Smith in his quest for comfort and companionship and she, too, immediately benefited from the union. During one of their first lunch dates, Marshall gave her an envelope with a thousand dollars in cash and told her she should quit her job at Gigi's. Marshall paid for country club visits, stays in hotel rooms, and expensive jewelry. He began sending her $2,000 checks every two weeks.[40] He called Smith "the light of his life" and told his attorney Harvey Sorensen that he wanted to marry her.[41] According to Smith, Marshall proposed to marry her repeatedly, each time offering a large engagement ring. On one occasion, Christmas Eve of 1993, Marshall purchased a $107,000 diamond ring for Smith from Neiman Marcus, one of the largest purchases in the store's history.[42] Smith steadfastly declined his marriage proposals. Years later, her attorney referred to her frequent refusals of his marriage offers as proof that she was not a gold digger. Tom Cunningham, her attorney, said, "They will say she is a gold digger, but gold diggers don't wait." Yet, Donna Hogan (Anna Nicole's half sister) speculated that she put off the marriage proposals in order to put her hooks more deeply into Marshall. She said Anna "waited three years before giving in and did everything in her power to make him rewrite his will and abandon any form of prenuptial agreement."[43] Her observation was not entirely accurate. According to documents uncovered during the discovery phase of the litigation over Marshall's will and estate, Marshall commanded his attorneys to create a prenuptial agreement that included a generous provision for Smith. He also sought to change his will in order to give Smith half of the wealth he earned during their time together. On December 22, 1992, Marshall directed his legal team to draft a prenuptial agreement, a catchall trust designed to give Smith a large donation, and a corporation for Smith's business. These legal moves worried his youngest son, Pierce Marshall. Pierce conferred with his father's lead attorney over his growing concern that Anna Nicole Smith was after his family's wealth.

Anna Nicole Smith's life and career reached unimaginable heights after she met J. Howard Marshall. In late 1991, soon after she quit Gigi's, she did test shots for *Playboy* magazine. In February 1992, she divorced Billy Smith and, the following month, she debuted on the cover of *Playboy*. In May 1992, *Playboy* featured her as a centerfold, earning her the title of Playmate of the Month and $20,000. A Houston modeling agency once told her that she would never find work as a model because she was "too big, too busty, and too blond."[44] But George Marciano saw Smith's *Playboy* photos and arranged for her to pose for some test shots for his brother Paul, the cofounder of Guess. At the time, she had never heard of Guess or Marciano. She told *People* magazine that she did not know what Guess jeans were because she "shopped at Wal-Mart and Kmart and stuff like that."[45]

Smith's photo shoot for Guess exuded allure and sophistication, and it astounded Marciano. "I couldn't believe what I was seeing," he said. "She gave me a hundred different looks." Her first test shot, one that played on her rural roots, featured Smith in a red-and-white checkered shirt, leaning against stacked hay bales, and holding a piece of straw in her open mouth. Marciano was so awestruck by the photograph that he used it for multiple international magazine advertisements. She was, in the words of journalist Andrew Gumbel, "a tall, voluptuous role model for retro vamps." Smith accepted the three-year contract offered by Guess, replacing supermodel Claudia Schiffer. Marciano also persuaded Smith to change her name from Vickie Lynn to Anna Nicole. The name change reflected a larger tension in the social construction of Smith's iconicity. Her background, a girl "plucked from Texas working-class obscurity," gave her story a comforting rags-to-riches narrative. As a high school dropout, former fast food worker, and single mom, she left her white trash origins to find international fame. Her impoverished background, however, threatened to undo the high-class and cultured image created by the Guess advertising team.[46]

The photos Smith took for Guess became legendary. Smith's strong resemblance to Marilyn Monroe was undeniable, a fact that Guess was quick to emphasize. Writing in 1993, Skip Hollandsworth from *Texas Monthly* commented on Smith, then twenty-five years old: "No one, it seems, can look at this unschooled, uncultured small-town girl without wondering whether she might turn into the next Marilyn Monroe." Shot in black and white, the photos deliberately conjured 1950s Hollywood and the pinup aesthetic. In one, Smith appeared leaning against a bare tree trunk, looking outward with a smoldering glare, her hair curled and piled high, holding a cigarette with her right hand. In another, reminiscent of a publicity still for Monroe's *Bus Stop*, Smith appears with her mouth open, her hand splayed against the side of her face, with her pinky finger poised between her teeth. A writer for the *Vancouver Sun* noted in 1992 that Smith's fame as a Guess model "defies all old agency standards."[47] The fashion industry in the early 1990s embraced the "waif look" that emphasized thinness and youth. Epitomized by the thin appearance of supermodel Kate Moss, the fashion industry increasingly moved away from models like Claudia Schiffer and Cindy Crawford who looked mature, tall, and healthy.[48] The Guess advertising campaign featuring Smith marked a bold departure from the fashion status quo and cemented Smith's star stature. The following year, 1993, Smith appeared in *Playboy* and was once again named Playmate of the Year.

In 1994, Anna Nicole Smith finally accepted J. Howard Marshall's marriage proposal. A month before the wedding, the couple had a "pre-honeymoon" in Bali. For Smith's half sister, Donna Hogan, the overseas trip was "one last chance at buttering him up."[49] The couple married on June 27, 1994, at the White Dove Wedding Chapel in Houston. She was aware of how the union appeared to outsiders and insisted to the owner of the chapel, "I'm not marrying him for his money."[50] The wedding was a small affair, attended by J. Howard's secretary, one of his nurses, and Smith's aunt and uncle. Notably, Pierce Marshall was not invited.[51]

FIGURE 15 Anna Nicole Smith, mid-1990s. Smith gained stardom as a model, Playboy playmate, and actor, but she was best known for marrying an eighty-six-year-old multimillionaire when she was twenty-four years old. Courtesy of PhotoFest.

Several sources reported on Anna Nicole Smith's cruelty toward her husband during their short marriage. According to many accounts, Smith's mistreatment of her husband occurred immediately after the marriage ceremony when, at the reception, Anna announced that she planned to leave for Greece for a photo shoot, leaving her husband crying in his wheelchair. "Please don't *cwy*," she purportedly told him.[52] When she returned, she avoided spending time with Marshall and, during their first six months of marriage, they were together only about two weeks. According to Pierce, "She worked hard to avoid being with my father but managed to call him constantly demanding more and more money."[53] Smith complained to *Playboy* talent scout D'eva Redding that she hated eating meals with Marshall because she had to spoon feed him and it was "nauseating" to watch him eat. According to Marshall's nurse, his life with Anna Nicole was "long, lonely, frustrating, and miserable."[54] She refused to sleep in the same bed with him because of his incontinence, a fact with which she cruelly taunted him. In Marshall's presence, she flirted with other men and flaunted her affairs, particularly with her bodyguard Pierre DeJean.[55] Other reports charged that Smith endangered Marshall's health on several occasions by improperly feeding him chicken soup such that he began choking, feeding him undercooked bacon that made him ill, and stranding him in the rain in his wheelchair on a cold December evening. During the rare times when they were together, Smith ran a video recorder and encouraged him to proclaim his desire to leave his estate to her and to adopt her son Daniel. At one point, she told Marshall that he could adopt Daniel and rename him "J. Howard Marshall III," unaware or not caring that Marshall already had a son by the same name. Although Marshall showed signs of senility, Smith's attempts to manipulate him into saying something legally binding for the video recorder were largely unsuccessful.[56]

Anna Nicole Smith disputed accounts of her greed and mistreatment of him. She stated, "I really do care for my husband. I don't care what people say about me. I am not a gold digger." On another occasion, she claimed, "I have known him a long time and we are deeply in love." After his death, Smith publicly professed her love for J. Howard Marshall. She told Larry King in 2002, "I loved him very much." Years later, Smith's attorney Tom Cunningham described the relationship as weighty and full of meaning. He said, "This is not about a gold digger sucking money. This is about a relationship that was very profound."[57] Nevertheless, Marshall's family, members of the media, and even those close to Anna Nicole Smith expressed skepticism about the depth and authenticity of her love for her husband. The talent scouts for *Playboy* who discovered Anna Nicole Smith said, "We all knew she didn't love J. Howard despite all her protests to the contrary." Smith seemed to confirm the suspicions about her motives in an interview with Larry King. She told King that she never had any physical attraction to him. When King asked, "What did a twenty-three-year-old girl see in an eighty-six-year-old man?" she replied, "I saw a very sick man. Someone that was just really, really sick."[58]

During their fourteen-month marriage, J. Howard spent a staggering sum of money on Anna Nicole. An accountant for Pierce Marshall testified in probate court that Marshall gave Anna Nicole approximately $6.7 million in cash, jewelry, and real estate. Marshall bought her a $900,000 ranch in Tomball, Texas, and a $650,000 home in Los Angeles. At one point in their marriage, when J. Howard Marshall was ill, Anna Nicole took him from the hospital to accompany her on an hour-long shopping trip to Harry Winston in Beverley Hills. Harry Winston was the jeweler famously referred to in Marilyn Monroe's number "Diamonds Are a Girl's Best Friend" in the film *Gentlemen Prefer Blondes*. Smith bought four jewels worth over a million dollars. A nurse for J. Howard Marshall testified that he agreed to buy Smith expensive jewelry at Harry Winston only after Smith drugged him with Valium. Smith later called the nurse a "damn liar." Pierce Marshall blocked the payment and Harry Winston Inc. sued Smith to recover the money or the jewels.[59]

Marshall died on August 4, 1995, with an estimated wealth of nearly $2 billion.[60] His death launched a legal battle that produced over two million pages of documents and lasted over twenty-five years, long past the deaths of both Anna Nicole Smith and Pierce Marshall. As *The Sunday Mirror* put it, Smith "was plunged into a bitter 'gold-digger' lawsuit" following her husband's death.[61] The conflict between Pierce Marshall and Anna Nicole Smith was brutal from the very start. Smith insisted on burying Marshall in a pink marble tomb, but Pierce used his power of attorney to have his father cremated. A judicial decision was required for the final dispensation of the ashes, with Anna and Pierce each taking half.[62] Anna Nicole Smith organized a funeral where, adorned in her wedding gown and veil, she sang Bette Midler's hit song, "Wind Beneath My Wings." Pierce Marshall banned Smith from a separate, much more staid ceremony.[63]

Anna Nicole Smith's attorneys moved to secure J. Howard Marshall's money within three days of his death. Smith, under her legal name of Vickie Lynn Marshall, petitioned a Texas probate court to assert that her husband died without a will and, therefore, she was entitled to the entirety of his wealth. Pierce Marshall submitted his father's last will and testament to the probate court to prove that Smith was excluded from it. He also filed a counterclaim to affirm the legality of the will and trust. Pierce showed that Marshall omitted Smith from any claim on his estate. His will left nearly everything to Pierce. J. Howard Marshall III, the eldest son, was also cut out of Marshall's will in 1980 after he sided with Frederick and William Koch against Charles and David Koch in the dispute over the control of the Koch Industries board of directors. J. Howard Marshall III and Anna Nicole Smith briefly joined forces during the legal fight.[64]

Smith was excluded from the will, but she claimed that Pierce exerted "undue influence" over J. Howard Marshall. Before J. Howard Marshall's death, Pierce Marshall allegedly used dishonesty to persuade his father to change the terms of his will. According to Smith, Pierce pressured Marshall to exclude Anna from the will, barred her from spending time with her husband, and visited Marshall's attorney to amend the will twenty-four times. Initially, Marshall had a living, "catchall" trust, one where he could give property to certain beneficiaries at death without the need for probate, the legal process to prove the validity of the will in court. According to Smith, Pierce pressured Marshall to change his trust into an irrevocable one, a hardened legal arrangement immune to amendments and alterations. A Texas probate court considered Smith's case.[65]

A year later, a bizarre sequence of events allowed Smith to make a new run at J. Howard Marshall's wealth, raising complicated legal questions that required two trips to the U.S. Supreme Court to resolve. In August 1995, Smith's longtime housekeeper Maria Antonia Cerrato sued Smith for sexual harassment and won an $830,000 judgment. After an unsuccessful attempt to appeal, Smith assumed residency in California and declared bankruptcy. This move allowed her to make a fresh claim on her deceased husband's estate by moving the legal decision-making from Texas to California. Smith said that her preexisting entitlement to Marshall's money gave her the financial resources needed to avoid bankruptcy, and that the bankruptcy court could decide the matter of her claim to Marshall's wealth in making their decision. In the weighing of liabilities and assets, a potential asset was the expectation that she could receive money from her husband's estate. Pierce brought a claim against Smith in her bankruptcy case as a creditor, essentially making an argument that if the bankruptcy court relieved Smith of her debt, then he should be first in line to be paid because of her malfeasance in the Texas probate matter. Specifically, Pierce accused Smith of defamation for telling journalists that he had engaged in, among other things, fraud and forgery. Smith asserted "truth as a defense" to his charge of defamation, which meant that the bankruptcy court could consider the fraud, forgery, and other claims Smith levied against Marshall. The opportunity for a court to evaluate Pierce's wrongdoing is why some observers considered the defamation claim to be one of his major blunders in the protracted legal battle.[66] Smith also filed a counterclaim of tortious interference, meaning that Pierce hindered J. Howard Marshall from giving her a gift of half of his wealth.

The involvement of multiple state courts, as well as the staggering sums of money at stake, made it a federal case, but probate decisions were typically exempted from federal jurisdiction, something known as the "probate exception." Pierce's entry into the bankruptcy case gave Samuel Bufford, the bankruptcy judge in Los Angeles, California, jurisdiction over questions of Marshall's estate. In September 2000, the bankruptcy court awarded Smith $449 million, later increased to $474 million. The court found that Pierce falsified and destroyed documents to prevent Smith from rightfully gaining access to her deceased husband's wealth. A secret document, later called the "Fine Tuning Memo," revealed that Pierce gave instructions to his financial team to drain his father's assets and put them in Pierce's control. He also used deceptive accounting practices to prevent Smith from tracking her husband's finances.[67]

The Construction of Anna Nicole Smith as a Gold Digger

Pierce countersued and served Smith with a subpoena, compelling her to appear in Harris County Probate Court presided by judge Mike Wood. Anna Nicole Smith's 2001 appearance in the Texas probate court connected the constellation of legal questions surrounding the case—issues of wills, inheritance, bankruptcy, torts, and jurisdiction—to the gold digger trope. In the decades-long legal battle over J. Howard Marshall's wealth, the gold digger and white trash stereotypes emerged in the legal realm most forcefully during the probate trial. The legal proceedings in Mike Wood's court, and their ensuing publicity, reinforced the broad strokes of the gold digger type; the construction of Anna Nicole Smith as a gold digger was loudly echoed in the worldwide journalistic coverage of the trial. This was the primary intent and strategy of Pierce Marshall's legal team. A writer for *The Australian* stated that Pierce's lawyers sought to "portray Smith as the quintessential gold digger who took advantage of a frail, if libidinous, old man." A writer for the *Contra Costa Times* observed, "Throughout the four-month trial, lawyers representing the estate have portrayed Smith as a transparent gold digger." The *New York Times* summarized the parties' clashing legal strategies: "Mr. Hardin worked to portray her as a gold digger. Ms. Smith portrayed herself as a good wife who provided love and companionship to a lonely man during his last days."[68]

Rusty Hardin, well-established in Houston's legal community, was the lead attorney representing Pierce Marshall. He had a perfect winning streak as a Harris County prosecutor, sending fifteen men to death row and securing convictions in over one hundred felony jury trials. As a defense attorney, his record was equally formidable. In a rare defeat, Hardin defended the Arthur Andersen accounting firm against federal obstruction of justice charges. The firm, which was one of the largest multinational companies during the 1990s, stood accused of shredding documents that would have shed light on the fraudulent business practices of the Enron energy corporation. Observers claimed that Hardin took what should have been an easy case for prosecutors and led jurors to a nearly hung verdict. The U.S. Supreme Court overturned the firm's conviction in 2005 in a unanimous ruling, and many people with legal training commented that Hardin laid essential groundwork for the Supreme Court's decision. Pierce Marshall could scarcely have selected a better attorney.[69]

In the final days of September 2000, attorneys for the opposing sides made their opening arguments in the Anna Nicole Smith probate case. Tom Cunningham, Smith's lawyer, argued that J. Howard Marshall had a morally binding oral contract with Smith despite the fact that he did not name her in any of his wills. Rusty Hardin depicted Smith as someone with an "insatiable appetite for money, jewelry and property." He told jurors, "This was not a woman who loved him, but a woman who took tremendous advantage of him."[70] The trial lasted months, but the most noteworthy moments occurred during Smith's four-day testimony. Anna Nicole Smith and Rusty Hardin (whom she called by his first name) frequently clashed, prompting the judge to intervene.

In his effort to cast Anna Nicole Smith as a gold digger, Hardin showed that J. Howard Marshall spent approximately $1.7 million on Smith in 1992. He bought her so much jewelry that she could not describe to Hardin a $455,000 ring Marshall purchased for her, and had trouble keeping track of Marshall's many gifts. Smith, in what appeared to be either carelessness or a counterintuitive legal strategy, played up her dumb blonde persona. For example, another member of Pierce Marshall's legal team, Lee Ware, asked Smith if she lost any of the jewelry. Smith replied, "I would hope not, but I used to be a real ditz, so it's possible." Hardin questioned Smith about the weekly allowance of $5,000 Marshall gave her: "Did you always spend it all before the end of the week?" Smith said, "Knowing me, probably." As Smith's comment suggests, she did not cast aside claims that she was a big spender. Rather, she emphasized the joy Marshall experienced when taking care of her. "It was his pleasure to please me," she insisted.[71] Smith complained that Pierce denied his father the gratification of spending money on her, leading to a revealing cross-examination about Smith's attitude toward wealth:

> *Smith*: He told me that Pierce would only give him $100,000 for my Christmas presents.
> *Hardin*: What kind of world is it when people start talking about only $100,000 for Christmas?
> *Smith*: $100,000 was not a lot of money to me.
> *Hardin*: Pardon me? $100,000 is not a lot of money to you?

Smith: No, sir. My husband threw money at me. You don't understand. You are trying to make it sound like this is a lot of money to me, because it's not. And that's how we lived, and that's how he made me live.[72]

She denied her agency and potential culpability by portraying herself as a kept woman. Like she told the press, Smith noted that she waited to accept his marriage proposal until her modeling career flourished. On the witness stand, she told Hardin that she decided to marry Marshall "after I make a name for myself, so nobody can call me a gold digger." Hardin asked, "How much gold did you get over the next two or three years?" She confirmed, "Quite a bit, Rusty."[73] Appropriating Hardin's characterization of her, perhaps as an ironic form of self-defense, Smith wore pink pants and a matching pink top to court. On the shirt, shiny jewels spelled the word "Spoiled." When Hardin asked Smith about her attire, she said that Marshall spoiled her on Valentine's Day, "and today is Valentine's Day."[74]

Rusty Hardin tried to persuade the jurors that Smith pressured her late husband to leave her his estate and adopt her fourteen-year-old son Daniel. Hardin had two purposes in playing for jurors the tapes Smith made of Marshall. Hardin wanted to establish her manipulative nature and he wanted to disprove the idea that Marshall and Smith had a verbal contract. The existence of the tapes suggested to the jurors that Smith had no reason to record her husband unless she knew he planned to exclude her from his will. Hardin also called to the witness stand health care worker Tish Hunt, who testified that she saw Smith offering her bare breast for Marshall to fondle while Smith encouraged him to state into a tape recorder his desire to adopt Daniel. Smith denied she bared her breast in an attempt to manipulate Marshall, and she called Hardin a pervert in open court.[75]

Smith stated that, although she did not sexually manipulate Marshall, she had a sexual relationship with him. Outside the courtroom, those close to the couple gave clashing descriptions of their sex life. Most accounts claimed that they never had intercourse, but Smith gratified him with phone sex and occasionally rubbed her breasts on his head.[76] Judge Wood reviewed an interview of Smith on the television show *A Current Affair* where she said, "I took care of my husband in a sexual way. I do my wifely duties."[77] Under direct examination from Smith's attorney, Anna Nicole said that she did not care about the age difference between her and her husband, and that the two of them discussed the possibility of having a child. She clarified during her testimony that their relationship was deeper than a sexual attraction. Smith brought a framed photo of Marshall with her to the witness stand, and she testified, "It wasn't a sexual 'baby, oh baby, I love your body-type love,' it was a deep 'thank you' for taking me out of this hole."[78] According to Smith, it was a meaningful relationship defined by neither sex nor money.

Hardin attempted to dispute the notion that Smith and Marshall carried on a healthy romantic and sexual relationship, and he sought to depict Anna Nicole Smith as cruel and abusive. Arnold Wyche, Marshall's former driver, cried on the witness stand when he recounted Smith mocking Marshall for his incontinence. He testified that Smith refused to eat with her husband. "It was terrible how she treated him," he told the jurors.[79] Testimony about food formed an area of conflict between the competing parties. Pierce Marshall's attorneys questioned J. Howard Marshall's assistant about a story that Anna Nicole Smith fed her husband uncooked bacon. "I'm real good at cooking bacon," Smith rebutted. "I always make it good and crispy. It's all lies."[80] Testimony about Marshall choking on soup spawned intense trial theatrics. Smith claimed that she saved Marshall's life after the soup caught in his throat: "That's the night he died on me and I brought him back to life." Others claimed that Smith caused the choking by feeding Marshall too aggressively and then panicking when he appeared to be in distress. Smith, however, used the 1995 soup incident as a way to accuse Pierce Marshall of killing, or attempting to kill, his father. "It was Pierce," she said, "Pierce was the one who made the order not to do anything because it wouldn't do any good."[81] She cried on the witness stand and said, "He killed my husband." Hardin questioned her about the allegations:

> *Hardin*: Do you seriously swear under oath that Pierce Marshall
>   ordered people to let his father choke to death?
> *Smith*: Yes.
> *Hardin*: Miss Marshall, have you been taking new acting lessons?
> *Smith*: Screw you, Rusty.[82]

News of Smith's insult traveled quickly. Later that evening, as Hardin left a Houston Rockets game, a man playfully shouted at him from the stands, "screw you, Rusty!" A few days later, maintenance workers at the Houston courthouse greeted him with the same phrase.[83]

Along with her allegation that Pierce was responsible for J. Howard Marshall's death, Smith also accused him of directing an anesthesiologist to kill Marshall's mistress, Lady Walker, while she was undergoing plastic surgery. She also suggested that Pierce plotted to electrocute her by putting live wires into her swimming pool. Smith testified that Pierce's attempts to kill her caused her life to spiral out of control. She had a nervous breakdown and began abusing drugs and alcohol because of Pierce's various conspiracies. Inquiring specifically about the claims that Pierce had Lady Walker killed, Hardin asked her if she had "any sense as to how outrageous that suggestion is?" "My whole life seems outrageous," she said.[84]

Anna Nicole Smith's outbursts brought strong rebukes from both the judge and Marshall's attorneys. Hardin told reporters outside the courthouse that everything she was saying about Pierce was "a flat-out lie."[85] Judge Wood scolded Smith the following day. He told her, "a lot of your testimony in the last day or so has been made-up stories," and he contacted the district attorney to inquiry into whether Smith committed perjury.[86] Tom Cunningham used Judge Wood's concerns about perjury as an argument for his recusal. Wood showed bias against his client, he alleged, by characterizing her statements as inescapably false. Cunningham's request was unsuccessful and Wood stayed on the trial but, years later in 2017, he begged the Marshall family to recuse him from the ongoing litigation over J. Howard Marshall's estate due to his exhaustion with the case and the personalities attached to it.[87]

In their closing arguments, the attorneys for the opposing sides sketched different stories about Smith's role in J. Howard Marshall's life. Smith's lawyer, Tom Cunningham, argued that Anna Nicole brought Marshall an invaluable sense of comfort during a depressing and tumultuous time. His wife and mistress had died, his sons were fighting over money, and Anna Nicole Smith gave him a reason to live. Cunningham asserted, as he did frequently throughout the trial, that Marshall referred to Smith as "the light of my life." According to Hardin, "the phrase was used so often that the jury was tired of it." To mock Smith and her attorney, Rusty Hardin used a portable music player to play Debby Boone's 1977 hit song "You Light Up My Life" as a prelude to his closing arguments. Hardin maintained that no one could corroborate Smith's assertion that J. Howard Marshall promised to give her half of his estate. The jury agreed. They deliberated for nearly three days and decided in favor of Pierce Marshall. As a fitting end to a trial punctuated by theatricality, the jurors serenaded Rusty Hardin with an impromptu rendition of "You Light Up My Life."[88]

Trial observers speculated that Smith's testimony harmed her case. A writer for *Texas Monthly* said, "as a trial witness on her own behalf, she seemed to be working overtime to persuade the jury to rule against her."

Jurors agreed with this observation about Smith's self-sabotage, and many of the jurors expressed strong opinions about the case. The *Houston Chronicle* reported that several "women jurors cried as Wood read the verdicts." One juror called Smith's testimony "far-fetched," and said that she gave himself and other jurors "headaches from trying to keep up with what she was saying." On *ABC News*, one of the jurors said, "I think it was a show of her acting like the dumb blond. So, she goes, 'Well, I'll—I'll play the part. Then I can lie and get away with it, you know, because I'm just dumb.'" Other jurors described Smith as "an opportunist," "manipulative," and "a sad little girl who has lost her way." One juror thought to herself "I'm done" when she saw Smith wearing the "Spoiled" shirt to court. The jury allegedly took only five seconds to arrive at a decision on the essential question of whether or not Smith was entitled to anything.[89]

Some spectators appreciated the entertaining qualities that the trial provided. Smith said during cross-examination, "I am, like, living a soap opera," and some found truth in that statement and lauded her performance.[90] A fifty-eight-year-old woman named Lilian Seifried attended the trial and called it "better than a soap opera." She observed Smith to be "very entertaining" and "fun to be with." A court assistant called her "adorable" and told a reporter from the *New York Times*, "You go, girl! That's all I can say. You go, girl!"[91] The strong emotions elicited by Anna Nicole Smith—crying jurors and cheering fans—reflect her celebrity status and her embodiment of the archetypal gold digger, and the folk devil and trickster qualities the gold digger carries. The powerful feelings and opinions about Smith also reveal the cultural power evoked by the gold digger label, which was the lens through which Smith was routinely viewed. As the legal battle ground onward during the early 2000s, Smith's iconicity expanded and solidified, but not in ways over which she had control.

Anna Nicole Smith as a Cultural Icon

Anna Nicole Smith's public image was molded through the character she created for herself, as well as by meanings generated from a conglomeration of media and celebrity interests, including members of the press, producers of her reality television show, and her biographers. Anna Nicole Smith was the product of overlapping constructions: as a personification of Marilyn Monroe, white trash, and a gold digger.

Anna Nicole drew on Marilyn Monroe as the dominant source of her style and persona. She claimed Monroe as her idol and told Larry King, "I just completely feel what she went through." The *Playboy* talent scouts that discovered her said that Smith was convinced that she was either the reincarnation of Marilyn Monroe or Monroe's secret daughter. Marilyn Monroe posters, pictures, and memorabilia littered her home. While in California, Smith rented Monroe's former house in Brentwood.[92] She stated her plans to fund an independent film studio where she intended "to make innocent, 1950s-style movies where she could play the 'Marilyn Monroe part.'"[93] On another occasion, she expressed her desire to design "Marilyn Monroe-style fashions."[94] Writer Mimi Swartz contends that Smith's invocation of Marilyn Monroe was a shrewd personal marketing strategy, and one that parlayed Smith's recollections of her troubled childhood into a hold on Monroe's life trajectory from abandoned child to international superstar.[95]

Others promoted and amplified the comparison between Marilyn Monroe and Anna Nicole Smith. A writer for the London *Independent* noted how Smith "was hyped as the new Marilyn Monroe" when she appeared in the Coen brother's 1994 film *The Hudsucker Proxy*. In 2004, she appeared in an ad for the People for the Ethical Treatment of Animals (PETA) that featured her in a pink satin dress similar to the one worn by Marilyn Monroe in *Gentlemen Prefer Blondes*. Smith posed with her mouth open, surrounded by tuxedo-clad men. The caption read, "Gentlemen Prefer *Fur-Free* Blondes." Articles about Smith's marriage and probate battles played off Monroe's gold digger movies of the 1950s. *Texas Monthly* titled a 1994 cover story about Smith "How to Marry a Millionaire." A year later, *People* ran an article about the Marshall estate battle titled "How to Bury a Millionaire."[96] The old Hollywood glamor summoned by Smith's black-and-white Guess ads, the unapologetic display of her full-figured body, her platinum hair, and "dumb blonde" persona drew inevitable comparisons to Monroe throughout her life. Yet, as the title of the *People* article suggests, the line on which Smith stood, the line between old Hollywood glamor and a pop culture punch line, was a thin one indeed. The associations with Marilyn Monroe allowed for a negative contrast between the two stars. Some used Monroe to draw a boundary of respectability beyond which Anna Nicole Smith was invariably placed. Writers for the London *Daily Mail* called her "the Marilyn Monroe of the fast food, throwaway consumer society." Mimi Swartz commented, "Monroe had talent, but Anna Nicole's gifts were limited."[97] The negative contrasts with Monroe underscored a common characterization of Smith as "white trash."

The white trash stereotype constructed Anna Nicole Smith as "famous for being famous" and, therefore, undeserving of legitimate celebrity. Media depictions of Anna Nicole Smith as white trash were not subtle. In 1997, a writer for the Montreal *Gazette* referred to Smith as an "overweight, drug-crazed, bimbo gold digger; drunk; and trollop." Another writer called her "an over-the-hill white trash ex-stripper from Texas with deluded fantasies of becoming the next Marilyn Monroe." An article in *Mail on Sunday* referred to Anna Nicole Smith as "the queen of trailer park trash." She was, according to her biographers, a "poor kid from nowhere, with no education, and no sophistication." The framing of Anna Nicole Smith as an embodiment of white trash selected and emphasized details from her past: high school dropout, fast food worker, and Walmart shopper. In August 1994, barely two years after the fashion industry heralded Smith's work as charting a revolutionary new direction in the modeling world, the cover of *New York* magazine featured a photo of Anna Nicole with her hand in a bag of potato chips under the headline "White Trash Nation."[98] She sued the magazine for defamation.[99]

Anna Nicole Smith carried a particularly gendered version of the white trash stereotype, a construction that tied together her promiscuity and low cultural capital. Her body was a site onto which individuals made claims about her sexuality, gender, social class, and (implicitly) her race. Media reports frequently commented on her large, surgically augmented breasts; and her breasts became a key part of her identity. According to the talent scouts from *Playboy*, Smith bragged about her breast implants, offered to have them feel her breasts, and boasted of the $14,000 cost, stating, "I could have bought myself a truck for what these damn things cost."[100] The reference to a truck (rather than any other point of comparison for an expensive purchase) reinforced her role in a social drama of a trashy Southern woman rising to fame due to her willingness to exploit her body. In 1995, Smith declared, "My whole life revolves around my breasts. Everything I have is because of them." Media reports amplified the attention to her breasts with creative comparisons. *Texas Monthly*, for example, stated that Smith had "breasts bigger than the state of Rhode Island." The *National Review* called her a "5' 11" harpy with DD bazooms." Her breasts became a symbol of her entire identity.[101]

Smith's body was a source of capital, but it also held the potential to undermine whatever glamorous image she built through it. As her weight increased, she more easily slid into a negative role model, fitting the main contours of the white trash stereotype. An article in *The Guardian* speculated that in her despair over her legal battles, she "tried to fill the emptiness with Twinkies, Ho-Hos and Dream Pies," foods coded in American society as belonging to white trash. The press, which previously celebrated her body type as a healthy departure from the then-popular waif look in elite modeling, fiercely criticized her. Cultural studies scholar Jeffrey Brown argues that Smith's fatness, coupled with her status as a "white trash gold-digger," made her a "female grotesque" that reinforced taken-for-granted standards of femininity and social class. Anna Nicole Smith's agency, her embrace and celebration of the things with which she should have had shame (like her donning a T-shirt that said "Spoiled" during the probate trial), made her an especially potent ideological threat, violating core ideas of deservingness and the Protestant work ethic so central to American neo-liberal thought.[102]

The construction of Smith as a gendered form of white trash presented her sexuality as an out-of-control force. *Playboy* scouts Eric and D'eva Redding detailed numerous examples of her supposedly insatiable sexual appetite. They stated that while working at Rick's strip club, clients and coworkers called Smith a "party girl" because she would engage in sex work in the parking lot. The Reddings alluded to an affair she had with actor Judd Nelson, her fondness for rubbing her bare breasts on J. Howard Marshall's head, and her masturbation habits.[103] They detailed her abuse of Xanax, Vicodin, and tequila, and said, "She liked partying, any kind, all kind. Sex, any sex. Drugs and alcohol as long as it was in excess."[104] Her hypersexuality, appetite, and substance abuse combined to create an image of a wild creature unmoored by social norms and undeserving of the vast wealth she was set to inherit. Her reality television show, which debuted in 2002, drew on and amplified her trashy, gold digger image.

The E! Entertainment Television network broadcast the first episode of *The Anna Nicole Show* in August 2002. The show ran for two full seasons and featured Smith in supposedly spontaneous real-life situations. *The Anna Nicole Show* aired during a time when "reality TV" soared in popularity, and the show appeared to be a ratings hit for E!. Inspired by the success of *The Osbournes*, the network rushed the show into production because they were concerned about the deluge of celebrity reality programming. Reviews of the show were harsh. The *Hollywood Reporter* argued that the show "served to glorify the woman's complicity in her own degradation." A writer for *Metro Magazine* argued that the show confirmed "money does not buy you 'class.'" British journalist Gaby Wood called the show "an unflinching self-portrait of a one-woman car crash." Donna Hogan declared, "'Dreadful' is far too complimentary a term to describe the series." Despite the scathing reviews, or because of them, the show began as a huge success, with over four million viewers tuning into the premiere. Its ratings, however, steadily dropped until the network cancelled it during the second season.[105]

The Anna Nicole Show, including the opening credits, explicitly drew humor from Smith's estate battle with Pierce Marshall and her reputation as a gold digger. The opening credits use fast-paced animation to tour the milestones of Smith's life: her small-town Texas roots, her work at a fried chicken restaurant, and her stripping. The opening sequence shows an image of her marrying J. Howard Marshall under wedding bells with diamonds, hearts, and dollar signs in the background. She kisses him and he disappears in a puff of ash. Her white wedding dress turns to black and a gavel bangs down in the center of the screen, segueing to a shot of Anna Nicole reclining on a giant scale in front of a courthouse counterbalanced with a pile of cash. The once-balanced scale tilts in her favor and she climbs off and dusts off her dress (now red), while her dog Sugar Pie pulls in the "Anna Nicole Show" title. The frenetic pace of the title sequence works to mirror the hectic life the show seeks to portray.

In every episode, following the animated opening, Smith directly faces the camera and says something apparently intended to be funny and self-deprecating. These moments, which appear to be highly scripted, often highlight her status as a gold digger. For example, in the first episode, "House Hunting," she tells the audience, "There's three things people think about me. I'm rich. I'm not rich. I'm gonna be rich. They think I'm a gold digger, and they think that I'm fat. Well, maybe I'm a little 'big-boned.'" In the fifth episode of the series, she opens the show with, "People always ask me did I ever learn anything as a stripper. Yah, I did. One man, plus two beers, equals twenty dollars." In these moments, Smith hugs and leans into the gold digger stereotype as a form of self-parody. Her Southern drawl and simplistic way of talking connects the gold digger stereotype to signifiers of white trash.[106]

The show focuses on different situations faced by Anna Nicole Smith, her assistant Kimmie, and her attorney Howard K. Stern, including their efforts to find Anna Nicole a new house, a trip to Las Vegas, and her visit to a dentist. Many of the episodes revolve around contrived arrangements, like when Anna Nicole takes her dog Sugar Pie to visit a pet psychiatrist. Other moments of the show twirl in self-referential loops: a scene where the audience watches Anna Nicole as she watches herself on the *Larry King Show*, when the show bases an entire episode around footage generated from the show's own publicity tour in New York City, or when Smith attends a drag show where the performers are dressed as Smith. Despite the banal subject matter and the show's deliberate attempt to display the ignorance and stupidity of its central subject, the *Anna Nicole Show* draws from complex and varied sources of humor.

The humor of the *Anna Nicole Show* stems from its camp sensibility, tongue-in-cheek corniness, and the "so-bad-it's-good" aesthetic of paracinema. E! executive Mark Sonnenberg said, "the appeal of the show lies in the fact that you can't quite tell if Smith is kidding or just dumb." The ambiguous spaces between parody and sincerity engender the comedy. For example, in an early episode, Anna Nicole searches for a new house with Howard and Kimmie. In a limousine ride on the way to look at a house, Howard K. Stern tries to explain to Anna Nicole the violence occurring in Israel during the Second Intifada: "People are dying in Israel and they're blowing themselves up in coffee shops, in ballrooms and stuff." Smith says, "Whoa, why would they do that? Don't they think it was kind of painful?" Like Peggy Hopkins Joyce complaining about World War I hurting her shopping opportunities in Paris, Anna Nicole Smith shows a lack of comprehension about major world events in a way that celebrates her frivolity. The uncertainty of whether her stupidity is deliberate is similar to the question jurors faced in the probate trial. Was it all an act? Or was Anna Nicole Smith toying with the expectations the public has for a gold-digging dumb blonde?[107]

Another source of the show's energy and humor directly centers on an explicit critique of Smith as white trash, drugged, and hypersexual. Here, Smith is not necessarily in on the joke, but is solely the target of it. Like so much of the show, it is difficult or impossible to separate Smith's presentation of herself from the editing decisions of the producers. Was she routinely using drugs or did the show editors simply choose to include her drugged moments during the short, twenty-two-minute episodes? In any event, her confused and dreamy comments, coupled with her frequently slurred speech, conveys a widespread impression that Smith was on depressants during filming.[108] The show itself plays on the tension between the evidence of drug use and her denials of it. The eighth episode of the first season follows her as she is interviewed by a Los Angeles radio station. The hosts of the station mention that she seems sedated, and Smith takes great offense. "You're calling me a fucking druggy!" she cries. She defends herself and tells them that she has "an accent from Texas and it's a lazy talk."[109]

A major part of the show's putative humor is the relentless sexualization of Anna Nicole. Talk of sex saturates the show. In a sequence that shows her dog Sugar Pie appearing to copulate with a teddy bear, Smith says, "One time, Sugar Pie saw me fucking this guy and the next day, it's like, she just started doing it. She's pretty good at it." She muses about receiving sexual satisfaction from the rumble of her father's pickup truck, stealing her mother's vibrator, and her need for "a fucking man-whore." The show's producers seem to script exaggerated sexuality into every episode. In the opening sequence of "The Driving Test," she deadpans to the camera, "a man once asked me what I knew about cars. I don't know nothing about power steering or radiators or crank shafts but I know everything there is to know about back seats." In the next episode, which focuses on her New York City publicity tour, she opens the episode with a reference to masturbation: "The New York reporters are crazy! They asked how I became such a good lover. I told 'em, 'a lot of practice on myself!'" In various episodes, the show follows her and her friends to a sex toy store, a Las Vegas strip club, a Chippendales show, and a performance called "Puppetry of the Penis."[110]

Depictions of her overt, cavalier, and adolescent attitude toward sex reinforce the presentation of Anna Nicole Smith as white trash. Her racialized class status is also underscored through a number of decisions made in the production and editing of the show. For example, in the episode "Cousin Shelly," Smith receives a visit from her cousin Michelle Cloud from Mexia, Texas. At first, Smith seems reluctant to meet with her, but they agree to convene for dinner at a steak house. Smith's discussion of cousin Shelly appears to emphasize her possible methamphetamine use: she refuses to eat and she talks nonstop. Calling forth a sign of white trash culture, Shelly reminisces about how they used to make macaroni and cheese out of the box and they would "eat it out of the pot."[111] In her biography of Anna Nicole Smith, *Train Wreck*, Donna Hogan expressed unique disgust for the episode focused on Smith's cousin, blaming the episode on a decision Anna Nicole made instead of understanding the role of producers in guiding reality television. She said, "out of all of Anna's respectable relatives, she decided to introduce her toothless cousin to her 4.1 million viewers." She added, "The worst thing about Anna parading this white trash relative of hers to the world is that everyone thinks it's me!" While viewers may have regarded the show as harmless fun, others (like Hogan) saw Anna Nicole Smith's image as a white trash gold digger as a source of interpersonal contamination.[112]

The Legal Impact of Anna Nicole Smith's Case

Five months before the premiere of the *Anna Nicole Show*, the United States District Court for the Central District of California revisited her $474 million bankruptcy award. In a lengthy decision, Judge David Carter carefully walked through the history of J. Howard Marshall, Anna Nicole Smith, and Pierce Marshall to conclude that Pierce engaged in "tortious interference," meaning that he illegitimately prevented Anna Nicole from rightfully receiving a monetary gift that J. Howard promised her while he was alive. Carter awarded Smith approximately $88.6 million, $44.3 million in compensatory damages and $44.3 million in punitive damages. The ruling created, as the Ninth Circuit Court of Appeals later noted, "one of the most extensive records ever produced in the Central District of California."[113]

The decision acknowledged Smith's mercenary motives. Carter wrote, "While she detested being thought of as a gold-digger, her actions leave little doubt that money was the central facet of her relationship with J. Howard." The decision, however, often cast her in a sympathetic light. Carter referenced her standoff with Rusty Hardin in Texas probate court, but characterized her performance as originating from poor communication skills. He said, "Her illiteracy is striking," and he took note of "her limited intelligence and understanding of business affairs."[114] Carter's decision stated that Smith's limitations, which were due to her educational and personal shortcomings rather than intentional malevolence, paled in comparison to the flagrant and calculated misuses of power by Pierce Marshall and J. Howard Marshall's lawyer Edwin Hunter.

The ruling documented Pierce's move to strip his father of wealth in order to hide it from both Anna Nicole Smith and the IRS. Harvey Sorenson, who was later removed by Marshall because of his poor dealings with the IRS, wrote a memo to capture Marshall's thoughts about a gift transfer to Smith. The so-called New Community Memo was a key piece of evidence gauging Marshall's "donative intent" (what he intended to give Anna Nicole) and showing Pierce's efforts to block his father's wishes. By "new community," Marshall referred to all of the assets that he developed from Koch Industries and Marshall Petroleum while he was married to Smith.[115] He wanted Smith to have half of his "new community," not half of his entire fortune, a distinction Smith never quite understood. Such a gift would concretize the value of Koch Industries and open them to substantial inquiries from the IRS. Judge Carter explained, "J. Howard's plan to give Vickie money based on the value of Koch Industries stock was immediately problematic," because "the teaming of a widowed wife with the IRS loomed as a bad combination in the goal of keeping down the value of Koch stock."[116] The District Court's ruling enumerated several steps Pierce Marshall and Edwin Hunter took to prevent Anna Nicole Smith from receiving J. Howard's wealth.

According to Judge Carter, the wedding between Anna Nicole and J. Howard triggered "a flurry of activity by Pierce, Hunter and others to alter J. Howard's estate plan so as to prevent Vickie from receiving a gift." After Pierce Marshall and Edwin Hunter learned about the marriage, they drafted a "Marshall post-matrimonial plan" which was later referred to in court as the "Fine Tuning Memo." The Fine Tuning Memo outlined a scheme to wrest control of J. Howard Marshall's wealth and change the catchall trust to an unalterable trust that excluded Smith. These changes, according to the memo, would leave "less for mischief (and Miss Cleavage)." The phrase "Miss Cleavage," which Hunter conceded was a reference to Smith, constituted a smoking gun of sorts because it showed a deliberate attempt to block Anna Nicole Smith from receiving J. Howard Marshall's money. Other details emerged in the court's inquiry that revealed a concerted effort to mislead both Smith and J. Howard Marshall. For example, Pierce hired a private investigator to trail his father in order to prevent him from signing a new will. Pierce's legal team argued that this was to protect J. Howard Marshall from Smith's bodyguard, but the logistics of the surveillance did not support that claim. The District Court decision also implied that Pierce forged his father's signature and altered the dates on the documents to make it appear as if Marshall intended to establish an irrevocable trust before he married Smith. They also submitted the trust in a way to shield it from any scrutiny. They filed the change of trust in Louisiana in order to "home town" the document, to place it in a favorable location under the power of friendly judges who had a familial connection to Edwin Hunter.[117]

Pierce Marshall and Edwin Hunter also stripped Marshall of his wealth, presenting the transfer of money from J. Howard to Pierce as a smart business decision, even though Pierce and his attorney knew Marshall did not have long enough to live to see a profit from the investment. The court noted, "Pierce and Hunter's actions of slowly draining J. Howard of assets in order to prevent a gift to Vickie were egregious in nature," and that "Pierce and Hunter engaged in a pattern of deceiving J. Howard for nearly two years." To calculate compensatory damages, Carter considered the wealth accrued by Marshall through his holdings in Koch Industries and Marshall Petroleum coterminous with his marriage to Anna Nicole Smith. Carter interpolated the value of Koch Industries stock based on different measures and, citing the rationale offered in the Exxon Valdez oil spill decision, arrived at punitive damages equal to the compensatory damages. Yet, Anna Nicole Smith never saw the $88,585,534.66 award. The ruling was appealed and the case slogged through the federal court system long after the deaths of both Smith and Pierce.[118]

After Judge Carter's ruling in District Court, the case landed at the feet of the Ninth Circuit Court of Appeals. They made their judgment on December 30, 2004. The court noted that three previous courts—the Texas probate court, the U.S. bankruptcy court, and the U.S. district court—had delivered conflicting and incompatible rulings. They also acknowledged the sprawling complexity of the case: "The route followed by the parties to this appeal on their epic journey is a tortured one indeed." The key issue in the case was jurisdiction. Which court had the power to decide the question of whether Smith was entitled to Marshall's wealth? Smith's case had elements that made it a federal matter. The litigation enveloped multiple states: California, Texas, and Louisiana (where Marshall's team filed his revised will in accordance with the Fine Tuning Memo). It also involved substantial sums of money, much more than the $75,000 needed to trigger federal jurisdiction. Under this interpretation, the District Court ruling would stand and Smith would be entitled to the $88 million. Yet, courts had long recognized a "probate exception" that gave states priority and broad latitude in deciding matters related to wills, property, and estate planning. Recognizing the probate exception gave jurisdiction to the Texas probate court. Accordingly, the ruling rendered in the five-month jury trial—the trial with the theatrical clash between Rusty Hardin and Anna Nicole Smith—would stand and Smith would get nothing. Ultimately, the Appeals Court sided with this latter interpretation and ruled that Carter's court lacked jurisdiction to hear the case.[119]

The Appeals Court ruling allowed the Supreme Court to address a set of vexing legal questions: How broad is the probate exception? Are there exceptions to the probate exception? What counts as a "core proceeding" in U.S. bankruptcy code (issues over which bankruptcy courts have jurisdiction)? The Supreme Court heard oral arguments on February 28, 2006. Smith attended the hearing dressed in a somber black outfit, but avoided making any statement. Different legal issues seemed to motivate the justices during oral arguments. Justice Ruth Bader Ginsburg saw the case as a way to eradicate the "vast confusion in the lower courts about the extent of the probate exception." Stephen Breyer mentioned Pierce's misconduct, that he "forged three pages of the will." John Roberts asked questions about previous courts' jurisdictions, preemptions, and preclusions. Despite different investments in the case, the justices arrived at the same conclusion. In May, the Court unanimously ruled in favor of Anna Nicole Smith, holding that federal courts have jurisdiction, under certain conditions, to "determine the rights of creditors, legatees, heirs, and other claimants relating to an estate."[120]

The Supreme Court's ruling did not mean that Smith would automatically receive the money. Rather, the Supreme Court remanded the decision back to the Ninth Circuit to determine whether her claim was, indeed, a "core proceeding." Although the Appeals court agreed that hers was a core proceeding, it held that the Texas probate court decision should be afforded the final judgment because it occurred first in the sequence of rulings. In their second and final consideration of the case in 2011, the Supreme Court ruled that a bankruptcy court lacked the constitutional authority to make a final judgment on Smith's claim of tortious interference. In his majority opinion, Justice John Roberts opened with a passage from Charles Dickens's *Bleak House*: "This 'suit has, in course of time, become so complicated, that no two lawyers can talk about it for five minutes, without coming to a total disagreement as to all the premises.'"[121]

Although Anna Nicole Smith was inarguably the archetypal gold digger of the late twentieth century, her legal impact was not in the realm of divorce law or alimony, but in bankruptcy law. The Supreme Court's 2011 decision in Stern v. Marshall was the most important bankruptcy decision in thirty years.[122] Writing in the *Loyola Law Review*, Jolene Tanner concluded that Anna Nicole Smith will "be remembered not only for the imprint that she left on pop culture, but also for rattling an entire legal institution."[123] The ruling restricted the power of bankruptcy courts, preventing them from having the authority to enter binding judgments on non-core matters. Some observers argue that the ruling increases the burdens on those filing for bankruptcy and hurts the appeals process for bankruptcy cases.[124] By limiting federal protection for bankruptcy, the ruling arguably advanced the neoliberal trend toward declining state protections for individuals' financial security.

The Death of Anna Nicole Smith

In 2006, Anna Nicole Smith's life moved forward with the interpersonal drama befitting a reality television star. On February 28, 2006, Smith left the Supreme Court Building surrounded by photographers.[125] Months later, she gave birth to her daughter Dannielynn in the Bahamas. Just three days after the birth of her child, Smith's son Daniel died of a drug overdose in his mother's hospital room at the age of twenty. An autopsy found toxic levels of antidepressants and methadone in his system. The death devastated Anna Nicole. She refused to leave her son's body, and hospital workers had to sedate her in order move her out of the hospital. Visibly distraught, Smith repeatedly screamed "I'm sorry, I'm sorry" at his coffin during his funeral.[126] Within weeks after her son's death, Anna Nicole's lawyer and ex-boyfriend filed conflicting lawsuits, each claiming to be the father of Dannielynn. In August, Anna Nicole Smith filed for permanent residency in the Bahamas. Minister of Immigration Shane Gibson personally approved her residency permit after visiting her home and receiving a $10,000 check. A photo of Gibson and Smith, and reports that he had improperly sped up the approval process for Smith's permit, caused a public uproar and led to his resignation. In the shadow of yet more scandal, Smith exchanged vows with her attorney and reality TV costar Howard K. Stern in a commitment ceremony off the coast of Paradise Island in the Bahamas on September 28, 2006. Three months later, the Los Angeles Superior Court ruled that Smith needed to bring Dannielynn to California for a paternity test. Holed up in the Bahamas, Stern and Smith fought the order, but a paternity test later showed that Larry Birkhead, photographer and Smith's former boyfriend, was Dannielynn's biological father.[127]

On February 8, 2007, Anna Nicole Smith died at the age of thirty-nine at the Seminole Hard Rock Hotel and Casino in Hollywood, Florida. A medical examiner stated that an accidental overdose caused her death. News coverage of Smith's death was unusually intense. Reports of her demise eclipsed all other major news stories, including developments in the U.S. war in Iraq (where over forty U.S. soldiers died in February) and a major scandal about staff neglect at the Walter Reed National Military Medical Center.[128] Some media figures, however, pushed back against the hype Smith's death generated. Anderson Cooper railed against the saturation coverage of her death provided by CNN, and reminded viewers of the Iraq war: "There's a war on, there's a war on, there's a war on." Joe Scarborough speculated, "Americans couldn't get enough" of Smith, "perhaps as a distraction from a disastrous war." On another network, Jack Cafferty on CNN turned to his colleague Wolf Blitzer and sardonically asked, "Is Anna Nicole still dead, Wolf?"[129]

· · · · · ·

In many ways, Anna Nicole Smith was the living embodiment of Madonna's "Material Girl." She was the torchbearer of the gold digger icon as it traveled from Jean Harlow to Marilyn Monroe. By the time of her death in 2007, the international press memorialized Smith—not for her talent as a model, actor, or sex symbol—but as "famous for being famous." CNN Entertainment Correspondent A. J. Hammer commented on her modeling career, yet concluded, "But she really was famous for the sake of being famous." Joe Scarborough claimed, "Smith was a new breed of celebrity who was famous simply because she was famous." Like Peggy Hopkins Joyce eighty years before, Anna Nicole Smith was "famous for being famous," a particularly gendered framing of fame that discounts women's talents, efforts, and sacrifices and, instead, attributes their fame to mercurial and mysterious social forces. Smith attained stardom in a media ecosystem that rewarded deviance and excess, yet reveled in its failure. Anna Nicole Smith's stardom helped produce, and was produced by, a complex swirl of celebrity culture motored by disgust and fascination.[130]

Part of the cultural energy of Anna Nicole Smith was her simultaneous defilement and imprinting of late twentieth-century gender norms and ideologies. In the eyes of some, she was a "stormtrooper for feminism," using her personality and wiles to attain undreamed-of wealth. Her attempts to control her image, from her self-mockery of her weight to her embrace of the gold digger persona, represented a kind of agency. As a media creation, however, she never had control over the production or interpretation of her image. As Jeffrey Brown has argued, the mass media portrayed Smith as a monstrosity who violated the accepted standards of femininity, especially after she gained weight in the early 2000s.[131]

Depictions of Anna Nicole Smith as white trash also made implicit arguments about race and social class. Anna Nicole Smith's life became a synecdoche for widespread social disorder. According to *Metro Magazine*, "the story of Anna's rise and fall provides a bird's-eye view of a society arguably in decline." For some, her behavior corrupted "the ideal of the virtues of solid hard work." The saga of Anna Nicole raises the question of who deserves what in the early twenty-first-century capitalist order. Her life story shows how the intersecting dimensions of race, class, gender, and sexuality drove assessments of deservedness.[132]

Those who argued that she deserved the money made their claim in terms of the reciprocal relationship she had with J. Howard. In this account, she traded fourteen months of pleasure for his wealth.[133] These assessments participate in neoliberal logic by characterizing Anna Nicole and J. Howard as autonomous entities entering into a contract. Journalist Carl Sarler, for example, criticized the "tut-tutting around the world's press that she is a 'gold digger.'" For Sarler, Marshall and Smith's marriage was "a deal freely entered into by adults who understand each other. Perfectly."[134] The rendering of the marriage as a business deal centers the discussion on the fairness of the exchange, but rarely, if ever, do commentators criticize the wealth itself. Few question the deservedness, or the economic and political context, in which J. Howard Marshall became a billionaire. This distraction is precisely the cultural magic that the gold digger stereotype performs. The story of Anna Nicole Smith demonstrates that histories of neoliberalism need to include a consideration of the cultural sources of its operations. The American political economy in the early twenty-first century drove forward on a particular cultural pavement smoothed by gender, race, and class stereotypes. The neoliberal economy, what economist Peter Fleming has described as "sugar daddy capitalism," developed a strong synergy with the gold digger stereotype.[135]

Anna Nicole Smith's role in the age of neoliberalism should be read alongside the histories of the Koch brothers and J. Howard Marshall. J. Howard Marshall was a quintessential member of what C. Wright Mills called the "power elite." During his work for the Department of the Interior, Marshall helped write oil industry rules that regulated the industry into which he assumed a commanding role. Through his associations with the Koch brothers, his wealth was part of a far-right network of political think tanks and influencers, and built upon unprecedented pollution and environmental damage.[136] Marshall, like his associates Charles and David Koch, despised the IRS and did everything in his power to avoid paying taxes. He skirted the lines of legality repeatedly by ignoring gift taxes, avoiding income taxes with bogus claims that Lady Walker and Anna Nicole Smith were "consultants," artificially suppressing the value of his corporate holdings, and engaging in other financial gimmickry.[137] Relatively few details of his wealth became part of the breathless reporting on Smith's legal battles. Journalists who upbraided Anna Nicole Smith for debasing the American work ethic never shifted their critical gaze on J. Howard Marshall.[138] While mass media and popular culture turned Anna Nicole Smith into a butt of jokes as a white trash, gold-digging monster, J. Howard Marshall was remembered as a self-made man who made poor choices in the name of love.

Epilogue

· ·

Twenty-First-Century Gold Diggers

Anna Nicole Smith's introduction of rap star Kanye West at the 2004 American Music Awards was unforgettable. She walked onto the stage waving her arms above her head, wearing a black dress with a silver necklace that spelled "Trimspa." In a sideways reference to her weight struggles, and what she later described as an endorsement of the new weight loss drug, she pointed to the necklace and asked the audience, "Like my body?" Next, her remarks about West, marked by barely coherent slurred speech, confirmed to many her suspected drug use. The moment was striking, not only because of Smith's strange behavior, but because the stage featured two cultural figures responsible for carrying the gold digger image into the twenty-first century. Kanye West released his hit song "Gold Digger" less than a year later. In "Gold Digger," West and guest vocalist Jamie Foxx criticize a woman for snaring an African American man in marriage for the sole purpose of acquiring money. The eponymous gold digger buys plastic surgery with money set aside for her children, owns a lavish house and car, and effectively traps the man in the relationship by becoming pregnant with his child. The song warns men to avoid such women and to obtain a prenuptial agreement before they marry.

It is difficult to overstate the song's commercial and cultural success. "Gold Digger" spent over ten weeks at the top of the Billboard Hot 100, broke a record for the fastest selling digital download, and was voted by VH1 as the twentieth greatest hip-hop song of all time. Kanye West won a Grammy Award for the Best Rap Solo Performance in 2005, and *Time* magazine recognized him as one of the 100 most influential people in the world. "Gold Digger" had enormous appeal outside of the hip-hop world, staking a high position on the mainstream Top 40 pop music charts. The song appealed to millions of Americans enthralled by West's clever word play and his vivid characterization of feminine greed. The video, which featured cameos by Beyoncé and John Legend, called up the retro pinup aesthetic of the 1950s, and connected the gold digger of the song with the rich history of the gold digger trope.

FIGURE 16 Kanye West at the 2004 Video Music Awards. Kanye West's enormously popular 2005 track "Gold Digger" underscored the racial, class, and gendered dimensions of the gold digger stereotype. The music video for "Gold Digger" invoked the retro pinup aesthetic of the 1950s, and connected the song with the rich history of the gold digger trope. Courtesy of PhotoFest.

While West's track "Gold Digger" did not introduce the expression into African American vernacular, it certainly helped to solidify it. The phrase "gold digger" and gold digger narratives have held a prominent place in rap music since the early years of the genre.[1] In fact, a 1990 song by rap artists EPMD called "Gold Digger" unfurled a scenario quite similar to the one Kanye West wrote about fifteen years later. EPMD's track describes a man lured into marriage by a gold digger. He experiences that his "brain locked" and his "whole damn head was malfunctional," prompting him to forget to sign a prenuptial agreement.[2] He feels trapped in the marriage because he knows that his wife will make substantial gains because of "the new divorce laws, which entitles them to half." The reference to community property laws and no-fault divorce succinctly shows how cultural representations of gold diggers drew on the law and how the legal system influenced the construction of the gold digger trope. Scholarship on race and gender has suggested how the cultural images prevalent in hip-hop during the 1990s and 2000s created a template for identities and practices among African American youth. The gold digger was one of the dominant sexual scripts created through rap music and hip-hop culture.[3]

Coinciding with the popularity of West's song, gold digger characters populated "street lit," a genre of popular fiction aimed at an African American audience. In Andrea Blackstone's 2004 *Schemin': Confessions of a Gold Digger*, nineteen-year-old Jalita is kick out of her dormitory and tries to find someone to house her.[4] She eventually meets Wes, a wealthy NBA player. Wes's fiancée finds out he is spending time and money on Jalita and attempts to murder them both. Eventually, Jalita finds companionship in her friend Seth, someone who has always seen right through her gold-digging schemes. Toward the end of the novel, Seth signs a million-dollar book contract and the novel's conclusion implies that he and Jalita become romantically involved. Like the *How to Marry a Millionaire* narrative, Jalita finds financial security by rejecting gold digging and pursuing true love. The 2007 novel *Gold Diggers* by Tracie Howard follows four women as they seek wealthy mates.[5] During the course of the novel, the gold diggers are routinely punished for their behavior. For example, Paulette conspires with her married lover to change a family member's will in order for her to inherit millions of dollars. She is killed when someone tampers with the brakes in her car. Reese pressures her fiancé, a man with a bright future in professional basketball, to sign an unfavorable prenup. Later, she is disfigured in a car crash. Similarly, a 2007 novel called *A Bona Fide Gold Digger* by Allison Hobbs shows the perils of gold digging. The 2007 novel follows a woman named Milan who becomes a sexual companion for a wealthy African American man named Noah Brockington who lives in an extravagant estate. Milan eventually marries Brockington and he compels her to sign a prenuptial agreement requiring her to try to bear his male heir.[6] The end of the novel reveals Brockington as not wealthy at all but rather the lover of another man who owns the estate. The novel concludes with Milan blackmailing both men and using the money to launch her own business venture. Like Depression-era cinematic depictions of gold diggers, the gold diggers in early-2000s street lit were sometimes punished for their gold-digging practices, but just as often celebrated for getting ahead in an unequal world.[7]

A second trajectory of the gold digger in the twenty-first century involved the growth of computing and telecommunications. The exponential progress of computing power and the development of the read-write internet propelled the gold digger into new digital domains. The durability of the gold digger trope was highlighted in 2007 by a personal ad that achieved "viral" status. Someone placed an advertisement on Craigslist, a popular online classified ad service, "to get married to a guy that makes at least half a million a year." The writer was allegedly twenty-five years old and "spectacularly beautiful." She had dated men who made $200,000 to $250,000, but lamented that "250,000 won't get me to central park west." She issued a challenge to her critics at the end of her request for a wealthy, marriage-minded man: "Please hold your insults—I'm putting myself out there in an honest way. Most beautiful women are superficial; at least I'm being up front about it. I wouldn't be searching for these kinds of guys if I wasn't able to match them—in looks, culture, sophistication, and keeping a nice home and hearth." Craigslist published a facetious reply, supposedly from a wealthy businessman, explaining why the woman found it difficult to find her ideal husband. Trading his wealth for her looks, the writer explained, "is plain and simple a crappy business deal." "In economic terms," he continued, "you are a depreciating asset and I am an earning asset." The original ad and its response "spilled over into the email world where it became a popular item to send to friends as a joke." Articles in the *New York Times* and *New York Post* speculated on the authenticity of the ad and its response. Urban legend archivist Barbara Mikkelson called it "the Craigslist gold digger ad," noted its popularity, and speculated that "the enhanced technology of the information age may have handed such gold diggers new tools with which to track down their prey." Although it was a tiny piece of internet ephemera, the Craigslist "gold digger ad" and the brief sensation it caused reveal the endurance and malleability of the gold digger stereotype in American culture.[8] Just as Chrissy Tate in 1915 blurred the boundaries between legitimate intimacy and sex work, the Craigslist gold digger likewise skirted that line. Both figures highlighted the monetization of romance, and the threat that the gold digger holds for dominant constructions of marriage, masculinity, and femininity.

Assessing the Cultural Power of the Gold Digger

This book has attempted to show the power of the gold digger stereotype to shape American culture. Throughout this book, I have used the phrases "cultural power" and "cultural work" to describe how the gold digger stereotype creates expectations and frames of reference for human behavior.

The gold digger exemplifies what sociologist Joel Best terms a "cultural resource."[9] The gold digger is a publicly available figure that can be mobilized for different political, social, and ideological projects. The gold digger exists in a field of symbols, in a space of social hierarchies and identities, in law, and in and at the edges of the institution of marriage. These fields by necessity overlap and intertwine. Within these domains, the gold digger stereotype creates a category of deviance by marking the limits of deserving and undeserving, establishing exchange rates and norms of commensuration, and describing and demarcating who and on what terms one should have access to resources.

The Gold Digger as Symbol

The gold digger stereotype works through a series of rhetorical movements inherent in the general operation of symbols and signs. In other words, the gold digger is a cultural phenomenon that generates meaning, and we can better appreciate the historical impact of the gold digger through an analysis of its symbolic processes. The symbol of the gold digger works in a few different, but interrelated, ways. It functions through condensation; it reduces a complex whole through a display of its representative parts. The gold digger symbol also operates by drawing a series of contrasts and juxtapositions, principally through highlighting the difference between the gold digger and her victims, and between the gold digger and respectable women. It works as a symbol through the creation of labels, and those labels become embodied in specific historical and fictional humans. Finally, the gold digger stereotype derives its power through the routine harnessing and mobilization of other stereotypes and symbols. Through these symbolic processes, the gold digger constructs social difference and inequality, influences the law, and shapes the spaces in and around marriage.

The gold digger stereotype condenses and organizes social complexity into a set of symbols and markers that allow romantic and dating behavior to be viewed through a lens of money-hungry acquisitiveness. Like all stereotypes, it functions through the dynamics of a part-whole relationship where broad and deep understandings of human behavior are derived from seemingly superficial and shallow signs: blonde hair, baby talk, love of jewelry, frivolity, and unintelligence. The gold digger enables a kind of vision where behavior can be read from appearance, distilling wide-ranging matter into smaller units that represent the whole. The pink elbow-length gloves of Marilyn Monroe in *Gentlemen Prefer Blondes* reappear in Madonna's "Material Girl" video and Anna Nicole Smith's PETA ad. The gloves, along with platinum hair and jewelry, mark Madonna and Anna Nicole Smith as gold diggers in advance of any action on their part that could be construed as gold digging. In this way, the gold digger, as a category of deviance, appears through stylization. Familiar ways of dress, speech, desire, bodily carriage, and manners of interacting are condensed into the gold digger trope.

As a symbol, the gold digger operates through contrast; gold diggers are only intelligible in relationship to respectable women and the holders of the gold.[10] First, the gold digger gains her symbolic importance through a contrast with the men upon which she preys. The men targeted by gold diggers are knowingly or unwittingly drawn into an unfair exchange whereby they trade wealth and security for the sex and companionship of the gold digger. Stanley Joyce, Lee Marvin, and J. Howard Marshall constituted, in the words of a 1930s heart balm critic, "poor weak susceptible" men.[11] These men reputably earned their wealth through honest means, but fell under the spell of manipulative women. Through this scenario, the construction of the gold digger calls into existence versions of masculinity. The gold digger helps sort a wide array of masculinities into a hierarchical order. Wealth, the gold digger reminds us, is not enough to secure hegemonic masculinity, and ineffable feminine power can suddenly unseat men's economic, political, and personal security. Gold diggers routinely appear in so-called crises of masculinity because of the relationship between the symbolic role of gold diggers and the instabilities and hierarchies inherent in dominant constructions of masculinity.

Second, the gold digger stands in contrast to respectable women. Lorelei Lee's quest for money is only fully appreciated next to Dorothy's pursuit of love. Women who refuse to use the legal tools of the gold digger underscore the problematic nature of gold digging. Bessie Cooley, the second wife of the creator of the Alimony Club of Illinois, contrasted sharply with his first wife, an alleged gold digger who sought a large alimony award. In an economy of respectability, Roberta West Nicholson (the creator of Indiana's ban on heart balm suits) gained prominence through a comparison to heart balm–seeking gold diggers, both real women like Peggy Garcia and Rhonda Doubleday as well as the characters in Depression-era movies looking to get rich from breach of promise lawsuits. Wartime Rosie the Riveter and the happy housewife of the 1950s also marked a divergence from the gold digger and, through interpolation, helped define the boundaries of both the gold digger stereotype and respectable womanhood.

Third, the symbol of the gold digger becomes a label, one that is affixed and embodied. The gold digger label fastens to specific women, and prominent gold diggers set a mold through which others follow. This mold establishes the edges and contours of how the women are viewed by different publics. The gold digger stereotype derives from popular and well-known women like Peggy Hopkins Joyce, Peaches Browning, and Anna Nicole Smith, as well as lesser-known women like Frances Singer, Peggy Garcia, Margaret Melter, and Grace Reinert. The gold digger type is also welded from fictional creations, like Lorelei Lee from *Gentlemen Prefer Blondes*, Lil from *Red-Headed Woman*, and the stars of *How to Marry a Millionaire*. The fluidity between the real and the fictional solidifies the cultural power of both.

Finally, the gold digger is not created out of whole cloth. It gathers up its potency by tapping into preexisting stories and harnessing the power of other, allied stereotypes. The cluster of traits that make up the gold digger are entangled with the "adventuress," the "vamp," and the "dumb blonde." The gold digger connects with long-standing gender stereotypes about women's cunning and destructiveness, but constructions of gold diggers also dovetail with historically specific stereotypes such as the "Welfare Queen," "dumb blonde," and "white trash." The use of these stereotypes charges the gold digger with heady meaning about race, gender, sexuality, and social class.

The Gold Digger and Social Inequality

The American gold digger is important because she is created from, and works through, intersecting identities and social locations. The gold digger serves as a useful figure in projects that mobilize understandings of gender, class, race, and sexuality to create social hierarchies. Most prominently, the gold digger glues together gender and social class. The gold digger, representing an illegitimate gender strategy for class advancement, fuses gender and social class through rhetoric about respectability. Gender and class respectability in marriage depend upon the proper combination of love and money and, importantly, the appropriate means through which both are acquired. Questions about money inevitably enter into matrimonial decision-making, but judgments about gold digging revolve around the level at which money, love, or family should direct and shape marriage. Peggy Hopkins Joyce, Michelle Triola, and Anna Nicole Smith were labeled gold diggers not because they married rich men but because the men's riches drove the union.

In this construction of the gold digger, the acceleration of Joyce, Triola, and Smith up the class ladder reflected poorly on them as women. At the same time, their gender strategy, use of sexuality, cultivated beauty, and the magnetic quality of their womanliness despoiled the legitimacy of their claims to wealth. Peggy Hopkins Joyce corrupted the reasoning abilities of Stanley Joyce. Heart balm gold diggers saved love letters for blackmail. Allotment Annies took advantage of the loneliness of soldiers. Michelle Triola made Lee Marvin feel trapped despite their lack of legal marriage. Anna Nicole Smith used her brazen sexuality to exert a toxic influence over J. Howard Marshall. Over and over, the American gold digger abused a gender role for social class purposes.

The gold digger also connects gender and racial identities in profound ways. The archetypal gold digger throughout most of the twentieth century is not just a white woman, but someone who carried a radiant and exaggerated whiteness: platinum blonde hair, white clothing, and diamond jewelry that reflects a piercing white glare. The gold digger traveled the twentieth century through the whiter-than-white presentations of Marilyn Monroe, Jean Harlow, Peggy Hopkins Joyce, and Anna Nicole Smith, as well as the often forgotten chorines of the Ziegfeld Follies and Busby Berkeley musicals. The gold digger is historically a white woman, not just white in terms of phenotype but a woman who participates in the ideological project of making whiteness. Gold diggers highlight the contingent quality of whiteness. Whiteness was a category one could defile by failing to uphold dominant notions of masculinity and femininity. Those who embodied whiteness had unique access to economic and social resources, but gold digging threatened the legitimacy of both the racial and gender status of those who engaged in it. In this way, the gold digger embodied a whiteness that spoke to an insecurity bubbling below the surface of white womanhood and manhood.

Gold diggers also unite sexual and racial threats. Racial status can be endangered through sexual practices where gold digging represents a denial of the romantic, affective, and sexual basis of companionship. The sexual practices of the gold digger stereotype perch on the borderlands of sex work where strategic and meretricious sex can contaminate the assumed purity of white womanhood. Heterosexual manhood, too, if not properly contained, threatens white hegemony. The heterosexual impulses of men who fall for gold diggers pose a threat to the whole edifice of racial and class power. This is why Charles Wilner, William Armstrong Fairburn, and others viewed gold diggers as a grave danger to the white race, and it is why the stereotypes of the gold digger and white trash neatly aligned at specific moments in American history.

Gold Diggers and Legal Culture

Stories direct the operation of law and our understanding of it. Storytelling and narrative processes are essential to how the law works, in the stories elicited in the examination of witnesses, the accounts of a legal case described in an appellate decision, and the ways newspapers narrate court cases and trials. The stories upon which law thrives connect with, and draw strength from, stories in the wider culture, in fields that spill outside the legal realm. The relationship between law and culture is an inextricable one, and sociologists of law have persuasively argued that law should not be thought of as a separate entity from culture, but that law *is* culture.[12] For most of the twentieth century, storytelling about gold diggers has shaped how and for whom laws are created, acted upon, and understood. Stories about gold diggers have influenced obvious domains of law like alimony, wills, and breach of promise, but understandings of gold diggers have been a part of legal storytelling in other legal realms, like the bigamy of the Allotment Annies and Anna Nicole Smith's impact on bankruptcy law. Gold diggers give a face to, and provide motivation to understand, otherwise abstract legal concepts and problematics.

Gold diggers in the American legal realm often appear in the form of exaggerated stories of lawsuits and crimes that contain political and social commentary about the state of society. Gold digger storytelling occurs in the context of moral panics about family and marriage, and in the context of recurring "crises" of masculinity. The rising divorce rate in the 1920s coincided with the popularization of stories about alimony-seeking gold diggers. Concerns about the Great Depression and its effect on family and marriage co-occurred with tort tales about heart balm. Stories about Allotment Annies, most of them apocryphal, circulated during a time when Americans expressed widespread anxiety about the disruptive effects of war on the American family structure. The postwar masculinity "crisis" among the white middle class, the sexual revolution during the 1960s and '70s, and the dislocations wrought by neoliberalism provided a continuous and ever-shifting context for gold digger narratives.

Characteristic of tort tales and moral panics, the outcomes of the stories failed to match the hyperbolic reporting of them. The press portrayed Peaches Browning as exploiting her rich husband, but she failed to win her lawsuit against him after their separation. Movie critic Rex Reed remembers Eleanor Holm as the "swimming gold digger," but the details of the case, and the relatively small amount she received in comparison to Billy Rose's overall wealth, have faded from public memory. Newspapers produced a flood of commentary about Michelle Triola's $1.8 million lawsuit, but she ended up with nothing. J. Howard Marshall spent lavishly on Anna Nicole Smith while he was alive, but she never lived to see any of the millions of dollars at stake in her legal battles against Pierce Marshall. The social threat of gold diggers was routinely lower than the rhetoric about them suggested.

Gold Diggers and Marriage

The historiography of marriage has shown that the dominance of romantic love as the basis of marriage, what Stephanie Coontz has described as the "love revolution," began in the eighteenth century and was firmly institutionalized in the West by the early twentieth century. The full adoption of love as the primary justification for marriage, and the growing acceptance of companionate marriage, coincided with the rise of the gold digger. Love came to dominate the reasoning behind marriage, but the love revolution was never complete. The gold digger prowls in the cracks of where the economic dimensions of romance persist. The gold digger is an interstitial figure who negotiates the cultural spaces between love and money. To the extent that marriage always entails an economic union as well as a romantic one, the gold digger stereotype hovers as an available cultural resource through which to make sense of the division of labor and allocation of resources within marriage.

The gold digger appears and reappears throughout the twentieth century because of continual crises in American marriage. The love-based justification for marriage guarantees a cyclical sense of undoing. The 1920s witnessed a rise in the divorce rate, and the seemingly limitless trend in divorce was once again a heated topic in the 1970s and into the 1980s. The Great Depression and World War II had unique and stressful impacts on the American family. Even periods when marriage appeared stable, like the 1950s, contained tensions and frustrations bubbling below the placid surface of the American family. In every epoch, the perceived crises of the American family were marked and understood through perspectives shaped by social class, gender, sexuality, and race. In each moment of crisis, the gold digger stood as a ready-made folk devil toward which to cast blame.[13] Through its symbolic utility, the gold digger construct engaged in a politics of recognition or, more precisely, a politics of misrecognition and misidentification. The gold digger allowed structural problems confronting the American family to be seen in an individualized, personalized, and stylized way. The effects of legal and economic change on American families was hard to grasp, but the gold digger was an easily accessible and understandable stereotype.

A powerful social construct, the gold digger weaves together its different dimensions into a coherent and identifiable whole. As a symbol, it works to craft understandings of the social order, and it stands at, and ties together, the major intersections of social difference and inequality. As a symbol of intersectional force, it intervenes in culture, law, marriage, and the connective tissue that brings these elements of social life together. The gold digger is a construct with consequences. Tracing the cultural force of the gold digger stereotype in the United States reveals powerful and intertwined relationships among law, popular culture, and social inequality. From chorus girl slang to a complicated folk devil, the gold digger has had a remarkable and important career over the twentieth century.

Notes

Introduction

1. Brooks, *My Battles with Vice*, 24, 114, 115. *My Battles with Vice* was part of a subgenre of books in the first two decades of the twentieth century that dealt with the alleged problem of "white slavery," or forced prostitution. Some of the books were fictional, but most claimed to recount true stories of immigrants abducting naive white women into sexual slavery. For a discussion of white slavery narratives, see Brian Donovan, *White Slave Crusades*.

2. In his study of New York City slang, Irving Allen contends that, "*Gold digger*, in the new, slang sense, came into American English around 1915." See Allen, *The City in Slang*, 80. According to theater scholar Angela Latham, Avery Hopwood's 1919 play *The Gold Diggers* created a kind of typecasting for women in theatrical choruses. See Latham, *Posing a Threat*, 116–17. Legal scholar Mary Coombs notes, "The derivation of the term 'gold-digger' for a woman who measures her charms on the gold standard is disputed. Some trace it to Loos' book [*Gentlemen Prefer Blondes*] and other popular literature of the 1920's . . . Others think it was first used to describe the much-married Peggy Hopkins Joyce." See Coombs, "Agency and Partnership," 12.

3. Brooks, *My Battles with Vice*, 116, 115.

4. On charity girls and the treating system, see Peiss, *Cheap Amusements*, and Clement, *Love for Sale*. On the categorical distinctions made by New York vice investigators, see Keire, "Swearing Allegiance," 260. In his 1932 ethnography of Chicago nightlife, sociologist Paul Cressey grouped together gold diggers, charity girls, and prostitutes. See Cressy, *Taxi-Dance Hall*, 289–90.

5. "How Avery Hopwood Discovered the Gold Diggers and Induced Them to the Stage." *Cleveland Plain Dealer*, November 16, 1919, D3.

6. See Rodgers, *Mencken*, 241–42.

7. Hayes, *On Reflection*, 93, 95; Mencken, *My Life as Author and Editor*, 83.

8. "How Avery Hopwood Discovered the Gold Diggers."

9. Sharrar, *Avery Hopwood*, 113–19.

10. "David Belasco's *Gold Diggers*." *Variety*, June 6, 1919, 14. The metaphor of gold, and the image of gold digging, was highly salient for Americans in the early twentieth century. The presidential race of 1896 underscored the role of gold in the American economy. The United States adopted the gold standard in 1900, and gold was effectively "naturalized" as a source of wealth. According to historian Kathryn Taylor Morse, "In the United States between 1900 and 1914, gold and money were identical." The slang meaning of gold digger might have eluded some Americans in 1919,

but the cultural resonance of "gold" and "gold digger" as signifiers of prosperity and resource extraction certainly did not. Morse, *Nature of Gold*, 36.

11. Quoted in Sharrar, *Avery Hopwood*, 115.

12. Sharrar, *Avery Hopwood*, 119. Jerome Charyn described Belasco's production of *The Gold Diggers* as "the great success of the season." See Charyn, *Gangsters and Gold Diggers*, 52. See also Hove, "In Search of Happiness," 18.

13. Stephen Sharot explains how, during the silent film era, the "gold digger" effectively replaced the "vamp" as the archetypal dangerous woman. See Sharot, *Love and Marriage*, 143–44.

14. Somewhat eliding the subcultural sources of the slang, Jerome Charyn claimed, "It's Hopwood who invents the term *gold digger.*" See Charyn, *Gangsters and Gold Diggers*, 52.

15. The gold digger ties together and travels between legal and cultural domains. The connection between law and culture illustrates what Pierre Bourdieu theorizes as the homologous relationships that exist among seemingly disparate fields. The concept of homology, and its implication of sharing and simultaneity, goes beyond the notion that law simply "reflects" culture (or vice versa). For a lucid description of Bourdieusian field theory and the concept of homology, see Thomson, "Field," 65–82.

16. For an overview of Friedman's concept of popular legal culture, see Carrillo, "Links and Choices."

17. "The deviant," sociologist Howard Becker argues, "is one to whom that label has been successfully applied; deviant behavior is behavior that people so label." Becker, *Outsiders*, 8–9.

18. Richard Dyer and Michael Pickering have emphasized how stereotypes are tools to create inequality. Once drawn, the boundaries of stereotypes are grafted onto institutions, organizations, and other loci of power. For example, Carol Groneman analyzes how the construction of nymphomania as a medical disorder leaked into the legal realm. "Nymphomania" as a medical category reinforced the legal category of nymphomania as a defense against rape charges and as a justification for institutionalizing nonconforming women. The constructivist approach, instead of simply identifying who is and who is not a "gold digger" or "nymphomaniac," shows how these acts of identification reinforce social inequality. See Dyer, *Matter of Images*; Pickering, *Stereotyping*; Groneman, *Nymphomania*, 95–121.

19. I agree with Gail Bederman that gender "is a historical, ideological process," and with Joan Scott that "gender is a primary way of signifying relationships of power." See Bederman, *Manliness and Civilization*, 7; Scott, *Gender and the Politics of History*, 42.

20. The rare moments when men are described as gold diggers do not undo the gendered valence of stereotype; they reinforce it. For example, Fairburn notes the existence of "male gold diggers" who seek European titles, but the bulk of his book excoriates gold diggers (who are presumed to be women). In the Busby Berkeley musical comedy *Gold Diggers of 1935*, Dick Powell plays a struggling medical student named Dick Curtis. The wealthy Mrs. Prentiss hires him to escort her daughter for the summer, but worries that he might be a "male gold digger." In 1950, actor and singer Dorothy Shay recounted her frustrations when dating men because she con-

stantly had to be on guard against being "a meal ticket for a lazy male gold digger." The military newspaper *Stars and Stripes* called comedian Martha Raye's husband a "male gold digger" for threatening to sue her for $100,000. In her syndicated advice column, Dorothy Dix warns a woman in 1959 against continuing her relationship with a "male gold-digger." These examples show that the phrase "male gold digger" implies that men, as gold diggers, are exceptional. The "male" modifier underscores womanhood as the default status of the gold digger. See Fairburn, *Law and Justice*, 397; *Gold Diggers of 1935*, directed by Busby Berkeley (Warner Brothers, 1935); Hal Boyle, "Oh, Shay, She Can't See Him," *Indiana Gazette*, April 3, 1950, 19; Dorothy Dix, "Escort Out for Soft Life," *The Morning Herald*, October 1, 1959, 23; "Raye's Husband Threatens to Sue," *Stars and Stripes*, October 30, 1959, 6.

21. On the "adventuress" and the use of breach of promise lawsuits, see Grossberg, *Governing the Hearth*, 57. On the "adventuress" type and property judgments in common law marriage see Goldberg, "Schemes of the Adventuress."

22. Sharot, *Love and Marriage*, 143–44.

23. Cressey, *Taxi-Dance Hall*, 100; Van Deventer, *Confessions of a Gold Digger*, 8; Loos, *Gentlemen Prefer Blondes*, 21.

24. The gold digger embodied a kind of "non-liberatory agency," one that invites the reader to recognize or take pleasure in the figure's freedom, but in a way that posed no real risk to dominant power relations. On "non-liberatory agency" in the context of feminism and Islam, see Mahmood, "Feminist Theory, Agency, and the Liberatory Subject"; Rounthwaite, "Veiled Subjects." On the concept's use in contemporary African American popular fiction, see Dunbar, "Reimaging Black Women and Agency"; Bragg, *Reading Contemporary African American Literature*, 63–82. Lori Landay notes, "In general, trickster figures are representations of liminality, duality, subversion, and irony." Landay, *Female Trickster*, 2. On the female trickster in American culture, see Landay, *Female Trickster*.

25. On "condensing symbols," see Jasper, *Art of Moral Protest*, 176.

26. In a discussion about Anna Nicole Smith, a *Herald Sun* columnist observed, "there are varying degrees of gold digging. Some are seen to be satisfied with a few nuggets. Others want the entire mine." See R. Brundrett, "Love That's Worth a Fortune," *Herald Sun*, August 12, 1995, 12.

27. Cohen, *Folk Devils and Moral Panics*.

28. Nathan and Snedeker, *Satan's Silence*.

29. Stuart Hall's classic study on mugging, for example, showed that politicians and print media overstated the threat of street crime and wrongly attributed it to immigrants and African Americans. Likewise, Gary Dowsett's analysis of the panic around AIDS in the 1980s and 1990s demonstrated that AIDS was portrayed as a kind of "gay plague" that authorities used as a justification to restrict the civil liberties of gay men. See Hall, *Policing the Crisis*; Dowsett, "The 'Gay Plague' Revisited."

30. Sarah Wright describes moral panics as an "enacted melodrama" that engulfs particular sectors of society at specific historical moments. See Wright, "Moral Panics as Enacted Melodramas."

31. Fred Strasser coined the term "tort tale" in 1987 and William Haltom and Michael McCann elaborated on the tort tale concept in their 2004 book *Distorting the*

Law. Haltom and McCann define tort tales as "moralistic parables that refocus general dissatisfaction with civil justice into particularized outrages or injustices." For Haltom and McCann, a lawsuit over a spilled cup of McDonald's coffee is the "quintessential tort tale." Strasser, "Tort Tales," 39; Haltom and McCann, *Distorting the Law,* 64–65, 67.

32. For example, excluded from the McDonald's tort tale are the facts that the coffee was at a dangerous temperature, McDonald's had been previously warned about the hazards in how they served coffee, and the amount they intended to give Liebeck to settle the case ($800) was woefully insufficient for covering the cost of her hospitalization and skin grafts. See Haltom and McCann, *Distorting the Law,* 67, 215.

33. The consideration of gold diggers in this book expands the historical reach of the tort tale concept. In its original formulation, sociologists of law describe tort tales as a product of post-1970s tort reform efforts by conservative groups and political entities, coinciding with a growing sense of a "litigation explosion" in American society (see Galanter, "Litigation Panic"). Tort tales were an element of the "culture wars" that have animated American politics with great intensity since the 1980s. A broader historical framework, however, uncovers tort tales that circulated long before the legendary McDonald's coffee case and the rise of tort reform as it is commonly understood. Tort tales, especially stories about breach of promise lawsuits, persisted many years before the late twentieth-century culture wars, and gold diggers were at the center of them.

34. This effort to instantiate a particular understanding of race is a process race theorists Michael Omi and Howard Winant call "racial projects." Omi and Winant, *Racial Formation in the United States.*

35. Intersectionality describes interlocking forms of social difference and inequality, and the concept has deep activist and academic roots. At its heart, the term denotes the simultaneity and inextricability of social identities and access to power. It refers to a subject position (the multiple identities one might have, for example, as a queer woman of color) but it also points to a form of praxis or political action (for example, the need for white feminist activists to fight racial inequality). Intersectionality accounts for how identities and power relations work together to form something greater than the sum of its parts. Scholars widely attribute the coinage of the term to legal scholar Kimberlé Crenshaw in the late 1980s. Others note a longer lineage of the concept that has its origins in black feminist activism in the 1960s, particularly the Combahee River Collective. Sociologist Shirley Hill argues that nineteenth- and early twentieth-century black feminists, like Sojourner Truth and Ida B. Wells, engaged in (what would now be seen as) intersectional analysis. See Hill, *Black Intimacies,* 5. See also Hancock, *Intersectionality;* Crenshaw, "Mapping the Margins."

36. Bailey, *From Front Porch to Back Seat;* Davis, *More Perfect Unions,* 12; Simmons, "Companionate Marriage," 245–48; Kuby, *Conjugal Misconduct,* 180; Zelizer, *Purchase of Intimacy,* 23–26.

37. Davis, *More Perfect Unions,* 17–19.

38. Kuby, *Conjugal Misconduct,* 9.

39. Roy J. Gibbons, "Militant Wife Launches War against Alimony in Chicago," *Freeport Journal-Standard*, July 8, 1927, 13.

40. In the 1990s, scholarship on racial "whiteness" showed how ethnic groups who were previously considered nonwhite or not-quite-white (like Italians and eastern Europeans) were folded into a broad category of whiteness. By the mid-1920s, the category "Caucasian" grouped together ethnicities and "races" who were previously regarded as socially and racially distinct. Simultaneously, these shifts in ethnic and racial categorization strengthened the black-white color line. Key texts documenting and analyzing these changes include Roediger, *Wages of Whiteness*; Ignatiev, *How the Irish Became White*; Allen, *Invention of Whiteness*. On the visual markers of race and the "seeing" of race, see Jacobson, *Whiteness of a Different Color*.

41. For a discussion of how cinematic depictions of blonde hair reinforce racial meaning in the first few decades of the twentieth century, see Tremper, *I'm No Angel*, 122–34.

42. The apparent crisis that faced modern marriage in the early twentieth century contained unexamined and taken-for-granted assumptions about power and race. See Carter, *Heart of Whiteness*.

43. Wilner, *Alimony*, 234.

44. Davis, *More Perfect Unions*, 187.

45. See, for example, Haag, *Consent*, 121–42; White, *First Sexual Revolution*.

46. On representations of whiteness in advertising, see Hale, *Making Whiteness*. For a discussion of the construction of whiteness in the Ziegfeld Follies, see Mizejewski, *Ziegfeld Girl*, 109–35.

Chapter One

1. The headlines included: "Klan Issue Looms as Factor Molding Democrats' Choice"; "Youthful Slayers to Plead Insanity, Attorneys Decide"; "Plot to Kill Rulers in Europe Charged"; "Peggy Joyce Again a Bride, Swedish Count Her Fourth," *Washington Post*, June 4, 1924, 1. Reporting often juxtaposed news about Peggy Joyce with important world events. For instance, a story about France and German World War I reparations in the *Chicago Daily Tribune* was followed by a report that "Peggy Joyce abandons discreet quiet and, loaded with jewels, is seen nightly in cafes she once frequented, accompanied always by the slight young man with a Rolls-Royce limousine." *Chicago Daily Tribune*, August 29, 1924, 2.

2. Rosenblum, *Gold Digger*, 5. I alternate between "Peggy Joyce" and "Peggy Hopkins Joyce" because these are the names she and the vast majority of news reports used to refer to her. Because names reflect marital status, the naming of Peggy Joyce had political stakes. Adding the family names of her ex-husbands stood as a way that journalists and others could underscore her multiple marriages and sexual reputation. For instance, Genevieve Forbes referred to her as "Mrs. 'Peggy' Upton-Archer-Hopkins-Joyce." Genevieve Forbes, "Stage Star's $750,000 Gems Stake in Suit," *CDT*, April 29, 1921, 1. A book on leadership skills, commenting on her ability to attract people, referred to her as "Peggy Upton Archer Hopkins Joyce." Laird and Laird, *Technique of Building Personal Leadership*, 23.

3. Historian and Chaplin biographer Kevin Lynn reported Peggy Joyce marrying five millionaires and added "(Not for nothing was it believed that the term 'gold digger' was coined in her honor, *circa* 1920)." See Lynn, *Charlie Chaplin and His Times*, 268. Constance Rosenblum notes, "Even if the phrase was not invented for Peggy, all agreed that she was the perfect embodiment of the type." See Rosenblum, *Gold Digger*, 85.

4. Rosenblum, *Gold Digger*, 83.

5. Extensive coverage of her divorce from Stanley Joyce occurred approximately halfway through the successful run of David Belasco's musical comedy *The Gold Diggers*.

6. Winthrop Sargent, "Fifty Years of American Women: A Prejudiced Survey of Their Role in the First Half of Our Century," *Life*, January 2, 1950; Spitzer, *The Palace*, 171; Brownlow, *The Parade's Gone By*, 34; Hudovernik, *Jazz Age Beauties*, 34.

7. Grossman and Friedman, *Inside the Castle*.

8. In Milwaukee in 1928, for example, less than 0.2 percent of alimony clients were men. See Charles C. Maas, "Has My Check Arrived?" *Marquette Law Review* 166 (1928–29), 166.

9. See Kuby, *Conjugal Misconduct*, 5.

10. Constance L. Shehan et al., "Alimony: An Anomaly in Family Social Science," 308–16.

11. John D'Emilio and Estelle Freedman give the clearest exposition of the structural origins of the first sexual revolution in the widely cited *Intimate Matters*. Their book synthesizes a large body of historical research on sexual norms, attitudes, and practices from Colonial times to the 1960s. They tie changes in sexual attitudes and practices to large-scale transformation in the American economy.

12. D'Emilio and Freedman, *Intimate Matters*, 58; Lystra, *Searching the Heart*, 77–80.

13. McGovern notes, "The great forward in women's participation in economic life came between 1900 and 1910; the percentage of women who were employed changed only slightly from 1910 to 1930." McGovern, "Freedom in Manners and Morals," 320; Kessner and Caroli, "New Immigrant Women at Work"; Odem, *Delinquent Daughters*. See also Hunt, "Regulating Heterosocial Space"; Meyerowitz, *Women Adrift*; Peiss, *Cheap Amusements*. By 1910, New York had 160 clubs for girls and young women. See Friedman-Kasaba, *Memories of Migration*, 152.

14. May, *Great Expectations*, 59; Simmons, *Making Marriage Modern*, 124; Kuby, *Conjugal Misconduct*, 6. On the varieties of marriage in the early twentieth century, see Simmons, *Making Marriage Modern*. On the controversies surrounding trial marriage, see Kuby, "Till Disinterest Do Us Part"; Kuby, *Conjugal Misconduct*.

15. Lindsey, *Companionate Marriage*. On the rise of companionate marriage, see Simmons, *Making Marriage Modern*, 105–37; Kuby, *Conjugal Misconduct*, 27.

16. Simmons, *Making Marriage Modern*, 172; May, *Great Expectations*, 77.

17. On regional divorce patterns in the late nineteenth-century and early twentieth-century United States, see Schultz, "Divorce Patterns in Nineteenth-Century New England"; Penningroth, "African American Divorce."

18. O'Neill, *Divorce in the Progressive era*, 20.

19. *Los Angeles Times*, March 7, 1920, II4. Sociologist Steven Seidman points to "a growing public perception in the early decades of the twentieth century that marital conventions were in a state of change and crisis." Historian William Kuby describes how intense public debate about marriage in the early twentieth century "reveals the deep sense of panic that accompanied shifting social and sexual mores." See Seidman, *Romantic Longings*, 66; Kuby, "Till Disinterest Do Us Part," 385.

20. Celello, *Making Marriage Work*, 21. The phrase "race suicide" was coined by sociologist Edward Ross in 1901 and popularized by Theodore Roosevelt. Bederman shows that the "race suicide" fear was about more than falling white birthrates. Race suicide had qualities of a catchall concept tied to broader concerns about threats to white male hegemony. Bederman, *Manliness and Civilization*, 196–206.

21. "Divorce, Alimony and Children," *LAT*, October 27, 1919, II4.

22. Samuel Saloman, "The Downtrodden Sex," *New York Times*, December 12, 1920, BR1.

23. Saloman, "The Downtrodden Sex," *NYT*.

24. Anne O'Hagan Shinn, "Women and Citizenship," *NYT*, December 26, 1920, 37; Mary Fisher Torrance, "The Protecting Sex," *NYT*, December 26, 1920, 37.

25. J. Herbie DiFonzo states that between 84 and 88 percent of divorces between 1922 and 1950 were uncontested. See DiFonzo, *Beneath the Fault Line*, 63.

26. DiFonzo, *Beneath the Fault Line*, 44. According to Grossman and Friedman, "spousal support awards have always been the exception rather than the rule." See Grossman and Friedman, *Inside the Castle*, 204.

27. Celello, *Making Marriage Work*, 21.

28. Grossman and Friedman, *Inside the Castle*, 196.

29. DiFonzo, *Beneath the Fault Line*, 63.

30. Grossman and Friedman state, "In practice, few wives were granted alimony awards; most ex-husbands failed to pay and ex-wives rarely went back to court to try to collect their money." Grossman and Friedman, *Inside the Castle*, 196. Likewise, in 1928, a writer for the *Marquette Law Review* noted, "The Clerk of the Circuit Court is so accustomed to listening to troubles in the cases of non-payment of alimony that he has become hardened." Charles C. Maas, "Has My Check Arrived?" *Marquette Law Review* 166 (1928–29), 167.

31. "New York Now Has an Alimony Club—Ten Thousand Alimony and Hundreds More Dodge the Court Order," *Fort Wayne Sentinel*, May 4, 1904, 5.

32. "New York Now Has an Alimony Club," *Fort Wayne Sentinel*.

33. Lillian G. Genn, "Marriage for Alimony Only a Public Menace Says Faith Baldwin," *Modesto News-Herald*, September 25, 1928, 26.

34. Gordon, *Pitied but Not Entitled*, 20. See also Hartog, *Man and Wife in America*.

35. Gordon, *Pitied but Not Entitled*, 23. Gordon's research shows a shockingly low level of child care facilities in the early twentieth century. Many Americans viewed day nurseries as an attack on the family structure, and "poor mothers used them only as a last resort." Gordon, *Pitied but Not Entitled*, 23.

36. On efforts to stop abandonment in New York City, which was perceived to be a growing problem in the early twentieth century, see Igra, *Wives without Husbands*.

37. Rosenblum, *Gold Digger*, 24–26.

38. Joyce, *Men, Marriage, and Me*, 80; Loos, *The Talmadge Girls*, 59.

39. Loos detailed her encounter with Madame Frances in her first autobiography. See Loos, *A Girl Like I*, 201–2.

40. According to Rosenblum, "her rise involved several detours to less glamorous venues." Rosenblum, *Gold Digger*, 45.

41. Snyder, "Vaudeville"; Snyder, "Palace Theatre."

42. Rosenblum, *Gold Digger*, 47, 61–62.

43. "Peggy in Paris Has Her First 'Morning After,'" *CDT*, February 17, 1922, 5; Genevieve Forbes, "Stage Star's $750,000 Gems Stake in Suit," *CDT*, April 29, 1921, 1; Rosenblum, *Gold Digger*, 5.

44. Mizejewski, *Ziegfeld Girl*, 110.

45. Kuby, *Conjugal Misconduct*, 110–15.

46. Mizejewski, *Ziegfeld Girl*, 117, 6.

47. Zora Neale Hurston, "How It Feels to Be Colored Me," *Pittsburgh Courier*, May 12, 1928, A1.

48. In 1914, a writer for *The Outlook* observed, "There is no doubt that the motion-picture show is America's most popular form of recreation." By 1920, half of the population went to the movie theaters weekly. Charles Stelzle, "How One Thousand Workingmen Spend Their Spare Time," *The Outlook*, April 4, 1914, 762–66; Ross, *Working-Class Hollywood*, 7.

49. *The Turmoil*, directed by Edgar Jones (Metro Pictures, 1916).

50. Rosenblum, *Gold Digger*, 64–65.

51. *The Woman and the Law*, directed by Raoul Walsh (Fox Motion Pictures, 1918); Cooper, *Dark Lady of the Silents*, 146.

52. Cited in Rosenblum, *Gold Digger*, 66.

53. Cooper, *Dark Lady of the Silents*. 146. A *Washington Post* profile of Peggy Hopkins Joyce noted that "schoolmates of Peggy remember her as rather dull with her lessons." See "Secret of Vamping, Says Peggy Hopkins Joyce, Depends upon Always Keeping the Man Guessing," *Washington Post*, March 18, 1923, 71.

54. Cooper, *Dark Lady of the Silents*, 147.

55. Joyce, *Men, Marriage, and Me*, 107; Rosenblum, *Gold Digger*, 69.

56. Joyce, *Men, Marriage, and Me*, 116; "Joyce on Stand Called 'Stage Door Johnny,'" *CDT*, June 10, 1921, 1; Joyce, *Men, Marriage, and Me*, 117; Genevieve Forbes, "Stage Star's $750,000 Gems Stake in Suit," *CDT*, April 29, 1921, 3. Forbes began her career at the *Chicago Daily Tribune* in 1921, the year of Stanley's divorce from Peggy. She later became a leading journalist of the 1920s, building her reputation with investigative reports of police, politics, and corruption. Her interview with Peggy Hopkins Joyce was an early career stepping-stone. See Whitt, *Women in American Journalism*, 17.

57. Rosenblum, *Gold Digger*, 79. The car was a Sheffield-Simplex, a luxury car. Joyce wrote, "I had never seen a Simplex and did not know what it was, so I said I did not like its looks, so Joyce said right away, 'Well I will get you any car you want.'" Joyce, *Men, Marriage, and Me*, 118.

58. "Divorce Price Put at Million by Peggy Joyce," *CDT*, April 13, 1921, 7.

59. Rosenblum, *Gold Digger*, 83; "Says Peggy Joyce Left Him for French," *NYT*, June 3, 1921, 15.

60. Rosenblum, *Gold Digger*, 91.

61. "Says Peggy Joyce Sold Her Jewelry," *NYT*, June 5, 1921, 20; Rosenblum, *Gold Digger*, 101; "Divorce Price Put at Million by Peggy Joyce," *CDT*, April 13, 1921, 7; "Kirkland, 87, Noted Leader in Law, Dies," *Chicago Tribune*, February 4, 1965, 1, 4; "A. S. Austrian Funeral Today," *CT*, January 27, 1932, 17; "Peggy Joyce Faces Attack," *LAT*, June 12, 1921, I6.

62. Genevieve Forbes, "Stage Star's $750,000 Gems Stake in Suit," *CDT*, April 29, 1921, 3.

63. Peggy Hopkins Joyce said, "He thought I would so hate the unpleasant publicity that this mess would bring that I would make him a settlement, but he is mistaken. I will fight him to the last ditch, although I would give him anything if it had not happened. I certainly think now that he married me for my money, and if he can't get it one way he will try another." "Joyce and Wife to Appear in Court," *NYT*, June 9, 1921, 19.

64. "Joyce on Stand Called 'Stage Door Johnny,'" *CDT*, June 10, 1921, 1; Allen, *The City in Slang*, 78.

65. Genevieve Forbes, "Stage Star's $750,000 Gems Stake in Suit," *CDT*, April 29, 1921, 1.

66. "Secret of Vamping, Says Peggy Hopkins Joyce, Depends upon Always Keeping the Man Guessing," *Washington Post*, March 18, 1923, 71.

67. "Men, Not Women, Wed for Money, Judge Finds," *Washington Post*, December 7, 1925, 1; "$1,350 a Month for Peggy Joyce," *NYT*, July 9, 1921, 6.

68. "Errázuriz, Blanca De Saulles' Brother, a Suicide in Paris over Peggy Joyce," *NYT*, May 2 1922, 1.

69. "Errázuriz, Blanca De Saulles' Brother, a Suicide in Paris over Peggy Joyce," *NYT*, May 2 1922, 1; "Peggy Joyce Home Again from Paris," *NYT*, May 13, 1922, 24; "Peggy Joyce Home Again from Paris," *NYT*, May 13, 1922, 24; Hemingway, *Complete Poems*, xxii.

70. For instance, a small item appeared in the *CDT*'s "Line 'O Type" section: "Absolute zero in suiciding is dying because Peggy Joyce had refused one's hand in marriage. But did Peggy say yes! AH! Mon Dieu! Ze rope, Seine, ze pistol, ze carbolic acid, ze bushel of dynamite!" *CDT*, May 3, 1922, 8.

71. The *Times* reported: "The motion picture theatre owners of America adopted today at their annual convention here a resolution declaring that it has been currently reported that motion pictures are to be produced featuring Peggy Joyce, and as the organization 'has always been opposed to the exploitation on our screens' of all 'such objectionable lines of conduct,' the delegates 'protest against the exhibition of all such picture in the interest of a clean screen and wholesome entertainment.'" "Movies Bar Peggy Joyce," *NYT*, May 12, 1922, 19.

72. "Peggy Joyce and the Film," *NYT*, May 14, 1922, 20. The article added: "He [Hays] said he did not think that any member producers would consent to any production with Peggy Joyce or Jack Dempsey." Joyce's biographer noted that this was the first time in motion picture history that a specific individual was banned from

film. While Rosenblum's claim is true in some respects, it should be noted that Congress passed a law in 1912 banning motion picture films of prizefights primarily because of the success of African American Jack Johnson. See Rosenblum, *Gold Digger*, 121; Bederman, *Manliness and Civilization*, 3, 42. Also, although Peggy Joyce was perhaps officially the first person to be targeted for a motion picture ban, the scandal over Roscoe "Fatty" Arbuckle over the 1921 death of Virginia Rappe shows that Hollywood responded fiercely to perceived moral transgressions of its stars. Some linked Joyce to Arbuckle. For instance, a Methodist bishop from Chicago claimed that while older Americans courted each other on the "way to church and prayer meeting, the present young folk adopt the way of Fatty Arbuckle or Peggy Joyce." "The Changing World," *CDT*, April 22, 1922, 13.

73. Loos, *Gentlemen Prefer Blondes*, 104.

74. *The Skyrocket*, directed by Walter Neilan (Celebrity Pictures, 1926). See Rosenblum, *Gold Digger*, 150; "This Week's Photoplays," *NYT*, January 31, 1926, X5; "Frivolous Photoplays," *NYT*, January 31, 1926, X5.

75. Cantor's song ends with a judge threatening a man with jail unless he pays alimony. Four Cole Porter songs refer to Peggy Hopkins Joyce. See Rosenblum, *Gold Digger*, 193–94.

76. "Who Is the World's Most Interesting Person Today?" *CDT*, April 19, 1926, 1.

77. Syrett, *American Child Bride*.

78. During the 1910s Alma Hirsig served as a disciple of Pierre Bernard in his "Secret Order of Tantriks," and she was an associate of occult leader Aleister Crowley. In 1928, Hirsig published an exposé under the pseudonym Marian Dockerill titled *My Life in a Love Cult: A Warning to All Young Girls*. See Sutin, *Do What Thou Wilt*, 273–74; Greenburg, *Peaches and Daddy*, 219.

79. Greenburg, *Peaches and Daddy*, 35, 19–20, 111–13.

80. Syrett, *American Child Bride*, 165, 169–70.

81. On the effect of the Peaches Browning scandal on American slang, see Creswell, "What Did Peaches Browning Say?"

82. Greenburg, *Peaches and Daddy*, 171.

83. Syrett, *American Child Bride*, 171. According to Syrett, the Peaches Browning scandal helped cast "adult-child marriages as sexually suspect" in the 1920s, and coverage of the case bolstered efforts to raise the age of consent. See Syrett, *American Child Bride*, 201.

84. "Hear Browning Case in Secret, Both Sides Plead," *NYT*, January 25, 1927, 3; "Say Browning Mixed Comedy and Sordidness," *CDT*, January 26, 1927, 1, 6; "'Peaches,' Weeping, Tells Tale of Life as Mrs. Browning," *Washington Post*, January 26, 1927, 1.

85. "Say Browning Mixed Comedy and Sordidness," *CDT*, January 26, 6; "Woman Fails to Push Suit against Peaches Browning," *CDT*, January 9, 1927, 24.

86. Peaches levied a "thinly-veiled insinuation that Browning was not above scarring her with acid and may have been the instigator of that distressing occurrence." See "'Peaches,' Weeping, Tells Tale of Life as Mrs. Browning," *Washington Post*, January 26, 1927, 1.

87. Greenburg, *Peaches and Daddy*, 242, 225; "Browning's Love Told," *LAT*, January 26, 1927, 3.

88. "Browning's Love Told," *LAT*, January 26, 1927, 3.

89. "Boy Friends of Peaches to Tell of Lovemaking," *CDT*, January 28, 1927, 7; Greenburg, *Peaches and Daddy*, 255.

90. Edward W. Browning v. Frances Heenan Browning, 129 Misc. 137; 220 N.Y.S. 651; 1927 N.Y.

91. Browning v. Browning.

92. "The Inquiring Reporter," *CDT*, March 31, 1927, 27; "'Peaches' Contract Canceled by Theater," *Washington Post*, March 31, 1927, 5; "'Peaches' Is Barred from 400 Theaters," *Washington Post*, April 1, 1927, 5.

93. Harry Carr, "A Dirty Case," *LAT*, March 23, 1927, A1; Harry Carr, "The Lancer," *LAT*, October 12, 1926, A1; Fairburn, *Justice and Law*, 374; "Gold Digging," *CDT*, March 25, 1927, 10; Richard Harding Armstrong, "Alimony as Abetting Divorce," *Virginia Law Register* 12, no. 10 (1927), 611.

94. "Judge Attacks Alimony-Seekers," *Ogden Standard-Examiner*, February 5, 1927, 2; Roy J. Gibbons, "Chicago Judge Denounces Childless Wives Who Demand Alimony with Divorces," *Manitowoc Herald-News*, December 24, 1925, 3; "American Wives Biggest Grafters Says Judge Strong of New York," *Laredo Times*, April 9, 1926, 2.

95. "Alimony Payers to Fight for Their Rights," *Washington Post*, May 22, 1927, SM2; "Valuation Absurdities," *Wall Street Journal*, April 7, 1927, 1; "Two Ways to Beat Alimony, Have Coin or Die," *The Morning Herald*, October 25, 1927, 10; "Alimony Payers to Fight for Their Rights," Anonymous, *Ogden Standard-Examiner*, May 22, 1927, 31.

96. "'Y' to War on Gold Diggers," *LAT*, September 27, 1927, A4; "Alimony Brides Make Business of Collecting," *The Lima News*, February 23, 1928, 8; Dorothy Dunbar Bromley, "The Ethics of Alimony," *Harper's Magazine* 154 (1927, 305–16), 315; "Two Prominent Women Differ over Present-Day Wives—Fannie Hurst and Mrs. J. Borden Harriman Take Opposite Views in Magazine War," *Dunkirk Evening Observer*, July 12, 1927, 7.

97. Kuby, "Till Disinterest Do Us Part," 395–99.

98. "Alimony Brides Make Business of Collecting," *Lima News*, February 23, 1928, 8; "Wow! Wait 'Till Peggy or Jack Hears of This," *CDT*, May 8, 1922, 21; "Doctor Battling Alimony Gets Bomb Threat," *CT*, June 28, 1927, 1; Hazel Canning, "The A.A.P.P. Is Out to Scotch Alimony Evil," *Boston Globe*, May 15, 1927, 8.

99. Canning, "Scotch Alimony Evil"; "Ex-Husbands Start Hot Fight on Alimony Racket," *Capital Times*, September 15, 1931, 2; Roy J. Gibbons, "Militant Wife Launches War against Alimony in Chicago," *Freeport Journal-Standard*, July 8, 1927, 13; "Getting After Our 'Alimony Heiresses,'" *Hamilton Evening Journal*, February 6, 1926, 22. In his history of divorce in the United States, DiFonzo explains, "The same cultural opening that perceived women's economic progress as generating virtual equality with men closed tightly against more women who received alimony." See DiFonzo, *Beneath the Fault Line*, 63.

100. Lillian G. Genn, "Marriage for Alimony Only a Public Menace Says Faith Baldwin," *Modesto News-Herald*, September 25, 1928, 26.

101. Baldwin, *Alimony*, 118, 10, 3, 8, 7.

102. Baldwin, *Alimony*, 196, 98, 198, 11, 109, 110.

103. Baldwin, *Alimony*, 108, 153, 198.

104. Baldwin, *Alimony*, 221, 113, 31, 208, 274.

105. As Jacobson documents, Jews in the United States were seen as racially distinct and inferior during the second half of the nineteenth century, a status that lingered into the 1920s. Jacobson writes, "Jews did not disappear from racial view overnight in the mid-1920s, nor had racial Jewishness vanished completely even by the 1940s." Jacobson, *Whiteness of a Different Color*, 187. On "probationary whiteness," see Jacobson, *Whiteness of a Different Color*, 176.

106. Vernon P. Cooley, "Purpose of Alimony Club Is Outlined by Dr. Cooley," *St. Petersburg Times*, August 13, 1927, 9. On the racial and gender politics of the Progressive-era crusades against white slavery, see Donovan, *White Slave Crusades*.

107. Fairburn, *Law and Justice*, 372. As Bederman notes, the term "sheik" as a description of a man with primitive and passionate sexuality to whom women were inescapably attracted "became a staple of the 1920s romantic vocabulary." Bederman, *Manliness and Civilization*, 233.

108. Fairburn, *Law and Justice*, 386, 388, 407.

109. Clem Whitaker, "World's Champion Alimony Martyr Is Asking Freedom," *The Victoria Advocate*, August 24, 1927, 4; "California's Embarrassing Problem of the First 'Alimony Martyr,'" *The American Weekly*, Sunday supplement to *The San Antonio Light*, December 25, 1927.

110. "Alimony Sam Sells Popcorn at Market," *Oakland Tribune*, December 14, 1928, 39.

111. For example, an ad in the January 30, 1929, *Oakland Tribune* (page 14) declared "Alimony Sam Says 'Arrival of a youngster in the Al Jolson home will give Al an excellent excuse for another 'Mammy' song.'"

112. "California's Embarrassing Problem of the First 'Alimony Martyr,'" *The American Weekly*, Sunday supplement to *The San Antonio Light*, December 25, 1927.

113. "California's Embarrassing Problem," *The American Weekly*; Phil J. Sinnott, "Buddies Go to the Rescue—and 'Alimony Sam' Is Free at Last," *Miami-News-Record*, October 25, 1928, 4; "'No Alimony' Martyr Works on State Road," *San Mateo Daily Times*, January 28, 1931, 5; "Sam Reid in Court Again as Divorced Wife Sues," *Woodland Democrat*, July 30, 1931, 1.

114. "Brooklyn Jail Alimony Payers Organize," *NYT*, January 25, 1927, 3; "Gold Diggers Denounced by Divorce Court Judge," *Washington Post*, February 5, 1927, 1.

115. "Alimony Club Outlines War on Gold Diggers," *CDT*, August 4, 1927, 21; "Alimony Club Opens Office," *CDT*, August 2, 1927, 3; *Xi Psi Phi Quarterly*, 19; "Nothing Wrong in Silk Nightie, Attorney Says," *CDT*, April 18, 1923, 17; "Mrs. Cooley to Get Her Decree; Judge Indicates," *CDT*, April 20, 1923, 2; Cooley v. Cooley, 244 Ill. App. 488, 1927.

116. Cooley v. Cooley, 244 Ill. App. 488, 1927, 491–92.

117. Cooley v. Cooley, 244 Ill. App. 488, 1927, 493. As evidence of the growing influence of legal realism, the opinion cited sociologist and legal scholar Roscoe Pound. Pound's jurisprudence was sensitive to the gap between the ideals of law and the pragmatics of legal administration.

118. "Calls Alimony Clubmen to Fight His Gay Ex-Wife," *CDT*, June 15, 1927, 19; "3 Million a Year Alimony Bill for Chicago," *Syracuse Herald*, July 17, 1927, 1.

119. For example, see "Chicago Alimony Rebels Form Club to Seek Fairer Divorces," *Kingsport Times*, July 21, 1927, 6; "Alimony Club to Ward Off Gold Diggers," *Daily Northwestern*, July 21, 1927, 3; "Alimony Club Opens Fight on 'Gold Digging,'" *Lima News*, August 5, 1927; "Wronged Husbands Form Alimony Club to Protect Cash," *Appleton Post-Crescent*, July 21, 1927, 1.

120. Roy J. Gibbons, "Militant Wife Launches War against Alimony in Chicago," *Ogden Standard-Democrat*, July 12, 1927, 4.

121. "Alimony Club Opens Office," *CDT*, August 2, 1927, 3. On Fjellander's background, see U.S. Census, 1920, Chicago Ward 27, Cook (Chicago), Illinois; Roll T625_339; Page: 4A; Enumeration District: 1634; Image: 493. Ancestry.com. *1920 United States Federal Census* [database on-line]. Provo, UT, U.S.: The Generations Network, Inc., 2005.

122. "Albany Witnesses Hit Alimony Law," *NYT*, February 27, 1929, 4; "Gold Diggers Denounced by Divorce Court Judge," *Washington Post*, February 5, 1927, 1.

123. William M. Marston, "Why Men Are Organizing to Fight Female Dominance," *Hamilton Evening Journal*, October 19, 1929, 1; "The Gold Digger," *LAT*, April 8, 1929, A4.

Chapter Two

1. "Woman Sues Rudy Vallee for $250,000 Heart Balm," *LAT*, September 5, 1934, 2; "Scouts Vallee's Charge," *NYT*, September 9, 1934, 11; "Never Met Girl Suing for $250,000 Balm, Rudy Vallee Says," *CDT*, September 7, 1934, 17.

2. "Rudy Vallee Sued for Heart Balm," *Washington Post*, September 5, 1934, 1; "Vallee's Lawyer Says Woman Wrote Crooner," *LAT*, September 5, 1934, 2; "Rudy Vallee Is Served in Suit for $250,000," *CDT*, September 5, 1934, 8; "Loses Point Against Vallee," *NYT*, September 16, 1934, 11; "Girl Asks $250,000 Balm from Vallee," *Pittsburgh Press*, September 5, 1934, 8; "Rudy Vallee Sued by Girl Performer," *Courier-Journal*, September 5, 1934, 3; "Typist Seeking Balm of Vallee Files Affidavit," *LAT*, September 9, 1934, 12; "Scouts Vallee's Charge," *NYT*, September 9, 1934, 11; "Never Met Girl Suing for $250,000 Balm, Rudy Vallee Says," *CDT*, September 7, 1934, 17; "Rudy Vallee Scoffs at Suit for Balm," *Washington Post*, September 7, 1934, 11.

3. According to Julie Berebitsky, "Historians have found nothing to substantiate the claim that heart balm cases were especially disposed to extortion or invention, and legal records show a diversity of plaintiffs. Substantiation is also lacking for reformers' assertion that juries handed down excessive awards to pretty plaintiffs playing innocent." See Berebitsky, *Sex and the Office*, 123–24.

4. See Werhnyak, "'O, Perjured Lover, Atone! Atone!'"

5. As Angus McLaren notes, "The press was not interested in the everyday complaints of the new army of shop girls and typists who fought off the sexual overtures of their employers." McLaren, *Sexual Blackmail*, 169.

6. "End of the Golden Heart-Balm Era as Vivid Vera Cashes In," *Salt Lake Tribune*, April 28, 1935, 6; Mary Day Winn, "The Love Racket," *Billings Gazette*, August 24, 1930, magazine section, 4.

7. Larson, "A Feminist Rethinking of Seduction."

8. Donovan, *Respectability on Trial*, 37–70.

9. Lawrence Friedman explains a typical scenario: "He had taken her off the marriage market during what might have been crucial marriageable years." See Friedman, *Guarding Life's Dark Secrets*, 113.

10. "Actress Assails Al Rogell's Marriage in Heart Balm Suit," *LAT*, July 30, 1939, 3; "Actress Describes Love-Making of Director in Heart Balm Suit," *LAT*, July 23, 1939, A6; "Actress Drops $125,000 Suit: Compromise Reached in Demand for Balm," *LAT*, December 27, 1939, A10.

11. Friedman, *Guarding Life's Dark Secrets*, 111; Lettmaier, *Broken Engagements*, 30; Coombs, "Agency and Partnership."

12. Friedman, *Guarding Life's Dark Secrets*, 111.

13. Simmons, *Making Marriage Modern*, 105–37.

14. Coontz, *Marriage*, 218; Davis, *More Perfect Unions*, 31.

15. Ware, *Holding Their Own*, 6–8. Based on her interviews with couples who lived during the Great Depression, sociologist Mirra Komarovsky observed, "Fear of pregnancy seems to be a specter haunting many of these families." See Komarovsky, *Unemployed Man and His Family*, 131.

16. Davis, *More Perfect Unions*, 32, 8; McElvaine, *Great Depression*, 175. Larissa Werhnyak argues that opposition to breach of promise lawsuits was a "direct response to this crisis of masculinity." See Werhnyak, "'O, Perjured Lover,'" 128.

17. Dickstein, *Dancing in the Dark*, 226.

18. In 1937, a woman's average pay was $525 a year compared to $1,027 for men. See Ware, *Holding Their Own*, 29. On labor segmentation by sex during the Great Depression, see Kessler-Harris, *Out to Work*; Milkman, "Women's Work and Economic Crisis."

19. McElvaine, *Great Depression*, 182.

20. Abelson, "Gender and Homelessness in the Great Depression."

21. Gordon writes, "In both contemporary and historical descriptions of the depression, it is remarkable how little attention was paid to the problems of women, let alone single mothers." See Gordon, *Pitied but Not Entitled*, 184; Terkel, *Hard Times*, 353.

22. According to McElvaine, widespread unemployment during the Great Depression "upset the traditional roles of father, mother, and children." McElvaine, *The Great Depression*, 180.

23. Ware notes that many housewives spent nearly sixty hours a week on housework during the Great Depression. See Ware, *Holding Their Own*, 5.

24. For an exemplary social history of the transition from silent film to the era of "talkies," see Eyman, *The Speed of Sound*.

25. Young and Young, *Great Depression in America*, 319.

26. Historian Robert McElvaine writes, "Movies were *the* preeminent form of popular culture in the 1930s." See McElvaine, *The Great Depression*, 209. Susan Ware concurs: "The movies dominated American popular culture from the 1920s through the 1940s, but they played an especially large role during the 1930s." See Ware, *Holding Their Own*, 178. On the pre-Code era, see Doherty, *Pre-Code Hollywood*. On the continuities between the pre-Code era and the Production Code era, and a critique of pre-Code cinema as unique, see Jacobs, *The Wages of Sin*.

27. The themes of class rise and cross-class romance had a strong presence in silent cinema. Films like *That Certain Thing* (1928), *Manhandled* (1924), and Clara Bow's *It* (1927) involved storylines that centered on working-class women leveraging their sex appeal to attract upper-class men. See Jacobs, *The Wages of Sin*, 12. Stephen Sharot notes a steep increase in the number of "class rise" films produced during the Great Depression. See Sharot, *Love and Marriage across Social Classes*.

28. Sharot, "Wealth and/or Love"; Dooley, *From Scarface to Scarlett*, 19.

29. Clarence Slavens observes that depictions of gold diggers in the 1920s rendered them as "spoiled, baby-ish party-girls" but, by the 1930s, "The gold digger is no longer the childish, spoiled baby who needs to learn a valuable lesson in American economics." Likewise, Janet Staiger argues that the "gold digger" figure humanized earlier filmic representations of "the vamp" in silent cinema. See Slavens, "Gold Digger as Icon," 71; Jacobs, *Wages of Sin*, 152; Staiger, *Bad Woman*, 180.

30. Jacobs, *Wages of Sin*, 152; Robertson, *Guilty Pleasures*; Jordan, *Sex Goddess in American Film*, 30. Jordan argues, "The gendered, and by definition, sexualized, and further, racialized body of the gold digger thus becomes a metonymic signifier for something quintessential about the American capitalist character." Jordan, *Sex Goddess in American Film*, 32.

31. Writing in the early 1970s, feminist film critic Molly Haskell criticized Harlow's roles as "vulgar," "sluttish," and "one of the screen's raunchiest inventions." For Haskell, Harlow's characters were antifeminist because they "were often used to put down other women." Haskell, *From Reverence to Rape*, 113–14, 113.

32. *Lawyer Man*, directed by William Dieterle (Warner Brothers, 1932). The film is based on Max Trell's 1932 book *Lawyer Man*. The book, like the movie, follows the rise, fall, and eventual rehabilitation of an energetic lawyer from the Lower East Side. In the novel, Horace Seagle represents musical comedy star Virginia Johns— "a woman made treacherous by love and self-love"—in a million-dollar breach of promise suit against her former lover and his brother, a New York State senator. Like in Faith Baldwin's novel *Alimony*, a Jewish lawyer assists the gold digger in her legal schemes. Unlike Baldwin's story, Seagle redeems himself at the end of the novel by marrying his wholesome and hardworking assistant and pledging to pursue honest legal work for the rest of his career. Trell, *Lawyer Man*, 223, 158. *Havana Widows*, directed by Ray Enright (First National Pictures, 1933); *Breach of Promise* directed by Paul L. Stein (Ben Verschleiser Productions); *I'm No Angel*, directed by Wesley Ruggles (Paramount Pictures, 1933).

33. The other films from this period that Busby Berkeley directed include *42nd Street* (Warner Brothers, 1933), *Dames* (Warner Brothers, 1934), and *Footlight Parade* (Warner Brothers, 1933).

34. Bergman, *We're in the Money*, 64.

35. *Gold Diggers of 1933*, directed by Busby Berkeley (Warner Brothers, 1933).

36. The threat of having to engage in sex work as a consequence of the Great Depression lurks in the background of *Gold Diggers of 1933*, including Trixie's admonition to Brad and the final musical number, "Remember My Forgotten Man," featuring Joan Blondell playing a sex worker.

37. Hove, *Gold Diggers of 1933*, 107.

38. Hove, "In Search of Happiness," 18, 19; Bergman, *We're in the Money*, 64; Rabinowitz, "Commodity Fetishism," 148. Rabinowitz contends, "The exuberant female presence and camaraderie of the narrative is effectively neutralized by the production numbers, confirming female passivity and isolation." See Rabinowitz, "Commodity Fetishism," 144.

39. Mellencamp, "Sexual Economics of *Gold Diggers of 1933*," 186; Robertson, *Guilty Pleasures*, 73.

40. Hove, *Gold Diggers of 1933*, 50.

41. Mellencamp argues that the presence of police is a reference to the general unrest of the Great Depression that lingers beneath the surface of the movie. See Mellencamp, "Sexual Economics of *Gold Diggers of 1933*," 179.

42. Hove, *Gold Diggers of 1933*, 75.

43. Hove, *Gold Diggers of 1933*, 65.

44. Hove, *Gold Diggers of 1933*, 108.

45. In his essay about *Gold Diggers of 1933* and *Footlight Parade*, Cheyney Ryan observes that these films were released during a time when "the breach of promise suit was coming under heavy attack from state legislatures," and that "the breach of promise suit is clearly where the question of law's relation to love is posed, if not resolved." See Ryan, "Lawyers as Lovers."

46. Hove, *Gold Diggers of 1933*, 167, 162.

47. Apstein, *The Parting of Ways*, 21, 22.

48. "Cleveland Dancer Wins $10,000 Heart Balm," *Cleveland Call and Post*, May 5, 1938, 11; "Seeks $75,000 Heart Balm," *LAT*, January 7, 1936, A8; "Woman Tells of Marriage Promise in Suit for $50,000," *LAT*, January 20, 1938, A2; "Tells of Love and Liquor in $100,000 Suit," *CDT*, February 10, 1937, 1; "Heart Balm Award Huge," *LAT*, April 2, 1936, 6.

49. Winn, "Love Racket"; John L. Coontz, "Heart Balm off the Gold Standard," *Charleston Daily Mail*, July 7, 1935, magazine section, 1; "Dinehart Suit Is Settled," *NYT*, October 5, 1933, 24; Winn, "Love Racket"; Apstein, *The Parting of Ways*, 24, 31.

50. "Heart Balm Award Huge," *LAT*, April 2, 1936, 6; "McCormick Settles with Mrs. Doubleday," *NYT*, May 19, 1934, 14; *American Weekly*. "The New Laws to Stop the 'Heart Balm' Suits," April 12, 1935, 11; "Miss Gay Wins $5000," *LAT*, April 13, 1934, A1, A13.

51. "A Blonde Hat-Check Girl Makes Gestures at a Famous Violinist," *Life*, March 1, 1937, 19; Charles Collins, "A Hang-Over from Golden Age of Heart Balm," *CDT*, April 25, 1937, G11; "Latest Message to Peggy Garcia," *CDT*, February 27, 1937, 7.

52. "Newark 'Daddy' Faces 'Peaches' in Love Suit," *Afro-American*, May 10, 1930, 1; "Daddy Must Pay Peaches $20,000 in Heart Balm," *Afro-American*, May 24, 1930, 1.

53. Everett Wadsworth, "Asks $10,000 from Iowa Specialist," *Chicago Defender*, February 29, 1936, 4; Everett Wadsworth, "White Nurse Wins Only $1 in Heart Balm Suit," *Chicago Defender*, May 23, 1936, 1.

54. "The New Laws to Stop the 'Heart Balm' Suits," *American Weekly*, April 12, 1935, 11; "Indiana House Votes against Heart Balm," *CDT*, February 2, 1935, 1.

55. Coontz, "Heart Balm off the Gold Standard," 11; E. L. Meyer, "Making Light of the Times," *Capital Times*, January 28, 1930, 16; Winn, "Love Racket," 4.

56. Winn, "Love Racket," 4; Alma Whitaker, "Alimony Law Held to Need Repair Work," *LAT*, August 15, 1934, A7. On the propensity for male jurors to favor female heart balm plaintiffs, see also Coontz, "Heart Balm off the Gold Standard"; "Muscling into a Good Racket," *Billings Gazette*, February 23, 1930, 4.

57. Winn, "Love Racket," 4; Frank A. Garbutt, "Women Beware," *LAT*, August 20, 1935, A4; "Heart Balm in the Legislature," *CDT*, April 1, 1935, 12; Roi Ottley, "This Hectic Harlem," *New York Amsterdam News*, March 17, 1934, 9.

58. According to Berebitsky, the anti–heart balm movement "harbored a deep, abiding suspicion of women." For Hirshman and Larson, "Repealing the heart-balm actions was a way to scale back women's bargaining power." See Berebitsky, *Sex and the Office*, 124; Hirshman and Larson, *Hard Bargains*, 166.

59. "No Balm for Blackmail," *Christian Science Monitor*, April 2, 1935, 16; Theodore Apstein, "Legal Blows Struck at Long-Flourishing Heart Balm Racket," *The Daily Times-News*, April 17, 1935, 7; Doris Blake (the pen name for Antoinette Donnelly), "Suit for Heart Balm Is Tawdry Label for Love," *CDT*, May 9, 1934, 19.

60. As Friedman notes, "whatever their station in life, breach of promise was definitely only for respectable women. It was definitely not an option for women of the type we would today call sexually active." See Friedman, *Guarding Life's Dark Secrets*, 115.

61. Apstein, *The Parting of Ways*, 26; Feinsinger, "Legislative Attack on 'Heart Balm,'" 984.

62. "Alimony and 'Heart Balm' for Men Urged by Leaders of the National Women's Party," *NYT*, June 24, 1935, 1; "Can Money Mend a Woman's Heart?" *LAT*, April 21, 1935, J3; John L. Coontz, "Heart Balm off the Gold Standard," *Charleston Daily Mail*, July 7, 1935, magazine section, 1.

63. "Balm Ban Made Law in Indiana," *LAT*, March 12, 1935, 1; Robert West Nicholson oral history transcript, Indiana State Oral History Project, page 47, accessed December 22, 2016, http://cdm16066.contentdm.oclc.org/cdm/ref/collection/p16066 coll40/id/207; "Indiana House Votes against Heart Balm," *CDT*, February 2, 1935, 1.

64. "Indiana House Votes sgainst Heart Balm," *CDT*, February 2, 1935, 1.

65. "Heart Balm Suits Barred in Indiana Bill," *CDT*, January 23, 1935, 19; "Indiana House Votes against Heart Balm," *CDT*, February 2, 1935, 1; "End of the Golden Heart-Balm Era as Vivid Vera Cashes In," *Salt Lake Tribune*, April 28, 1935, 6; "Gold Digger War Brought Here by Indiana Woman," *CDT*, March 28, 1935, 16.

66. "Indiana House Votes against Heart Balm," *CDT*, February 2, 1935, 1; "Gold Digger War Brought Here by Indiana Woman," *CDT*, March 28, 1935, 16; Kathleen Norris, "The Blight on the Great American Heart Balm Racket," *Salt Lake Tribune*, June 2, 1935, 6.

67. "Gold Digger War Brought Here by Indiana Woman," *CDT*, March 28, 1935, 16; "Foe of Heart Balm to Make U.S. Fight," *Mansfield News-Journal*, March 22, 1935, 4; "The New Laws to Stop the 'Heart Balm' Suits," *American Weekly*, April 12, 1935, 11.

68. Robert West Nicholson oral history transcript, Indiana State Oral History Project, page 49, accessed December 22, 2016, http://cdm16066.contentdm.oclc.org /cdm/ref/collection/p16066coll40/id/207. She said she was inspired to create the bill after receiving a letter from a lawyer in Hammond, Indiana.

69. Friedman, *Guarding Life's Dark Secrets*, 107–9.

70. "Heart Balm," *CDT*, November 15, 1936, 16; *American Weekly*, "New Laws," 11.

71. "Perkins 'Snub' Hit by Mrs. Roosevelt," *NYT*, March 26, 1935, 21; "Ban on Heart Balm Is Made State Law," *NYT*, March 30, 1935, 3; "Move Planned in 8 Other States," *NYT*, March 30, 1935, 3.

72. "Both Houses in N.Y. Vote Bar on Love Suits," *CDT*, March 20, 1935, 1; "Women Scorned," *NYT*, March 24, 1935, E2; "Rush to Start Suits for Balm as Law Changes," *CDT*, May 28, 1935, 9; "Ban on Heart Balm Is Made State Law," *NYT*, March 30, 1935, 3.

73. Fearon v. Treanor, 248 App. Div. 225, N.Y., (1936), 10–11; "Heart Balm Law Upheld by Court," *NYT* May 30, 1936, 18; "United States Supreme Court," *NYT*, May 25, 1937, 54.

74. "Ban on Alienation Suits Held Voice: Husband's Actions Backed by Court," *NYT*, March 1, 1936, 1; "Alienation Issue Argued in Appeal," *NYT*, March 3, 1937, 19; Hanfgarn v. Mark, 159 Misc. 122; 286 N.Y.S. 335, (1936).

75. Hanfgarn v. Mark, 274 N.Y. 22; 8 N.E.2d 47, (1937); "'Heart Balm' Ban Upheld on Appeal," *NYT*, April 28, 1937, 16.

76. "Foe of Heart Balm to Make U.S. Fight," *Mansfield News-Journal*, March 22, 1935, 4; "Iowa Offers Fines to Heal Broken Hearts," *CDT*, February 11, 1937, 1; "Colorado Puts Ban on Suits," *NYT*, April 28, 1937, 16; "New Bay State Law Gives Man Right to Change His Mind, Too," *CDT*, May 26, 1937, 1.

77. Berebitsky, *Sex and the Office*, 122.

78. Lettmaier, *Broken Engagements*; Coombs, "Agency and Partnership"; Werhnyak, "'O, Perjured Lover.'"

79. Saskia Lettmaier explains, "With the advent of women's social and sexual autonomy, the action for breach of promise became as musty and out-of-date as the feminine ideal it enshrined." See Lettmaier, *Broken Engagements*, 170.

80. Werhnyak notes that Mary Risteau, who led Maryland's effort to ban heart balm, came from a wealthy family, and that Eudochia Bell Smith from Colorado was a former debutante. See Werhnyak, "'O, Perjured Lover,'" 201–2.

Chapter Three

1. Crist v. Crist, 62 N.E.2d 252 (1942), 255, 256. Her name is listed as "Margery" in the Appellate Court decision, but it is spelled "Marjorie" in key genealogical documents. As a minor, Marjorie was not able to sue, so Clara Swick, her mother by adoption, acted as her legal "next friend" to file the suit.

2. Crist v. Crist, 176. Herbert's father acted as a "next friend" by initiating the divorce proceedings but, the Appellate Court ruled, it was improper to presume from this action that he was alienating the affection of his son toward his daughter-in-law.

3. Class differences, and the accompanying dispositions inculcated by class status, likely influenced Archie and Rose Crist labeling Marjorie as a gold digger. The Crists experienced a measure of class mobility between 1930 and 1940. Archie Crist was promoted from a cashier's assistant to a cashier, allowing his family to go from renting to owning a home worth approximately $11,000. Walter Swick, by comparison, only completed some school and was employed in construction. These findings are from the 1930 and 1940 censuses. *1930*; Census Place: *Columbus, Franklin, Ohio*; Page: *11A*; Enumeration District: *0003*; FHL microfilm: *2341527*. *1940*; Census Place: *Columbus, Franklin, Ohio*; Roll: m-t0627-03242; Page: *6A*; Enumeration District: 93-47. Ancestry.com. *1940 United States Federal Census*. For Walter Swick, see *1930*; Census Place: *Columbus, Franklin, Ohio*; Page: *23A*; Enumeration District: *0095*; FHL microfilm: *2341531*, Provo, UT, USA: Ancestry.com Operations, Inc., 2012.

4. Leder, *Thanks for the Memories*, 98; Lloyd Wendt, "What Experts Say About War Marriages," *CT*, February 1, 1942, D1.

5. Zeiger, *Entangling Alliances*, 7.

6. According to Pascoe, the War Brides Act weakened state and local antimiscegenation laws. See Pascoe, *What Comes Naturally*, 92. See also Zeiger, *Entangling Alliances*, 164–65.

7. Zeiger, *Entangling Alliances*, 127–63; Pascoe, *What Comes Naturally*.

8. Honey, "Maternal Welders," 484, 485.

9. "Vote Allotment Bill for Service Men's Families," *CDT*, May 20, 1942, 11; "Draft Bill Raises Wife's Allotment," *NYT*, May 27, 1942, 8.

10. On the allotment system, see Cline, "Allowances to Dependents of Servicemen in the United States," *Annals of the American Academy of Political and Social Science* (May 1943): 1–8, (see especially page 4); Grossman and Cole, "Some Observations on the Distribution of Family Allowance Benefits in World War II," *American Sociological Review* 10:5 (October 1945): 614–18.

11. Lever and Young, *Wartime Racketeers*, 76; Geraldine Smith, "Mother-In-Law as Informer," *St. Louis Post-Dispatch*, March 18, 1945, 4; Frances Spatz, "Allotment Annies Are At It Again," *San Antonio Light*, December 17, 1950, 2. Spatz claimed that 246 women were convicted of abusing the allotment system in 1946; Clifton L. Williams, "Looking on Norfolk," *New Journal and Guide*, January 10, 1948, 10.

12. "Sailor's Bride Convicted Here of Bigamy," *Washington Post*, February 5, 1943, B5; "Girl, 20, Gets 1 to 3 Years for Bigamy," *Washington Post*, October 9, 1943, B1.

13. Lever and Young, *Wartime Racketeers*, 82; Ruth Reynolds, "The 'Victory Girls'; Bigamy Is Their Racket, Though They Claim Marriages to Servicemen Are Prompted by Love and Patriotism—Government Calls It Greed for Allotment Checks," *St. Louis Post-Dispatch*, October 31, 1943, 1.

14. Lever and Young, *Wartime Racketeers*, 83.

15. Reynolds, "Victory Girls"; Lever and Young, *Wartime Racketeers*, 76; Mickey MacDougall, "Legions of Larceny: No. 2—Allotment Brides," *American Weekly*, June 4, 1944, 1.

16. Pfau, "Allotment Annies and Other Wayward Wives," 101. Reports of Elvira Tayloe have been repeated, largely in an uncritical fashion, in a number of histories of World War II, including a popular textbook. See Costello, *Love, Sex, and War*, 269; Costello, *Virtue Under Fire*, 195; Berkin et al., *Making America*, 677.

17. Pfau, "Allotment Annies," 99–100.

18. "Allotment Wives," *The Republic*, February 7, 1946, 10; "Allotment Wives," *Denton Record-Chronicle*, March 17, 1946, 11.

19. *Allotment Wives*, directed by William Nigh (Monogram Pictures, 1945).

20. Weiss, *To Have and To Hold*, 179.

21. Weiss, *To Have and To Hold*, 53.

22. "Gold-Digging Secrets Told," *LAT* October 2, 1949, D8; Powel, *Good Jobs for Good Girls*, xix, 147.

23. "Teenage Poison," *Ladies' Home Journal* 66, no. 11 (November 1949), 64; Bailey, *From Front Porch to Back Seat*, 57–76. On the hierarchy of corsages, see the interfolio photos between pages 96 and 97.

24. Stokes v. Stokes, 222 S.W.2d 108 (1949), Springfield Court of Appeals, Missouri, 111.

25. Stokes v. Stokes, 113–14.

26. Stokes v. Stokes, 117, 125.

27. During the fifteen years following the end of World War II the gross national product increased by close to 250 percent and the per capita income grew by 35 percent. Real wages grew during the 1950s by more than they had during the previous fifty years. See Coontz, *The Way We Never Were*, 24.

28. As Coontz notes, only 43 percent of American families owned homes in 1940 but, by 1960, 62 percent of American families owned their own home. Coontz, *The Way We Never Were*, 24, 31.

29. Leder, *Thanks for the Memories*, 144.

30. Coontz, *The Way We Never Were*, 76–77; Bailey, *Sex in the Heartland*, 83; Davis, *More Perfect Unions*, 99.

31. According to Altschuler and Blumin, "The GI Bill was the most egalitarian and generous initiative blacks had ever experienced." They acknowledge, however, that the act did little to overcome Jim Crow and that the "GI Bill did not reduce racial disparities in the United States." See Altschulter and Blumin, *The GI Bill*, 129. Turner and Bound show that blacks made only small educational gains from the bill, and Southern blacks were especially deprived of the act's benefits. See Turner and Bound, "Going to War and Going to College," 784–815. See also Katznelson, *When Affirmative Action Was White*.

32. Margot Canaday shows how servicemen suspected of being gay were denied G.I. benefits. She writes, "The military establishment used the GI Bill to build a closet within federal social policy." See Canaday, *The Straight State*, 170.

33. May, *Homeward Bound*.

34. Weiss, *To Have and To Hold*, 223, 228–29; Coontz, *The Way We Never Were*, 28.

35. Despite the rhetoric of male breadwinners and female homemakers during the 1950s, shared breadwinning was extremely prevalent. See Weiss, *To Have and To Hold*, 28–29.

36. For all of the promotion of conservative gender norms during the 1950s, there were pushbacks and protests that varied in scale. According to Coontz, family and gender relations that developed during the 1950s "contained some time bombs" activated during the sexual revolution. Joanne Meyerowitz has convincingly argued that understanding the 1950s requires rejecting the simple stereotypes of the era and recognizing the "ambivalences and contradictions in postwar domestic ideology." Susan Lynn contends that scholars overemphasize postwar domesticity by focusing on the media campaign to ensconce women in the domestic sphere, and by taking Betty Friedan's description of the 1950s as an uncomplicated portrait of reality. She shows how organizations like the American Association of University Professors, League of Women Voters, National Council of Negro Women, and the American Friends Service Committee made radical claims for racial and social justice long before the full development of second wave feminism and the New Left. Amanda Littauer locates the origins of the 1960s sexual revolution in female countercultures of the 1940s and 1950s, including "B-girls" who worked for bars enticing men to spend money on drinks. Littauer also demonstrates how sexual experimentation in mainstream middle-class dating culture defied the stereotypes of the 1950s and established the groundwork for the 1960s sexual revolution. In short, the 1950s were more complicated than the mass media images of the time, or popular cultural reminiscences, suggest. See Coontz, *The Way We Never Were*, 38; Meyerowitz, "Beyond the Feminine Mystique," 238; Lynn, "Gender and Progressive Politics"; Littauer, *Bad Girls*.

37. Rex Reed, "From Brando to Scavullo: 2004's Many Losses," *The Observer*, January 10, 2015, accessed June 30, 2017, http://observer.com/2005/01/from-brando -to-scavullo-2004s-many-losses/.

38. Rumors of Holm drinking with playwright Charles MacArthur strained his marriage with actor Helen Hayes. See Conrad, *Billy Rose*, 112–13; Maraniss, *Rome 1960*, 415. According to Earl Conrad, she "became almost as famous for her liking champagne as for her abilities as a swimmer." See Conrad, *Billy Rose*, 110.

39. *LAT*, July 24, 1984, part 8, 3; Sheilah Graham, "Eleanor Holm, Thrown in Mud, Retaliates," *LAT*, November 5, 1937, 21. Her "champagne and cigarettes" quip is also featured in Conrad, *Billy Rose*, 112.

40. "Orchestra Leader Jarrett Divorces Eleanor Holm," *LAT*, June 10, 1938, A1; "Jarrett Sues Eleanor Holm," *LAT*, December 3, 1937, A1.

41. On the lack of romance in Billy Rose's marriage with Fanny Brice, see Cohen, *Not Bad for Delancey Street*, 55–58. On his discomfort with being known as "Mr. Brice," see Gottlieb, *Nine Lives of Billy Rose*, 94. Because of Holm's departure from the film, *Tarzan's Revenge* has an unusually abrupt ending. See Gottlieb, *Nine Lives*, 131.

42. Cohen, *Not Bad for Delancey Street*, 135–36. See also Conrad, *Billy Rose*, 140.

43. Joe Donnelly, "Eleanor Holm, 59, Peppery as Ever," *LAT*, June 13, 1972, F1.

44. "Report Stirs Fannie Brice," *LAT*, November 13, 1937, A1.

45. "Life Calls on Billy Rose and Wife," *Life* (8:20), May 13, 1940, 112–17; "Eleanor Holm Suing for Separation," *LAT*, November 20, 1951, 2.

46. "Gentlemen Prefer Blondes," *Life* (27:26), December 26, 1949, 69; Cohen, *Not Bad for Delancey Street*, 202.

47. Gottlieb, *Nine Lives*, 44. See also Conrad, *Billy Rose*, 96–97. On his attitudes toward women, see Gottlieb, *Nine Lives*, 95.

48. In his biography of Billy Rose, Mark Cohen cites sources that claim that Holm called Rose a "dirty Jew" and a "little Jew bastard." See Cohen, *Not Bad for Delancey Street*, 109, 206.

49. Cohen, *Not Bad for Delancey Street*, 199–200.

50. "Eleanor Holm Reported Separated from Billy Rose," *LAT*, October 11, 1951, 2; "Joyce Matthews Attempts Suicide," *NYT*, July 16, 1951, 16; "Eleanor Holm Reported Separated from Billy Rose," *LAT*, October 11, 1951, 2; "Eleanor Holm," *LAT*, July 24, 1984, H3; Cohen, *Not Bad for Delancey Street*, 206.

51. "Eleanor Holm 'Locks Out' Billy Rose," *LAT*, October 12, 1951, 2; Gottlieb, *Nine Lives*, 187; "Eleanor Holm Hits Back at Rose in Marital Row," *LAT* August 8, 1952, 8; Nizer, *My Life in Court*, 163.

52. "Eleanor Holm Hits Back at Rose in Marital Roe," *LAT*, August 8, 1952, 8; Nizer, *My Life in Court*, 163–64.

53. Nizer, *My Life in Court*, 165–66; "Report Rose, Eleanor Holm in Agreement," *CDT*, January 5, 1954, 6; "Rose's Ex Sees 'Lady' as Untrue," *LAT*, March 28, 1975, G11; Conrad, *Billy Rose*, 223; "'War of the Roses' Ended, and It's Costly to Billy," *CDT*, January 8, 1954, 6; Harold Farber, "Eleanor Holm Wins Separation Suit after Billy Rose Drops All Charges," *NYT*, September 11, 1952, 34.

54. Nizer, *My Life in Court*, 167.

55. Brodkin, *How the Jews Became White Folks*; Berman, "Sociology, Jews, and Intermarriage," 47; Cohen, *Not Bad for Delancey Street*, 109.

56. Cohen, *Not Bad for Delancey Street*, 168.

57. James Gilbert, for instance, points to different models of manhood in the 1950s that stood in contrast to the rugged individualism of John Wayne's cowboy mystique, including the self-effacement of Ozzie Nelson and the pious surrender of Billy Graham. He writes, "This was never entirely John Wayne's world any more than it ever belonged to Liberace." See Gilbert, *Men in the Middle*, 8. For criticism of the "crisis" concept applied to 1950s masculinities, see Traister, "Academic Viagra"; May, *Homeward Bound*, 85–88; Gilbert, *Men in the Middle*. Writing about the late nineteenth and early twentieth century, Bederman argues that accounts of a masculinity crisis wrongly imply that masculinity is a transhistorical entity instead of a construct undergoing constant transformation. See Bederman, *Manliness and Civilization*, 11.

58. Davis, *More Perfect Unions*, 99.

59. Wilner, *Alimony*.

60. "Books Published Today," *NYT*, September 3, 1952, 27; Anthony M. Ludovici, "The Alimony Racket," *The International Journal of Sexology* 6 (1952–53): 236–39.

61. Wilner, *Alimony*, 215, 220.

62. Wilner, *Alimony*, 4, x, xii, 5, 11, 6, 41.

63. "Burt Zollo, 1924–2014," *CT*, March 25, 2014.

64. "Miss Gold Digger," *Playboy*, December 1953, 6–8.

65. "Miss Gold Digger," *Playboy*, December 1953, 7.

66. "Miss Gold Digger," *Playboy*, December 1953, 7.

67. "Miss Gold Digger," *Playboy*, December 1953, 8.

68. Molly Mayfield, "Here's Challenge to College Gals," *News-Herald*, May 4, 1955, 5; "Dear Molly Mayfield," *News-Herald*, May 21, 1955, 13.

69. Bowman, *Marriage for Moderns*; *Who's Right?*, 1954, McGraw Hill, Internet Archive, accessed July 10, 2018.

70. Bullock's Downtown ad, *LAT*, December 20, 1955, 19; *LAT*, January 8, 1956, K55.

71. Spoto, *Marilyn Monroe*, 219.

72. Dyer, *Heavenly Bodies*, 40.

73. This argument is widespread among scholars studying Monroe. Richard Dyer claims, "Monroe became virtually a household word for sex." Laura Mulvey claims that she is the "ultimate signifier of sexuality." Will Scheibel describes Monroe as "the quintessential female sex symbol of 1950s Hollywood." See Dyer, *Heavenly Bodies*, 21; Mulvey, "Thoughts on Marilyn Monroe," 209; Scheibel, "Marilyn Monroe."

74. May, *Homeward Bound*, 62. For the Groucho Marx quote, see Spoto, *Marilyn Monroe*, 148. Scheibel, "Marilyn Monroe, 5; Cohen, "Horizontal Walk," 267; Mulvey, "Thoughts on Marilyn Monroe," 209.

75. Spoto, *Marilyn Monroe*, 46, 36, 74. Lois Banner concurs: "Grace dreamed of being Jean Harlow, and she projected that dream onto Norma Jean." See Banner, *Marilyn Monroe*, 38.

76. Banner, *Marilyn Monroe*, 21, 343, 118.

77. Spoto, *Marilyn Monroe*, 146.

78. According to Spoto, "More than any other portraits of a nude woman in the history of photography, those of Marilyn Monroe taken in 1949 became virtual icons, everywhere recognizable, ever in demand." See Spoto, *Marilyn Monroe*, 153.

79. Spoto, *Marilyn Monroe*, 210–13.

80. Spoto noted that she "turned potential personal and professional disaster into conquest." See Spoto, *Marilyn Monroe*, 211–12.

81. Spoto, *Marilyn Monroe*, 229.

82. Mulvey, "Unmasking the Gaze," 28. As Spoto described it, "The role of Lorelei Lee fixed Marilyn in the world's consciousness as the exaggeratedly, dishily seductive blonde." Spoto, *Marilyn Monroe*, 331.

83. A film critic for the *Washington Post* speculated, "When Miss Loos wrote *Gentlemen Prefer Blondes*, it is highly probable that she had a definite person in mind, and though the identity of the character is not divulged through the entirety of the story—nor is there a name assigned to Lorelei in the opus—I'd be willing to bet two bits that the person referred to has a prominent part in the forthcoming world beater [record-setter], 'The Skyrocket.'" See Jack Y. Lad, "Photoplays and Players," *The Washington Post*, April 11, 1926, F2. Constance Rosenblum writes, "Loos could not have avoided the endless newspaper accounts of Peggy's past, which resembled a souped-up version of Lorelei's story while perfectly capturing its flip, mercenary tone." See Rosenblum, *Gold Digger*, 156. Eve Golden claims that Joyce was "the inspiration for the literary, stage and film anti-heroine Lorelei Lee, in Anita Loos' *Gentlemen Prefer Blondes*." See Eve Golden, "Peggy Hopkins Joyce: The Gentleman Preferred Blonde," *Films of the Golden Age* 17 (Summer 1999). Maya Cantu also

maintains that Lorelei is modeled after Joyce. See Cantu, *American Cinderellas*, 60. Others speculate that Loos constructed Lorelei based on the exploits of Ziegfeld Follies star Lillian Lorraine (See Wallace, *Capital of the World*, 162). Loos's explanation of the origins of Lorelei Lee is inconsistent. In 1963, Loos stated that she based the character on Ziegfeld performer Mabel Minnow, a woman with whom publisher H. L. Mencken had an infatuation. See Anita Loos, "The Biography of a Book," in *Gentlemen Prefer Blondes: The Illuminating Diary of a Professional Lady*, 13. In her 1966 memoir, Loos claimed that she modeled Lorelei Lee after Mae Davis, another of Mencken's lovers. She said, "The satisfaction of getting even with Mae Davis for seducing the man I loved more than paid for the pains of bringing Lorelei into the world." Loos, *A Girl Like I*, 272. In the same work, Loos claimed that she drew inspiration for Lorelei from observing sex workers in San Diego. She wrote, "Those San Diego ladies of the evening may have given me a slant on that timeworn profession which I was to capitalize on when I wrote *Gentlemen Prefer Blondes*. For I couldn't take seriously the lost virtue of a heroine who was too dense to have any kind of emotional experience at all." See Loos, *A Girl Like I*, 54–55. Maya Cantu identifies another potential inspiration for Lorelei Lee, the fictional Lulu Lorrimer. Roy McCardell's comic novels *Conversations of a Chorus Girl* (1903) and *The Show Girl and her Friends* (1904) featured Lorrimer as a gold-digging chorus girl with wise-cracking brunette sidekick similar to Lorelei's friend Dorothy Shaw. Cantu writes, "While Anita Loos never acknowledged reading McCardell's work, it's likely that *Gentlemen Prefer Blondes*' Lorelei Lee inherited some literary DNA from Lulu Lorrimer." Cantu, *American Cinderellas*, 51.

84. It was the second most popular novel of 1926 and reached its ninth edition in March of that year. See Wood, "Gentlemen Prefer Adaptations," 567. Frost, "Blondes Have More Fun," 292.

85. Scholars have presented Lorelei Lee as a hero who, in one fell swoop, subverts the hierarchical gender order and the capitalist economy on which it depends. Bethany Wood argues that Lorelei mocks consumer capitalism, especially the luxury market in which upper-class women are embroiled. Jason Barrett-Fox uncovers "Loos' radical though coded feminist critique." He argues that Lorelei Lee was not just a superficial flapper, but a character who exemplified "types of feminist-coded rhetorics that were largely nonexistent in the 1920s." Cultural studies scholar Lori Landay describes Lorelei Lee as the "consummate Jazz Age female trickster" and, although Lorelei "is a gold digger who is motivated by gem lust, her trickery leads to endless possibilities and strengthens the economy and society." Legal scholar Saskia Lettmaier contends that Loos uses Lorelei to simultaneously embody and condemn Victorianism. Lorelei's dependence on men for material support, fused with the crafty way she extracts gifts from men, pillories the gender system. Lettmaier writes, "Her gold-digging blonde enacts a critique of the system of commodification and objectification that nineteenth-century gender ideology upholds." See Wood, "Gentlemen Prefer Adaptations," 566; Barrett-Fox, "Rhetorics of Indirection, Indiscretion, Insurrection," 222, 235; Landay, *Female Trickster*, 55, 20. Lettmaier, *Broken Promises*, 185.

86. In the novel, Lorelei Lee encourages Spoffard to send her love letters, which she photographs for legal proof in case she loses them. She thinks about marrying him, but concludes that it's "quite a quandary because it might really be better if Henry should happen to decide that he should not get married, and he should change his mind, and desert a girl, and then it would only be right if a girl should sue him for a breach of promise." Loos, *Gentlemen Prefer Blondes*, 129.

87. Coombs, "Agency and Partnership," 7. Christina Simmons considers how novels of the 1920s introduced characters who "served to legitimize or delegitimize for readers certain kinds of subjectivities and forms of heterosexual relations that facilitated or obstructed the achievement of modern marriage. They helped to normalize certain character types and demonize others." See Simmons, *Making Marriage Modern*, 139.

88. "Diamonds Are a Girl's Best Friend," Leo Robin and Jule Styne, 1949.

89. *Gentlemen Prefer Blondes*, directed by Howard Hawks (Twentieth Century Fox, 1953).

90. Hegeman, "Taking *Blondes* Seriously," 525.

91. Mulvey, "Visual Pleasure and Narrative Cinema."

92. H. Alpert, "Bumps and Grinds," *Saturday Review* 36 (August 1953): 27–28; *Catholic World*, "Gentlemen Prefer Blondes," 177 (August 1953): 384; Scheibel, "Marilyn Monroe," 6.

93. Haskell, *From Reverence to Rape*, 256, 254; Spoto, *Marilyn Monroe*, 331.

94. For Susan Hegeman, "Lorelei and Dorothy are represented as pure fetish objects" in the opening "Little Rock" song-and-dance number but, as the film progresses, the film features men as objects to be admired and scrutinized. According to Will Scheibel, the antics of Dorothy and Lorelei sabotage "the patriarchal viewing economy" that the movie established for its viewers. For Mulvey, the comedy of *Gentlemen Prefer Blondes* partakes and centers on the male gaze, but it also satirizes it. "Ultimately," she writes, "comedy subverts and overrides the conventions of 'visual pleasure' by making its textual construction comically visible, and the spectator is unavoidably distanced by laughter." Mulvey points to an early scene where Lorelei and Dorothy make an entrance onto the ship. The sequence "satirizes cinematic voyeurism" because the women walk onto the ship with the intent to be looked at and appreciated, but are ultimately ignored. In this and other ways, the film subverts the male gaze and engages in feminist messaging that is radical for the early 1950s. See Hegeman, "Taking *Blondes* Seriously," 547; Scheibel, "Marilyn Monroe," 9; Mulvey, "Unmasking the Gaze," 21, 19.

95. See Arbuthnot and Seneca, "Pre-Text and Text in *Gentlemen Prefer Blondes*," 18. They write, "We could think of no other film in which women so consistently subverted the objectifying male gaze." See Arbuthnot and Seneca, "Pre-Text and Text," 16. Arbuthnot and Seneca borrow the phrase "mammary madness" from Rosen, *Popcorn Venus*, 267–82.

96. Banner, "Creature from the Black Lagoon," 19; Cohen, "Horizontal Walk."

97. Spoto, *Marilyn Monroe*, 219. According to Mulvey, "Monroe became a superstar quite suddenly in 1953." See Mulvey, "Thoughts on Marilyn Monroe," 205.

98. Konkle, "Marry a Millionaire," 364.

99. On these pressures, see, for example, Whyte, *Organization Man*.

100. For example, in his 1950 study *The Lonely Crowd*, David Riesman discussed the "uneasinesses caused by the newly liberated." See Riesman, *Lonely Crowd*, 280.

101. Konkle, "Marry a Millionaire," 374, 366.

102. My description here only touches on one of a number of important points Konkle makes about the film, including its messages about social class and masculinity. She explores the film as "a democratic fantasy of classlessness, while also reiterating that marriage was a means of changing class." See Konkle, "Marry a Millionaire," 366.

103. "Loco the Heiress," *How to Marry a Millionaire*, CBS Home Entertainment, NTA Film Network, 1957.

104. The women recite this oath in the episode "Alias the Secretary" (season 1, episode 9).

105. "Alias the Secretary," *How to Marry a Millionaire*, CBS Home Entertainment, NTA Film Network, 1957.

106. "Peaches Browning Autopsy," *NYT*, August 25, 1956, 32.

107. "Peaches Browning Is Dead at 46; Child-Bride Symbol of Twenties," *NYT*, August 24, 1956, 19.

108. Pitzulo, *Bachelors and Bunnies*, 7; Banner, *Marilyn Monroe*, 6.

Chapter Four

1. H. B. Kenny, "Cap Kenny Calling," *News-Herald*, April 5, 1960, 4; Hal Boyle, "There's Just One More Shopping Day before It's 'Valentine Day,'" *The Plain Speaker*, February 12, 1960, 8; "Dear Abby," *Warren Times Mirror*, March 12, 1963, 3.

2. Abigail Van Buren, "Dear Abby: Never Trust a Gold-Digger," *The Bristol Daily Courier*, March 26, 1962, 7; "Dear Abby," *Warren Times Mirror*, February 1, 1963, 3; Sally Shaw, "Dear Sally," *New Oxford Item*, October 4 1962, 4.

3. Dorothy Dix, "He's Being Played for Sucker," *The Evening Standard*, May 2, 1957, 38; "Dear Abby: American vs. Oriental," *Bristol Daily Courier*, March 1, 1961, 9; "Ann Landers," *The Evening Sun*, June 4, 1963, 10.

4. See Rosen, *World Split Open*.

5. Rosen, *World Split Open*, 204–5. See also Davis, *More Perfect Unions*, 183.

6. Davis, *More Perfect Unions*, 179.

7. On the collective action that preceded Stonewall, see Elizabeth Armstrong and Suzanna Crage, "Movements and Memory: The Making of the Stonewall Myth," 724–51. In 1970, two men, Richard Baker and James Michael McConnell, unsuccessfully applied for a marriage license in Minnesota, and thereby took the first steps in a decades-long battle to establish the legality of gay marriage. Their appeal to the Minnesota Supreme Court was unsuccessful. See Baker v. Nelson, 291 Minn. 310, 191 N.W.2d 185 (1971).

8. See Bailey, *Sex in the Heartland*.

9. D'Emilio and Freedman, *Intimate Matters*, 330–31; Lefkovitz, *Strange Bedfellows*, 11.

10. D'Emilio and Freedman, *Intimate Matters*, 331; Ciji Ware, "Economics of Divorce," *New West*, March 28, 1977, 8.

11. Friedman, *Law in America*, 63–65.

12. "Divorce: Make Sense, Not War," *Money* (2), February 1973, 28.

13. "No-Fault: New Emphasis in Divorce Cases," *LAT*, February 14, 1977, 1.

14. William Flanagan, "You Don't Need a Lawyer to Get a Divorce . . . But It Helps," *New York*, December 6, 1976, 107.

15. In her study of the effect of no-fault divorce in California, Lenore Weitzman famously found that the woman's standard of living decreases by seventy-three percent following a divorce while a man's standard of living increases by forty-two percent. See Weitzman, *Divorce Revolution*, 274.

16. As Martha Fineman explains, "In light of the different structural positions women and men occupy, it seems obvious that to impose sameness of treatment, particularly within the context of family laws, simply perpetuates inequality." See Fineman, *Illusion of Equality*, 35.

17. Weitzman, *Divorce Revolution*, 147.

18. Mary Ellen Haskett, "Equal Alimony under the Law," *LAT*, March 2, 1980, K10.

19. "Divorcees and Dollars," *Human Behavior* (4), September 1975, 60.

20. Marguerite Tarrant, "The Divorcee's Dilemma, or Making Do with Less," *Money*, December 1974, 86.

21. Weitzman, *Divorce Revolution*, 152.

22. Weitzman, *Divorce Revolution*, 162.

23. Weitzman shows that in Los Angeles County, permanent, or open-ended, alimony awards fell from 62 percent to 32 percent in just four years, between 1968 and 1972. See Weitzman, *Divorce Revolution*, 164, 177.

24. Tarrant, "The Divorcee's Dilemma," 85.

25. Lefkovitz, *Strange Bedfellows*, 54.

26. Marguerite Tarrant, "The Divorcee's Dilemma, or Making Do with Less," *Money*, December 1974, 86.

27. Orr v. Orr, 440 U.S. 268 (1979).

28. Paul C. Glick, "Some Recent Changes in American Families," *Current Population Reports* (Washington, D.C.: U.S. Government Printing Office, 1976); Lawrence Van Gelder, "Cohabitation and the Courts: The Stigma Is Beginning to Fade," *NYT*, September 2, 1976, 44. D'Emilio and Freedman cite evidence that cohabitation tripled in frequency from the 1960s. See D'Emilio and Freedman, *Intimate Matters*, 331. Sociologist Arielle Kuperberg has shown that women of color were early innovators of premarital cohabitation, and did so at a rate of two times that of white women. See Kuperberg, "Premarital Cohabitation," 454–55.

29. Carol Kleiman, "Playing House: The Stakes Are Rising," October 1, 1978, D1.

30. Dorothy Storck, "Oops, There Goes Another Social Custom," *CT*, August 19, 1979, L1.

31. Pleck, *Not Just Roommates*, 19.

32. Thompson, "In Defence of the 'Gold-Digger,'" 1239.

33. Thompson, "In Defence of the 'Gold-Digger,'" 1237.

34. According to the attorneys Thompson interviewed, "their clients or client's partners viewed the agreement as almost a litmus test for gold digging." See Thompson, "In Defence of the 'Gold-Digger,'" 1240.

35. "Prenuptial Contract: Realistic or 'Cold'?" *NYT*, March 19, 1977, 35.

36. "Personal Finance: Premarriage Contracts," *NYT*, August 28, 1975, 49.

37. "State High Court Upholds Premarital Agreements," *NYT*, June 30, 1976, 3; "Prenuptial Contract: Realistic or 'Cold'?" *NYT*, March 19, 1977, 35; "His and Hers—Is It Theirs?" *Los Angeles Time*, July 10, 1978, H1.

38. Throughout this chapter, I use the name Michelle Triola for the sake of consistency, despite the fact that she changed her name to Michelle Marvin shortly before the end of her relationship with Lee Marvin.

39. "Everything he had was mine," cited in Marvin, *Lee*, 232. The book uses long passages of court testimony from the *Marvin v. Marvin* civil trial: "What I have is yours, and what you have is mine." Cited in Claudia Luther, "Ms. Marvin Takes Stand, Tells of Actor's Promises," *LAT*, January 17, 1979, A1.

40. Pleck, *Not Just Roommates*, 1.

41. Galanter, "Litigation Panic.

42. Marvin, *Lee*, 206.

43. Marvin, *Lee*, 200; "After Singer 'Met Lee Marvin,' Her Life 'Was Never the Same,'" *NYT*, April 19, 1979, B13. During the trial, many of her singing engagements proved difficult or impossible to verify. For example, of her Playboy Club performances, Triola could prove having only one two-week stint in Phoenix. According to Pamela Marvin, "Appearances in Europe couldn't be checked at all." See Marvin, *Lee*, 223.

44. Marvin, *Lee*, 208.

45. "After Singer 'Met Lee Marvin,' Her Life 'Was Never the Same,'" *NYT*, April 19, 1979, B13; Claudia Luther, "Ms. Marvin Takes Stand, Tells of Actor's Promises," *LAT*, January 17, 1979, A1. On "The Year of Lee Marvin," see "Marvin Means Mucho Macho," *Baltimore Sun*, April 25, 1979, 26.

46. Claudia Luther, "Didn't Want Ms. Marvin on Location Marvin Says," *LAT*, March 9, 1979, 30.

47. Ronnie Cowan, "Divorce without Marriage," *Ladies Home Journal*, October 1973 (90), 78.

48. Luther, "Didn't Want Ms. Marvin." Marvin testified that he supported Triola's singing career, even going so far as to set up a recording company for her. Others noted that Marvin used the recording company as a tax break. "Use of Recording Fees for Tax Gain by Marvin Told," *LAT*, February 8, 1979, A4.

49. Roderick Mann, "Quiet Legend Has Spotlight on His Past," *LAT*, December 17, 1978, O85.

50. Ronnie Cowan, "Divorce without Marriage," *Ladies Home Journal*, October 1973 (90), 80.

51. Claudia Luther, "Something for Everyone,'" *LAT*, February 3, 1979, A12. On the witness stand during the trial, Marvin said that Triola threatened to "reveal certain private matters, items to the press and the public at large, and she would tell

of my problems with my ex-family and those of my children; of my fears, my worries, my self-doubts." See Marvin, *Lee*, 299.

52. Claudia Luther, "Ex-Lover Made Suicide Threats, Marvin Testifies," *LAT*, February 1, 1979, D1.

53. Claudia Luther, "Marvin Asked to Define Love,'" *LAT*, January 31, 1979, 1.

54. Cross-examination of Marvin as recorded in Marvin, *Lee*, 306.

55. Marvin, *Lee*, 342.

56. Claudia Luther, "Michelle Marvin Recounts 2 Abortions, Miscarriage during Her Years with Actor," *LAT*, January 18, 1979, A8.

57. Ronnie Cowan, "Divorce without Marriage," *Ladies Home Journal*, October 1973 (90), 84. On the staged accidents, see Marvin, *Lee*, 187.

58. Mitchelson, *Made in Heaven*, 15, 19–20.

59. Mitchelson, *Made in Heaven*, 10.

60. Mitchelson, *Made in Heaven*, 43–48.

61. Myrna Oliver, "Judge May Kill Ex-Singer's Suit to Share Lee Marvin Property," *LAT*, December 5, 1973, A1; Myrna Oliver, "Suit Dismissed in Lee Marvin Case," *LAT*, December 6, 1973, B1; "Court Rejects Property Split for Unmarrieds," *LAT*, June 25, 1975, 3.

62. On Tobriner and the role of second wave feminism on the *Marvin* decision, see Pleck, *Not Just Roommates*, 153–54.

63. *In Re: Marriage of Cary*, 1973, Court of Appeals, First District, California, 34 Cal. App. 3d 345.

64. *Estate of Atherley*, 1975, Court of Appeals, Third District, California, 44 Cal. App. 3d 758.

65. Marvin v. Marvin, 18 Cal. 3d 660, December 27, 1976.

66. Judith Michaelson, "The Marvin Rule," *LAT*, May 17, 1978, B12; Marcia Seligson, "Marvin Mitchelson: The Amazing Palimony Man," *Cosmopolitan* (September 1979): 251; "Morals from Marvin," *CT*, April 22, 1979, A6.

67. Barry Siegel, "Will Legal Agreements Be the Death of Romance?" *LAT*, November 24, 1977, H16.

68. Michael Coakley, "Rock Stars Sing Blues over Ruling on 'Live-In' Girls," *CT*, August 28, 1977, 5.

69. Sue Mittenthal, "Aftershocks of Lee Marvin Case," *NYT*, February 22, 1979, C1.

70. "When Love Is Ended, What's Left?" *People*, May 7, 1979, 85.

71. "Marvin 'Palimony' Suit Only a Beginning," *Paris News*, April 25, 1979, 16. A writer for the *LAT* declared that "shock waves" from the court's decision were "reverberating across the country." Lorraine Bennett, "His and Hers—Is It Theirs?" *LAT*, July 10, 1978, H1.

72. Sonelick, *The Legality of Love*, 48–49.

73. Gene Blake, "Bill on Property Rights of Unwed Hit at Hearing," *LAT*, November 23, 1977, D1.

74. Pleck, *Not Just Roommates*, 160.

75. See Pleck, *Not Just Roommates*, 164.

76. Pleck, *Not Just Roommates*, 149.

77. Carol Kleiman, "Playing House: The Stakes Are Rising," October 1, 1978, D4; "Illinois High Court Bars Property Suits among Lovers Who Are Not Married," *LAT*, September 20, 1979, B10.

78. Claudia Luther, "Lee Marvin Case on Waiting List," *LAT*, December 3, 1978, B1.

79. Marvin, *Lee*, 177; Pleck, *Not Just Roommates*, 154; Claudia Luther, "Marvin Trial Testimony Ends after 11 Weeks," *LAT*, March 28, 1979, 3.

80. Marvin, *Lee*, 177; "Michelle Wails after Remark about Hooker," *LAT*, February 23, 1979, A3; Claudia Luther, "Shortcut Taken in Marvin Trial," *LAT*, March 16, 1979, B3.

81. "Of Love and Nonmarriage," *LAT*, April 19, 1979, F6.

82. Claudia Luther, "Ms. Marvin Claims Fraud by Actor," *LAT*, February 10, 1979, A18; Claudia Luther, "Testimony Given by Marvin's Spouse," *LAT*, February 15, 1979, E21.

83. Luther, "Lee Marvin Case on Waiting List," *LAT*, December 3, 1978, B1.

84. Claudia Luther, "Ms. Marvin Takes Stand, Tells of Actor's Promises," *LAT*, January 17, 1979, A1.

85. Claudia Luther, "Ms. Marvin Challenged on Motive for Changing Name," *LAT*, January 20, 1979, A23; Marvin, *Lee*, 196.

86. Claudia Luther, "Nagging Drove Actor to Drink, Court Told," *LAT*, February 7, 1979, C2.

87. Claudia Luther, "Marvin Tells of 'Idle Male Promises,'" *LAT*, January 27, 1979, A24.

88. Luther, "Marvin Tells of 'Idle Male Promises.'"

89. Claudia Luther, "Marvin Asked to Define Love,'" *LAT*, January 31, 1979, 1.

90. Marvin, *Lee*, 193; Claudia Luther, "Don't Love Girlfriend, Marvin Says," *LAT*, January 26, 1979, C1.

91. Claudia Luther, "Topics from Sex to Food Covered by Ms. Marvin," *LAT*, March 27, 1979, C1.

92. Claudia Luther, "Something for Everyone,'" *LAT*, February 3, 1979, A12.

93. Marvin, *Lee*, 298; Triola testified that she lost her singing job at the Holiday House in Malibu because Marvin showed up to her performances drunk and made trouble. Claudia Luther, "Marvin Trial Winding Down," *LAT*, March 24, 1979, A27.

94. Claudia Luther, "Marvin Trial Winding Down," *LAT*, March 24, 1979, A27; Marvin, *Lee*, 228–29; Claudia Luther, "Nagging Drove Actor to Drink, Court Told," *LAT*, February 7, 1979, C2.

95. According to Claudia Luther, Marvin Mitchelson "attempted to demonstrate that she cared for the actor as would a wife whose husband drank." See Claudia Luther, "Nagging Drove Actor to Drink, Court Told," *LAT*, February 7, 1979, C2.

96. Claudia Luther, "Agent Blames One Marvin Drinking Bout on Ex-Lover," *LAT*, February 7, 1979, A1; Marvin, *Lee*, 354, 300–301, 338–39.

97. Claudia Luther, "Testimony on Lee Marvin Sex Life Barred by Judge," *LAT*, March 15, 1979, B3; Marvin, *Lee*, 210; "Use of Recording Fees for Tax Gain by Marvin Told," *LAT*, February 8, 1979, A4.

98. As Elizabeth Pleck has noted, an irony of the case was its resuscitation of adversarial legalism during a time when no-fault divorce boomed in popularity. See Pleck, *Not Just Roommates*, 168.

99. Claudia Luther, "Michelle Marvin Recounts 2 Abortions, Miscarriage during Her Years with Actor," *LAT*, January 18, 1979, A8.

100. Claudia Luther, "Marvin Asked to Define Love,'" *LAT*, January 31, 1979, 1.

101. Claudia Luther, "Testimony Given by Marvin's Spouse," *LAT*, February 15, 1979, E21. Also, Patricia Hulsman, whom Triola claimed went with her to the doctor's office for the abortion, denied that she accompanied Triola. See Claudia Luther, "Witness Claims He Had Affair with Ms. Marvin," *LAT*, February 21, 1979, C1; Claudia Luther, "Ex-Lover Made Suicide Threats, Marvin Testifies,'" *LAT*, February 1, 1979, D1.

102. Claudia Luther, "Actor Claims Fling with Michelle," *LAT*, February 20, 1979, A1; Marvin, *Lee*, 279.

103. Marvin, *Lee*, 273.

104. Luther, "Actor Claims Fling"; Claudia Luther, "Testimony About Affair False, Attorney Asserts," *LAT*, March 14, 1979, D13.

105. Claudia Luther, "Shortcut Taken in Marvin Trial," *LAT*, March 16, 1979, B3.

106. Luther, "Actor Claims Fling."

107. Luther, "Shortcut Taken in Marvin Trial."

108. Claudia Luther, "Final Briefs Are Offered in Marvin Case," *LAT*, April 5, 1979, A6.

109. Noel Myricks, "'Palimony': The Impact of Marvin v. Marvin," *Family Relations* 29, no. 2 (April 1980): 211.

110. According to Pamela Marvin, "in the eyes of the public Lee was very much a hero." See Marvin, *Lee*, 357.

111. Sonelick, *Legality of Love*, 3; Nora Ephron, "The Gold Digger Standard," *Washington Post*, April 20, 1979, A15.

112. Art Hoppe, "The Wages of Sin," *Chula Vista Star News*, April 25, 1979, 45; Howard Rosenberg, "Burnett—for the Fun of It," *LAT*, August 17, 1979, G37; on Johnny Carson's friendship with Lee Marvin, see Marvin, *Lee*, 178.

113. *Saturday Night Live*, Complete Fifth Season 1979–1980, Universal Home Entertainment, 2009.

114. Claudia Luther, "Something for Everyone,'" *LAT*, February 3, 1979, A12; Ephron, "The Gold Digger Standard"; Bill Raspberry, "Lee Marvin Case Puzzle for Wives," *CT*, April 26, 1979, B3; Ann Rinaldi, "Incredible Naivete of Michelle Triola Is Difficult to Believe," *Indianapolis Star*, May 30, 1979, 17; George Will, "The Marvining of America," *Washington Post*, April 22, 1979, C7.

115. Michael Seiler, "Like Trial, Reaction Runs a Gamut," *LAT*, April 19, 1979, A22.

116. "Of Love and Nonmarriage," *LAT*, April 19, 1979, F6; "A Sorry Spectacle," *Iola Register*, April 20, 1979, 4; Will, "Marvin-ing of America"; "'It's a Good Lesson': Reactions to the Marvin Decision," *LAT*, April 19, 1979, H1.

117. Art Buchwald, "Romeo vs. Juliet," *Garden City Telegram*, April 26, 1979, 4; Sue Mittenthal, "Aftershocks of Lee Marvin Case," *NYT*, February 22, 1979, C1; Jacque Jones, "Beds Stuffed with Gold Are Lumpy and Cold," *LAT*, February 8, 1979,

D7; Terry Clifford, "Lovesuits: A New Social Disease Now Is Epidemic," *CT*, March 28, 1982, M1; Steven Brill, "Revenge for the Jilted?," *Esquire*, May 9, 1978, 16; Joan Beck, "Legal Traps of Unwedded Bliss," *CT*, May 18, 1981, 23; Zelizer, *Purchase of Intimacy*.

118. Marvin, *Lee*, 266; Michael Seiler, "Like Trial, Reaction Runs a Gamut," *LAT*, April 19, 1979, A22; Jacque Jones, "Beds Stuffed with Gold Are Lumpy and Cold," *LAT*, February 8, 1979, D7; Ann Rinaldi, "Incredible Naivete of Michelle Triola Is Difficult to Believe," *Indianapolis Star*, May 30, 1979, 17.

119. Claudia Luther, "Gloria Allred Hits 'Sexist Reporting' of Marvin Trial," *LAT*, March 14, 1979, A3; Michael Seiler, "Like Trial, Reaction Runs a Gamut," *LAT*, April 19, 1979, A22. On Steinem's reaction, see "'It's a Good Lesson': Reactions to the Marvin Decision," *LAT*, April 19, 1979, H1.

120. "It's a Good Lesson."

121. "It's a Good Lesson."

122. "It's a Good Lesson"; Hochschild, *The Second Shift*. On the importance of Hochschild's work, see Kristin Celello, *Making Marriage Work*, 142–43.

123. Quoted in Pleck, *Not Just Roommates*, 157.

124. Robert Lindsey, "Lee Marvin Told to Pay $104,000 but Judge Prohibits Property Split," *NYT*, April 19, 1979, A1.

125. Sonelick, *Legality of Love*, 53.

126. Pat B. Anderson, "Lovers' Property Law Predicted," *LAT*, March 20, 1977, 1; Marvin Mitchelson, "Living Together," *CT*, June 1, 1981, K1. The piece in the *CT* was excerpted from Mitchelson's 1980 book, *Living Together*.

127. On Mitchelson's failed lawsuit to recoup court costs, see Claudia Luther, "Mitchelson Seeks Fee from Marvin," *LAT*, May 16, 1979, B20. Triola received an advance for her memoir, but she never finished it. Dorothy Townsend, "Marvin Appeals Award to Ex-Lover," *LAT*, September 20, 1979, A26; Linda Deutsch, "Despite Scars, Michelle Marvin Writes, Lectures and 'Survives,'" *LAT*, May 9, 1980, C1.

128. Linda Deutsch, "Despite Scars, Michelle Marvin Writes, Lectures and 'Survives,'" *LAT*, May 9, 1980, C1; "Court Reverses $104,000 Award for Ex-Companion of Lee Marvin," *NYT*, August 13, 1981, A12; "Michelle Marvin Pleads Innocent, Seeks Trial on Shoplifting Charge," *LAT*, October 1, 1980, E8.

129. Marvin, *Lee*, 361.

130. David Margolick, "Celebrity Lawyer Defending Himself from Accusations on Several Fronts," *NYT*, July 3, 1988, 10.

131. Marcia Seligson, "Marvin Mitchelson: The Amazing Palimony Man," *Cosmopolitan* (September 1979): 253.

132. "Attorney Marvin Mitchelson Convicted of Tax Evasion," *AP*, February 9, 1993, accessed November 2, 2018, https://www.apnews.com/e915155ab3e1d6089d bb794fdb6498f7.

133. Judith Michaelson, "The Marvin Rule," *LAT*, May 17, 1978, B12; Mitchell Locin and Mark Polzin, "Bill Seeks to Thwart 'Marvin Cases' Here," *CT*, April 6, 1979, 3; Gene Blake, "Bill on Property Rights of Unwed Hit at Hearing," *LAT*, November 23, 1977, D1.

134. Lefkovitz, *Strange Bedfellows*, 40. Rebecca Davis's analysis of "pro family" legislation in the 1990s and early 2000s shows the contradictory qualities of neo-

liberal family policy. On the one hand, state and court affirmations of prenuptial agreements and no-fault divorce worked to position marriage as an individual contract distant from state involvement. On the other, states made strong interventions into marriage, seeing the institution as a solution to various social problems. In 1997, Louisiana adopted "covenant marriage." In the early 2000s, Minnesota lowered fees, and South Carolina offered tax credits, for marriage licenses if the couples received marriage counseling prior to marriage. States' investments in "healthy marriage" illuminate the neoliberal ideology of seeing personal behavior as an answer to structural, public, social problems. See Davis, *More Perfect Union*, 232–54.

Chapter Five

1. Prieto-Arranz, "Performance and Success in Madonna," 181.
2. Madonna, "Material Girl," 1984, Sony/ATV Music Publishing.
3. Masuda, "Analyzing 1980's Gender and Materiality"; Camille Paglia, "Madonna—Finally, a Real Feminist," *NYT*, December 14, 1990, 39. On Paglia's turn against Madonna, see Aida Edemariam, "Why Have Camille Paglia and Co. Turned on Madonna?," *The Guardian*, August 18, 2008. Guilbert, *Madonna as Postmodern Myth*, 43–44. Ann Kaplan and Ramona Curry also highlight the use of pastiche in Madonna's "Material Girl" video. See Kaplan, *Rocking around the Clock*, 120; Curry, "Madonna From Marilyn to Marlene."
4. Ehrenreich, *Worst Years of Our Lives*, 202.
5. Harvey, *Brief History of Neoliberalism*, 1.
6. For example, see Barbara Ehrenreich's collection of essays during the 1980s (most of which appeared in *Mother Jones*), *Worst Years of Our Lives*.
7. Harvey, *Brief History of Neoliberalism*, 65; Hancock, *Politics of Disgust*.
8. "'Welfare Queen' Becomes Issue in Reagan Campaign," *NYT*, February 15, 1976, 51; Kohler-Hausmann, "The Crime of Survival," 335.
9. Hancock, *Politics of Disgust*, 57. See also "Dethroning the Welfare Queen: The Rhetoric of Reform," *Harvard Law Review* 107 (8), June 1994, 2013–2030.
10. The earliest record of the term "white trash" is from 1821, but the term gained popularity in the 1850s. See Isenberg, *White Trash*, 135–36. On "white trash" marking the deserving from the undeserving, see Isenberg, *White Trash*, 275–76.
11. In her account of growing up in a self-described white trash culture, Roxanne A. Dunbar discusses how members of her husband's family accused her of being a gold digger for trying to marry someone above her social class status. See Dunbar, "Bloody Footprints," 73–86.
12. On the Koch Industries' collaborations with the Soviet Union, see Mayer, *Dark Money*, 27–34; Mayer, *Dark Money*, 39; Koch, *A Business Man Looks at Communism*.
13. Mayer, *Dark Money*, 43.
14. Mayer, *Dark Money*, 53.
15. *Dark Money*, 2.
16. Quoted in Schulman, *Sons of Wichita*, 78.
17. Schulman, *Sons of Wichita*, 122–23, 129, 130–37.

18. Andrew Gumbel, "What's $800M Got to Do with It?," *Independent*, October 30, 1999, W15.

19. I use the name "Anna Nicole Smith" throughout this chapter for the sake of consistency, even though court records often used the name "Vickie Lynn Smith" and some of the events described occurred before she changed her name to Anna Nicole Smith at the suggestion of fashion designer Paul Marciano.

20. Susan Schindehette and David Hutchings, "Anna Nicole Smith Models for Guess Jeans," *People*, April 12, 1993, accessed September 26, 2018, https://people .com/tbd/from-the-archives-anna-nicole-smith-models-for-guess-jeans-1993.

21. Redding and Redding, *Great Big Beautiful Doll*, 13.

22. "The Dentist," *The Anna Nicole Show*, E! Entertainment, 2002, Lion's Gate Home Entertainment.

23. Jason Kerrigan, "Billy and the Billionaire's Bride," *Sunday Mirror*, October 1, 2000, 12–13.

24. "I kicked her once is all," Billy Wayne said. See Peter Fearon, "How the GBP 150 Showgirl Became a GBP 300M Widow," *The Express*, September 29, 2000. On his failure to pay child support, see Donna Hogan, *Train Wreck*, 16.

25. Hogan and Tiefenthaler, *Train Wreck*, 17.

26. Hogan and Tiefenthaler, *Train Wreck*, 17–18.

27. Marshall, *Done in Oil*, 27–28.

28. Pierce Marshall, J. Howard's son, believed that his father had a long-term affair with Bettye during J. Howard's marriage to Eleanor. See In re Marshall v. Marshall (in re Marshall), 275 B.R. 5, United States District Court of the Central District of California, March 7, 2002, 13.

29. Marshall, *Made in Oil*, 254.

30. The exact amount of J. Howard Marshall's wealth was disputed. In 2000, his son, Pierce Marshall, estimated his fortune as somewhere between $48 to $60 million. *Forbes* magazine stated that he was worth $1.2 billion when including his Koch Industries stock. See Bruce Nichols, "Row Bigger than Texas," *Sunday Mail*, September 24, 2000, 38; Marego Athans, "Texas-Size Battle for Money," *Baltimore Sun*, October 4, 2000, accessed July 5, 2018, http://articles.baltimoresun.com/2000-10 -04/news/0010040195_1_anna-nicole-smith-howard-marshall-smith-story.

31. Jerry Reed's single "She Got the Goldmine (I Got the Shaft)," written by Tim DuBois and recorded by RCA Records, spent two weeks as the number one U.S. country song in September 1982 and three months in the top forty.

32. Mimi Swartz, "How to Marry a Millionaire," *Texas Monthly*, October 1994, accessed September 12, 2018, https://www.texasmonthly.com/articles/how-to -marry-a-millionaire.

33. In re Marshall v. Marshall (in re Marshall), 275 B.R. 5, United States District Court of the Central District of California, March 7, 2002, 29; Shelby Hodge, "For Wealthy Car Lovers, RR Is the Ultimate Seduction," *Houston Chronicle*, June 16, 1991, 6.

34. Swartz, "How to Marry a Millionaire." Swartz notes that Walker spent $1.2 million of Marshall's wealth in 1984 alone.

35. She attended events like a "Best Dressed Luncheon" sponsored by the March of Dimes, a Saks Fifth Avenue fashion show, and a children's hospital charity ben-

efit. Linda Griffin, "Best Dressed Lunch in Style," *HC*, March 1, 1990, 9; "Michele Meyer, "A Luncheon That Sparkled," *HC*, August 30, 1990, F6; "Gala Benefits Hospital," *HC*, February 21, 1991, F14.

36. Swartz, "How to Marry a Millionaire."

37. Swartz, "How to Marry a Millionaire."

38. Duggan v. Marshall II, https://caselaw.findlaw.com/tx-court-of-appeals /1384053.html.

39. Swartz, "How to Marry a Millionaire."

40. Graham Dudman and Harry Siskind, "How Sexy Anna Bust Out to Become a B-I-G Star," *The People,* October 30, 1994, 8–9. On Marshall's spending on Smith, see In re Marshall v. Marshall (in re Marshall) 275 B.R. 5, United States District Court of the Central District of California, March 7, 2002, 42.

41. Marshall said, "She is the light of my life. I think maybe Pierce is a little jealous." See "The Widow Wore White: Anna Nicole Smith Wore Her Wedding Dress to Mourn Howard Marshall," *Daily Record*, August 9, 1995, 5.

42. "The Widow Wore White," 44.

43. "$450M Anna Nicole Is No Gold Digger, Says Her Lawyer," *The Evening Standard*, October 3, 2000, 4; Hogan and Tiefenthaler, *Train Wreck*, 71–72.

44. Skip Hollandsworth, "The Making of a Sex Symbol," *Texas Monthly*, July 1993, accessed September 25, 2018, https://www.texasmonthly.com/articles/the-making -of-a-sex-symbol-1993.

45. Susan Schindehette and David Hutchings, "Anna Nicole Smith Models for Guess Jeans," *People*, February 9, 2007, accessed September 25, 2018, https://people .com/tbd/from-the-archives-anna-nicole-smith-models-for-guess-jeans-1993.

46. Schindehette and Hutchings, "Anna Nicole Smith Models for Guess Jeans"; Andrew Gumbel, "What's $800M Got to Do with It?," *Independent*, October 30, 1999, W15; On being "plucked from obscurity," see Hollandsworth, "The Making of a Sex Symbol."

47. According to Guess photographer Daniela Fereici, "We haven't seen that kind of charisma since Marilyn Monroe." See Schindehette and Hutchings, "Anna Nicole Smith Models for Guess Jeans"; Skip Hollandsworth, "The Making of a Sex Symbol"; Vida Roberts, "Face of Fashion, '90s-Style, Naturally Turning a New Cheek," *Vancouver Sun*, December 15, 1992, C2.

48. See, for example, Natalie Angier, "Fashion's Waif Look Makes Strong Women Weep," *NYT*, April 11, 1993, section 4, page 2.

49. Hogan and Tiefenthaler, *Train Wreck*, 73.

50. Swartz, "How to Marry a Millionaire."

51. Hogan and Tiefenthaler, *Train Wreck*, 72.

52. Redding and Redding, *Great Big Beautiful Doll*, 125; Swartz, "How to Marry a Millionaire."

53. Hogan and Tiefenthaler, *Train Wreck*, 104–5.

54. Redding and Redding, *Great Big Beautiful Doll*, 186; Hogan and Tiefenthaler, *Train Wreck*, 100.

55. Bill Murphy, "Ex-Driver Disputes Smith 'Terrible How She Treated' Husband," *HC*, February 21, 2001, 26; Hogan and Tiefenthaler, *Train Wreck*, 97.

56. Hogan and Tiefenthaler, *Train Wreck*, 96, 93.

57. "I've Turned into a Basket Case," *Sunday Mail*, March 5, 1995, 4; "Interview with Anna Nicole Smith," *CNN*, aired May 29, 2002; "Former Stripper Sues for Inheritance," *The Globe and Mail*, September 27, 2000, R2.

58. Redding and Redding, *Great Big Beautiful Doll*, 185; "Interview with Anna Nicole Smith," *CNN*, aired May 29, 2002.

59. "Smith Got $6.7 Million During Marriage," *HC*, January 26, 2001, 20; Bill Murphy, "Emotional Accusations Smith Alleges Stepson Tried to Have Her Killed," *HC*, January 31, 2001, 13; Hogan and Tiefenthaler, *Train Wreck*, 91.

60. In re Marshall v. Marshall (in re Marshall) 271 B.R. 858, 3.

61. Caroline Sutton and Terry Willows, "Playboy Offers Anna Nicole Smith £300,000 to Lose Weight," *Sunday Mirror*, May 12, 1996, 2–3.

62. Redding and Redding, *Great Big Beautiful Doll*, 208; "Put My Tycoon in Tomb," *Daily Record*, August 12, 1995, 3; Bruce Nichols, "Row Bigger than Texas," *Sunday Mail*, September 24, 2000, 38.

63. Mark Dowdney, "The Widow Wore White," *Daily Record*, August 9, 1995, 5.

64. Peter Fearon, "How the GBP 150 Showgirl Became a GBP 300M Widow," *The Express*, September 29, 2000; Hogan and Tiefenthaler, *Train Wreck*, 245–46.

65. Deborah Orr, "Don't Be Fooled: She May Be Rich but She's a Victim," *The Independent*, September 29, 2000, 5; Grossman, "The End of the Road."

66. Joanna Grossman called it a "grave tactical error." See Grossman, "The End of the Road."

67. Nicola Pittman, "Judge Awards Model $449M," *Evening Standard*, September 28, 2000, 1; Paul Thompson and Antonella Lazzeri, "From a Chicken Shack to Pounds 315M Treasure Chest," *The Sun*, September 29, 2000.

68. Stephen Romei, "Tycoon's Widow $817M Merrier," *The Australian*, September, 29, 2000, 32; "News," *Contra Costa Times*, January 30, 2001, A02; Jim Yardley, "Honky-Tonk Love Gets Its Day in Probate Court," *NYT*, February 2, 2001, 12.

69. Pamela Colloff, "The Trick Is Not to Act Like a Lawyer," *Texas Monthly*, September 2002, accessed September 24, 2018, https://www.texasmonthly.com/politics/the-trick-is-not-to-act-like-a-lawyer.

70. "My Stepmom 'Miss Cleavage,'" *The Straits Times*, October 8, 2000.

71. Bill Murphy, "Anna and Her King," *HC*, January 30, 2001, 15; Bill Murphy, "Smith Denies Selling $4 Million in Lost Jewelry," *HC*, February 13, 2001, 25.

72. Bill Murphy, "Smith: $100,000 Wasn't Much Money to Her in '94," *HC*, February 14, 2001, 21.

73. Bill Murphy, "Anna and Her King."

74. Bill Murphy, "Smith Finished Trial Testimony She Denies Getting Husband Fondle Her to Get Son Adopted," *HC*, February 15, 2001, 31.

75. Bill Murphy, "Smith Finishes Trial Testimony," *HC*, February 15, 2001, 31.

76. Redding and Redding, *Great Big Beautiful Doll*, 130; Hogan and Tiefenthaler, *Train Wreck*, 87, 98; Nicola Pittman, "Judge Awards Model $449M," *Evening Standard*, September 28, 2000, 1–2.

77. Bill Murphy, "Smith: $100,000 Wasn't Much Money to Her in '94."

78. "Expensive to Be Me," *The Toronto Star*, January 30, 2001.

79. Bill Murphy, "Ex-Driver Disputes Smith," *HC*, February 21, 2001, 26.

80. Andy Lines, "Angry Widow Anna's Courtroom Bust-Up," *Daily Record*, February 2, 2001, 9.

81. "Tears in Anna's Latest Production," *Daily Telegraph*, February 2, 2001, 28.

82. Doug Camilli, "Big-Buck Ruckus," *The Gazette*, February 6, 2001; Bill Murphy, "Emotional Accusations Smith Alleges Stepson Tried to Have Her Killed," *HC*, January 31, 2001, 13.

83. Pamela Colloff, "The Trick Is Not to Act Like a Lawyer," *Texas Monthly*, September 2002, accessed September 24, 2018, https://www.texasmonthly.com/politics/the-trick-is-not-to-act-like-a-lawyer; Jim Yardley, "Co-star of a Juicy Texas Trial Enjoys His High Profile," *NYT*, March 11, 2001, accessed September 24, 2018, https://www.nytimes.com/2001/03/11/us/co-star-of-a-juicy-texas-trial-enjoys-his-high-profile.html.

84. Bill Murphy, "Emotional Accusations Smith Alleges Stepson Tried to Have Her Killed," *HC*, January 31, 2001, 13.

85. Murphy, "Emotional Accusations."

86. Jim Yardley, "Honky-Tonk Love Gets Its Day in Probate Court," *NYT*, February 2, 2001, 12.

87. Bill Murphy, "Smith Lawyer Wants Judge to Be Recused," *HC*, February 6, 2001, 21; Dianna Wray, "Judge Begs Family of Anna Nicole Smith's Husband to Let Him Quit Case," *Houston Press*, January 27, 2017, accessed September 20, 2018, https://www.houstonpress.com/news/judge-begs-family-of-anna-nicole-smiths-husband-to-let-him-quit-case-9147055.

88. John Council, "Blonde Bombshell Implodes on Witness Stand," *Texas Lawyer*, March 19, 2001.

89. Mimi Swartz, "The Punch Line," *Texas Monthly*, April 2007, 125; Bill Murphy and Susan Bardwell, "Jury: Smith Has No Share of Estate," *HC*, March 7, 2001, accessed September 20, 2018, https://www.chron.com/news/houston-texas/article/Jury-Smith-has-no-share-of-estate-2007015.php; *ABC News 20/20*, "Anna Nicole Smith: Jurors Discuss Anna Nicole Smith's Legal Battle over Late Husband's Estate," June 18, 2001.

90. Murphy, "Emotional Accusations," 13.

91. Jim Yardley, "Honky-Tonk Love Gets Its Day in Probate Court," *NYT*, February 2, 2001, 12.

92. "Interview with Anna Nicole Smith," *CNN*, aired May 29, 2002; Redding and Redding, *Great Big Beautiful Doll*, 105; Deborah Orr, "Don't Be Fooled: She May Be Rich but She's a Victim," *The Independent*, September 29, 2000, 5; Hogan and Tiefenthaler, *Train Wreck*, 89.

93. Andy Lines, "Anna Nicole Gets Half of Husband's Pound 600M," *Daily Record*, October 4, 1999, 23.

94. Sarah Chalmers, "The Merry Widow," *Daily Mail*, September 29, 2000, 3.

95. Mimi Swartz, "The Punch Line," *Texas Monthly*, April 2007, 240.

96. Deborah Orr, "Don't Be Fooled: She May Be Rich but She's a Victim," *The Independent*, September 29, 2000, 5; "PETA: Anna Was a Friend to Animals," *TMZ*, February 8, 2007, accessed September 27, 2018, http://www.tmz.com/2007/02/08

/peta-anna-was-a-friend-to-animals; Mimi Swartz, "How to Marry a Million-aire," *Texas Monthly*, October 1994, accessed September 27, 2018, https://www.texasmonthly.com/articles/how-to-marry-a-millionaire; Anne Maier and Laurel Brubaker Calkins, "How to Bury a Millionaire," *People*, August 21, 1995, accessed September 26, 2018, https://people.com/archive/how-to-bury-a-millionaire-vol-44-no-8.

97. Sharon Churcher and Peter Sheridan, "The Queen of Trailer Park Trash Divides America Over Her Billion Dollar Battle," *Daily Mail*, October 17, 1999, 32; Mimi Swartz, "The Punch Line," *Texas Monthly*, April 2007, 240.

98. Doug Camilli, "Anna Nicole Smith Swears Off Drugs, Sex, Shopping, Etc.," *The Gazette*, January 15, 1997, C7; Andrew Gumbel, "What's $800M Got to Do with It?," *Independent*, October 30, 1999, W15; Sharon Churcher and Peter Sheridan, "The Queen of Trailer Park Trash Divides America over Her Billion Dollar Battle," *Mail on Sunday*, October 17, 1999, 32; Redding and Redding, *Great Big Beautiful Doll*, 62; Tad Friend, "White Hot Trash!" *New York Magazine*, August 22, 1994, accessed September 27, 2018, http://nymag.com/news/features/46608/.

99. The suit was likely settled out of court. See "Anna Nicole and 'New York': A No-Love-Lost Story," *New York Magazine*, February 12, 2007, accessed October 8, 2018, http://nymag.com/intelligencer/2007/02/anna_nicole_and_new_york_a_no1_1.html.

100. Redding and Redding, *Great Big Beautiful Doll*, 25.

101. Ian Markham-Smith, "Sexpot Takes on Oil Family," *Daily Mirror*, August 7, 1995, 17; Skip Hollandsworth, "The Making of a Sex Symbol"; Florence King, "For Whom the Bell (Really) Tolls," *National Review*, April 2007 (59:5), 42.

102. Michael Ellison, "How 405 Days of Wedded Bliss Adds Up to a $450M Fortune," *The Guardian,* September 29, 2000, 3. Humorous books by self-identified members of white trash culture refer to Twinkies as a white trash food. See Lamar and Wendland, *White Trash Mom Handbook*, 110; Hays, *When Did White Trash*, 22, 53, 85, 106. A 2014 article in the *Thrillist* mentioned Twinkies as one of "America's Most White Trash Snacks," accessed September 26, 2018, https://www.thrillist.com/travel/nation/europeans-on-american-food-europeans-taste-test-american-junk-food. Brown, "Class and Feminine Excess."

103. Redding and Redding, *Great Big Beautiful Doll*, 24, 130, 155, 61.

104. Redding and Redding, *Great Big Beautiful Doll*, 72.

105. Ray Richmond, "An Inevitable Demise for All the World to See," *Hollywood Reporter*, February 13, 2007 (398:16); "2007 Idiot's Box Award," *Metro Magazine* 156, March 2008, 175; Gaby Wood, "Chronicle of a Death Foretold," *The Observer*, May 13, 2007, 40; Hogan, *Train Wreck*, 132. According to Brown, the show was E!'s "most successful series ever." See Brown, "Class and Feminine Excess," 92.

106. "House Hunting," *The Anna Nicole Show*, E! Entertainment, 2002, Lion's Gate Home Entertainment; "Las Vegas Part 1," *The Anna Nicole Show*, E! Entertainment, 2002, Lion's Gate Home Entertainment.

107. On paracinema and the "so-bad-it's-good" sensibility, see Bonnstetter, "Legacy of *Mystery Science Theater 3000*." Joel Stein, "Anna Goes Prime Time," *Time* 2002 (160:4), 48. "House Hunting," *The Anna Nicole Show*.

108. CNN correspondent Carol Costello said, "Everyone was wondering whether she was on something during the shooting of the show." Likewise, the editor of *In Touch* magazine observed, "anybody who ever saw her E-Entertainment reality series will never forget how incoherent she always was." Donna Hogan observed, "she is quite obviously on an assortment of drugs and alcohol." See Wolf Blitzer, "The Situation Room," *CNN*, February 8, 2007; Tom O'Neil, Paula Zhan Now, *CNN*, February 8, 2007, Cable News Network; Hogan, *Train Wreck*, 133.

109. "Cousin Shelly," *The Anna Nicole Show*, E! Entertainment, 2002, Lion's Gate Home Entertainment.

110. "House Hunting," *The Anna Nicole Show*, E! Entertainment, 2002, Lion's Gate Home Entertainment. On her discussion of masturbation, see "The Dentist," *The Anna Nicole Show*. For her reference to a male prostitute, see "NYC Publicity Tour," *The Anna Nicole Show*. "The Driving Test," *The Anna Nicole Show*; "NYC Publicity Tour," *The Anna Nicole Show*.

111. "Cousin Shelly," *The Anna Nicole Show*.

112. Hogan, *Train Wreck*, 134–35.

113. Marshall v. Marshall (In re Marshall), 32 F. 3d 1118, United States Court of Appeals for the Ninth Circuit, San Francisco California, 30.

114. In re Marshall v. Marshall (in re Marshall) 275 B.R. 5, United States District Court of the Central District of California, March 7, 2002, 37–38, 72.

115. In re Marshall v. Marshall, 61.

116. In re Marshall v. Marshall, 88–89.

117. In re Marshall v. Marshall, 95, 74, 96.

118. In re Marshall v. Marshall, 45, 57. Both parties appealed the ruling to the Ninth Circuit. Smith wanted the original bankruptcy court decision of $449 million to stand because it would preclude the Texas probate ruling (and because it was a much higher award). Pierce appealed because he believed the Texas probate decision should be the final judgment.

119. Marshall v. Marshall (In re Marshall), 32 F. 3d 1118, United States Court of Appeals for the Ninth Circuit, San Francisco California, 11. The court ruled: "We apply the probate exception to federal court jurisdiction and hold that all judgments awarded to Vickie Lynn Marshall against E. Pierce Marshall should be reversed." See Marshall v. Marshall (In re Marshall), 32 F. 3d 1118, United States Court of Appeals for the Ninth Circuit, San Francisco California, 51.

120. Marshall v. Marshall, U.S. Supreme Court Oral Arguments, February 28, 2006, https://www.oyez.org/cases/2005/04-1544. See also Tom Goldstein, "The Marshall v. Marshall Oral Argument," *Scotusblog*, March 1, 2006, accessed October 4, 2018, http://www.scotusblog.com/2006/03/the-marshall-v-marshall-oral-argument/; Marshall v. Marshall, 547 U.S. 293 (2006).

121. Stern v. Marshall, 564 U.S.

122. See, for example, Dalton, "Stern v. Marshall."

123. Tanner, "Earthquake that Hit the Bankruptcy Courts," 588.

124. See Fillippi, "Legacy of the Anna Nicole Smith Case."

125. Joan Biskupic, "Anna Nicole Smith Stirs Up High Court," *USA Today*, March 1, 2006, 3.

126. "Funeral Held for Smith's Son," *Townsville Bulletin*, October 21, 2006, 36.

127. "Hurricane Anna Nicole Wreaks Havoc in the Bahamas," November 15, 2006, accessed October 8, 2018, https://wikileaks.org/plusd/cables/06NASSAU1711_a.html; "Inside Anna Nicole's Surprise Ceremony," *People*, October 5, 2006, accessed October 8, 2018, https://people.com/celebrity/inside-anna-nicoles-surprise-ceremony.

128. For example, on February 8, 2007, NBC Nightly News showed fourteen seconds of coverage of the Iraq war, but devoted over three minutes to the death of Smith. References to Anna Nicole Smith on MSNBC were 522 percent more frequent than references to Iraq. These statistics come from the blog *Think Progress*, accessed October 4, 2018, https://thinkprogress.org/video-compilation-anna-nicole-smith -and-our-national-media-embarassment-d826fo5fcd4e/.

129. https://thinkprogress.org/gibson-reporters-who-ignore-anna-nicole-smith -to-focus-on-iraq-war-are-snobs-3a2d32682515/, accessed October 4, 2018; Joe Scarborough, Scarborough Country, MSNBC, February 8, 2007; "Media Analysis: Nontraditional Outlets Fuel Smith Coverage," *PR Week*, February 2007, 10.

130. *Paula Zahn Now*, 2007, Cable News Network, February 8, 2007; Scarborough, J. M. Potter, and S. Risdon, Scarborough Country, MSNBC, *MSNBC Scarborough Country*, February 8, 2007. On the "famous for being famous" construct, see Gerd, "Famous for Being Famous."

131. For Smith as a "stormtrooper," see Melanie Reed, "Why Can't We All Be as Upfront as Anna?," *Sunday Mail*, October 31, 1999, 23. On Anna Nicole Smith as a feminist icon, see also Philippa Snow, "Reappraising the Fabulous Feminist Legacy of Anna Nicole Smith," *Vice.com*, February 9, 2017, https://i-d.vice.com/en_us/article /gyqbx4/reappraising-the-fabulous-feminist-legacy-of-anna-nicole-smith; Brown, "Feminine Excess."

132. "2007 Idiot's Box Award," *Metro Magazine* 156, March 2008, 175; Sharon Churcher and Peter Sheridan, "The Queen of Trailer Park Trash Divides America over Her Billion Dollar Battle," *Mail on Sunday,* October 17, 1999, 32.

133. Reed, "Why Can't We All Be as Upfront as Anna?"

134. Carol Sarler, "His 'N' Her Big Assets Make a Perfect Union," *The People*, July 1994, 23. Anna Nicole's half sister Donna Hogan shared this sentiment in an otherwise scathing account of Smith. She said, "In one respect, J. Howard was using my sister as much as she was using him." See Hogan and Tiefenthaler, *Train Wreck*, 232.

135. Fleming, *Sugar Daddy Capitalism*.

136. Koch Industries faced more than $400 million in fines through penalties and judgments. David Evans and Asjylyn Loder, "Koch Industries Has Pattern of Violating Ethics, Environmental Laws," *Seattle Times*, October 8, 2011, accessed October 11, 2018, https://www.seattletimes.com/business/koch-industries-has-pattern-of-vio lating-ethics-environmental-laws. A Texas jury in 1999 slapped the company with a $296 million verdict in a wrongful death suit stemming from a butane pipeline rupture that killed two teenagers. See Tim Dickinson, "Inside the Koch Brothers' Toxic Empire," *Rolling Stone*, September 24, 2014, accessed October 30, 2018, https://www .rollingstone.com/politics/politics-news/inside-the-koch-brothers-toxic-empire -164403/. Koch Industries was allegedly responsible for over 300 oil spills between 1990 and 1995. See Mayer, *Dark Money*, 126.

137. According to Justice David Carter, Marshall was "hiding and manipulating his assets in aggressive accounting gimmicks." See In re Marshall v. Marshall (in re Marshall), 275 B.R. 5, United States District Court of the Central District of California, March 7, 2002, 36.

138. Sharon Churcher and Peter Sheridan, "The Queen of Trailer Park Trash Divides America over Her Billion Dollar Battle," *Mail on Sunday*, October 17, 1999, 32.

Epilogue

1. Jennifer Pemberton documented the prominence of gold digger themes in hip-hop music. See Pemberton, "Now I Ain't Sayin' She's a Gold Digger."

2. EPMD, "Gold Digger," 1990, EMI Publishing.

3. Stephens and Phillips. "Freaks, Gold Diggers, Divas, and Dykes."

4. Blackstone, *Schemin'.*

5. Howard, *Gold Diggers.*

6. Hobbs, *A Bona Fide Gold Digger.*

7. A full consideration of the gold digger in early twenty-first-century African American vernacular is outside the historical scope of the present study, but it merits further attention. Part of the context includes the expansion of the African American middle and upper classes (see Hill, *Black Intimacies*, 1). By the late 1990s and into the 2000s, there was more proverbial gold to dig while, at the same time, African Americans continued to face racism, discrimination, and blocked opportunities in labor and marriage markets. Other important factors include lower marriage rates among African Americans and the disjuncture between the experiences of African Americans and the expectations of traditional marriage, particularly the expectations placed on Black wives (see Johnson and Loscocco, "Black Marriage"; Raley et al., "Growing Racial and Ethnic Divide"). In this way, structural and economic forces established the groundwork for specific cultural representations of gold diggers in hip-hop and street lit.

8. Cited in Barbara Mikkelson, 2007, "Fool's Gold Digger," snopes.com, accessed February 17, 2014, http://www.snopes.com/love/dating/golddigger.asp; Andrew Newman, "Acquisitive Craigslist Post Reddens Faces All Around," *NYT*, October 8, 2007; Ethan Rouen, "Gold Digger Posts Craigslist Ad to Find Rich Husband," *New York Post*, October 8, 2007.

9. Best, *Random Violence*, 86–91.

10. As Michael Schudson observes, "The power of a cultural object or message exists by virtue of contrastive relationships to other objects in its field." See Schudson, "How Culture Works," 166.

11. Frank A. Garbutt, "Women Beware," *LAT*, August 20, 1935, A4.

12. See Saguy and Stuart, "Culture and Law"; Rosen, *Law as Culture.*

13. As Coontz explains, "The history of love-based marriage from the late eighteenth to the mid-twentieth century is one of successive crises, as people surged past the barriers that prevented them from achieving marital fulfillment and then pulled back." See Coontz, *Marriage*, 5.

Bibliography

Primary Sources

Books

Apstein, Theodore. *The Parting of Ways: An Exposé of America's Divorce Tangle.* New York: Dodge Publishing, 1935.

Baldwin, Faith. *Alimony.* New York: Triangle Books, 1928.

Blackstone, Andrea. *Schemin': Confessions of a Gold Digger.* Annapolis, MD: Dream Weaver Press, 2004.

Bowman, Harry. *Marriage for Moderns.* New York: McGraw Hill, 1954.

Brooks, Virginia. *My Battles with Vice.* Chicago: Macaulay Company, 1915.

Brownlow, Kevin. *The Parade's Gone By.* Berkeley: University of California Press, 1976.

Cressey, Paul. *The Taxi-Dance Hall: A Sociological Study in Commercialized Recreation and City Life.* Chicago: University of Chicago Press.

Fairburn, William Armstrong. *Law and Justice.* New York: National Press Printing Company, 1927.

Hayes, Helen. *On Reflection: An Autobiography.* New York: Lippincott, 1968.

Hays, Charlotte. *When Did White Trash Become the New Normal?* Washington, D.C.: Regnery, 2013.

Hemingway, Ernest. *Ernest Hemingway: Complete Poems.* Edited by Nicholas Gerogiannis. New York: Bison Books, 1983.

Hobbs, Allison. *A Bona Fide Gold Digger.* Largo, MD: Strebor Books, 2007.

Hogan, Donna, and Henrietta Tiefenthaler, *Train Wreck: The Life and Death of Anna Nicole Smith.* Beverly Hills: Phoenix Books, 2007.

Hove, Arthur. *Gold Diggers of 1933.* Edited by Arthur Hove. Madison: University of Wisconsin Press, 1980.

Howard, Tracie. *Gold Diggers.* New York: Broadway Books, 2007.

Joyce, Peggy Hopkins. *Men, Marriage, and Me.* New York: Macauley, 1930.

Koch, Fred C. *A Business Man Looks at Kansas.* Wichita: printed by the author, 1961.

Komarovsky, Mirra. *The Unemployed Man and His Family: Status of the Man in Fifty-Nine Families.* New York: AltaMira Press, 2004 [1940].

Laird, Donald A., and Eleanor Laird. *The Technique of Building Personal Leadership: Proven Ways for Increasing the Powers of Leadership.* New York: McGraw-Hill, 1944.

Lamar, Michelle, and Molly Wendland. *The White Trash Mom Handbook.* New York: St. Martin's Press, 2008.

Lever, Harry, and Joseph Young. *Wartime Racketeers.* New York: G.P. Putnam's Sons, 1945.

Lindsey, Benjamin. *Companionate Marriage.* New York: Brentano's, 1929.

Loos, Anita. *Gentlemen Prefer Blondes: The Illuminating Diary of a Professional Lady.* New York: Penguin, 1992.

———. *A Girl Like I.* New York: Viking, 1966.

———. *The Talmadge Girls.* New York: Viking, 1978.

Marshall, J. Howard. *Done in Oil: An Autobiography of J. Howard Marshall II.* College Station, TX: Texas A&M Press, 1994.

Mencken, H. L. *My Life as Author and Editor.* New York: Knopf, 1993.

Mitchelson, Marvin. *Living Together.* New York: Simon and Schuster, 1980.

———. *Made in Heaven, Settled in Court.* Los Angeles: J. P. Tarcher, 1976.

Nizer, Louis. *My Life in Court.* New York: Doubleday, 1961.

Powel, Harford. *Good Jobs for Good Girls.* New York: Vanguard, 1949.

Redding, Eric, and D'eva Redding. *Great Big Beautiful Doll: The Anna Nicole Smith Story.* Fort Lee, NJ: Barricade Books, 1996.

Riesman, David. *The Lonely Crowd: A Study of the Changing American Character.* New Haven: Yale University Press, 2001.

Sonelick, Jerry. *The Legality of Love.* New York: Jove, 1981.

Spitzer, Marian. *The Palace.* New York: Atheneum, 1969.

Trell, Max. *Lawyer Man.* New York: Macaulay, 1932.

Van Deventer, Betty. *Confessions of a Gold Digger.* Girard, KS: Haldeman-Julius, 1929.

Whyte, William H. *The Organization Man.* New York: Simon and Schuster, 1956.

Wilner, Charles. *Alimony: The American Tragedy.* New York: Vantage Press, 1952.

Xi Psi Phi Quarterly. Illinois: Ovid Bell Press, 1930.

Court Cases

Baker v. Nelson, 291 Minn. 310, 191 N.W.2d 185 (1971).

Browning v. Browning, 129 Misc. 137, 220 N.Y.S. 651; N.Y. (1927).

Cooley v. Cooley, 244 Ill. App. 488 (1927).

Crist v. Crist, 62 N.E.2d 252, 1942 Ohio App. LEXIS 760, 43 Ohio L. Abs. 170 (Court of Appeals of Ohio, Second District, Franklin County. October 13, 1942).

Estate of Atherley, Court of Appeals, Third District, California, 44 Cal. App. 3d 758 (1975).

Fearon v. Treanor, 248 App. Div. 225, N.Y. (1936).

Griswold v. Connecticut, 381 U.S. 479 (1965).

Hanfgarn v. Mark, 159 Misc. 122; 286 N.Y.S. 335 (1936).

Hanfgarn v. Mark, 274 N.Y. 22; 8 N.E.2d 47 (1937).

Hewitt v. Hewitt, 77 Ill. 2d 49, 31 Ill. Dec. 827, 394 N.E.2d 1204 (1979).

In re Marriage of Cary, Court of Appeals, First District, California, 34 Cal. App. 3d 345 (1973).

In re Marshall v. Marshall (in re Marshall) 275 B.R. 5, United States District Court of the Central District of California (2002).

In re Marshall v. Marshall (in re Marshall) 271 B.R. 858.

Knebel v. Knebel, 189 S.W.2d 464 (Mo. App. 1945).

Marshall v. Marshall (In re Marshall), 32 F. 3d 1118, United States Court of Appeals for the Ninth Circuit, San Francisco, California.

Marvin v. Marvin, 18 Cal. 3d 660 (1976).

Orr v. Orr, 440 U.S. 268 (1979).

Stokes v. Stokes, 222 S.W.2d 108, Springfield Court of Appeals, Missouri (1949).

Newspapers

Afro-American
American Weekly
Appleton Post-Crescent
Australian
Baltimore Sun
Billings Gazette
Boston Globe
Bristol Daily Courier
Capital Times
Charleston Daily Mail
Chicago Daily Tribune
Chicago Defender
Christian Science Monitor
Chula Vista Star News
Cleveland Call and Post
Cleveland Plain Dealer
Contra Costa Times
Courier-Journal
Daily Mirror
Daily Northwestern
Daily Telegraph
Daily Times-News
Daily Record
Denton Record-Chronicle
Dunkirk Evening Observer
Evening Standard
Evening Sun
Express
Freeport Journal-Standard
Fort Wayne Sentinel
Gazette
Globe and Mail
Guardian
Hamilton Evening Journal
Hamilton Spectator
Houston Chronicle
Independent

Indiana Gazette
Indianapolis Star
Iola Register
Kingsport Times
Laredo Times
Lima News
Los Angeles Times
Mail on Sunday
Manitowoc Herald-News
Mansfield News-Journal
Miami-News-Record
Modesto News-Herald
Morning Herald
New Journal and Guide
New Oxford Item
News-Herald
New York Post
New York Amsterdam News
Oakland Tribune
Observer
Ogden Standard-Democrat
Ogden Standard-Examiner
Paris News
Pittsburgh Press
Plain Speaker
Republic
Sunday Mirror
Salt Lake Tribune
San Antonio Light
San Mateo Daily Times
Saturday Review
Seattle Times
Stars and Stripes
Straits Times
St. Louis Post-Dispatch
St. Petersburg Times
Sun

Sunday Mail
Syracuse Herald
Toronto Star
Townsville Bulletin
USA Today
Vancouver Sun

Victoria Advocate
Wall Street Journal
Warren Times Mirror
Washington Post
Woodland Democrat

Journals and Magazines

American Sociological Review
Annals of the American Academy of
    Political and Social Science
Catholic World
Cosmopolitan
Current Population Reports
Esquire
Family Relations
Harper's Bazaar
Harper's Magazine
Hollywood Reporter
Human Behavior
International Journal of Sexology
Ladies Home Journal
Life
Marquette Law Review
Metro Magazine

Michigan Law Review
Money
National Review
New West
New York Magazine
New York Times
The Outlook
People
Playboy
Rolling Stone
Texas Lawyer
Texas Monthly
Time
Variety
Virginia Law Register
Woman's Day

Movies and Television Series

42nd Street (1933)
All About Eve (1950)
Allotment Wives (1945)
The Anna Nicole Show (2002–2004)
Asphalt Jungle (1950)
Breach of Promise (1932)
China Seas (1935)
Dames (1934)
Dancing Mothers (1926)
Dinner at Eight (1933)
The Dirty Dozen (1967)
Double Indemnity (1944)
Father Knows Best (1954–1960)
A Fool There Was (1915)
Footlight Parade (1933)
Gentlemen Prefer Blondes (1953)
Gold Diggers of 1933 (1933)
Gold Diggers of 1935 (1935)

Gold Diggers of Broadway (1929)
The Greeks Had a Word for It (1932)
Havana Widows (1933)
Hell in the Pacific (1968)
How to Marry a Millionaire (1953)
How to Marry a Millionaire (1957–1958)
I'm No Angel (1933)
International House (1933)
It (1927)
The Jazz Singer (1927)
Lawyer Man (1932)
Leave It to Beaver (1957–1963)
Libeled Lady (1936)
The Love Boat (1977–1986)
Love Happy (1949)
Manhandled (1924)
Niagara (1953)
Pandora's Box (1929)

Red-Headed Woman (1932)
Saturday Night Live (1979–1980)
The Seven Year Itch (1955)
Ship of Fools (1965)
The Skyrocket (1926)
Synanon (1965)

Tarzan's Revenge (1938)
That Certain Thing (1928)
The Turmoil (1916)
Who's Right? (1954)
The Woman and the Law (1918)

Songs

"Diamonds Are a Girl's Best Friend." Leo Robin and Jule Styne, 1949.
"Gold Digger." EPMD, EMI Publishing, 1990.
"Gold Digger." Kanye West, Roc-A-Fella, Def Jam, 2005.
"Makin' Whoopee." Walter Donaldson, 1928.
"Material Girl." Madonna, Sony/ATV Music Publishing, 1984.
"My Heart Belongs to Daddy." Cole Porter, 1938.
"Pettin' in the Park." Harry Warren and Al Dubin, 1933.
"Remember My Forgotten Man." Harry Warren and Al Dubin, 1933.
"She Got the Goldmine (I Got the Shaft)." Jerry Reed and Tim DuBois, 1982.
"We're in the Money." Harry Warren and Al Dubin, 1933.

Secondary Sources

Books

Allen, Irving Lewis. *The City in Slang: New York Life and Popular Speech*. New York: Oxford University Press, 1993.

Allen, Theodore W. *The Invention of Whiteness: Racial Oppression and Social Control*. 2nd ed. New York: Verso, 2012.

Altschuler, Glenn C., and Stuart M. Blumin. *The GI Bill: A New Deal for Veterans*. New York: Oxford University Press, 2009.

Bailey, Beth. *From Front Porch to Back Seat: Courtship in Twentieth-Century America*. Baltimore, MD: Johns Hopkins University Press, 1988.

———. *Sex in the Heartland*. Cambridge: Harvard University Press, 2002.

Banner, Lois. *Marilyn Monroe: The Passion and the Paradox*. New York: Bloomsbury, 2012.

Becker, Howard. *Outsiders: Studies in the Sociology of Deviance*. New York: Free Press, 1964.

Bederman, Gail. *Manliness and Civilization: A Cultural History of Gender and Race in the United States, 1880–1917*. Chicago: University of Chicago Press, 1995.

Berebitsky, Julie. *Sex and the Office: A History of Gender, Power, and Desire*. New Haven: Yale University Press, 2012.

Bergman, Andrew. *We're in the Money: Depression America and Its Films*. New York: Harper Row, 1971.

Berkin, Carol, Christopher Miller, Robert Cherny, and James Gormly. *Making America: A History of the United States, Volume II: Since 1865*. Boston: Cengage Learning, 2012.

Best, Joel. *Random Violence: How We Talk About New Crimes and New Crime Victims.* Berkeley: University of California Press, 1999.

Bragg, Beauty. *Reading Contemporary African American Literature: Black Women's Popular Fiction, Post-Civil Rights Experience, and the African American Canon.* New York: Lexington, 2015.

Brodkin, Karen. *How the Jews Became White Folks and What That Says About Race in America.* New Brunswick, NJ: Rutgers University Press, 1998.

Canaday, Margot. *The Straight State: Sexuality and Citizenship in Twentieth-Century America.* Princeton: Princeton University Press, 2009.

Cantu, Maya. *American Cinderellas of the Broadway Stage: Imagining the Working Girl from Irene to Gypsy.* New York: Palgrave, 2015.

Carter, Julian. *The Heart of Whiteness: Normal Sexuality and Race in America, 1880–1940.* Durham, NC: Duke University Press, 2007.

Celello, Kristin. *Making Marriage Work: A History of Marriage and Divorce in the Twentieth-Century United States.* Chapel Hill: University of North Carolina Press, 2009.

Charyn, Jerome. *Gangsters and Gold Diggers: Old New York, the Jazz Age, and the Birth of Broadway.* New York: Da Capo Press, 2004.

Clement, Elizabeth. *Love for Sale: Courting, Treating, and Prostitution in New York City, 1900–1945.* Chapel Hill: University of North Carolina Press, 2006.

Cohen, Mark. *Not Bad for Delancey Street: The Rise of Billy Rose.* Waltham, MA: Brandeis University Press, 2018.

Cohen, Stanley. *Folk Devils and Moral Panics: The Creation of the Mods and Rockers.* New York: Routledge, 2011.

Conrad, Earl. *Billy Rose: Manhattan Primitive.* New York: World Publishing, 1968.

Coontz, Stephanie. *Marriage, A History: From Obedience to Intimacy, or How Love Conquered Marriage.* New York: Viking, 2005.

———. *The Way We Never Were.* New York: Basic Books, 1992.

Cooper, Miriam. *Dark Lady of the Silents.* New York: Bobbs-Merrill, 1973.

Costello, John. *Love, Sex, and War: Changing Values 1939–45.* London, WI: Collins, 1986.

———. *Virtue under Fire: How World War II Changed Our Social and Sexual Attitudes.* New York: Fromm International Publishing, 1986.

Davis, Rebecca L. *More Perfect Unions: Americans Search for Marital Bliss.* Cambridge: Harvard University Press, 2010.

D'Emilio, John, and Estelle Freedman. *Intimate Matters: A History of Sexuality in America.* New York: Harper and Row, 1988.

DiBattista, Maria. *Fast-Talking Dames.* New Haven: Yale University Press, 2001.

Dickstein, Morris. *Dancing in the Dark: A Cultural History of the Great Depression.* New York: Norton, 2009.

DiFonzo, J. Herbie. *Beneath the Fault Line: The Popular and Legal Culture of Divorce in Twentieth-Century America.* Charlottesville: University of Virginia Press, 1997.

Doherty, Thomas. *Pre-Code Hollywood: Sex, Immorality, and Insurrection in American Cinema, 1930–1934.* New York: Columbia University Press, 1999.

Donovan, Brian. *Respectability on Trial: Sex Crimes in New York City, 1900–1918.* Albany: State University of New York Press, 2016.

———. *White Slave Crusades: Race, Gender, and Anti-Vice Activism.* Champaign: University of Illinois Press, 2006.

Dooley, Roger. *From Scarface to Scarlett: American Films in the 1930s.* New York: Harcourt, Brace, and Jovanovich, 1979.

Dyer, Richard. *The Dumb Blonde Stereotype: Documentation for EAS Classroom Materials.* London: British Film Institute, 1979.

———. *Heavenly Bodies: Film Stars and Society.* New York: Routledge, 1986.

———. *The Matter of Images: Essays on Representations.* New York: Routledge, 2002.

Ehrenreich, Barbara. *The Worst Years of Our Lives: Irreverent Notes from a Decade of Greed.* New York: Pantheon, 1990.

Eyman, Scott. *The Speed of Sound: Hollywood and the Talkie Revolution.* New York: Simon and Schuster, 1997.

Fineman, Martha. *The Illusion of Equality: The Rhetoric and Reality of Divorce Reform.* Chicago: University of Chicago Press, 1991.

Fleming, Peter. *Sugar Daddy Capitalism: The Dark Side of the New Economy.* New York: Polity, 2019.

Friedman, Lawrence. *Guarding Life's Dark Secrets: Legal and Social Controls over Reputation, Propriety, and Privacy.* Palo Alto: Stanford University Press, 2007.

Friedman-Kasaba, Kathie. *Law in America: A Short History.* New York: Random House, 2002.

———. *Memories of Migration: Gender, Ethnicity, and Work in the Lives of Jewish and Italian Women in New York, 1870–1924.* Albany: State University of New York Press, 1996.

Gilbert, James. *Men in the Middle: Searching for Masculinity in the 1950s.* Chicago: University of Chicago Press, 2005.

Gordon, Linda. *Pitied but Not Entitled: Single Mothers and the History of Welfare, 1890–1935.* Cambridge: Harvard University Press, 1998.

Gottlieb, Polly Rose. *The Nine Lives of Billy Rose.* New York: Crown, 1968.

Greenburg, Michael. *Peaches and Daddy: The Story of the Roaring 20s, the Birth of Tabloid Media, and the Courtship that Captured the Heart and Imagination of the American Public.* New York: Overlook Press, 2008.

Groneman, Carol. *Nymphomania: A History.* New York: Norton, 2000.

Grossberg, Michael. *Governing the Hearth: Law and the Family in Nineteenth-Century America.* Chapel Hill: University of North Carolina Press, 1985.

Grossman, Joanna L., and Lawrence M. Friedman. *Inside the Castle: Law and the Family in 20th Century America.* Princeton: Princeton University Press, 2011.

Guilbert, Georges-Claude. *Madonna as Postmodern Myth: How One Star's Self-Construction Rewrites Sex, Gender, Hollywood and the American Dream.* Jefferson, NC: McFarland, 2002.

Haag, Pamela. *Consent: Sexual Rights and the Transformation of American Liberalism.* Ithaca, NY: Cornell University Press, 1999.

Hale, Elizabeth Grace. *Making Whiteness: The Culture of Segregation in the South.* New York: Vintage, 1999.

Hall, Stuart. *Policing the Crisis: Mugging, the State, and Law and Order.* New York: Palgrave, 1978.

Haltom, William, and Michael McCann. *Distorting the Law: Politics, Media, and the Litigation Crisis.* Chicago: University of Chicago Press, 2004.

Hancock, Ange-Marie. *Intersectionality: An Intellectual History.* New York: Oxford University Press, 2016.

———. *The Politics of Disgust: The Public Identity of the Welfare Queen.* New York: New York University Press, 2004.

Hartog, Hendrik. *Man and Wife in America: A History.* Cambridge: Harvard University Press, 2000.

Harvey, David. *A Brief History of Neoliberalism.* New York: Oxford University Press, 2005.

Haskell, Molly. *From Reverence to Rape: The Treatment of Women in the Movies.* New York: Penguin, 1973.

Hill, Shirley A. *Black Intimacies: A Gender Perspective on Families and Relationships.* New York: AltaMira, 2005.

Hirshman, Linda R., and Jane E. Larson. *Hard Bargains: The Politics of Sex.* New York: Oxford University Press, 1999.

Hochschild, Arlie. *The Second Shift: Working Parents and the Revolution at Home.* New York: Viking, 1989.

Hudovernik, Robert. *Jazz Age Beauties: The Lost Collection of Ziegfeld Photographer Alfred Cheney Johnston.* New York: Universe Publishing, 2006.

Ignatiev, Noel. *How the Irish Became White.* New York: Routledge Classics, 2008.

Igra, Anna. *Wives without Husbands: Marriage, Desertion, and Welfare in New York, 1900–1935.* Chapel Hill: University of North Carolina Press, 2007.

Isenberg, Nancy. *White Trash: The 400-Year Untold History of Class in America.* New York: Penguin, 2016.

Jacobs, Lea. *The Wages of Sin: Censorship and the Fallen Woman Film, 1928–1942.* Berkeley: University of California Press, 1997.

Jacobson, Matthew Frye. *Whiteness of a Different Color.* Cambridge: Harvard University Press, 1998.

Jasper, James. *The Art of Moral Protest.* Chicago: University of Chicago Press, 2008.

Jordan, Jessica Hope. *The Sex Goddess in American Film, 1930–1965.* Amherst, NY: Cambria Press, 2009.

Kaplan, Ann E. *Rocking around the Clock: Music, Television, Postmodernism, and Consumer Culture.* London: Methuen, 1987.

Katznelson, Ira. *When Affirmative Action Was White: An Untold History of Racial Inequality in Twentieth-Century America.* New York: Norton, 2005.

Kessler-Harris, Alice. *Out to Work: A History of Wage-Earning Women in America.* Oxford: Oxford University Press, 1982.

Kuby, William. *Conjugal Misconduct: Defying Marriage Law in the Twentieth-Century United States.* Cambridge: Cambridge University Press, 2018.

Landay, Lori. *Madcaps, Screwballs, and Con Women: The Female Trickster in American Culture.* Philadelphia: University of Pennsylvania Press, 1998.

Latham, Angela J. *Posing a Threat: Flappers, Chorus Girls, and Other Brazen Performers of the American 1920s*. Hanover, NH: Wesleyan University Press, 2000.

Leder, Jane Mersky. *Thanks for the Memories: Love, Sex, and World War II*. Westport, CT: Praeger, 2006.

Lefkovitz, Alison. *Strange Bedfellows: Marriage in the Age of Women's Liberation*. Philadelphia: University of Pennsylvania Press, 2018.

Lettmaier, Saskia. *Broken Engagements: The Action for Breach of Promise of Marriage and the Feminine Ideal, 1800–1940*. New York: Oxford University Press, 2010.

Littauer, Amanda. *Bad Girls: Young Women, Sex, and Rebellion before the Sixties*. Chapel Hill, NC: University of North Carolina Press, 2015.

Lynn, Kevin S. *Charlie Chaplin and His Times*. New York: Simon and Schuster, 1997.

Lystra, Karen. *Searching the Heart: Women, Men, and Romantic Love in Nineteenth-Century America*. New York: Oxford University Press, 1989.

Maraniss, David. *Rome 1960: The Olympics That Changed the World*. New York: Simon and Schuster, 2008.

Marvin, Pamela. *Lee: A Memoir*. Boston: Faber and Faber, 1997.

May, Elaine Tyler. *Great Expectations: Marriage and Divorce in Post Victorian America*. Chicago: University of Chicago Press, 1980.

———. *Homeward Bound: American Families in the Cold War Era*. New York: Basic Books, 1988.

Mayer, Jane. *Dark Money: The Hidden History of the Billionaires behind the Rise of the Radical Right*. New York: Doubleday, 2016.

McCann, Graham. *Marilyn Monroe*. New Brunswick, NJ: Rutgers University Press, 1987.

McElvaine, Robert. *The Great Depression: America, 1929–1941*. New York: Times Books, 1984.

McLaren, Angus. *Sexual Blackmail: A Modern History*. Cambridge: Harvard University Press, 2002.

Meyerowitz, Joanne J. *Women Adrift: Independent Wage Earners in Chicago, 1880–1930*. Chicago: University of Chicago Press, 1988.

Mizejewski, Linda. *Ziegfeld Girl: Image and Icon in Culture and Cinema*. Durham, NC: Duke University Press, 1999.

Morse, Kathryn Taylor. *The Nature of Gold: An Environmental History of the Klondike Gold Rush*. Seattle: University of Washington Press, 2003.

Mulvey, Laura. "Unmasking the Gaze: Feminist Film Theory, History, and Film Studies." In *Reclaiming the Archive: Feminism and Film History*, edited by Vicki Callahan, 17–31. Detroit: Wayne State University Press, 2010.

Nathan, Debbie, and Michael Snedeker. *Satan's Silence: Ritual Abuse and the Making of a Modern American Witch Hunt*. New York: Basic, 1995.

Odem, Mary. *Delinquent Daughters: Protecting and Policing Adolescent Female Sexuality in the United States, 1885–1920*. Chapel Hill: University of North Carolina Press, 1995.

Omi, Michael, and Howard Winant. *Racial Formation in the United States*. New York: Routledge, 2014.

O'Neill, William L. *Divorce in the Progressive era.* New Haven: Yale University Press, 1968.

Pascoe, Peggy. *What Comes Naturally: Miscegenation Law and the Making of Race in America.* New York: Oxford University Press, 2010.

Peiss, Kathy. *Cheap Amusements: Working Women and Leisure in Turn-of-the-Century New York.* Philadelphia: Temple University Press, 1986.

Pickering, Steven. *Stereotyping: The Politics of Representation.* New York: Palgrave, 2001.

Pitzulo, Carrie. *Bachelors and Bunnies: The Sexual Politics of Playboy.* Chicago: University of Chicago Press, 2011.

Pleck, Elizabeth H. *Not Just Roommates: Cohabitation after the Sexual Revolution.* Chicago: University of Chicago Press, 2012.

Robertson, Pamela. *Guilty Pleasures: Feminist Camp from Mae West to Madonna.* Durham, NC: Duke University Press, 1996.

Rodgers, Marion Elizabeth. *Mencken: An American Iconoclast.* New York: Oxford University Press, 2005.

Roediger, David. *The Wages of Whiteness: Race and the Making of the American Working Class.* New York: Verso, 2007.

Rosen, Lawrence. *Law as Culture: An Invitation.* Princeton: Princeton University Press, 2008.

Rosen, Marjorie. *Popcorn Venus: Women, Movies, and the American Dream.* New York: Avon, 1974.

Rosen, Ruth. *The World Split Open: How the Modern Women's Movement Changed America.* New York: Viking, 2000.

Rosenblum, Constance. *Gold Digger: The Outrageous Life and Times of Peggy Hopkins Joyce.* New York: Henry Holt, 2000.

Ross, Steven. *Working-Class Hollywood: Silent Film and the Shaping of Class in America.* Princeton: Princeton University Press, 1998.

Schulman, Daniel. *Sons of Wichita: How the Koch Brothers Became America's Most Powerful and Private Dynasty.* New York: Grand Central, 2014.

Scott, Joan Wallach. *Gender and the Politics of History.* New York: Columbia University Press, 1988.

Seidman, Steven. *Romantic Longings: Love in America, 1830–1980.* New York: Routledge, 1992.

Sharot, Stephen. *Love and Marriage across Social Classes in American Cinema.* New York: Palgrave, 2017.

Sharrar, Jack F. *Avery Hopwood: His Life and Plays.* Ann Arbor: University of Michigan Press, 1989.

Simmons, Christina. *Making Marriage Modern: Women's Sexuality from the Progressive era to World War II.* New York: Oxford University Press, 2011.

Smith-Rosenberg, Carroll. *Disorderly Conduct: Visions of Gender in Victorian America.* New York: Oxford University Press, 1985.

Spoto, Donald. *Marilyn Monroe: The Biography.* New York: Cooper Square Press, 1993.

Staiger, Janet. *Bad Woman: Regulating Sexuality in Early American Cinema*. Minneapolis: University of Minnesota Press, 1995.

Sutin, Lawrence. *Do What Thou Wilt: A Life of Aleister Crowley*. New York: St. Martin's Press, 2002.

Syrett, Nicholas L. *American Child Bride: A History of Minors and Marriage in the United States*. Chapel Hill: University of North Carolina Press, 2018.

Terkel, Studs. *Hard Times: An Oral History of the Great Depression*. New York: Pantheon, 1970.

Tremper, Ellen. *I'm No Angel: The Blonde in Fiction and Film*. Charlottesville: University of Virginia Press, 2006.

Wallace, David. *Capital of the World: A Portrait of New York City in the Roaring Twenties*. New York: Lyons Press, 2011.

Ware, Susan. *Holding Their Own: American Women in the 1930s*. Boston: Twayne Publishing, 1982.

Weiss, Jessica. *To Have and to Hold: Marriage, the Baby Boom, and Social Change*. Chicago: University of Chicago Press, 2000.

Weitzman, Lenore. *The Divorce Revolution: The Unexpected Social and Economic Consequences for Women and Children in America*. New York: Free Press, 1985.

White, Kevin. *The First Sexual Revolution: The Emergence of Male Heterosexuality in Modern America*. New York: New York University Press, 1992.

Whitt, Jan. *Women in American Journalism: A New History*. Champaign: University of Illinois Press, 2008.

Young, William H., and Nancy K. Young. *The Great Depression in America: A Cultural Encyclopedia*. Vol. 2. Westport, CT: Greenwood Press, 2007.

Zeiger, Susan. *Entangling Alliances: Foreign War Brides and American Soldiers in the Twentieth Century*. New York: New York University Press, 2010.

Zelizer, Viviana. *The Purchase of Intimacy*. Princeton: Princeton University Press, 2005.

Articles and Chapters

Abelson, Elaine S. "'Women Who Have No Men to Work for Them': Gender and Homelessness in the Great Depression, 1930–1934." *Feminist Studies* 29, no. 1 (Spring 2003): 104–27.

Arbuthnot, Lucie, and Gail Seneca. "Pre-Text and Text in *Gentlemen Prefer Blondes*." *Film Reader* 5 (1982): 13–23.

Armstrong, Elizabeth, and Suzanna Crage. "Movements and Memory: The Making of the Stonewall Myth." *American Sociological Review* 71 (October 2006): 724–51.

Banner, Lois. "The Creature from the Black Lagoon: Marilyn Monroe and Whiteness." *Cinema Journal* 47, no. 4 (Summer 2008): 4–29.

Barrett-Fox, Jason. "Rhetorics of Indirection, Indiscretion, Insurrection: The 'Feminine Style' of Anita Loos, 1912–1925." *JAC* 32, no. 1 (2012): 221–49.

Berman, Lila Corwin. "Sociology, Jews, and Intermarriage in Twentieth-Century America." *Jewish Social Studies* 14 (Winter 2008): 32–60.

Bonnstetter, Beth E. "The Legacy of *Mystery Science Theater 3000*: Text, Textual Production, Paracinema, and Media Literacy." *Journal of Popular Film and Television* 40 (2012): 94–104.

Brown, Jeffrey A. "Class and Feminine Excess: The Strange Case of Anna Nicole Smith." *Feminist Review* 81 (2005): 74–94.

Carrillo, Jo. "Links and Choices: Popular Legal Culture in the Work of Lawrence M. Friedman." *Southern California Interdisciplinary Law Journal* 17, no. 1 (2007): 1–22.

Cline, Denzel C. "Allowances to Dependents of Servicemen in the United States." *Annals of the American Academy of Political and Social Science* (May 1943): 1–8.

Cohen, Lisa. "The Horizontal Walk: Marilyn Monroe, CinemaScope, and Sexuality." *Yale Journal of Criticism* 11, no. 1 (Spring 1998): 259–83.

Coombs, Mary. "Agency and Partnership: A Study of Breach of Promise Plaintiffs." *Yale Journal of Law and Feminism* 2, no. 1 (1989): 1–23.

Crenshaw, Kimberlé. "Mapping the Margins: Intersectionality, Identity Politics, and Violence against Women of Color." *Stanford Law Review* 43, no. 60 (1991): 1241–99.

Creswell, Thomas. "What Did Peaches Browning Say?" *American Speech* 37, no. 1 (February 1962): 27–40.

Curry, Ramona. "Madonna from Marilyn to Marlene: Pastiche and/or Parody." *Journal of Film and Video* 42, no. 2 (1990): 15–30.

Dalton, Bryce K. "Stern v. Marshall: How Anna Nicole Smith Almost Stripped Bankruptcy Courts of Jury Trials." *Iowa Law Review* 98, no. 1 (2012): 337–63.

Dowsett, Gary. "The 'Gay Plague' Revisited: AIDS and Its Enduring Moral Panic." In *Moral Panics, Sex Panics: Fear and Fight over Sexual Rights*, edited by Gilbert Herdt, 130–56. New York: New York University Press, 2009.

Dunbar, Eve. "Hip Hop (Feat. Women Writers): Reimagining Black Women and Agency through Hip Hop Fiction." In *Contemporary African American Literature: The Living Canon*, edited by Lovalerie King and Shirley Moody-Turner, 91–112. Bloomington: Indiana University Press, 2012.

Dunbar, Roxanne A. "Bloody Footprints: Reflections on Growing Up Poor White." In *White Trash: Race and Class in America*, edited by Matt Wray and Annalee Newitz, 73–86. New York: Routledge, 1997.

Fillippi, Jamie G. "The Legacy of the Anna Nicole Smith Case in Bankruptcy Courts." *Duquesne Business Law Journal* 14 (Winter 2012): 19–46.

Frost, Laura. "Blondes Have More Fun: Anita Loos and the Language of Silent Cinema." *Modernism/Modernity* 17, no. 2 (April 2010): 291–311.

Galanter, Marc. "Beyond the Litigation Panic." *Proceedings of the American Academy of Political Science* 37, no. 1 (1988): 18–30.

Gerd, Jenna. "Famous for Being Famous: Celebrity Socialites and the Framework of Fame." In *Simulation in Media and Culture: Believing in the Hype*, edited by Robin DeRosa, 9–24. New York: Lexington Books, 2011.

Goldberg, Charlotte K. "Schemes of the Adventuress: The Abolition and Revival of Common-Law Marriage." *William and Mary Journal of Women and the Law* 13 (2007): 483–538.

Golden, Eve. "Peggy Hopkins Joyce: The Gentleman Preferred Blonde." *Films of the Golden Age* 17 (Summer 1999). Accessed September 9, 2013. http://filmsofthegoldenage.com/foga/1999/summer99/peggyjoyce.html.

Grossman, Harry, and Robert H. Cole. "Some Observations on the Distribution of Family Allowance Benefits in World War II." *American Sociological Review* 10, no. 5 (October 1945): 614–18.

Grossman, Joanna. "The End of the Road: The Late Anna Nicole Smith's Quest to Inherit Is Over." *Verdict* (September 2, 2014). Accessed October 3, 2018. https://verdict.justia.com/2014/09/02/end-road.

Hegeman, Susan. "Taking *Blondes* Seriously." *American Literary History* 7, no. 3 (1995): 525–54.

Honey, Maureen. "Maternal Welders: Women's Sexuality and Propaganda on the Home Front during World War II." *Prospects* 22 (1997): 479–519.

Hove, Arthur. "In Search of Happiness." In *Gold Diggers of 1933*, edited by Arthur Hove, 9–31. Madison: University of Wisconsin Press, 1980.

Hunt, Alan. "Regulating Heterosocial Space: Sexual Politics in the Early Twentieth Century." *Journal of Historical Sociology* 15, no. 1 (March 2002): 1–34.

Johnson, Kecia R., and Karyn Loscocco. "Black Marriage through the Prism of Gender, Race, and Class." *Journal of Black Studies* 46, no. 2 (March 2015): 142–171.

Keire, Mara L. "Swearing Allegiance: Street Language, US War Propaganda, and the Declining Status of Women in Northeastern Nightlife, 1900–1920." *Journal of the History of Sexuality* 25, no. 2 (May 2016): 246–66.

Kessner, Thomas, and Betty Caroli. "New Immigrant Women at Work: Italians and Jews in New York City, 1880–1905." *The Journal of Ethnic Studies* 5, no. 4 (1978): 19–31.

Kohler-Hausmann, Julilly. "'The Crime of Survival': Fraud Prosecutions, Community Surveillance, and the Original 'Welfare Queen.'" *Journal of Social History* 41, no. 2 (December 2007): 329–54.

Konkle, Amanda. "How to (Marry a Woman Who Wants to) Marry a Millionaire." *Quarterly Review of Film and Video* 31, no. 4 (March 2014): 364–83.

Kuby, William. "Till Disinterest Do Us Part: Trial Marriage, Public Policy, and the Fear of Familial Decay in the United States, 1900–1930." *Journal of the History of Sexuality* 32 (September 2014): 383–414.

Kuperberg, Arielle. "Premarital Cohabitation and Direct Marriage in the United States, 1956–2015." *Marriage and Family Review* 55 (2019): 447–75.

Larson, Jane E. ""Women Understand So Little, They Call My Good Nature 'Deceit'": A Feminist Rethinking of Seduction." *Columbia Law Review* 93, no. 2 (1993): 374–472.

Lynn, Susan. "Gender and Progressive Politics: A Bridge to Social Activism of the 1960s." In *Not June Cleaver: Women and Gender in Postwar America, 1945–1960*, edited by Joanne Meyerowitz, 103–27. Philadelphia: Temple University Press, 1994.

Mahmood, Saba. "Feminist Theory, Agency, and the Liberatory Subject: Some Reflections on the Islamic Revival in Egypt." *Cultural Anthropology* 16, no. 2 (2001): 202–36.

Masuda, Wakako. "Analyzing 1980's Gender and Materiality: Madonna's *Material Girl.*" *Studies in English and American Literature* 48 (2013): 169–78.

McGovern, James R. "The American Woman's Pre-World War I Freedom in Manners and Morals." *Journal of American History* 55, no. 2 (September 1968): 315–33.

Mellencamp, Patricia. "The Sexual Economics of *Gold Diggers of 1933.*" In *Close Viewings: An Anthology of New Film Criticism,* edited by Peter Lehman, 177–99. Tallahassee: Florida State University Press, 1990.

Meyerowitz, Joanne. "Beyond the Feminine Mystique: A Reassessment of Postwar Mass Culture, 1946–1958." In *Not June Cleaver: Women and Gender in Postwar America, 1945–1960,* edited by Joanne Meyerowitz, 229–62. Philadelphia: Temple University Press, 1994.

Milkman, Ruth. "Women's Work and Economic Crisis: Some Lessons of the Great Depression." *Review of Radical Political Economics* 8, no. 1 (1976): 73–97.

Mulvey, Laura. "Thoughts on Marilyn Monroe: Emblem and Allegory." *Screen* 58, no. 2 (Summer 2017): 202–9.

———. "Visual Pleasure and Narrative Cinema." *Screen* 16, no. 3 (October 1975): 6–18.

Penningroth, Dylan C. "African American Divorce in Virginia and Washington, D.C., 1865–1930." *Journal of Family History* 33 (January 2008): 21–35.

Pfau, Ann. "Allotment Annies and Other Wayward Wives: Wartime Concerns About Female Disloyalty and the Problem of the Returned Veteran." In *The United States and the Second World War,* edited by Sidney Pash and G. Piehler, 99–128. New York: Fordham University Press, 2010.

Prieto-Arranz, Jose I. "The Semiotics of Performance and Success in Madonna." *The Journal of Popular Culture* 45, no. 1 (February 2012): 175–95.

Rabinowitz, Paula. "Commodity Fetishism: Women in *Gold Diggers of 1933.*" *Film Reader* 5 (1982): 140–49.

Raley, R. Kelly, Megan M. Sweeny, and Danielle Wondra. "The Growing Racial and Ethnic Divide in U.S. Marriage Patterns." *The Future of Children* 25 no. 2 (Fall 2015): 89-109.

Rounthwaite, Adair. "Veiled Subjects: Shirin Neshat and Non-liberatory Agency." *Journal of Visual Culture* 7, no. 2 (2008): 165–80.

Rubin, Gayle. "The Traffic in Women: Notes on the 'Political Economy' of Sex." In *Toward an Anthropology of Women,* edited by Rayna R. Reiter, 175–210. New York: Monthly Review, 1975.

Ryan, Cheyney. "Lawyers as Lovers: *Gold Diggers of 1933* or 'I'd Rather You Sue Me than Marry Me.'" *University of San Francisco Law Review* (Summer 1996): 1123–30.

Saguy, Abigail, and Forrest Stuart. "Culture and Law: Beyond a Paradigm of Cause and Effect." *Annals of the American Academy of Political and Social Science* 619 (September 2008): 149–64.

Scheibel, Will. "Marilyn Monroe, 'Sex Symbol': Film Performance, Gender Politics and 1950s Hollywood Celebrity." *Celebrity Studies* 4, no. 1 (March 2013): 1–13.

Schudson, Michael. "How Culture Works: Perspectives from Media Studies on the Efficacy of Symbols." *Theory and Society* 18 (1989): 153–80.

Schultz, Martin. "Divorce Patterns in Nineteenth-Century New England." *Journal of Family History* 15 (1990): 101–15.

Sharot, Stephen. "Wealth and/or Love: Class and Gender in the Cross-Class Romance Films of the Great Depression." *Journal of American Studies* 47, no. 1 (2013): 89–108.

Shehan, Constance L., Felix M. Berardo, Erica Owens, and Donna H. Berardo, "Alimony: An Anomaly in Family Social Science." *Family Relations* 51 (2001): 308–16.

Simmons, Christina. "Companionate Marriage." In *International Encyclopedia of Human Sexuality*, edited by Patricia Whelehan and Anne Bolin, 245–48. New York: Wiley Blackwell, 2015.

Slavens, Clarence. "The Gold Digger as Icon: Exposing Inequity in the Great Depression." *Studies in Popular Culture* 28, no. 3 (2006): 71–92.

Snyder, Robert W. "Palace Theatre." In *The Encyclopedia of New York City*, edited by Kenneth T. Jackson, 876. New Haven: Yale University Press, 2003.

———. "Vaudeville." In *The Encyclopedia of New York City*, edited by Kenneth T. Jackson, 1226. New Haven: Yale University Press, 2003.

Stephens, Dionne P., and Layli D. Phillips. "Freaks, Gold Diggers, Divas, and Dykes: The Sociohistorical Development of Adolescent African American Women's Sexual Scripts." *Sexuality & Culture* (December 2003): 3–49.

Strasser, Fred. "Tort Tales: Old Stories Never Die." *National Law Journal* (February 16, 1987): 39.

Tanner, Jolene. "Comment: Stern v. Marshall: The Earthquake that Hit the Bankruptcy Courts and the Aftershocks that Followed." *Loyola L.A. Law Review* 45, no. 2 (Winter 2012): 587–612.

Thompson, Sharon. "In Defence of the 'Gold-Digger.'" *Oñati Socio-Legal Series* 6, no. 6 (2016): 1225–48.

Thomson, Patricia. "Field." In *Bourdieu: Key Concepts*, edited by Michael Grenfell, 65–82. New York: Routledge, 2008.

Traister, Bruce. "Academic Viagra: The Rise of American Masculinity Studies." *American Quarterly* 52 (June 2000): 274–304.

Turner, Sarah, and John Bound. "Going to War and Going to College: Did World War II and the G.I. Bill Increase Educational Attainment for Returning Veterans?" *Journal of Labor Economics* 20, no. 4: 784–8115.

Wood, Bethany. "Gentlemen Prefer Adaptations: Addressing Industry and Gender in Adaptation Studies." *Theatre Journal* 66 (2014): 559–79.

Wright, Sarah. "Moral Panics as Enacted Melodramas." *British Journal of Criminology* 55 (2015): 1245–62.

Dissertations and Theses

Pemberton, Jennifer. "'Now I Ain't Sayin' She's a Gold Digger': African American Femininities in Rap Music Lyrics." PhD diss., Florida State University, 2008.

Werhnyak, Larissa Marie. "'O, Perjured Lover, Atone! Atone!': A Legal and Cultural History of Breach of Promise to Marry, 1880–1940." PhD diss., University of Iowa, 2015.

Index

Page locators in italics indicate figures

Austrian, Alfred, 33
Aykroyd, Dan, 149

Bailey, Beth, 93
Baldwin, Faith, 26, 55, 129–30, 217n32
Bankhead, Tallulah, 4
bankruptcy law, 16, 172, 173, 184, 187–88, 200, 241n118
Banner, Lois, 118, 125
Bara, Theda, 7
Barry Ashton Dancers, 134
beauty: physical measurements, 107; racial, class, age, and sexual criteria for, 29; success of lawsuits and, 74, 149–50
Beck, Joan, 151
Bederman, Gail, 204n19, 209n20, 224n57
Belsaco, David, 2, 4, 203–4n10
Bergman, Andrew, 67
Berkeley, Busby, 4, 66, 204n10
Berle, Milton, 102
Bernstein, Carl, 149
Best, Joel, 196
Beyoncé, 192
bigamy, 72, 88–89, 200
Billings Gazette, 74
Birkhead, Dannielynn, 188–89
Birkhead, Larry, 189
birth control, 128
birth rate, 13; among "native-born" whites, 25, 30
Black Cat raid (Los Angeles), 128
Blackstone, Andrea, 194
Bleak House (Dickens), 188
Blitzer, Wolf, 189
blonde hair, 12, 78; "amusement blondes," 72, 78, 105; "blonde bombshell," 21, 111, 115; "dumb blonde," 7, 23, 96, 111, *112,* 115–16, 174, 178–79, 183, 198; "proverbial blonde," 105, 110
Blondell, Joan, 12
A Bona Fide Gold Digger (Hobbs), 194
Boon, Debbie, 177

Bourdieu, Pierre, 204n15
Boyle, Hal, 126
Breach of Promise (movie), 64
breach of promise lawsuits, 7, 10, 17, 56, 197, 220n79; in African American media, 70, 72–73, *73;* gender and class dynamics of, 59; as gendered litigation, 59; high-profile, 71; in movies, 64, 66, 68–70; nineteenth century, 58–59; tort tales, 70–76
Breen, Joseph, 117
Brice, Fanny, 30, 100, 223n41
The Bride (movie), 31
Brill, Steve, 151
Bromley, Dorothy Dunbar, 46–47
Brooks, Louise, 7
Brooks, Virginia, 1, 203n1
Brown, Harry Joe, 71
Brown, Jeffrey, 181, 190
Brownell, Phoebe, 51
Browning, Edward, 38–46
Browning, Frances "Peaches" Heenan, 38–46, *42,* 54, 72, 78, 198, 200–201; death of, 124
Brownlow, Kevin, 21
Brundage, Avery, 99
Buchwald, Art, 150
Bufford, Samuel, 172
Burgess, Ernest, 86–87
Burnett, Carol, 149
A Business Man Looks at Communism (Koch), 161
Bus Stop (movie), 168
Butler, Bettie, 59

Cafferty. Jack, 189
California, divorce laws, 130
California Family Law Act of 1969, 130
California Federation of Women's Clubs, 76
California Supreme Court, 15, 18; nonmarital support case, 139–42
Cannon, Ethel, 72
Cantor, Eddie, 37, 144, 212n75
capital exchange, logic of, 43

capitalism, 18, 64, 160, 217n30. *See also* neoliberalism

capitalist-patriarchy, 67

Carol Burnett Show, 149

Carr, Henry, 44

Carson, Johnny, 149

Carter, David, 185–87, 243n137

Cary, Paul, 140

Catholic World, 117

Celello, Kristin, 25

censorship, 117

Cerrato, Maria Antonia, 172

Champlin Reining Company v. Oklahoma Corporation Commission, 164–65

Chanel, Gabrielle, 44

Channing, Carol, 101

"charity girls," 2

Chicago Daily Tribune: alimony discussed in, 29, 36, 39, 42–43, 53–54; heart balm suits discussed in, 74

Chicago Defender, 72, 73

Chicago Tribune, 33, 34, 74, 141, 150–51, 159; Mitchelson's article, 153

"child brides," 38, 212n83

childhood sexual abuse, trivialization of, 38–39, 42, 43

Children's Bureau, 62

China Seas (movie), 113

Chisholm, Shirley, 127

chorus girls, 12

Christian Science Monitor, 75

Cinderella figure, 7

CinemaScope, 118–19

Claire, Ina, 4

class context, 198–99, 221n3, 228n102; African Americans and, 72; breach of promise lawsuits, 59; class rise and cross-class romance in movies, 63–64, 217n27; consumer culture and, 110; dating, 11; heart balm lawsuits and, 75–76, 83–84; Marvin-Triola palimony suits and, 148–55; palimony suits and, 148–49, 151–52; poverty, class dynamics of, 78–79;

sexuality and, 12; social mobility through gold digging portrayed in film, 63–64; "white trash," 159–61. *See also* intersection of gender, race, and class; middle-class domesticity

Clifford, Terry, 150–51

Cloud, Michelle (Smith's cousin), 184

cohabitation, 15, 18, 129, 132, 229n28; community property standards, 139–40; "Living Together (in California)" workshop, 141. *See also* Marvin, Lee; palimony; Triola, Michelle

Cohen, Lisa, 112–13, 118

Cohen, Mark, 104

Cohen, Stanley, 9

Cohn, Roy, 137

Cold War era, 98, 124–25

college-educated women, 109

commodity fetishism, 67

common law, 58, 82

common-law marriage, 7, 138

communism, 14, 161

community property standards, 139–40

companionate marriage, 11, 23–24, 59–60

Companionate Marriage (Lindsey), 11, 24

computing and telecommunications trajectory, 194–95

condensing symbol, 8

Confessions of a Gold Digger (Van Deventer), 7

conformity, attributed to 1950s, 98, 105, 125, 223n36

constructivist perspective, 6, 204n18

consumer culture, 93–94, 110, 118; 1980s materialism, 158–59; "yuppie" social type, 158

consumerism, 14, 24

Contra Costa Times, 173

contract law, 58, 59; heart balm law as, 81; implied contracts, 140, 144, 156

contrast, 196–97

Cooley, Bessie, 54, 197

Cooley, Vernon P., 52–54

Coombs, Mary, 115–16
Coontz, John, 76
Coontz, Stephanie, 98, 201, 243n13
Cooper, Anderson, 189
Cooper, Miriam, 31
Cosmopolitan, 155
courtship, 11
coverture, 21–22
Craigslist "gold digger" ad, 195
Crawford, Cindy, 168
Crenshaw, Kimberlé, 206n35
Cressey, Paul, 7
criminal conversation, 57, 58, 70
Crist, Archie, 85
Crist, Herbert, 85
Crist, Rose, 85
Crist v. Crist, 85, 220n1, 221n3
Cukor, George, 64
cultural capital, 27, 43, 149, 160, 180–81
Cunningham, Tom, 167, 170, 174, 177
A Current Affair (television show), 175
Curtin, Jane, 149

damages, marriageability and, 58–59, 69–70
Dane, Charlotte (character, *Alimony*), 48
dating, 11; 1960s, 126; liminal space between sex work and, 2; mid-twentieth century, 93–94; monetization of, 127
Davis, Rebecca, 15, 60, 105, 128
"Dear Abby" column, 126
DeJean, Pierre, 169
Dempsey, Jack, 36, 211n72
Department of Defense, 14
de Saulles, Blanca, 31, 36
de Saulles, Jack, 31, 36
desertions, 26–27
deservedness, 16, 160, 181, 190–91
deviant behavior, 21, 204n17
"Diamonds Are a Girl's Best Friend" *(Gentlemen Prefer Blondes),* 110, 157, 170
Dickens, Charles, 188
Dickstein, Morris, 61

Dietrichson, Phyllis, 7
DiFonzo, J. Herbie, 26, 213n99
Dinehart, Alan, 71
Dinner at Eight (movie), 64, 113
The Dirty Dozen (movie), 135, 144
Distefano, Sam, 146
District of Columbia Supreme Court, 54
divorce: alimony blamed for, 25–26, 45–50; "collusion," 130; do-it-yourself, 130; fault system, 129–30, 146; grounds for, 15, 24, 129; no-fault, 15, 129–31, 140, 229n15; post–World War I trends, 26; rate of, 15; rate of, 1880 to 1930, 24–25; rate of, late 1920s, 16; sexual revolution, 1960s, 129–33; stigma of, 131–32; uncontested, early twentieth century, 26; women's standard of living and, 130
Divorce Yourself, 130
Dix, Dorothy, 127, 205n20
Donnelly, Antoinette, 75
Dooley, Roger, 64
Dorothy (character, *Gentlemen Prefer Blondes*), 115–18, 197
Doubleday, Felix, 71
Doubleday, Rhoda Tanner, 10, 71, 78, 197
Doughty, Richard (witness in trial), 146–47
dowry, 50
Dunbar, Jane, 152
Dunbar, Roxanne A., 235n11
Dyer, Richard, 111

Earl Carroll Vanities of 1923, 37
Ecob, Robert, 47–48
economy: anxieties displaced onto lower class and African Americans, 159; Great Depression, 12–13, 68–69; postwar, 96–98, 120, 222n27; women's management of household, 62. *See also* structural and economic conditions
E! Entertainment Television network, 181–83
Eilers, Sally, 71

Gay, Marjorie, 71
gaze, male, 117–18, 157, 225n80
Gazette (Montreal), 180
gender ideology, 5, 60; 1970s, 143–45; 1980s, 154–55; deviance of portrayed in terms of race, 49–50; double-edged quality of 1950s, 113, 223n36; gold diggers as threat to, 17–18, 94; during Great Depression, 60–61; sexual division of labor, 128. *See also* intersection of gender, race, and class
General Federation of Women's Clubs, 76
Gentlemen Prefer Blondes (Loos), 6–7, 12, 17, 55, 105, 196–98; Billy Rose and, 101; "Diamonds Are a Girl's Best Friend," 110, 157, 170; film scholarship on, 115, 117–18; friendship between women as main text, 118, 121; Joyce as model for, 37, 115, 225–26n83; "Little Rock" number, 227n94
Gentlemen Prefer Blondes (movie, 1953), 7, 14–15, 17, 105, 110, 111, 115–18, 196–97
GI Bill (Servicemen's Readjustment Act of 1944), 14, 96–98, 222nn31, 32
Gibson, Shane, 189
Gilbert, James, 224n57
Gimbel, Frederic, 71
Ginsburg, Ruth Bader (justice), 187
"girl-next-door," 107
Glenn County Jail (California), 51
"Glorified American Girl," 29
Goddard, Paulette (Pauline Marion Levy), 30
gold, role of in American economy, 203–4n10
gold digger: Anna Nicole Smith and trope of, 173–78; categorical labor of, shifts in, 110; as category of woman-hood, 4, 5; as comedic, 12–15; cultural capital of, 27, 43, 149, 160, 180–81; cultural power of, 195–200; defined, 1–2, 203n2; development of stereo-type, 6–8; dissatisfied housewife as,

109–10; double bind facing women, 34, 95; as expression of white men's anxieties, 5–6; failed, movie trope of, 123; labeling of, 6, 198; late twentieth-century, 15–16; Marilyn Monroe in genealogy of, 110; men as, 204–5n10; self-parody of, 182, 190; as social force, 5–6; as societal threat, 7–8; as subversive cultural force, 64, 112, 118, 153, 205n24; as symbol, 196–98
"Gold Digger" (EPMD), 193–94
"Gold Digger" (West), 192–94, *193*
Gold Diggers (Howard), 194
Gold Diggers of 1933 (musical), 4, 65, 66–70, 123, 218n36; analyses of, 67–68; "Pettin' in the Park" number, 66, 68
Gold Diggers of 1935 (movie), 4, 65–66, 204n10
Gold Diggers of 1937 (movie), 4
Gold Diggers of Paris (movie), 4
"The Gold Digger Standard" (Ephron), 148–49
The Gold Diggers (Hopwood), 3–4, 66
The Gold Diggers (movie), 4
The Gold Diggers of Broadway (musical), 4
Golden Dreams (nude photo shoot), 114–15
Goldman, Lois, 143
Good Jobs for Good Girls (Powel), 92–93, *93*
Gordon, Linda, 26–27, 61, 216n21
Great Depression era, 12–13, 17, 56, 57–84, 201; Black Tuesday, 60; breach of promise tort tales during, 70–76; employment of women during, 61–62, 216n18; marriage and, 60–62; movies, 12–13, 57–70, 197; sex work, fears of, 62, 218n36
Great Lakes Exposition Aquacade, 100
Great Northern Oil Company, 162
Great Society, 160
Greed Decade, 158–59

marriage, 201–2; common-law, 7, 138; companionate, 11, 23–24, 59–60; as contract, 130, 132–33; decline in rate of, 129; desertions, 26–27; economic model, 23; "feminist," 23; "flapper marriage," 23; Great Depression and, 60–62; interracial, 106; in nineteenth century, 21–22; "partnership," 23; rate, Great Depression, 13; rate, World War II era, 14; separation, lifestyle-based justifications for, 25; sexual revolution, 1960s, 129–33; structural changes in, 9; "traditional," 128; trial, 11, 15, 23
marriageability, 58–59, 69–70
Marriage for Moderns (textbook), 109
"Marriage Without License" extension course (University of California at Los Angeles), 141
Married Women's Property Acts, 22
Marshall, Arthur K., 147
Marshall, Bettye Bohannon, 165, 166, 236n28
Marshall, J. Howard, II, 162–63, 164–88, 197, 236n30; Anna Nicole Smith's marriage to, 163; tax avoidance schemes, 191; will of, 171–72
Marshall, J. Howard, III, 163, 171
Marshall, Pierce, 162–63, 167–77, 182, 185–87, 201; defamation claim, 172; "Fine Tuning Memo," 172–73, 186; "New Community Memo," 185
Marshall Petroleum, 185
Marshall v. Marshall, 187–88, 241nn118, 119
Marvin, Betty, 135, 140
Marvin, Lee, 10, 18, 133–42, *136*, 197, 199; Los Angeles trial of, 142–48
Marvin, Pamela, 137, 147, 151
"Marvin Doctrine," 141
Marvin-Triola palimony suits, 133–42; 1976 ruling, 140–41; California Supreme Court nonmarital support issue, 139–42; constructing gender

and social class in, 148–55; core components, 143–44; domestic arrangements, importance of to, 145–47; love letters as evidence in, 145–46. *See also* Marvin, Lee; Triola, Michelle
Marx, Groucho, 111
Marx, Karl, 67
masculinity: crises of, 61, 105–7, 124, 197, 200, 216n16, 224n57; economic crisis and, 13; failures of, 125; gender relations, gold diggers as threat to, 17–18; Great Depression's effects on, 61; lack of wealth as feminizing, 122–23; Marilyn Monroe and crisis of, 111–24; mid-twentieth century anxieties, 93; models of, 224n57; "poor weak susceptible" men, 74, 197; postwar crisis, 105–10; white, threatened by "dumb blondes," 96; World War II era, 14
Masuda, Wakako, 157
matchmaking services, 24
"Material Girl" (Madonna), 157–58, 189–90, 196–97
Matthews, Joyce, 102, 103, 104–5
May, Elaine Tyler, 24, 98, 111
Mayer, Jane, 162
Mayfield, Molly, 109
McCann, Michael, 205–6n31
McCormick, Harry F., 71
McDonald's lawsuit tort tale, 9, 206nn32, 33
McDowell, James C., 94, 95
McElvaine, Robert, 61, 216n22
McGraw-Hill, 109
McHugh, Edna, 144
McKee, Grace, 113
McNaboe, John, 79–81
meaning, 196
media narratives, 9–10; 1960s representations of women, 152; of alimony, 22, 25, 36–40, 55; Great Depression, 62; heart balm laws and, 13, 57, 59, 62, 64, 70, 72–79, *73*, *77*, *80*, 83; midcentury, 98–99;

during neoliberalism, 159, 161. *See also* tort tales
Mellencamp, Patricia, 67–68, 218n41
Melter, Margaret, 52–53, 198
Men, Marriage, and Me (Joyce), 27
Mencken, H. L., 2
Mendal, Lilian, 71
Metro Magazine, 181, 190
middle-class domesticity, 85–125, 197, 200, 222n27; Cold War era anxieties, 98, 124–25; complexity of, 223n36; conformity attributed to 1950s, 98, 105, 125, 223n36; contradictory messages about, 17, 99, 111–15, 120; double binds faced by women, 34, 95; media narratives, 98–99; postwar economic expansion, 96–98; postwar transition era, 92–96; World War II era, 86–92. *See also* class context; intersection of gender, race, and class
Midler, Bette, 171
Mikkelson, Barbara, 195
military, fears of gold diggers, 14, 17
Mills, C. Wright, 191
Mises, Ludwig von, 162
"Miss Gold Digger" (Zollo), 107–8, 119
Mitchelson, Marvin M., 137–38, 143, 147, 155; gender equality comments, 153
Mittenthal, Sue, 150
Mizejewski, Linda, 29–30
Monroe, Marilyn, 196–97; archetype of, 157, 225n73; in cultural imagination, 110; early life, 113, 164, 179; in *Gentlemen Prefer Blondes,* 7, 14–15, 17, 108, 110, *112,* 115–18, 196–97; *Golden Dreams* (nude photo shoot), 114–15; "Marilyn clones," 125; postwar masculinity crisis and, 111–24; Smith influenced by, 178–79; star persona, 112–13
moral panic, 9, 200–201, 205nn29, 30; about alimony, 46; heart balm lawsuits and, 83; palimony suits, 141, 154–56; in roaring twenties, 10–11; World War II era, 14, 86, 89

Morse, Kathryn Taylor, 203–4n10
Mortenson, Norma Jeane. *See* Monroe, Marilyn
Moss, Kate, 168
mother-daughter melodramas, 91–92
mother-in-law gold diggers, 45
mothers, single, 27, 61–62
mothers' aid programs, 61–62
Motion Picture Production Code, 63, 114
Motion Pictures Producers and Distributors Association, 36–37
Motion Picture Theatre Owners of America, 36–37, 211n71
Mouvet, Maurice, 33
A Moveable Feast (Hemingway), 36
movies, 56; breach of promise lawsuits in, 64, 66, 68–70; CinemaScope, 118–19; class rise and cross-class romance, 63–64, 217n27; Depression-era, 12–13, 57–70; economy portrayed in, 68–69; failed gold digger trope, 123; friendship between women as main text, 118, 121, *122;* gold digger as heroic figure, 64; gold digger as subversive cultural force, 64, 112, 118; Great Depression era, 17, 62–76, 197; legal themes in, 65–66, 68; pre-Code era (1929–1934), 63–70, 84, 119; protofeminist agency in 1930s, 64, 67–68, 70; World War II era, 14, 90–92
Mulvey, Laura, 67, 113, 115, 117, 227n94
Munnell, William, 139
musicals, gold digger theme, 4
My Battles with Vice (Brooks), 1, 203n1
"My Heart Belongs to Daddy" (song), 7

National Abortion Rights Action League (NARAL), 127
National Divorce Reform League, 70
National Labor Board, 76
National Organization for Women (NOW), 127, 152
National Review, 180
National Sociological League, 48

National Women's Party (NWP), 76, 82
"native-born" whites, 25, 30, 50
nativist movements, 30
Neiman Marcus, 166–67
Nelson, Judd, 181
neoliberalism, 16, 156, 190–91, 200; family policy, 234–35n134; free market ideology, 158–59, 161; Koch brothers and, 161–73; legal realism and, 164–65; media narratives, 159, 161; Protestant work ethic, 181, 190; think tanks, 161, 162, 191; welfare policies dismantled, 158; world economy and, 158
neutrality, legal, 133
"Never Trust a Gold-Digger" (Dear Abby column), 126
New Amsterdam Theatre, 29
New Deal, 60
Newsweek, 149
New York Court of Appeals, 82
New York heart balm laws repealed, 80–81
New York nightspots, 27–28
New York Society for the Prevention of Cruelty to Children, 38
New York State Appellate Court, 81
New York State Supreme Court, 82
New York Times, 25, 32, 39, 106; Anna Nicole Smith coverage, 173, 178
New York World's Fair (1939), 100
Nicholson, Roberta West, 76–80, 82, 197
Nineteenth Amendment, 25
nineteenth century, marriage in, 21–22
nineteenth-century lawsuits, 58–59
Ninth Circuit Court of Appeals, 185, 187, 188, 241n119
Nizer, Louis, 102–4, 137–38
"non-liberatory agency," 205n24
Norris, Kathleen, 78–79, 82
nuclear weapons, 98
Nugent, John P. (New York Democrat), 55
"nymphomania," 204n18

Oakland Tribune, 51
O'Day, Judy, 71
Office of Dependency Benefits (ODB), 90
Ogden Standard-Examiner, 54
Ohio Court of Appeals, 85
oil industry, 164–65, 191
Olympics, 99
opportunity cost, 59
Ottley, Roi, 74–75

Packard, Kitty (character, *Dinner at Eight*), 64
Paglia, Camille, 157
Palace Theater (New York), 28
palimony, 10, 15, 18, 133–39; defined, 138; in popular culture, 153–55; suits since 1978, 155–56. *See also* Marvin, Lee; Marvin-Triola palimony suits; Triola, Michelle
Pandora's Box (silent movie), 7
"partnership marriage," 23
People magazine, 141, 163, 179
Pfau, Ann, 89
phrenology, 30
Pierce, Eleanor, 165
Pine Bend Refinery, 162
Piper, Alice, 72, *73*
Pisarra, Vincent, 38, 44–45
Pitzulo, Carrie, 125
A Place in the Sun (Broadway production), 32
Playboy magazine, 17–18, 107–8, 119, 125, 167, 168, 170, 180
Pleck, Elizabeth, 132, 134, 142, 156, 233n98
politicians, women, 76–80, 83–84, 127, 197
postwar transition era, 92–96
poverty: class dynamics of, 78–79; due to desertions, 26–27; marriage as path to avoidance of, 60, 62
Powel, Harford, 92–93, *93*
power relations, 10, 19, 26, 55, 205n24, 206n35

Strong, Selah B., 45–46
structural and economic conditions: 1980s, 158–59; alimony and, 22–25, 27, 46–47, 49–50, 55; breach of promise laws, 13; caricatured by gold digger, 19; gold digger blamed for, 8–9, 13, 47, 84, 129, 159, 201–2; Great Depression era, 57, 68–69; individual or marginalized group blamed for, 9–10, 13, 86, 151, 159, 201–2; late twentieth-century, 18; mid-twentieth century, 86. *See also* economy
stylization, 196–97, 202
subversive cultural force, gold digger as, 64, 112, 118, 153, 205n24
suffrage, 25, 76
"sugar daddy capitalism," 191
The Sunday Mirror, 171
Sunshine, Dorothy, 40–41
Supreme Court, 16, 82, 137; Anna Nicole Smith bankruptcy case and, 172, 173, 184, 187–88; Arthur Anderson ruling, 173–74; Griswold v. Connecticut, 128; Orr v. Orr, 132
Swartz, Mimi, 165, 179
Swick, Clara, 85, 220n1
Swick, Marjorie, 85, 220n1
Swick, Walter, 85
symbol, gold digger as, 196–98, 202
Synanon (movie), 134
synchronized swimming, 100

Tanner, Jolene, 188
Tarzan's Revenge (movie), 100, *101*
Tate, Chrissy (sex worker), 1, 195
Tayloe, Elvira ("Allotment Annie"), 89, 222n16
Taylor, Linda (Welfare Queen stereotype), 159–60
Tea Party movement, 162
Terkel, Studs, 62
Texas Monthly, 165, 168, 177, 179, 180
think tanks, 161, 162, 191
Thompson, Sharon, 133
Tobriner, Matthew, 139

tort law: marriageability as damages, 58–59, 69–70
tort tales, 8–10, 200, 205–6n31, 206n33; heart balm laws, 70–76, 84, 215n3; Marvin-Triola case and, 134; post-1970s tort reform and, 206n33. *See also* media narratives
Train Wreck (Smith), 184
Treanor, Charles, 81
"treating," 2
Trevor, Norman, 32
trial marriage, 11, 15, 23
trickster, 7, 8, 15, 66, 112, 117, 178
Triola, Michelle, 10, 18, 133–39, *136,* 155, 198–99, 201; California Supreme Court nonmarital support issue, 139–42; Los Angeles trial of Lee Marvin and, 142–48; name change, 144; public criticism of, 148–51
The Turmoil (movie), 31
Twentieth Century Fox Film Corporation, 114, 118–19
The Twentieth Century Market, 51
twenty-first century gold diggers, 192–200; African American discourse of, 192–94, *193,* 243n7; computing and telecommunications trajectory, 194–95

United States District Court for the Central District of California, 184–87
Upton, Marguerite "Peggy." *See* Joyce, Peggy Hopkins
urbanization, 26–27
utilitarian law, 164–65

Vallee, Rudy, 57, 62, 66, 71
vamp figure, 7, 167, 217n29
Van Buren, Abigail, 126
Vancouver Sun, 168
Van Deventer, Betty, 7
Van Doren, Mamie, 125
Variety, 4
vaudeville, 28–29, 31, 37
victimization, 38, 148–49

Victorianism, decline of, 11, 23, 83
Vietnam War, 132
"Visual Pleasure and Narrative Cinema" (Mulvey), 117
Vockler, Paul, 158

Wagner Act, 76
Walker, Jewell DiAnne "Lady," 165–66, 176–77, 191
Wall Street Journal, 46
Walsh, Raoul, 31, 36
"war brides," 87, 127
War Brides Act of 1945, 87
Ward, Skip, 134–35
War Department Office of Dependency Benefits, 87
Ware, Lee, 174
Ware, Susan, 60–61, 216n15
Warner, Irma, 59
Warner, Jack, 59
Warner Brothers, 4, 66
"The War of the Roses," 98–105
Wartime Racketeers (Lever and Young), 88
Washington, William Henry, 72
Washington Post, 148; alimony discussed in, 20, *35,* 39–40, 46
Weiss, Jessica, 92, 98
Weitzman, Lenore, 130–31, 229n15
Welch, Robert, 161
welfare and social support programs, 27, 158–59
"Welfare Queen" figure, 159–60
Wells, Ida B., 1
Werhnyak, Larissa, 83, 216n16
West, Kanye, 192–94, *193*
West, Mae, 64, 65
Whitaker, Alma, 74
"white," as category in flux, 12, 16, 207n40

whiteness, 17, 199; fears of middle and upper classes, 25; Joyce's beauty aligned with, 29–30; Monroe as emblem of, 111; "probationary," 50, 104, 214n105; "racial purity," 30, 106–7, 199–200; shifts in response to immigration, 30
"white slavery" (prostitution), 1, 50, 203n1
"white trash," 159–61, 168, 240n102; Anna Nicole Smith as, 161, 179–80, 184
Whitney, Cornelius Vanderbilt, 71
Who's Right? (educational film), 109–10
Will, George, 150
Williams, Clifton, 88
Wilner, Charles, 15, 106–7, 199
Wilson, Frances. *See* Browning, Frances "Peaches" Heenan
"Wind Beneath My Wings," 171
Winn, Mary Day, 58, 71, 74
The Woman and the Law (movie), 31, 36
Wood, Gaby, 181
Wood, Mike, 173, 175, 177
World War II era, 14–15, 17, 86–92, 201
Wyche, Arnold (driver for Marshall), 176

Yale Law School, 164
"You Light Up My Life" (Boon), 177
Young, C. C., 51
Young, Joseph, 88
"yuppie" social type, 158

Zeiger, Susan, 87
Zelizer, Viviana, 11, 151
Ziegfeld Theatre, 101
Ziegfield, Florenz, 28–30
Ziegfeld Follies, 2, *3,* 6, 16, 20, 29, 71, 99; "Glorified American Girl," 29; *Miss 1917,* 29; racial whiteness delineated by, 29–30
Zollo, Burt, 107–8, 119

CPSIA information can be obtained
at www.ICGtesting.com
Printed in the USA
LVHW111141280920
667187LV00007B/59

9 781469 660288